Critical Food Issues: Problems and State-of-the-Art Solutions Worldwide

Critical Food Issues: Problems and State-of-the-Art Solutions Worldwide

Volume 1: Environment, Agriculture, and Health Concerns

Edited by

Laurel E. Phoenix

PRAEGER
An Imprint of ABC-CLIO, LLC

A B C ⬤ C L I O

Santa Barbara, California • Denver, Colorado • Oxford, England

Library of Congress Cataloging-in-Publication Data
Critical food issues : problems and state-of-the-art solutions worldwide.
    p. cm.
  Includes index.
    ISBN 978-0-313-35444-1 (set: hard copy: alk. paper)—ISBN 978-0-313-35446-5 (vol. 1:
hard copy: alk. paper)—ISBN 978-0-313-35448-9 (vol. 2: hard copy: alk. paper)—
ISBN 978-0-313-35445-8 (set: ebook)—ISBN 978-0-313-35447-2 (vol. 1: ebook)—
ISBN 978-0-313-35449-6 (vol. 2: ebook)
1. Food supply. 2. Food consumption. 3. Food—Social aspects.
4. Agriculture. 5. Produce trade. 6. Nutrition policy. I. Phoenix, Laurel E.
II. Walter, Lynn, 1945-
  HD9000.5.C733 2009
  363.8—dc22   2009018999

13 12 11 10 9   1 2 3 4 5

This book is also available on the World Wide Web as an eBook.
Visit www.abc-clio.com for details.

ABC-CLIO, LLC
130 Cremona Drive, P.O. Box 1911
Santa Barbara, California 93116-1911

This book is printed on acid-free paper ∞

Manufactured in the United States of America

This work is dedicated to future generations.
We will learn to save the seed corn for you.

Contents

Foreword

Lynn Walter and Laurel E. Phoenix

Eating is one of the first things we do in life and one of the last things we do. In between our first and last bite, food sustains us, orders our days, celebrates our lives, stimulates our senses, brings us together, and sets us apart. Food is so central to our individual and collective experience that we are intimately familiar with it. But, even with all we know about food, we need to know much more; and this is as true of gourmet "foodies" as it is of those who consider food a trifle. First, we need to identify how the way that food is produced, distributed, and consumed affects human well-being as well as that of our environment and communities. *Critical Food Issues: Problems and State-of-the-Art Solutions Worldwide* examines many of the problems that derive from our prevailing agrifood system—from environmental degradation, resource depletion, and disordered eating, to declining rural livelihoods, food insecurity, unjust labor practices, and animal mistreatment.

Second, we need to know how to address these critical food issues, which is the key question of this collection. Each chapter focuses on strategies and practices that will enhance the synergy between sustainable agrifood systems and a sound environment, healthy people, and equitable communities, locally and globally. As befits the scope of the problems, the solutions are wide-ranging—from local markets, appropriate technologies for pest management and soil improvements, and policies for better working conditions for agricultural workers to social movements for land equity and environmental quality, political consumerism, and creative and scholarly work in the arts and sciences.

The critical food issues are examined by specialists from many academic disciplines who analyze the current state of research on both specific problems and potential solutions. They bring authoritative depth to their analysis of the current literature based in their specific disciplinary specializations, from environmental, nutritional, soil, and agricultural sciences; public health and dietetics; education; literature; history; philosophy; economics; sociology; anthropology; and gender studies. Most of the chapters examine case studies from around the world, wherever problems are being addressed effectively; others concentrate on the United

States, where the research in agrifood studies is growing in concert with the rapidly increasing number of communities, schools, farms, agencies, and businesses working on sustainable agrifood projects.

Each chapter is written in jargon-free language to inform citizen and consumer engagement in the future of food and agriculture and to advance interdisciplinary agrifood studies. The breadth of the problems and solutions is examined in two volumes, generally divided into more bioenvironmental issues or more sociocultural ones. Volume 1 covers *Environment, Agriculture, and Health Concerns*, while Volume 2 focuses on *Society, Culture, and Ethics*. To an extent, the partitions between the volumes and among the sections within them are simply paper ones, because addressing the problems and solutions requires integrating knowledge from the natural sciences with the social sciences and humanities. As farmer and writer Wendell Berry observed, "Eating is an agricultural act."[1] Because eating links our bodies to the Earth, developing strategies to sustain agriculture requires considering nature in relationship to the ways humans transform it into culturally appropriate foods through social processes.

Therefore, while the contributors analyze specific problems and solutions with the depth that comes from their specialization in one of the many academic disciplines represented in this collection, they share an overarching interdisciplinary problem-focus that integrates their work as a whole. That focus is on strategies to promote a sustainable symbiosis among viable agrifood systems, a sound environment, healthy people, and equitable communities. Scholars of "agro-ecology" and "the ecology of food" have conceptualized the holistic, interdisciplinary character of agrifood studies with various ecological models. The value of ecology as a framework for agrifood studies is that it takes the long-term sustainability of natural resources, the economy, and human health into consideration. As it is understood here, the ecology of agrifood framework also includes values, tastes, traditions, and an ethic of equity and justice. Because an ecology of food links health, economy, environment, community, culture, and ethics, strategies based on it should (1) provide food security for all, (2) renew and sustain the natural resource base and the biodiversity of the environment to ensure future food security, (3) build viable agrifood systems that provide for decent rural livelihoods, and (4) promote democratic access to agrifood decision-making as a basis for just and equitable communities.

Encompassing all of these factors in the creation of sustainable agrifood systems will take serious thought on all our parts and knowledge of the models, ideas, and information with which to consider the problems and solutions. Whenever we think seriously about food, we evoke the past millennia during which times turning soil, water, and sunshine into sustenance was understood to depend on prayer, since food was such a precious and precarious thing. The rising call to return food to its central place in our imaginations and our politics indicates that we are once again uncertain about the future of food. *Critical Food Issues: Problems and State-of-the-Art Solutions Worldwide* examines the bases of our fears and ways that we might address them.

NOTE

1. Wendell Berry, "The Pleasures of Eating," in *American Food Writing*, ed. Molly O'Neill (New York: Library Classics of the United States, 2007), 551–58, 552.

Preface

Lynn Walter and Laurel E. Phoenix

A project of the scope of *Critical Food Issues: Problems and State-of-the-Art Solutions Worldwide* requires a collaborative effort. Especially critical has been the work of the forty-one university researchers from around the country and around the world who have provided their academic expertise to this collection. They were asked to present complex information and ideas in a way that not only revealed the complexity of their subjects but also communicated it across the disciplinary boundaries. Communication among the many different disciplinary specialists depended on their commitment to the goals of the project as a whole—first, to provide the public with the information necessary to address the critical foods issues confronting the world today; and second, to contribute to the development of a new interdisciplinary field of food studies. Given the range of disciplines represented here—from environmental, nutritional, and agricultural sciences, to literature, history, philosophy, economics, sociology, anthropology, and psychology—this was no easy task.

The knowledge integration process has been institutionally supported by the fact that the editors and some of the contributors are faculty members at the Center for Food in Community and Culture at the University of Wisconsin–Green Bay. The mission of the center is reflected in the central interdisciplinary problem-focus of this collection, which is to promote "interdisciplinary scholarship to enhance the synergy between sustainable food systems and a sound environment, healthy people, and equitable communities, locally and globally." Its work is reinforced by the innovative, interdisciplinary structure of the university's mission, in which the faculty is encouraged to cross the traditional boundaries of knowledge within the broad frameworks of ecology and engaged citizenship.

We are indebted to Debora Carvalko and Elizabeth Potenza from Praeger and Rebecca L. Edwards of Cadmus Communications for their editorial support. At the University of Wisconsin–Green Bay, we relied on Katie Stilp for editorial assistance with the manuscript production. We are grateful for their efforts, their talents, and their encouragement.

Lynn Walter personally thanks her friends and colleagues Katherine Hall, Diane Legomsky, and Judy Martin for reading and reviewing her work throughout the process.

Finally, none of this would have been possible if it were not for the fact that people around the world, farmers and farmworkers, chefs, family cooks, gardeners, artisan food producers, community activists, journalists, and scientists, are awakening us to the critical food issues and to ways that we might learn from their experience. We recognize their work in ours and hope we have done it justice.

Introduction to Volume 1

Laurel E. Phoenix

Food binds us—to past generations of peoples and places, and across oceans to those who benefit or suffer from our food choices. Food unites us—when we have time to share a meal. It divides us through access—the haves and have nots in city, nation, and world. Eating also shapes us—much of our health and happiness is derived from our relationship with food. For something we need so critically, it is worrying that we do not know what we *should* know about what we eat. Complex systems prompt growers to select their seeds, coax crops to harvest, transport food from farm to factory to market, and entice us to buy and consume. *What* we buy then perpetuates the current agrifood system, while weakening human health and destabilizing Earth's environmental systems. *Critical Food Issues: Problems and State-of-the-Art Solutions Worldwide* identifies a variety of traditional and innovative strategies to restructure policies and practices related to food.

Urbanization has distanced many generations from their rural beginnings and the arts of agriculture. Seldom do we think of the soil, air, sunlight, and water as elements within our daily meals. These fundamentals, so basic that they are easily overlooked, were once acknowledged by cultures offering prayers to Earth, Air, Fire, and Water.[1] Industrial development based on fossil fuel use moved people out of the fields into urban factories. The subsequent application of fossil fuels and new technology to farming evicted even more farmers and farmworkers from the land, a trend that continues to this day.

The last three generations have witnessed an accelerating use of and dependence on fossil fuels and technology that have reshaped our food systems and promoted Western cultural and agricultural ideals around the world. These energy and technology inputs were lauded in the Green Revolution, which helped to feed another doubling of the world's population. Thus, millions more were added to the planet before the constraints of land, soil, water, energy, and technology became evident.[2] The consumption patterns of the global north and the rising populations of the global south now reinforce each other in their pressure on agricultural lands.

We are surely at, or beyond, the natural limits of the Earth to supply our needs unless we begin to change our approach to food and agriculture.

A range of disciplinary research is collected here to demonstrate multilevel approaches and strategies to solve the environmental and access problems related to food. The purpose of this volume is to draw the reader's eye to a web of systems, natural and human, that currently produce and deliver our food: the natural resources providing the agricultural inputs to grow the crops and the policies and practices that either obstruct or promote sustainable agriculture and healthy populations.

The fifteen chapters of Volume I are divided into three parts: Environment, Agriculture and Fisheries, and Health. The environment section lays the ground-work for reviewing the status of the natural resources upon which our food supply depends: soil, water, plants, animals, and energy. Next, the relationship between natural resources and laws, policies, and grassroots efforts to achieve sustainable agriculture and fisheries are examined. Finally, the health section discusses the connection between poverty and access to food security, the ways government or corporate policies affect access to food and affect its nutritional content, and the spectrum of health disorders related to our food choices.

ENVIRONMENT

We cannot ensure food security if we degrade our environment. How we manage the land and water and organisms that live on or within them determine not only the quality of the food we eat, but how quickly we destroy the environment's capacity to support current populations, much less future ones. In chapter 1, Laurel E. Phoenix introduces the issues of the fragmentation of water- and land-use policies in the United States, and how these policies affect or are affected by agriculture. The lack of coherent policy acknowledging the fundamental physical linkage between land and water results in policy too narrowly focused on land or on water. The lack of policy coordination leads to contradictory decisions being made at different government levels. Because the allocation, use, and environmental protection policies of land and water are developed independently and without a focus on food security, they simultaneously encourage the loss of agricultural farmland and perpetuate the unsustainable externalities (i.e., soil, water, and habitat degradation and low-quality food) of industrial agriculture. Because elements, nutrients, pathogens, and chemicals are endlessly transported and recycled between soil, water, and crops, land- and water-use policies must be integrated together with agricultural policy. And, yet, she argues that citizens have powerful ways to influence the way municipalities develop their comprehensive land-use plans. More challenging for citizen action is the strengthening of laws that allocate or protect water so that waters can be managed sustainably. Phoenix provides models for legal and administrative reformation at state and federal levels.

In chapter 2 on soil degradation and conservation, Patricia E. Norris and John M. Kerr further examine the land allocation policies or agricultural practices that degrade soil, and point out numerous strategies used around the world to improve and rehabilitate it. They note that soil degradation has on- and off-site impacts and emphasize that beyond typical regulation and subsidy policies, socioeconomic factors that are barriers to adopting conservation practices must also be addressed. For example, they examine issues beyond farmers' personal annual income that constrain soil conservation, such as cash flow, access to credit, or lack of collective action by all farmers in the landscape.

In addition to concerns about the impacts of soil, land, and water depletion on agricultural production, another problem is getting crops to harvest without losing too much to pests or disease. Providing a detailed examination of the Integrated Pest Management (IPM) system, Michael J. Brewer and Marcia Ishii-Eiteman in chapter 3 discuss the history and current practice of IPM, and survey policy options for supporting it. They explore the difficulty of balancing the risks to the environment, human health, and societal consequences when selecting particular methods for pest management and offer a rubric by which the sustainability of an IPM tactic can be determined. A case study in Indonesia provides a powerful illustration of how to introduce a new strategy to farmers in a way that they will accept it and ultimately promote it themselves. This example underscores the fact that top-down regulation is not effective by itself, but that the knowledge base and constraints of farmers doing the actual work for any sustainable practice has to be considered. The Farmer Field Schools described in this case study are a powerful peer method to promote sustainable practices.

A discussion of animals as pests is only one aspect of the relationship of plants and animals to agriculture. In contrast to the focus of chapter 3, beneficial plant and animal species in agriculture are viewed through the lens of agrobiodiversity in Vicki L. Medland's chapter 4. She examines the planned biodiversity of the domesticated species on a farm as well as the wild species (i.e., worms, mites, beetles) that support agricultural productivity. To reverse the trend of industrial monocultures, agrobiodiversity emphasizes the resilient nature of biodiverse ecosystems and the free inputs they supply that reduce agricultural input costs. Medland describes several organizations supportive of revitalizing traditional agricultural knowledge. For example, DIVERSITAS conducts and shares research in many countries. It is focused on using the natural capital of ecosystem services combined with increasing diversity of seed and animal species. Many of these practices are drawn from more traditional, indigenous practices.

Sustainable agriculture is not just about what happens on a farm. After the crops are harvested, how they get from rural farms to urban consumers is also a critical issue. A study of energy inputs for U.S. food transportation provides data highlighting the enormous amount of fossil fuel energy expended on contemporary U.S. food distribution relative to the energy provided by the food itself. David Pimentel's chapter 5 contrasts the "fuel" in the food (i.e., cabbage and lettuce) with the fuel expended to traverse vast distances. The relative energy inefficiencies of trucks are detailed and compared to the even greater inefficiencies generated by transporting food by air. He focuses on fossil fuel inputs because our future no longer includes cheap, plentiful oil. Roughly half of the current fossil energy use could be saved, states Pimentel, if changes were made at every step of the food system, including on-site farm production, processing and packaging, various transportation modes, and consumption choices. We learn, for example, that junk food is high in fossil fuel inputs: you should look at your next soda, french fries, and hamburger and remember the fossil fuel that made them. Pimentel poses several useful strategies to reduce the fossil fuel inputs hidden in our food supply. His study has implications not only for the United States with its far-flung transportation network, but all countries using industrial farming methods and shipping food by truck or plane.

AGRICULTURE AND FISHERIES

For a brief but limited period of time, industrial agriculture temporarily increased Earth's carrying capacity (for humans), engendering a false sense of security that nature is still bountiful and we can scoff at the word "scarcity." But research has proven that such intensive production cannot continue. We face ever-diminishing returns from depleted soils producing food with little nutrition but numerous contaminants. As the previous chapters introduced various natural resources upon which agriculture depends, this next section provides a broader picture of production and harvest on land and sea. Beginning with the concept of "sustainable agriculture," examples of effective methods and policies are highlighted in the rural lands of the industrial and developing countries. This concept is extended into the cities, where numerous examples of urban agriculture are described. And what is probably the most unfamiliar to most readers is the critical status of ocean fisheries and the uncertainty of what can still be harvested. For land and sea we now explore the possibilities.

Providing an overview of sustainable agriculture and the various alternative methods it employs, Daniel A. Cibulka (chapter 6) introduces and defines sustainable agriculture as it is practiced in selected postindustrial (i.e., wealthier) countries of the world. Hydroponics, cover crops, perennial grains, and rotational grazing are some of the methods he describes. After surveying movements promoting these alternatives, Cibulka identifies some of their founders to reveal how these initiatives began, and where they are supported or opposed by governments, industries, or other interest groups.

Sustainable agriculture is also growing in the developing countries, with some shared and some unique variations. Chapter 7 by Richard H. Bernsten and Sieglinde Snapp sets the stage by revealing trends toward resource depletion that these countries share that underscore the need for sustainable methods. Poor countries, particularly in Africa, are suffering from increasing populations, decreasing food productivity, decreasing worker productivity from HIV/AIDS, poverty that precludes the use of high-yield seed varieties that require expensive chemicals and fertilizers, and sometimes unreliable irrigation, and global climate changes causing even more droughts or floods. They explore the successes of organizations such as the Consultative Group for International Agriculture Research (CGIAR) and its agricultural research centers, and the Collaborative Research Support Programs that link countries with agricultural research at U.S. land-grant universities. Bernsten and Snapp argue that strategies for promoting successful sustainable agriculture must include research-driven, market-driven, or extension-driven approaches. To make their case, they point to programs around the world using each of these, and the various collaborations between agencies, governments, and farmers that were successful. Projects can aim at hillside production systems, more efficient water management suited for a particular site, using different seed varieties, connecting farmers to more markets or developing their own "value-added" products, sustainably harvesting agroforestry products, and much more.

Food production is no longer solely a rural pursuit. In what they call a "quiet revolution" in chapter 8, Jim Bingen, Kathryn Colasanti, Margaret Fitzpatrick, and Katherine Nault note that urban agriculture and gardening are currently undergoing enthusiastic acceptance in many cities. These pursuits provide an additional means to food security. There is surprising diversity in stakeholders as well as their reasons for participating. Individuals, various coalitions of neighbors, civic or social service groups, and even commercial entities are being drawn to this renaissance of growing fresh food and reaping the additional benefits of health, education, feeling part of your community, and ultimately, food security. Food is grown on public and private land, empty lots, and even on balconies, windowsills, parking lots, and roofs. Bingen, Colasanti, Fitzpatrick, and Nault describe city farms and gardens, the intersection of city land-use planning with political interest groups to achieve support for urban agriculture, and learning to value multiple agendas to achieve these more comprehensive goals. Some of the critical questions they ask are: "How are urban farm and garden activities both shaped by, and active in shaping, instances of disinvestment and/or investment in cities?" and "Do urban agriculture activities and programs create the conditions for grassroots and neighborhood groups and coalitions to emerge in defense of urban agriculture in public policymaking and planning?"

Turning to fisheries, both wild and farmed, Tracy Dobson (chapter 9) presents the history and current status of global fisheries, highlighting current literature to identify and describe declining biodiversity, ever-shrinking annual harvests, degraded marine environments, and destructive harvesting methods. In addition, inequality of fishing access is the result of wealth and technology combining to "vacuum" the ocean in waters that are deeper than fishers with small boats can reach. To the degree that there is any management of fisheries (since it is next to impossible to police the oceans), Dobson highlights different approaches that have been taken to slow this "race to the bottom" in marine harvests and discusses the role of capture fisheries (i.e., farmed fish) in mitigating these shrinking marine harvests. She describes the role of regional agencies in public education and monitoring coastal or lacustrine (i.e., lake) fisheries where equitable quota systems can be enforced. The more difficult issue of deepwater fisheries outside of national controls, she notes, is being tackled by nongovernmental organizations (NGOs) such as Greenpeace and the International Union for Conservation of Nature (IUCN).

HEALTH

Human health and well-being are nourished and supported by food that is accessible, affordable, and nutritious. Without these prerequisites, hunger, disease, and poor social and academic skills result. This section introduces the critical issues of food security, the science of nutrition, national or corporate policies affecting access or quality of food, and various aspects of our relationship with food and more extreme manifestations of food-related health problems.

John T. Cook (chapter 10) incorporates multiple household-level studies to document food security in the United States. Using the food security definition, "access by all people at all times to enough food for an active, healthy life," he outlines the relationship of food insecurity to poverty, child health and development, maternal depression, and academic and social risk. Cook concludes that food insecurity in the poor and near-poor U.S. population is "one of the most readily measured as well as one of the most rapidly remediable by policy changes."

If there is political will, wealthy countries can readily achieve food security for their populations. However, the magnitude of the problem in developing nations makes it more difficult to solve. To address the constellation of factors affecting food security in poorer countries, John M. Staatz, Duncan H. Boughton, and Cynthia Donovan (chapter 11) focus on Sub-Saharan Africa and South Asia to illustrate the complicated trade-offs policymakers face to address food security in impoverished areas. Because the real cost of food includes productivity of each step in the food system, from farm to "agricultural input markets, assembly markets, processing, wholesaling, and retailing," it is a delicate business indeed to devise practicable interventions at each step that increase productivity and reduce costs without harming the current workers or owners. Moreover, food might be available at the markets but remain inaccessible because someone cannot afford it. Thus, different approaches to improving food security sometimes need to be adopted in unison to solve the multiple aspects of food security problems. The authors argue that the biggest challenge is in addressing transitory and chronic food insecurity simultaneously. The multiple factors of human, biological, and physical capital tied to food security are explored and then placed in the context of state institutional capital, which determines land and resource tenure and how they can be equitably exchanged in working markets. Staatz, Boughton, and Donovan point to government and nongovernmental programs currently promoting food security programs to demonstrate strategies have been tried and achieved success.

Another aspect of food security is the nutritional quality of food, which is affected by the ways that it is grown, harvested, stored, and transported. Consumers cannot tell from looking at produce if it is highly nutritious as well as without blemish. Imagine two heads of broccoli: same size and color, but containing vastly different nutrients. What are the factors of soil, seed, fertilizer, and grower preference (i.e., pest resistance, capacity to withstand mechanical harvesting/sorting) that determine how one head is nutritionally superior to the other? Debra Pearson's chapter 12 illuminates how different aspects of agricultural practices alter the nutrient profile of the food you buy and gives examples of other varieties that you would select using nutritional rather than aesthetic criteria. She traces the history of overall crop nutrient density decline over multiple decades, and then further examines particular varieties to assess their differential nutrient densities as well as the effect of organic versus industrial farmed on the same variety. In addition to analyzing the familiar minerals, vitamins, and macronutrients (i.e., protein, carbohydrate, and fats) Pearson also unearths how agricultural practices affect the roughly eight thousand phytochemicals in food that are also important to human health. Even the common practice of harvesting before the plant is ripe reduces its phytochemical content. To promote good health and reduce common diseases linked to malnutrition, she argues that agricultural production must consider the nutritional qualities of varieties as well as their yield. She suggests that more local production of fruits and vegetables for sale in local markets might improve their nutrient quality.

Nutrition and national food policies are merged in Sandra M. Stokes's (chapter 13) history and analysis of federally funded school lunch and breakfast programs.

She outlines how a federal policy ostensibly aimed at feeding children became a support program for agriculture, and then became co-opted by food industries setting further lucrative conditions on schools before they could be accepted into receiving this federal support. For example, schools are required by federal law to buy up to 80 percent of their food from one central supplier. To demonstrate how this trend of poor-quality food supplied for school children has been reversed, she provides a case study of an award-winning elementary school that has taken an innovative and comprehensive approach to improving the food it serves while educating the children and families as well. After analyzing the weaknesses and roadblocks of current federal policy, Stokes gives nine recommendations that would result in healthier school lunches.

Popular culture not only tells us what to eat, but also increasingly stresses body image and ever-more-emaciated models wearing clothes no larger than size four. Is this merely a passing American fad or modern phenomenon of the global north, or do its roots go deeper? Disordered eating and body image is examined in chapter 14 by Cheryl Toronto Kalny, who relates historical cases from Christian, medieval Europe of voluntary food denial among young women through the 1600s. Researchers in the last half-century in the Western world have studied anorexia and bulimia, a related eating disorder, in greater depth, developing and revising theories on causation and treatment. From this data, Kalny summarizes several American demographic studies on eating disorder patients by age, income, and ethnicity. Most were white, middle-class, young women. In other studies, risk criteria are documented for women in Western and Eastern Europe, finding increased incidence of food disorders in Eastern Europe as Western influence strengthened (e.g., after the collapse of communist power in 1989). Kalny analyzes studies from Africa, Asia, and Latin America, all of which demonstrate greater risk and higher incidence of disordered eating as closer links are forged with Western culture. Anorexia has even emerged in cultures with traditional preferences for fat body types, but studies suggest causation and therefore, risk factors are more circumscribed. For example, a Hong Kong, China, study noted that most of the patients were from lower economic classes, and the fewer from higher classes used disordered eating as a way to show their rebellion. Kalny concludes by surveying treatment modalities used in various countries.

Adult obesity is also a growing problem, initially seen in Western countries but now spreading to developing nations. The rising incidence rates now seen in children and teens are generating multiple target populations for which strategies must be found. Joanne Gardner (chapter 15) identifies U.S. obesity rates for age, race, and gender, and analyzes the incidence and the massive costs to treat these health problems related to obesity. She notes that simple taking in more caloric than what's expended is part, but not the only cause. The ratio of fats, sugars, and other components of food calories not only make critical differences, but act differently on very young children than adults. In particular, she explores recent research on high-fructose corn syrup as having effects on body metabolism different from other sweeteners of the same calories. Advertising, popular culture, restaurant food portions, federal subsidies for corn, personal income, and lack of nutrition education are some of the factors she discusses that combine to exacerbate this obesity epidemic. Gardner surveys contemporary programs now aimed at reducing the "supersizing" of America.

As our current food systems push the limits of both natural systems and our own bodies, we impoverish our current generations and endanger our descendants. We need to realize that what happens on farms and fishing vessels not only changes the physical systems providing the harvest, but also changes our physical and mental health. In other words, "we are what we eat" means our bodies carry the memories of the harvesters and the harvested, the water and the land. We can no longer pretend that we are separate from these environmental or agricultural systems. The authors of *Critical Food Issues* demonstrate that we are capable of learning to grow food with wisdom and without harm.

NOTES

1. Jill Ker Conway, Kenneth Keniston, and Leo Marx, *Earth, Air, Fire, Water: Humanistic Studies of the Environment* (Amherst: University of Massachusetts Press, 1999).
    2. Richard Heinberg, *Peak Everything: Waking up to a Century of Declines* (Gabriola Island, Canada: New Society Publishers, 2007).

Abbreviations

ACOE	Army Corps of Engineers
AFS	American Fisheries Society
AHA	American Heart Association
ANDES	Association for Nature and Sustainable Development
APA	American Planning Association
ARS	Agricultural Research Service
AU	Africa Union
BAPPENAS	Badan Perencanaan Pembangunan Nasional
BMI	body mass index
BRFSS	Behavioral Risk Factor Surveillance System
BVCs	Beach Village Committees
CAADP	Comprehensive African Agricultural Development Program
CAFOs	Concentrated Animal Feed Operations
CBT	Cognitive Behavioral Therapy
CCHIP	Community Childhood Hunger Identification Program
CCX	Chicago Climate Exchange
CDC	Centers for Disease Control and Prevention
CFSP	California Fresh Start Program
CFSS	Children's Food Security Scale
CGIAR	Consultative Group for International Agricultural Research
CHCC	California Healthy Cities and Communities
CIAL	Comité de Investigación Agricola Local (Local Agricultural Research Committee)
CIFOR	Center for International Forestry Research
CIP	International Potato Center
C-SNAP	Children's Sentinel Nutrition Assessment Program
COFI	Committee on Fisheries
COMACO	Community Markets for Conservation
CPI	Consumer Price Index

CPS	Current Population Survey
CRP	Conservation Reserve Program
CRSP	Collaborative Research Support Program
CSPI	Center for Science in the Public Interest
CWA	Clean Water Act
DSM	Diagnostic and Statistic Manual of Mental Disorders
ECAF	European Conservation Agriculture Federation
ECLS	Early Childhood Longitudinal Study
EEZ	exclusive economic zone
EPA	Environmental Protection Agency
EQIP	Environmental Quality Incentives Program
ERS	Economic Research Service (of U.S. Department of Agriculture)
FAFS	Framework for African Food Security
FAO	Food and Agriculture Organization of the United Nations
FASEB	Federation of American Societies for Experimental Biology
FDA	Food and Drug Administration
FFS	Farmer Field Schools
FNS	Food and Nutrition Services
FSP	Food Stamp Program
FSS	U.S. Food Security Scale
FTC	Federal Trade Commission
FTS	farm-to-school [programs]
FWPCA	Federal Water Pollution Control Act
FWS	U.S. Fish and Wildlife Service
GLASOD	Global Assessment of Soil Degradation
GLFC	Great Lakes Fishery Commission
GMOs	genetically modified organisms
H&CFI	household and child food insecurity
HFCS	high fructose corn syrup
HFI	household food insecurity
HOPS	Healthier Options for Public Schoolchildren
IAAD	International Association of Agricultural Development
IAASTD	International Assessment of Agricultural Knowledge, Science and Technology for Development
ICARDA	International Center for Agricultural Research in the Dry Areas
ICAT	International Center for Tropical Agriculture
icipe	African Insect Science for Food and Health
ICRAF	World Agroforestry Center
ICRISAT	International Crops Research Institute for the Semi-Arid Tropics
IDA	iron deficiency anemia
IFDC	International Fertilizer Development Center
IFPRI	International Food Policy Research Institute
IOM	Institute of Medicine
IOPs	Intensive Outpatient Programs
IPM	Integrated Pest Management
IPM CRSP	Integrated Pest Management Collaborative Research Support Program
IPT	Interpersonal Psychotherapy

ITQs	individual tradable quotas
IUCN	International Union for Conservation of Nature
IUU	illegal, unregulated, and unreported [fishing]
IWMI	International Water Management Institute
LOS	United Nations Law of the Sea Treaty
LSRO	Life Sciences Research Office
LTRAS	Long-Term Research on Agricultural Systems
MET	Motivational Enhancement Therapy
MMSD	Madison (Wisconsin) Metropolitan School District
MRL	maximum residue level
MSC	Marine Stewardship Council
NAWQA	National Water-Quality Assessment
NGOs	nongovernmental organizations
NHANES	National Health and Nutrition Examination Survey
NHLBI	National Heart, Lung, and Blood Institute
NPDES	National Pollutant Discharge Elimination System
NPS	nonpoint source pollution
NRI	National Resources Inventory
NSLP	National School Lunch Program
OCD	Obsessive Compulsive Disorder
OMB	Office of Management and Budget
OMB Watch	Office of Management and Budget Watch
OPEC	Organization of Petroleum Exporting Countries
PACE	Purchase of Agricultural Easements
PCBs	polychlorinated biphenyls
PDS	positive depressive symptoms
PEDS	Parent's Evaluation of Developmental Status
PES	payment for environmental services
POPs	persistent organic pollutants
PSC	Pediatric Symptom Checklist
QSR	quick-serve restaurants
rBGH	recombinant bovine growth hormone
REACH	Responsive Education for All Children
RFMOs	regional fisheries management organizations
SAN	Sustainable Agricultural Network
SANREM CRSP	Sustainable Agriculture and Resource Management Collaborative Research Support Program
SSA	Sub-Saharan Africa
TBL	Triple Bottom Line
TDR	Transfer of Development Rights
TMDL	total maximum daily load
UNDP	United Nations Development Program
UPA	Urban and Peri-Urban Agriculture Alliance
USAID	U.S. Agency for International Development
USDA	U.S. Department of Agriculture
USGS	U.S. Geological Survey
VAT	value added tax
WFC	World Fish Center

WFP	United Nations World Food Programme
WHO	World Health Organization
WIC	Special Supplemental Nutrition Program for Women, Infants, and Children
WPA	Works Progress Administration
WWF	World Wide Fund for Nature

PART I

Environment

1

Water and Land-Use Policies in the United States

Laurel E. Phoenix

All of us need a place to live, water to drink, and food to eat. Because these are the most critical items for survival, land-use and water-use issues are most fiercely contested or assiduously avoided, resulting in fragmented or nonexistent management structures. In the United States, land-use regulation tends to be created and enforced in most states at the local level, and water allocation law is promulgated at the state level. Underenforced water-quality regulations flow from the federal level. Laws regarding ownership and use of land and water vary across regions and rarely incorporate concerns about the externalities, such as water and soil contamination caused by poor management practices—agricultural or otherwise. This lack of coherent policy over land and water use can affect where and how food is grown, with consequential repercussions on land, water, animals, and people.

Land and water policy arenas are not to be confused with agricultural policy, which is reauthorized roughly every five years at the federal level with no thought given to local land use or water issues. Thus, the United States has policies and laws regarding land, water, and food, each of which are created in a vacuum—that is, at different levels by different interest groups with no thought to the interconnections between these systems. This chapter briefly introduces the effects of agrifood production on land and water in the United States, focuses on how land-use regulations or water laws inadvertently affect food production, and offers suggestions for improvement.

EFFECTS OF FOOD PRODUCTION

Agriculture is concentrating in fewer and much larger farms. Increased mechanization, coupled with the few dominant agrifood corporations, has turned the majority of farming into factory farming—creating many of the same problems that factories have: polluting air, water, and soil while reducing the quality of the finished product. This brief selection of industrial farm impacts on soil and land use, water quality, and water loss provides a preface and counterpoint to the chapter's focus on how land use and water policies affect agriculture.

Effects on Soil and Land Use

Soil is permanently damaged by industrial farming. As machinery, wind, and water erode topsoil, nutrients, micronutrients, and organic matter are lost. The micronutrients are not replaced by chemical fertilizer applications, and the organic matter is never replaced. Without these, soil biota, needed for breaking down and recycling these constituents, are lost. As soil is compacted by heavy farming equipment, soil pores are permanently reduced, making it harder for roots, oxygen, and water to penetrate the soil. Moreover, this compaction not only increases surface runoff from the fields, exacerbating erosion and flooding, but also prevents water from infiltrating down past the root zone to recharge the aquifer.

Soils can build up toxic quantities of agrochemicals. Industrial farming with its monoculture crops requires repeated applications of new pesticides to make up for the lack of resilience to pests in monoculture cropping. Pesticides, some listed as Persistent Organic Pollutants (POPS), can linger in the soil for decades, as the longevity of DDT (dichloro-diphenyl-trichloroethane) can attest. Whether long or short-lived, pesticides are often indiscriminate in the range of biota they kill, resulting in soil virtually void of organisms that can break down nutrients and aerate the soil. Lead arsenate pesticides commonly used in cherry and apple orchards leave high levels of arsenic in the soil. Landspreading of animal manure from Concentrated Animal Feed Operations (CAFOs) typically overloads soil with too much nitrogen, thus altering or killing soil biota. Landspreading of fly ash, sewage sludge, or other industrial wastes adds more than beneficial nutrients to the soil. Studies have shown these practices to add polychlorinated biphenyls (PCBs) and a variety of heavy metals to the soil, some of which are taken up by the crops.[1]

In hot and dry regions of the interior U.S. West where crops must be irrigated, salts are drawn up through the soil and left in the root zone as soil surface evaporation draws the soil water up. These salts can build up to levels that are toxic to plant roots, and land has been permanently abandoned because of soil salinization.

Industrial farming has negative effects beyond farm land quality. The ability of industrial farming to produce a cheaper product drives smaller farmers out of business. Besides creating economic and social problems, this industrial dominance can create land-use issues if the small farmer requires rezoning to attract a buyer.

The proliferation of industrial farming tends to predetermine possible uses of lands adjacent to the factory farms, since nothing other than more industrial farming is compatible. CAFOs, in particular, cause so many off-site externalities that no one wants to live near them. Although the majority of land-use plans and regulations are developed in cities, county planners are historically supportive of, and influenced by, primary extractive industries such as farming, ranching, mining, and forestry that predominate in rural locales; consequently, they will not obstruct agriculture of any size. Agricultural lobbyists pressure officials from the federal to the local level to prevent any regulation of industrial farming, thus continuing the concentration of farming in giant agribusiness corporations and the ease with which CAFOs are established on county lands.

Effects on Water Quality

Soil erosion transports sediments into streams and lakes, covering former gravel or sandy bottoms with silt and destroying the natural habitat for stream and lake biota. Enough soil deposition on a stream or river bottom raises the riverbed, exacerbating the damage of future floods because the river can no longer hold the same amount of floodwaters within its banks.

Erosion and runoff also transport nutrients from fertilizer or CAFO manure; altering chemical and biotic composition of waterbodies. The most common result is eutrophication, where the resulting algal bloom removes oxygen from the water as it decomposes. The bloom carpets the water body and prevents sunlight from reaching submerged plants, and the subsequent deoxygenation of the water kills off many aquatic animals.

Too many nutrients also percolate down into the groundwater, primarily from landspreading of CAFO manure. The heavy load of nitrogen is converted in the soil to nitrate, which builds up in groundwater. Children under two years of age drinking nitrate-contaminated well water suffer from methemoglobinemia, or blue-baby syndrome, and babies under six months can die, as nitrates reduce their bloodstream's oxygen. Moreover, the presence of high nitrate levels often indicates other contaminants likely to be in the well water.

Effects on Water Quantity

Most states lack tight regulation of groundwater withdrawals. This lack of regulation encourages the use of the cheapest and most inefficient irrigation methods, which use the most groundwater. Many users pumping large amounts of water inevitably lower the water tables and drain the aquifer of water faster than natural recharge can replenish it. This results in a permanent reduction of water available to the local area. If a farm operation switches to a more water-intensive crop (e.g., rice or cotton) because new subsidies or higher demand raises the profitability of those crops, even more water will be pumped from the aquifer, thus using the groundwater unsustainably and possibly dropping the water table beyond the reach of other users' wells. Industrial farming tends to use high-capacity wells that are efficient in mining groundwater. This is true whether they are irrigating crops or pumping water for CAFO operations.

In states like Colorado with its strict "use it or lose it" doctrine, farms will use their whole water allowance even though they could easily use less or install efficient irrigation. But this doctrine requires that they use the *entire* portion of their water right, or risk losing their water right completely. This law prevents badly needed agricultural-efficiency technologies from being employed, and theoretically prevents others from being able to buy a water right for the portion of water that could be saved.

Another issue in dry western climates is that inefficient agricultural irrigation essentially removes water from a river or aquifer and exposes it more broadly to evaporative forces. Thus, some of what was local water and could have percolated back down through the soil has now floated downwind to benefit the neighboring state.

Industrial agriculture has enormous effects both on and beyond property boundaries. Not only are there permanent environmental damages to soil and water, but actual and well-documented permanent losses of topsoil and groundwater as well. In addition, industrial agriculture generates economic repercussions regarding land value, land ownership, and local job availability. The next section describes selected effects of land-use decisions from the federal, state, and local levels that shape agricultural production and begins to clarify why local governments do little about the negative externalities of industrial agriculture despite its effect on local citizens and the environment.

LAND USE

Most counties and cities in the United States have some form of land-use regulations, although a few rural counties have none. Land-use decisions historically have been left to the local level. Some states take a more active role either in a few subject areas, such as agriculture, power plants, or mining, or take a central role by drawing up a general land-use plan that all municipalities must use as their base plan. This general land-use plan ensures that municipalities at least will be consistent with minimum state requirements. Some states contain federal land, in which case the local or state government has either little or no voice over how that public land is managed, limiting local land planning options.

Typical land-use regulations flow from a local land-use plan created from urban perspectives by planners with traditional urban land-use training. Basic plans map out densities of particular land uses that are already in place or permitted in specific areas of that municipality. Simple plans may only consider the built environment, while more comprehensive plans also look at transportation, economic development, extension of city services, and a host of other topics that combine to form a particular quality of life for that area.

Although land use is primarily a local prerogative, policies or laws are going to constrain local plans in some way. For this reason, this section begins with the federal level and then examines the state and local level.

Federal

Clean Water Act Section 404 Permits

Lands defined as wetlands by the federal government require a Section 404 permit from the Army Corps of Engineers (ACOE) before any dredging or filling can occur. The degree to which the ACOE permits dredging and filling then determines what lands in any state can be developed, unless the state has written a more stringent state law.

Federal Lands

Many types of federal lands are located across the United States, although the majority of them are found in the western states. These can include National Park, National Forest, Bureau of Land Management, or reserved lands like military bases and Indian reservations, among others. The degree to which these federal lands affect neighboring local land-use planning depends on how these lands are managed, for what purpose, and whether the local area benefits or not from their proximity.

State

States choose the degree to which they will control local land use and whether they do this by statutes mandating municipal compliance or by providing helpful information and guidelines that municipalities can use on a voluntary basis. The most stringent state oversight is through mandating local plans consistent with the state plan. Variability between states requiring local planning is evident: ten states say local planning is optional, twenty-five states require local planning on some conditions, and fifteen states require local plans of all their municipalities.[2] However, most states leave the vast majority of land-use planning and power to the local level.

Local

Planning

Local planners develop a plan of what they would like their city (or county) to look like in twenty to thirty years. From this blueprint, municipalities create zoning ordinances (i.e., land-use regulations) that provide the framework for implementing the plan. Because much of a twenty- to thirty-year plan is based on best-case scenario outcomes and predictions of population growth and economic growth coupled with local desires, revisions of the plan are inevitable when initial ideas do not comport with future realities. Unexpected growth in population, sudden shifts in the local or national economy, emerging political pressure, or other unforeseen events require plan revision. Although ill-advised, plan variances (e.g., changing densities or type of use) are often given. A plan by itself carries no legal mandate but is merely a document of guidance. Only local ordinances focusing on specific parts of a plan, such as the density of houses allowed in one part of town, or the specification of where certain commercial activity may occur, require compliance to that part of the plan. Thus, the existence of a written plan does not, in itself, result in logical and orderly growth of a city.

Traditional Assumptions in Planning

Traditional assumptions of land use, whether or not they have been clearly articulated, shape the type of plans and subsequent ordinances that are written. The undeveloped spaces outside of a city are viewed as a *tabula rasa*, or a blank slate, upon which many new uses can be projected. Because agricultural lands are considered undeveloped, and thus inefficiently used until converted to a more profitable use, they have suffered from this urge to turn them into something else.

Another assumption is that growth is good, necessary, inevitable, and perpetual. This has justified the expansion of development into formerly low-density areas, open space, and agricultural areas. Although urban areas expanded through this century because of the amount of land available (unlike, for example, in Europe), cities are now bumping up against boundaries constraining their growth, whether they are physical (i.e., a river or mountain) or political (i.e., another city's boundary).

An interesting and currently changing assumption is that house buyers want low-density, single-use, suburban sprawl. Although developers have argued that they are merely building what buyers want, this justification obscures the fact that land at the edge of or outside of the city is always cheaper, gives developers more latitude in using the same formula design, and, in the case of agricultural land, is fairly flat. All of these factors raise the potential profits for the developers. If this land is outside of city limits, developers may benefit from the far-less-stringent county ordinances.

Aside from the space available for new buildings, assumptions about inputs to city life are overlooked and taken for granted. First, it is assumed that relatively cheap energy and materials will always be available to build the longer roads, pipelines, and electric lines and then to service these widely dispersed developments with utilities, police and firefighters, and schools. Related to this cornucopian vision of natural resources is the assumption that we will all continue to drive our own cars, thereby negating any need for walkable neighborhoods.

Perhaps the most remarkable thing taken for granted is food. Zoning local agriculture out of existence has been common, as planners assume the food will just be grown somewhere else. Several factors have encouraged this assumption. Decades of cheap oil and interstate highways overcame the constraints of geography to encourage planners to rid their area of cheaper agricultural land and give it instantly increased value by zoning it for residential, commercial, or industrial use. Any local loss of food production could be replaced easily by shipping it in from another region. Similarly, because most economic production occurs in cities, states historically have given cities the prerogative to unilaterally annex adjacent county land for expansion. Consequently, cities continue to overtake surrounding countryside and push agriculture to the margins, or sometimes out of the county entirely.

Pothukuchi and Kaufman explored this lack of involvement by planners in food issues, and found that planning literature does not address food systems. Moreover, when numerous planners were interviewed, seven categories of reasons were given for not doing so:

- It is not our turf.
- It is not an urban issue; it is a rural issue.
- The food system is driven primarily by the private market.
- Planning agencies are not funded to do food system planning.
- What is the problem? If it ain't broke, why fix it?
- Who is addressing the community food system with whom we can work?
- We do not know enough about the food system to make a greater contribution.[3]

Consequently, lack of knowledge, mandates, and perspective combine to allow ongoing urbanization of agricultural land and the undervaluing of agriculture that this loss implies.

Valuing Agricultural Land

Land value is derived not from the natural services it provides, but from the human economic activity that occurs on it. Once agricultural land is eyed by planners or developers for conversion, its soil fertility or groundwater recharge potential has generally been ignored. Local food security and the potential future need for that land for food production is rarely considered. Despite the fact that planners and city officials are supposed to make decisions for the long-term good of a city, it is far easier to aim for quick returns than long-term investment.

Food has been relatively cheap in this country for decades, as long as cheap oil and government subsidies were able to keep food prices down. This means that agricultural acres are valued for the dollar amount of the crops grown. The sale value of an acre of corn or soybeans is insignificant compared with the money garnered from one acre of developed uses. Agricultural land prices can reflect only the current value of crops, and thus tend to be priced significantly lower than industrial, commercial, or residential land. Although city planners ostensibly work from a twenty- to thirty-year plan, the current financial pressures of cities needing ever more property tax revenue causes planners to zone fewer acres as agricultural and to zone current agricultural lands for their future development potential. This is a signal for developers to pressure farmers to sell so the developers can subdivide the land for a different profitable use.

In some cases, the working farms in an area have no interest in selling their land for development, and their right to continue farming as development creeps around them has been established under common law. One tactic used to drive out local agriculture is to start taxing the working farmland as though it had already been developed (i.e., taxing it on its future presumed value). This is legal as long as all agricultural property within the district is levied the same higher rate. Most farmers cannot absorb the blow of higher taxes and still keep farming.

Politics of Land Use

The idea behind creating a plan and implementing it through zoning regulations implies a rational, orderly, and equitable process done in the name of the public good. However, zoning property for a particular use directly affects its market value, either limiting it to much less than the owner hoped for or increasing its value by zoning it for higher-density residential or commercial or industrial purposes. Consequently, the act of zoning confers or takes away current or future value. Because of this, planners and city officials are pressed by developers to provide variances or rezone parcels to increase the land value or the profit that can be made from higher-density or higher-value construction. Developers are not only looking to make more profit and make more land available for construction, but also can argue that variances and rezoning will help maintain or provide new construction jobs in the area. City officials are loathe to plan or zone in ways that would slow growth, shed jobs, or shrink the flow of money through the local economy. It is this short-term growth perspective that circumvents the more rational nature of a plan and pulls planners away from long-term visions toward short-term gains.

Summary of Land-Use Policy Decisions on Agriculture

Although local planners are constrained by some federal or state land uses or consistency requirements, they still have great latitude in their local planning. And despite the yearly statistics available from the U.S. Department of Agriculture on agricultural land loss through urbanization,[4] planners still create plans focused on the built environment to maximize their current local benefits while leaving the externalities, especially the loss of local food supply, to fate. This "tyranny of small decisions"[5] moves cities and the nation further from food security. Of course, planners are a product of their education and their professional organization. If one goes to the American Planning Association Web site, there is no listing of "Agriculture" under their "search by topic" pull-down menu. Thus, even planning's professional organization is still trapped by old and limited views of what urban planning should initially consider as primary concerns.

Advocates for Change

Those who have pointed out the weaknesses of urbanizing agricultural land come from a broad swath of backgrounds. Food security and farming advocates, researchers, progressive states, planners, and those concerned with sustainable living or energy concerns have all written about the need for protection of agricultural land. One group dealing directly with the issues of agriculture and land-use planning and zoning is the Food Security Learning Center.[6] It not only offers specific land-planning and zoning tools to protect local agriculture (both urban and rural), but it frames the issue within the broader topic of food security. It suggests comprehensive plans that allow farmers markets and zoning agricultural properties in large enough parcels that they are unlikely to be profitably convertible to any other use but farming.

The American Farmland Trust[7] Web site links to examples from around the country where zoning tools can protect agriculture. Its "Farmland Protection Toolbox" explains a variety of strategies:

- States can create Agricultural Districts, within which agriculture is protected from annexation or eminent domain by local municipalities.
- Governors can write executive orders to direct their agencies not to institute policies or programs that will encourage farmland conversion.
- States can offer Circuit Breaker tax programs or Differential Assessment tax programs in which agricultural land gets property tax credits.
- Municipalities can create Agricultural Protection Zoning where zoning is very low-density and land uses incompatible with farming are not allowed.
- The Purchase of Agricultural Easements (PACE) can be used where the municipality or nonprofit organization like American Farmland Trust or Trust for the Public Land can pay the farmer the difference of the higher price she could get from developers, in return for putting an easement on her land requiring it to stay agricultural. Such an easement stays in force through subsequent sales of the property.
- Cities, counties, and states can use Transfer of Development Rights (TDR) programs to give incentives to developers to build at higher-than-normal densities in "receiving zones" (where planners want to direct growth) rather than in the "sending zones" (where planners want to protect agricultural areas).

These voluntary or mandatory agricultural protection programs are described in *Land Use in a Nutshell*[8] and some comprehensive plans around the country.

Some academics study the big picture of American land use. Rutherford Platt,[9] a prominent land-use geographer, notes that over time, the federal government's response to agricultural acres lost to urbanization has been to encourage better soil management practices on the lands that are left, but do nothing about the fact that acreage is being lost. Others described the value of agricultural land as including two categories: (1) the capacity of the land to provide enough food and fiber, and (2) other intangible "amenity" values.[10] As long as the public is unaware that farmland loss is reaching a critical point, the amenity values of agricultural land will outweigh its capacity values.

Oregon is a shining example of a state realizing agriculture's importance and how to protect it. Oregon's Department of Land Conservation and Development[11] illustrates what comprehensive planning at the state level can do to actively protect agriculture. Through Oregon's 1973 Growth Management Statute, cities were mandated to create urban growth boundaries, beyond which a city could not expand. Other areas were zoned as urbanizable or rural, with rural lands including open space, agriculture, and forest to remain low density. Reflecting the more comprehensive approach of urban and rural interrelationship, Portland has merged its Bureau of Planning and Office of Sustainable Development into the Bureau of Planning and Sustainability.[12]

Randall Arendt, a planner looking at the strains of growth pressures on rural towns, has written *Rural by Design: Maintaining Small Town Character*,[13] listing numerous strategies to protect local agriculture.

Other "big picture" thinkers write from the perspective of strengthening local economies, sustainable growth, and peak oil constraints.[14] James Howard Kunstler has long raged against the ills of suburbs and the American rationalization to grow incessantly, expect something for nothing, and consume its way into a poverty of natural resources and social capital.[15] The Transition Town movement and similar groups pushing for conversion to local, sustainable living[16] have recognized that communities must start functioning like ecosystems to remain viable, and that energy and food and all other inputs assumed to perpetually support us at current consumption rates will be drastically reduced without a sea change of behavior.

WATER QUALITY

As is typical with other common pool resources, water-quality degradation benefits a few users with the costs shared by all. The unidirectional nature of water flow complicates incentives to keep waters clean, as states, cities, or individuals can pollute water to the detriment of downstream neighbors while feeling little of the harm. Because of this, water-quality laws tend to be promulgated at the federal level.

Federal

The Federal Water Pollution Control Act (FWPCA) of 1972 (hereafter referred to as the Clean Water Act [CWA]) was the first federal water-quality law that achieved significant national water-quality improvement. The CWA initially focused on point source discharges from industries (factory outfall pipes into water bodies) and cities (wastewater treatment plant outfalls). The CWA's National Pollutant Discharge Elimination System (NPDES) was instituted to measure type and amount of pollutants being discharged into water and permit it, if the U.S. Environmental Protection Agency (EPA) decided this was a reasonable amount and reduced concentration of effluent from best management practices. Consequently, the EPA could tally cumulative totals of all pollutants to make sure that collectively they did not exceed the Total Maximum Daily Load (TMDL) a water body could accept without degradation. This law gave factories incentive to improve their in-house recycling of substances, such as metal-plating plants, so fewer pollutants went into the waters. In addition, a historic amount of money was made available through this bill to improve wastewater treatment plants as well, both by building wastewater plants where they did not exist and upgrading existing plants to secondary treatment.

After initial improvements of waterways (i.e., no more rivers catching on fire, far less noxious sewage in the rivers), improvement stopped as more industries and wastewater plants began exceeding their NPDES permits and were still allowed to operate by the EPA.

The CWA also addressed nonpoint source (NPS) pollution, emanating from diffuse sources like agriculture, mining, forestry, and urban runoff. Because this is harder to measure at the source, and even more difficult to monitor and enforce, NPS pollution was initially addressed by education programs and voluntary reductions. As they remain voluntary, polluters do not comply. Agriculture is the biggest source of NPS pollution.

Nonagricultural Requirements and Effects on Food

The main pollutants serving as measures of NPS pollution are heavy metals, sediment, salinity, bacteria, and nutrients. Reduction of toxic chemicals, heavy metals, and pathogens would no doubt better protect our food supply although it is hard to find studies looking at these issues. The effects of NPS pollutants in irrigation water are not widely known. We know plants take up chemicals such as perchlorate, with perchlorate found in irrigated vegetables and milk.[17] We know plants take up heavy metals, as they are studied for their efficacy in removing heavy metals from streams contaminated with mining effluent.[18] We also know pathogens from untreated or incompletely treated sewage effluent can spread salmonella,[19] *E. coli*,[20] and cholera[21] on food irrigated with this water.

Agricultural Requirements and Effects on Food

The agricultural lobby has been successful so far in avoiding any kind of requirements under the CWA. Even the relatively new problem of CAFOs has been skillfully maneuvered by industrial farms merely writing a "Manure Management Plan" and then "voluntarily" following the plan. This results in continued water pollution with nutrients and pathogens, which can then be taken up again by the next downstream irrigators, possibly contaminating their crops. OMB-WATCH,[22] a watchdog over the President's Office of Management and Budget, has long followed this disregard by the EPA of CAFO externalities. Besides manure and fertilizer runoff, farms still apply enough pesticides (some of questionable safety) that run off aboveground or are transported through subsurface flow back into waterways.

At least in regard to nutrients and sediment, CWA guidelines for agricultural TMDLs for phosphorus and total suspended solids are now available to state environmental agencies, with expected compliance deadlines in 2012. Guidelines serve only as suggestions, however, so these deadlines are not enforceable.

State

Theoretically, states must be minimally consistent with CWA requirements and enforce them through their own state environmental departments. In practice, there has long been a pronounced variability between states in regard to enforcement depending on the environmental awareness of the citizens, the wealth of the state, and the strength of the industrial, agricultural, and municipal lobbies.

Local

In rare instances, a city can control the water quality of its source water. If the city's lake is its sole source of drinking water, it may regulate what activities may occur on or near the water, up to denying access to the water surface and requiring buffer zones around the lake where certain land uses, roads, or chemical applications may not occur. Similarly, if a city is sitting over the recharge zone of its own aquifer, it may place strict regulations on above- or below-ground chemical use or additional construction of impervious surfaces. Outside of these two scenarios, a city must use water of variable quality over which it has no control.

WATER QUANTITY

How much water is available to any state, city, or individual depends on long-term and short-term regional precipitation, how many external or internal water sources they may draw from, the degree to which they are constrained by interstate compacts and state water law, and how many others compete for the same water.

Interstate Compacts

Interstate water compacts are primarily allocation agreements between states over shared rivers to prevent upriver areas from damming or diverting more than a reasonable share of the river. Like any political agreement, they reflect the relative strength of the various signatories. As of 2009, thirty-five compacts had been adopted.[23]

Colorado River

The Colorado River Compact of 1922 resulted in the Upper Basin (Wyoming, Colorado, Utah, and New Mexico) and the Lower Basin (Nevada, California, and Arizona) each being allotted 7.5 million acre feet (MAF) per year of water. The Lower Basin (with a greater population) was also given a guarantee of 7.5 MAF over a ten-year rolling average.[24] This gives Lower Basin cities and agriculture slightly less incentive to use water efficiently since they are guaranteed roughly the same amount each year. This is unfortunate since irrigated lands in the lower basin are hot deserts where much more irrigation water evaporates from cropland. Upper Basin states are left to share the shortage burden in drought years.

Because populations are growing in all of these states, some water will move out of agriculture, since it uses 70 to 80 percent of water in these states. Cities needing more water will surely buy more water rights from agriculture. A 2008 book, *Unquenchable: America's Water Crisis and What to Do About It*,[25] gives numerous examples of western farmers who are innovating ways to use less water as demand for water increases and cities look to agriculture to purchase water rights.

State Laws

State water law generally refers to how the waters of the state are allocated within the state and to what use they may be put. Historically, these laws concern only quantity and not quality issues. Moreover, nonhuman uses of water by flora and fauna are rarely considered. State water laws are not only complex, but also differ greatly between the drier and wetter regions of the country. A brief summary of the different surface-water laws and groundwater laws are given to underscore how water is so mismanaged in most areas.

Prior Appropriation

Prior appropriation is used in the dry inland western states. Water must be diverted from a watercourse onto that land no matter how distant it is, and it must be put to beneficial use. The initial date when each water right was developed forever remains with that water right, and the older the right, the greater priority the owner has to use her full allocation of water before anyone else on the river (upstream or downstream) who has rights junior to hers. This "first come, first served" system was developed for dry lands where drought is common. In dry times, owners with senior water rights may access their water, and the owners with junior water rights get nothing.

Riparian

Riparian water law is used in the wetter, eastern states and generally ties water use to land bordering water. Owners of riparian land (on lakes or rivers) automatically have a right to a reasonable use of waters, if it does not prevent other riparians from reasonable use of the waters. This implies that all will suffer equally in times of shortage, but many states using riparian law do not measure what each user takes, so they can scarcely enforce an equitable reduction in use.

Regulated Riparian

Regulated riparian, or hybrid states, use a mix of riparian and prior appropriation because their states are part arid and part humid. These states include the coastal western states and the lower plains states along the one hundredth meridian. There is more regulation, measurement, and oversight of water in these states than in riparian states.

Groundwater Issues

The laws governing groundwater use not only vary from state to state but also within states that use the same type of surface-water law. Use of groundwater can range from the strict laws to "take all you want." In Colorado, every water right is quantified, every well is metered, and water commissioners (water police) in every watershed basin monitor all wells and surface-water diversions to prevent cheating. Then, there is Texas. The Texas "rule of capture" asserts that landowners have the right to pump as much water as they can from beneath their property, even if it harms other groundwater users.

Advocates for Change

State water laws for the most part are extremely antiquated and hinder states from sustainably using water. One advocate for change to improve water laws is a professional organization trying to update water laws. The American Society of Civil Engineers wrote two manuals,[26] the *Appropriative Rights Model Water Code* and the *Regulated Riparian Model Water Code*, to assist states with improving their water laws. In particular, they advocate conjunctive use of ground and surface waters (i.e., manage and measure both of them, not just surface water), metering all water use, and converting all riparian states to regulated riparian.

CONCLUSION

To a large degree, land and water use cannot be disentangled with regard to the impacts they have on industrial agriculture and the effects they suffer from it. At the same time, the world's population continues to grow, creating an increased demand on diminishing agricultural acres. Since land use, water use, and food production are decided and acted on by a relatively small proportion of the population, most people are unaware that the trends in each (i.e., more resource demand and less quality) are converging to a crisis point.

Clearly, individuals can do many things to address these issues. At the local level, proven strategies have been implemented for protecting large-scale rural agricultural land, while encouraging the remaining agriculture within city boundaries to convert to more profitable, intensive production of vegetables and fruits. Zoning to allow farmers markets in town would link urban residents with local farms. But most planners developing the plans and regulations have a traditional planning background, which is to say there is little knowledge of larger-scale resource constraints or environmental systems. This lack of knowledge means that individuals must press their city officials to improve their planning vision. But citizens must do more than work to change local land uses. Every state has room to improve the way it allocates water, enforces federal water quality laws, or mandates stricter ones, and protects agricultural lands from sprawl while reducing or recycling the pollution they create. State legislators must be lobbied by citizen groups to debate and address these issues at the state level. The same applies to the federal level. Imagine how much cleaner our water, land, and air would be if executive and legislative branches were pressed to address food security and to realize that food security cannot be achieved without comprehensively managing land and water resources at every level. Industrial agriculture is not sustainable, and the shift toward sustainable agriculture cannot be achieved by merely purchasing organic or local food. Beyond individual behavior, citizens must reach out to teach and reform every level of government. Government systems have long viewed law and policy about land, water, and food as discrete subjects. Wendell Berry spoke to the futility of such isolated pursuits when he wrote,

> And so I must declare my dissatisfaction with movements to promote soil conserva-
> tion or clean water or clean air or wilderness preservation or sustainable agriculture
> or community health or the welfare of children. Worthy as these and other goals may
> be, they cannot be achieved alone. I am dissatisfied with such efforts because they are
> too specialized, they are not comprehensive enough, they are not radical enough,
> they virtually predict their own failure by implying that we can remedy or control
> effects while leaving causes in place.[27]

The framework to nurture sustainable agriculture is built with citizens who fight the causes of natural resource decline at every level. If you want food security, look to yourselves and your government, look to your precious lands and waters.

NOTES

1. Duff Wilson, *Fateful Harvest: The True Story of a Small Town, A Global Industry, and a Toxic Secret* (New York: Harper Collins, 2001).

2. American Planning Association, http://www.planning.org/growingsmart/guide-book/seven07.htm (accessed January 4, 2009).

3. Kameshwari Pothukuchi and Jerome L. Kaufman, "The Food System: A Stranger to the Planning Field," *Journal of the American Planning Association* 66, no. 2 (2000): 113–24.

4. USDA Economic Research Service, "Land Use, Value, and Management," http://www.ers.usda.gov/Briefing/LandUse/ (accessed January 4, 2009).

5. Alfred E. Kahn, "The Tyranny of Small Decisions: Market Failures, Imperfections, and the Limits of Economics," *Kylos* 19 (1966): 23–47.

6. The Food Security Learning Center, "Land Use Planning," http://www.whyhunger.org/programs/fslc/topics/land-use-planning.html (accessed April 12, 2008).

7. American Farmland Trust, http://www.farmland.org/ (accessed December 2, 2008).

8. John R. Nolon and Patricia E. Salkin, *Land Use in a Nutshell* (St. Paul, MN: West Publishing, 2006).

9. Rutherford H. Platt, *Land Use Control: Geography, Law, and Public Policy* (Washington, DC: Island Press, 2004).

10. Pierre Crosson and R. Hass, "Agricultural Land," *Current Issues in Natural Resource Policy* (Washington, DC: Resources for the Future, 1982).

11. Oregon's Department of Land Conservation and Development, http://www.lcd.state.or.us/ (accessed November 4, 2008).

12. Portland Bureau of Planning and Sustainability, http://www.portlandonline.com/planning/index.cfm?c=28534 (accessed November 4, 2008).

13. Randall Arendt, *Rural by Design: Maintaining Small Town Character* (Chicago: Planners Press, 1994).

14. Peak oil refers to the moment at which 50 percent of the known reserves of global oil have been pumped, after which there is an inevitable decline of oil production. Traditional liquid fuel production peaked in 2005.

15. James H. Kunstler, *The Geography of Nowhere: The Rise and Decline of America's Man-Made Landscape* (New York: Simon & Schuster, 1993); James H. Kunstler, *The*

Long Emergency: Surviving the Converging Catastrophes of the Twenty-First Century (New York: Atlantic Monthly Press, 2005).

16. Pat Murphy, *Plan C: Community Survival Strategies for Peak Oil and Climate Change* (Gabriola Island, BC: New Society Publishers, 2008); Peter Newman and Isabella Jennings, *Cities as Sustainable Ecosystems: Principles and Practices* (Washington, DC: Island Press, 2008); Rob Hopkins, *The Transition Handbook: From Oil Dependency to Local Resilience* (Foxhole, Devon, England: Green Books, 2008).

17. Environmental Working Group, Rocket Fuel (Perchlorate) Studies, http://www.ewg.org/featured/225 (accessed November 15, 2008).

18. See, for example, Monica O. Mendez and Raina M. Maier, "Phytostabilization of Mine Tailings in Arid and Semiarid Environments—An Emerging Remediation Technology," *Environmental Health Perspectives* 116, no. 3 (2008): 278–83.

19. Gail Cordy et al., "Do Pharmaceuticals, Pathogens, and Other Organic Wastewater Compounds Persist When Wastewater Is Used for Recharge?" *Ground Water Monitoring and Remediation* 24, no. 2 (2004): 58–69.

20. Natural Resources Conservation Service, "Water Quality – Reducing Risk of E. Coli 0157:H7 Contamination" (Water Quality Technical Note No. 19, October 29, 2007), http://www.nm.nrcs.usda.gov/technical/tech-notes/water/water19.pdf (accessed November 11, 2008).

21. Dennis L. Corwin and Scott A. Bradford, "Environmental Impacts and Sustainability of Degraded Water Reuse," *Journal of Environmental Quality* 37 (2008):S1–S7; Matthew McKinney, "Linking Growth and Land Use to Water Supply," *Land Lines* 15, no. 2 (2003): 4–6.

22. OMBWATCH, http://www.ombwatch.org (accessed November 4, 2008).

23. Thomas Cech, *Principles of Water Resources: History, Development, Management, and Policy*, 2nd ed. (New York: Wiley, 2005).

24. Ibid.

25. Robert Glennon, *Unquenchable: America's Water Crisis and What to Do About It* (Washington, DC: Island Press, 2009).

26. Joseph W. Dellapenna, ed., *Appropriative Rights Model Water Code* (Reston, VA: ASCE, 2007); Joseph W. Dellapenna, ed., *Regulated Riparian Model Water Code* (Reston, VA: ASCE, 2004).

27. Wendell Berry, "In Distrust of Movements," *Resurgence Issue* January/February (2000): 198; reprinted at http://thegreenhorns.wordpress.com/essays/essay-in-distrust-of-movements-by-wendell-berry/ (accessed December 31, 2008).

RESOURCE GUIDE

Suggested Reading

Arendt, Randall. *Rural by Design: Maintaining Small Town Character*. Chicago: Planners Press, 1994.
Getches, David H. *Water Law in a Nutshell*. St. Paul, MN: West Publishing, 1997.
Glennon, Robert. *Water Follies: Groundwater Pumping and the Fate of America's Fresh Waters*. Washington, DC: Island Press, 2002.
Glennon, Robert. *Unquenchable: America's Water Crisis and What to Do About It*. New York: Island Press, 2009.
Hopkins, Rob. *The Transition Handbook: From Oil Dependency to Local Resilience*. Foxhole, Devon, England: Green Books, 2008.

Kunstler, James H. *The Long Emergency: Surviving the Converging Catastrophes of the Twenty-First Century*. New York: Atlantic Monthly Press, 2005.

Murphy, Pat. *Plan C: Community Survival Strategies for Peak Oil and Climate Change*. Gabriola Island, BC: New Society Publishers, 2008.

Newman, Peter, and Isabella Jennings. *Cities as Sustainable Ecosystems: Principles and Practices*. Washington, DC: Island Press, 2008.

Nolon, John R., and Patricia E. Salkin. *Land Use in a Nutshell*. St. Paul, MN: West Publishing, 2006.

Pothukuchi, Kameshwari, and Jerome L. Kaufman. "The Food System: A Stranger to the Planning Field." *Journal of the American Planning Association* 66, no. 2 (2000).

Web Sites

American Farmland Trust, http://www.farmland.org/.

Local Harvest: Real Food, Real Farmers, Real Communities, www.localharvest.org.

The Food Security Learning Center, http://www.worldhungeryear.org/fslc/faqs2/ria_801. asp?section=18&click=2.

Smart Growth Online, http://www.smartgrowth.org/.

2

Soil Degradation and Soil Conservation

Patricia E. Norris and John M. Kerr

Soil degradation and conservation are inextricably linked to food production. Globally, some countries face more serious constraints to food production than others. Everywhere, though, protecting soil requires understanding soil degradation, methods for conserving soil, constraints to soil conservation investment, and policies to promote conservation. We focus on three main points. First, soil degradation takes many forms and has on- and off-site impacts. Second, discussions of soil conservation are commonly connected to controlling soil erosion. This chapter focuses largely on soil erosion, but recognizes that conservation is about controlling soil degradation more generally. Third, numerous socioeconomic factors explain why farmers may or may not adopt conservation practices to address erosion and other problems. To be effective, policies aimed at increasing the adoption of conservation must address these underlying constraints.

TYPES AND EXTENT OF SOIL DEGRADATION

Soil degradation is "any change or disturbance to the soil perceived to be deleterious or undesirable" and normally connotes change or disturbance in soil quality, including soil structure and biological productivity or complexity.[1] Reducing soil quality reduces its capacity "to function, within natural or managed ecosystem boundaries, to sustain plant and animal productivity, maintain or enhance water and air quality, and support human health and habitation."[2] While soil erosion is the most commonly described type of soil degradation, other physical, chemical, and biological changes in soils also reduce soil quality. More generally, physical degradation results from water or wind erosion or from changes in soil structure,[3] such as compaction, crusting and sealing, or water-logging and subsidence of organic soils.[4] Chemical degradation involves processes such as salinization, alkalinization, or acidification of soils, and biological degradation occurs from a reduction in soil humus, vegetation, or soil biota.[5] Not all soil degradation is caused by human activities, but modern scientific and popular environmental literature almost always uses the term degradation in reference to perceived decreases in natural conditions caused by changes or disturbances made by humans.[6] Natural changes to soils (caused, for example, by shifts in vegetation, glaciation, and climate change) occur slowly, so that soils are able to adjust or adapt, although some natural changes do occur rapidly and with drastic results (e.g., volcanic eruptions). Most changes in soil quality are human induced, however, and are "rapid, disturb the delicate balance between soil and its environment, and lead to drastic alterations in soil properties and processes."[7] Information on the extent of soil degradation worldwide is limited. The most comprehensive assessment of global soil degradation was sponsored by the United Nations Environment Programme and was completed in 1990. The Global Assessment of Soil Degradation (GLASOD) categorized types of soil degradation according to water erosion, wind erosion, chemical degradation, and physical degradation. While extensive, GLASOD represented a gross assessment and does not necessarily assist with understanding soil degradation issues regionally or locally.

Table 2.1 summarizes GLASOD's findings. In total, human-induced soil degradation worldwide has affected 1966 million hectares, or 15 percent of total land area. The study concluded that human-induced soil degradation has affected 24 percent of inhabited land area. Values ranged from 12 percent in North America, 18 percent in South America, and 19 percent in Oceania to 26 percent in Europe, 27 percent in Africa and Central America, and 31 percent in Asia.[8]

In the United States, the National Resources Inventory (NRI) provides the most comprehensive look at the extent and severity of soil degradation. The NRI is a survey of land use and natural resource conditions and trends on nonfederal land in the United States, focusing primarily on soil erosion.[9] In 2003, just under 41.3 million hectares of cropland in the United States (28 percent of all cropland) were eroding above soil loss tolerance rates, while 107.6 million hectares of cropland (72 percent) were eroding at or below soil loss tolerance rates. This compares to 1982 when the area eroding above soil loss tolerance rates was 40 percent

Table 2.1.
Extent of Soil Erosion Globally as Estimated by the Global Assessment of Soil Degradation (GLASOD) Project

	Water Erosion	Wind Erosion	Chemical Degradation	Physical Degradation
	(million hectares)			
Africa	227	186	62	19
Asia	441	222	74	12
South America	123	42	70	8
Central America	46	5	7	5
North America	60	35	+*	1
Europe	114	42	26	36
Oceana	83	16	1	2
World	1094	548	240	83

Source: Adapted from L. R. Oldeman, "The Global Extent of Soil Degradation," in *Soil Resilience and Sustainable Land Use*, ed. D. J. Greenland and I. Szabolcs (Wallingford, UK: CAB International, 1994).
*"+" denotes an area smaller than one million hectares.

(68.4 million hectares).[10] A tolerance rate is a soil-specific sustainable level of erosion; soil quality and productivity can be maintained when erosion is at or below tolerance rates.[11] Lal and others report the extent of water erosion on grazing land and Conservation Reserve Program (CRP) land in the United States between 1982 and 1997 using NRI data. (CRP land is retired from crop production for a specified period of time and planted with permanent vegetative cover to protect against soil erosion.) About 12.1 percent of pastureland and rangeland acres (approximately twenty-six million hectares) was affected by water erosion during the period 1982–1992. Over that time, water erosion increased slightly on areas being grazed and declined slightly on areas remaining ungrazed. Although CRP acreage increased from 5.59 million hectares in 1987 to 13.24 million hectares in 1997, the amount of CRP land affected by water erosion dropped from 12.9 percent in 1987 to 1.2 percent by 1997.[12]

CAUSES AND IMPACTS OF SOIL DEGRADATION

Table 2.2 lists causes of soil degradation. Clearly, most causes are largely associated with agriculture, although soil degradation is observed across forestland, urban land, and developed areas. According to GLASOD, agricultural practices are the principle cause of soil degradation worldwide (see Table 2.3). However, it is not clear whether soil degradation on agricultural land is more or less damaging than, for example, soil erosion from construction sites, mining operations, or other disturbed areas. Nevertheless, the balance of this chapter focuses on the impacts of agricultural soil degradation and on conservation practices that reduce these impacts.

Table 2.2.
Causes of Soil Degradation

Type	Causes
Physical	Deforestation
	Biomass burning
	Denudation
	Tillage up and down the slope
	Excessive animal, human, and vehicular traffic
	Uncontrolled grazing
	Monoculture
Chemical	Excessive irrigation with poor quality water
	Lack of adequate drainage
	No, little, or excessive use of inorganic fertilizers
	Land application of industrial/urban wastes
Biological	Removal and/or burning of residues
	No, little, or excessive use of biosolids (e.g., manure, mulch)
	Monoculture without growing cover crops in the rotation cycle
	Excessive tillage

Source: Adapted from R. Lal et al., *Soil Degradation in the United States: Extent, Severity, and Trends* (Boca Raton, FL: CRC Press, 2004).

Table 2.3.
Extent of Soil Degradation Types and Causes, Worldwide (million hectares)

Types of Soil Degradation	Causes			
	Deforestation of Natural Vegetation	Overexploitation of Natural Vegetation	Agricultural (Crop and Livestock) Activities	Bio-industrial Activities
Water erosion	471	36	586	–*
Wind erosion	44	85	419	–
Chemical degradation	62	10	147	23
Physical degradation	1	+†	80	–

Source: Adapted from L. R. Oldeman, "The Global Extent of Soil Degradation," in *Soil Resilience and Sustainable Land Use*, ed. D. J. Greenland and I. Szabolcs (Wallingford, UK: CAB International, 1994).
* "–" indicates none were identified.
† "+" indicates area smaller than one million hectares.

Soil degradation impacts are observed in agricultural fields when soil quality is reduced and off-site when water quality, air quality, or other ecosystem functions are impaired. The principal on-site impact is reduced crop yields. In general, erosion-induced reductions in crop yields result from reduction in rooting depth, loss of plant nutrients and soil organic matter, loss of plant available water and soil water-holding capacity, and damage to young plants.[13] Chemical degradation, such as the buildup of soluble salts in the root zone common in some heavily irrigated areas, reduces crop yields because of toxicity to plants or negative impacts on soil physical properties.[14] For all types of soil degradation, crop yield effects will vary with soil type, crop, initial soil conditions, and severity of degradation. Declining productivity may not be realized in high-input production systems until yields are near their maximum and declining soil quality is manifested in higher input costs (e.g., fertilizer or water) rather than lower yields.[15]

Water and wind erosion generally move the most fertile soils. When erosion removes those soils from a field, soils of poorer structure with less available organic matter and lower water-holding capacity are left behind.[16] In some regions, farmers depend on the deposition of sediment that has been washed or blown in from somewhere else, improving rooting depth and soil moisture, to maintain agricultural production.[17] In other cases, crops may be damaged or even buried by water- and wind-borne sediments.[18] Water- and wind-borne sediments also commonly are deposited in lakes and streams, increasing turbidity, shortening reservoir life spans, impeding navigation, and damaging fish spawning habitats.[19] When runoff or eroded sediment from agricultural fields carry nutrients and pesticides, receiving waters are contaminated, nutrients accelerate the eutrophication of lakes and reservoirs, and pesticides can be toxic to fish.[20] However, recent research has shown that sedimentation tends to have specific sources and sediment deposited in waterways tends to come largely from adjacent land. Soil eroded from land farther from waterways may leave the farmer's field from which it originates but tends to be trapped by natural filters in the landscape before it can reach a waterway.[21]

Concerns about the relationship between soil erosion, atmospheric carbon, and climate change are receiving increasing attention from soil scientists and others exploring whether soil degradation plays a role in greenhouse gas emissions. Organic carbon stored within soil resources has been called the largest active pool of organic carbon, excluding fossil organic carbon.[22] Thus, the role of healthy soil resources in global carbon sequestration is of interest, as is the fate of soil organic carbon when soils are disturbed, whether through tillage or through erosion and other causes of soil degradation. Lal describes two distinct schools of thought about whether soil erosion serves as a carbon sink or a carbon source and, similarly, whether soil tillage increases carbon sequestration or carbon emissions.[23] He suggests that additional research is needed to determine whether more of the soil organic carbon that is moved by erosion is buried in deposition or in aquatic ecosystems and thus protected against mineralization, or if more is redistributed over the landscape, subjected to mineralization, and thus available to the atmospheric carbon pool.

SOIL CONSERVATION

Soil conservation traditionally has been equated with erosion control. However, there is increasing recognition that serious soil degradation problems can occur in areas where erosion is not a problem and that soil conservation is about addressing all causes of declining soil quality. More broadly, references to soil and water conservation reflect a focus on agronomic practices that control soil degradation, reduce runoff of water from agricultural fields, and reduce water-quality problems related to erosion and other soil-related problems.

A 2006 review of the benefits of conservation on cropland takes this broad view and describes conservation practices for soil, water, nutrient, pest, and landscape management.[24] Not surprisingly, the authors offer a lengthy list of conservation practices. The soil management chapter alone describes eight categories comprising twenty-nine different practices.[25] The U.S. Department of Agriculture's (USDA) Natural Resources Conservation Service recommends combining individual practices to maximize benefits across soil, water, and other natural resource conservation needs. This chapter reviews selected conservation practices, focusing on erosion reduction and soil quality.

Residue management practices are designed to "manage the amount, orientation, and distribution of crop and other plant residue on the soil surface year-round."[26] Conservation tillage practices, for example, maintain residue cover on the soil (30 percent to 100 percent cover depending on the practice adopted). No-till is a type of conservation tillage that involves planting crops directly into narrow slots in otherwise untilled soil. Alternatively, in mulch tillage, the field is tilled but the tillage equipment leaves at least 30 percent of the soil surface covered with crop residue. Conservation tillage minimizes water and wind erosion, maintains or improves soil organic carbon, and conserves soil moisture. In 2004, no-till was practiced on 25 percent of U.S. cropland. Farmers in parts of South America use no-till much more than do U.S. farmers (45 percent to 60 percent of cropland in Argentina, Brazil, and Paraguay), but no-till accounts for only about 2 percent of cropland in Africa, Asia, and Europe combined.[27]

Cover crops are another example of residue management. They are "close-growing crops grown primarily for the purpose of protecting and improving soil between periods of regular crop production or between trees and vines in orchards and vineyards."[28] Cover crops prevent erosion and help build soil organic matter. Long-term conservation cover also involves using vegetation to protect soil, although this is not technically considered a cover crop. Instead, land is fully removed from crop production and replaced by permanent vegetation.

Whereas residue management and cover crops cover soil to hold it in place, other practices limit movement of soil within a field or prevent its movement across the field boundary or into water bodies. Buffer strips (vegetative barriers) are strips of permanent vegetation that buffer movement of water or wind and associated sediment or runoff. Filter strips are a special form of buffers planted along shorelines to capture sediment and runoff before it moves into water. Generally, vegetative strips of all sorts are combined with other in-field practices to maximize conservation benefits.[29]

Carefully arranging field rows can reduce water movement across fields. Contour planting refers to orienting tillage and planting so that rows follow along the contour of a field, rather than running up and down a slope. This type of arrangement enables individual rows to capture rainfall, maximizing water infiltration and minimizing runoff. Contour farming is not as well suited to rolling topography with irregular slopes, and generally it should be used in combination with other conservation practices to maximize conservation benefits. In many cases, contour farming has been replaced by conservation tillage and cover crops.[30]

To summarize, many approaches can be followed to conserve soil on agricultural land. Some of these approaches can be used jointly, and the best approach depends on the specific situation. The most drastic approach is to take land out of production altogether and protect soil with permanent vegetation.

SOCIOECONOMIC BARRIERS TO CONSERVATION PRACTICE

Given the numerous practices available to prevent soil erosion and associated soil degradation, why do some farmers allow land to become degraded and fail to invest in soil conservation? Understanding which of the many possible reasons are applicable in a particular case is essential in designing project and policy interventions. A policy tool that targets the wrong constraint to investment will not work. This section summarizes several constraints; the next section reviews potential corresponding policy approaches to help overcome them.

Lack of Information

Researchers and program managers often assume that farmers do not invest in soil conservation because they do not understand it. Some degradation processes like sheet erosion are difficult to perceive, so the assumption that farmers are not aware of these processes is understandable and sometimes is correct. However, in countries around the world where officials believed that farmers did not understand or perceive erosion, research found that in fact they did, and other reasons explained lack of investment.[31] This is important, because working to make farmers aware of erosion will have little impact if real constraints to investment lie elsewhere.

Off-Site Nature of Damages or Benefits of Conservation

As described earlier, soil erosion can have both on-site and off-site impacts. Naturally, a farmer's bottom line is affected primarily by on-site costs of erosion, whereas off-site costs affect other people or society in general. Research from around the world has explored the nature and location of costs of soil erosion. If the benefits of soil conservation are realized primarily off-site, a farmer who invests in soil conservation will see most of the benefit go to others. Not surprisingly, many farmers will find it difficult to justify such investments.

Offsetting Productivity Enhancements

Even where erosion costs are incurred primarily on-site, farmers may choose not to invest in soil conservation if they have alternative means of overcoming those costs. For example, if soil erosion reduces soil fertility, farmers can offset productivity losses by adding more fertilizer. They may choose to do this if fertilizer is a much cheaper alternative. Of course, depending on soil type and depth, continued erosion might cause greater and greater productivity losses requiring increasing amounts of fertilizer each year to offset damage. This depends heavily on soil type and depth and whether decreased productivity results from loss of fertile organic matter or loss of depth. On very deep soil, initial erosion might cause a loss of fertile organic matter that reduces productivity but fixed increases in the amount of fertilizer year after year would overcome productivity loss. If, on the other hand, productivity loss stems from reduced soil depth, the ability to offset productivity losses with fertilizer applications would be limited.

As mentioned earlier, eroding soil often just moves from one place to another, and research in many places has found that farmers actively "harvest" soil that moves onto their field from another field further up the slope. A farmer who is confident in the possibility of harvesting soil deposited from up the slope may be unconcerned about losing some soil from his own field.[32]

Planning Horizons

Soil erosion is a gradual process, and soil conservation often has gradual benefits, both in terms of on-site productivity and off-site pollution.[33] A farmer with a short-term planning horizon may be unwilling to invest in soil conservation that would yield only long-term benefits. The most likely reason for a short planning horizon is if a farmer does not expect to be on the land for very long and does not expect to be affected by erosion. This helps explain why research from around the world shows that farmers using land on short-term rental leases rarely invest in soil conservation, unless it is stipulated in rental agreements or has some short-term benefits.[34]

This issue is more policy relevant in developing countries than in the United States, and two main scenarios arise. First, numerous farmers in many developing countries do not have formal legal title to land they farm. If they fear eviction from their lands, they certainly will have a short planning horizon, with little incentive to invest in conservation. The second scenario concerns "land to the tiller" laws found in many developing countries. They specify that someone who leases the same piece of land year after year eventually can claim ownership to it. In India and many other countries, landowners avoid leasing the same piece of land to the same farmer for more than one season, and it is unsurprising that such lands tend to suffer disproportionately from soil erosion.[35]

Land Prices Do Not Reflect Damage or Protection

Farmers who plan to sell land soon may invest in conservation if erosion and conservation status affect the sale price. For example, if buyers of sloping land are willing to pay more for land that is protected, then a farmer planning to sell may want to invest in conservation to capture its value in the sale price. If the land will be converted to buildings or is considered valuable for real estate development, the sale price is unlikely to reward conservation investments. In such a case, the relevant aspects of the time horizon concern the likely future land use rather than the likely occupant. There is little point in allocating resources to conserve soil on agricultural land that will be paved over. Such a scenario may be part of a separate problem: land markets that do not reflect the full value of agricultural land. This problem requires its own chapter.

Poverty

Poverty makes it difficult to invest in soil conservation. Where costs are on-site, it will be difficult for an impoverished farmer to make an expensive conservation investment that yields only gradual benefits. Poverty can take different forms that create different kinds of constraints to investment.[36] In particular, soil conservation might require cash, or labor, or both. Some farmers have little cash but plenty of family labor. Such a family would be in a good position to invest in labor-intensive soil conservation, but not in soil conservation that requires a cash outlay. A farmer with cash on hand but not much labor faces the opposite problem.

Credit Constraints

Where soil conservation investment requires cash, an obvious potential constraint to investment is that the farmer knows it would be profitable but the long-term payoff creates a cash flow problem. In such a case, credit is the constraint to investment, not necessarily poverty. Many countries have poorly functioning credit markets that could create such a constraint. In India, for example, farmers can easily get bank credit to invest in irrigation or to improve irrigated fields, but the same credit is not usually available for rain-fed (unirrigated) fields.

Credit constraints vary between countries. Loans may not be given to farmers with land holdings below a certain size, or credit is available only for some kinds of land improvements. Government policy may stipulate that formal credit from banks be offered at below-market interest rates. This means that the lender loses money on every loan offered, so fewer loans are made.

Competing Objectives

In much of the world, technical solutions to soil conservation are known, but resource constraints make them difficult to implement. For example, using cover crops to protect soil quality is well known, but careful management is required to plant cover crops early enough to gain sufficient biomass for soil protection and then kill them in a timely manner to retain that biomass for soil protection while not competing with the main crop. Competition for available soil moisture and time and labor taken from income-earning enterprises are also concerns. However, organizations like the Sustainable Agriculture Network in the United States are working to provide information to farmers about cover crop benefits and management needs.[37] Also, as prices of nitrogen fertilizer track with petroleum prices, use of soil-incorporated cover crops to replace some or all fertilizer may increase. If a cover crop could be harvested for some gain—for example, as biomass for energy production—without sacrificing conservation benefits, then use of cover crops may grow.

In India, crop residue and manure cannot be retained easily on agricultural fields because of their high value as animal feed and fuel, respectively. In addition, on rainfed land, Indian farmers rarely adopt contour farming because it interferes with other aspects of their farming systems.[38] For example, in the Indian system of land inheritance, a farmer's land is divided among all the sons in a household. On mildly sloping land in rain-fed areas, lower areas tend to have deeper and more fertile soil than land farther up the slope. A father dividing land for inheritance gives each son a mixture of land in lower and higher areas to minimize disparities in land quality. Accordingly, many Indian farms consist of steep, narrow plots that run up and down slopes. Also, because long crop rows facilitate oxen-driven farming operations, farmers orient their crop rows up and down the slope rather than along the contour.

Constraints to Collective Action Where It Is Required

In many cases, a soil conservation investment requires coordinated or collective action by more than one person. This can take several forms. One example concerns gully erosion, which can be controlled by planting permanent vegetation throughout the gully to bind the soil and placing barriers across the gully to intercept runoff. When a gully is large enough, it must be treated in several places to ensure that runoff water cannot gain enough momentum to breach any given barrier. Typically, the more farmers whose action is required, the more difficult it is to make the investment, because the chances are greater that at least one party will be constrained from investing for some reason.

Another problem arises when land is not owned individually. This may refer to ownership by the state, by the community as a group (common property), by no one in particular (open access), or when ownership is not enforced and people treat the land as unowned. Under common property, decisions to invest in soil conservation are complicated by the challenge of convincing all the users to invest jointly. This is conceptually equivalent to the case described above of the gully that runs through several properties. Under open access, investment almost certainly will not be forthcoming. The reason is related to the case in which the costs of soil erosion occur off-site—that is, those who undertake the investment would bear the cost, but they would have to share the benefits with all the others.

CONSERVATION POLICY APPROACHES

Several policy approaches to encourage soil conservation have been applied to effectively address various barriers to adoption. Sometimes, the lack of conservation investment may call for unique, innovative policy tools.

A common conservation policy is public investment in conservation education and technical assistance for farmers, especially when the lack of information constrains conservation investment. In the United States, for example, adoption was low when no-till was first introduced, because it contradicted centuries of farming tradition that involved clean fields and neat rows of crops. USDA agency personnel, conservation districts, and extension educators then helped farmers adapt no-till to meet their needs and collaborated with companies to conduct research to develop the necessary equipment and chemicals.

Education and technical assistance may not be effective when costs are incurred primarily off-site and farmers do not invest in conservation because they foresee no profit or when farmers have competing interests for the use of their scarce labor, capital, and other resources. Instead, policy approaches like regulation or, more commonly, subsidization are more likely to increase conservation. Regulations making soil conservation a legal requirement have been used widely around the world. This policy approach was found in colonial India and several British colonies in Africa.[39] Even after independence, various former colonies have pursued the same approach. Some countries have land-use policies that prohibit farming on slopes above a certain grade, but such policies are difficult to enforce.

Iowa authorized soil conservation districts to adopt mandatory soil erosion limits in 1973. Farmers who objected to conservation requirements questioned their constitutionality in court and, ultimately, the limits and conservation obligations were upheld by Iowa's Supreme Court.[40] Nevertheless, laws requiring investment in soil conservation need to be undertaken with care as they can create bad relationships between government and farmers.

The most realistic way to encourage soil conservation where it is not profitable to the farmer or where competition exists for the resources needed for conservation is to help pay for it. Subsidizing conservation is also a consideration when poverty constrains conservation investments; poor farmers may need assistance that is specifically targeted to help them overcome labor or cash constraints. A common approach is government subsidization of soil conservation's startup costs. However, subsidies may not overcome barriers related to long-lived customs such as the Indian land inheritance system.

The U.S. CRP program is a notable effort to help farmers pay for the cost of conservation through long-term retirement of cropland. CRP was authorized to protect highly erodible land and water quality. Participating landowners are paid to retire land from crop production for a ten- to fifteen-year contract period and to plant and maintain a protective vegetative cover.[41] The CRP functions like a long-term easement; participating landowners retain rights to use land subject to easement provisions that restrict uses that reduce erosion protection provided by the vegetative cover. In some parts of the United States, improved wildlife habitat has been a significant benefit, and landowners have been able to lease hunting rights for additional income. Periodically, especially during periods of tight animal feed supplies, landowners have been allowed to use CRP acreage for grazing or hay production for a limited period. As of April 2008, the CRP was providing for permanent cover on almost thirty-five million acres.[42]

Because CRP contracts are not permanent, continuing conservation on land being released from CRP is of considerable concern. With grain prices at record levels and demand for biofuel feed stocks growing, CRP lands are converting to row-crop production in some regions. Erosion control and soil organic matter benefits of long-term cover can be lost, depending on how the newly converted land is managed. Some suggest that the soil quality benefits of CRP can be retained if land is returned to crop production with no-till or conservation tillage,[43] citing as an example the growth of soybean production in Brazil that occurred largely on native grassland converted to no-till soybeans with little or no loss of soil organic matter.[44]

Unfortunately, many farmers have abandoned subsidized conservation practices soon after special programs end and program officials no longer monitor compliance.[45] Because ongoing government monitoring is costly, searches for effective alternatives led to an approach known as payment for environmental services (PES). The key distinction in this approach is that ongoing subsidy payments are conditional on the farmer's compliance in maintaining the agreed-upon conservation practice. Still, the viability of PES as a policy instrument is limited because identifying and measuring environmental services and linking them to a particular land use are often difficult and costly.[46] One example of PES is found in many small Latin American cities where municipal water services pay farmers living upstream to protect the water source that supplies the city.[47] A small tax on water customers provides the funds for the environmental service payment.

A similar situation occurred in the United States when gradual land-use change in upstate watersheds began to threaten New York City's water quality. Faced with the prospect of spending more than six billion dollars to build and operate a water filtration plant, the city instead negotiated in upstate areas to acquire land, purchase conservation easements, and establish setbacks and buffer zones throughout the source watersheds. New York City paid land users less than one billion dollars to undertake these measures to protect water sources and make the filtration plant unnecessary.[48]

The Chicago Climate Exchange (CCX) pays farmers for land management practices that sequester carbon dioxide (that is, capture carbon dioxide from the atmosphere and store it in the soil). Conservation tillage sequesters carbon dioxide as does converting cropland to grassland. Depending on soil conditions, farmers are eligible to enroll with CCX to earn such payments.[49] Under certain conditions, the same land can be enrolled both with CCX and CRP.[50]

If short planning horizons constrain farmers from investing in soil conservation, policies that help lengthen the planning horizon are appropriate where feasible. Where ownership of land is unclear, changes in land tenure rules can be made. For example, legalizing farmers' occupation of land even though they do not hold title would help ensure that farmers have incentive to care for the land. In one Indonesian program, farmers on government land are allowed to remain there as long as they undertake conservation farming practices.[51] Where land-leasing laws, such as those in the "land to the tiller" scenario, discourage conservation, governments could change laws to encourage longer leases.

Finally, promoting collective action is notoriously difficult. Even after decades of study, researchers have made little progress in predicting the conditions under which it will take place. For some problems, a local authority could perhaps be responsible for helping to coordinate the actions of neighboring farmers. For open access and common property situations, success of different property rights arrangements varies by situation and location, so blanket recommendations are impossible. Location-specific research and experimentation are needed to find out what kinds of property rights arrangements work.[52]

CONCLUSION

Soil degradation comes in many forms with different degrees of severity and different measures available to correct it. Scherr concluded that soil degradation appears not to threaten aggregate global food supply by 2020, although in some regions the effects of soil degradation on food consumption by rural poor and on agricultural markets and incomes may be significant.[53] Overcoming soil degradation requires understanding specific problems and their biophysical causes, but also socioeconomic causes. For policy and program interventions to be successful, they must accurately target the underlying determinants of soil degradation and recognize the capacity of farmers and other land managers to respond effectively to the threat of degradation.

NOTES

1. D. L. Johnson et al., "Meanings of Environmental Terms," *Journal of Environmental Quality* 26, no. 3 (1997): 584.

2. D. L. Karlen et al., "Soil Quality: a Concept, Definition, and Framework for Evaluation," *Soil Science Society of America Journal* 61, no. 1 (1997): 6.

3. R. Lal, "Soil Degradation by Erosion," *Land Degradation and Development* 12, no. 6 (2001): 520.

4. L. R. Oldeman, "The Global Extent of Soil Degradation," in *Soil Resilience and Sustainable Land Use*, ed. D. J. Greenland and I. Szabolcs (Wallingford, UK: CAB International, 1994), 103.

5. R. Lal, "Soil Degradation," 520; L. R. Oldeman, "Global Extent," 102–3.

6. D. L. Johnson et al., "Meanings," 583.

7. R. Lal et al., *Soil Degradation in the United States: Extent, Severity, and Trends* (Boca Raton, FL: CRC Press, 2004), 5.

8. Ibid., 108.

9. Information on and reports from the NRI are available at http://www.nrcs.usda.gov/technical/NRI/ (accessed December 5, 2008).

10. USDA, Natural Resources Conservation Service, "National Resources Inventory, 2003 Annual NRI: Soil Erosion," http://www.nrcs.usda.gov/technical/NRI/2003/SoilErosion-mrb.pdf (accessed December 5, 2008).

11. R. Lal et al., *Soil Degradation in the U.S.*, 47.

12. R. Lal et al., *Soil Degradation in the U.S.*, 86–89.

13. R. Lal, "Soil Erosion Impact on Agronomic Productivity and Environment Quality," *Critical Reviews in Plant Sciences* 17, no. 4 (1998): 329.

14. I. Szabolcs, "Salt Buildup as a Factor of Soil Degradation," in *Methods for Assessment of Soil Degradation*, ed. R. Lal et al. (Boca Raton, FL: CRC Press, 1998), 256.

15. S. J. Scherr, *Soil Degradation: A Threat to Developing-Country Food Security by 2020?* (Washington, DC: International Food Policy Research Institute, 1999), 8.

16. R. Reeder and D. Westermann, "Soil Management Practices," in *Environmental Benefits of Conservation on Cropland: The Status of Our Knowledge*, ed. M. Schnepf and C. Cox (Ankeny, IA: Soil and Water Conservation Society, 2006), 3.

17. J. M. Laflen and E. J. Roose, "Methodologies for Assessment of Soil Degradation Due to Water Erosion," in *Methods for Assessment of Soil Degradation*, ed. R. Lal et al. (Boca Raton, FL: CRC Press, 1998), 32.

18. R. Lal, "Soil Erosion Impact," 333.

19. P. Crosson, "Impact of Erosion on Land Productivity and Water Quality in the United States." in *Soil Erosion and Conservation*, ed. S. A. El-Swaify, W. C. Moldenhauer and A. Lo (Ankeny, IA: Soil Conservation Society of America, 1985), 231.

20. E. H. Clark, J. A. Haverkamp, and W. Chapman. *Eroding Soils: The Off-Farm Impacts* (Washington, DC: The Conservation Foundation, 1985), 7.

21. M. van Noordwijk, J. Poulsen, and P. Ericksen, "Quantifying Off-Site Effects of Land Use Change: Filters, Flows and Fallacies," *Agriculture Ecosystems and Environment* 104, no. 1 (2004): 19–34.

22. S. V. Smith et al., "Budgets of Soil Erosion and Deposition for Sediments and Sedimentary Organic Carbon across the Conterminous United States," *Global Biogeochemical Cycles* 15, no. 3 (2001): 697.

23. R. Lal, "Soil Erosion and Carbon Dynamics," *Soil and Tillage Research* 81, no. 2 (2005): 137–42.

24. M. Schnepf and C. Cox, eds., *Environmental Benefits of Conservation on Cropland: The Status of Our Knowledge* (Ankeny, IA: Soil and Water Conservation Society, 2006).

25. R. Reeder and D. Westermann, "Soil Management," 5.

26. Ibid., 4.

27. R. Reeder and D. Westermann, "Soil Management," 6–7.

28. Ibid., 35.

29. R. Reeder and D. Westermann, "Soil Management," 49.

30. Ibid., 64.

31. J. Kerr and J. Pender, "Farmers' Perceptions of Soil Erosion and its Consequences in India's Semi-Arid Tropics," *Land Degradation and Development* 16, no. 3 (2005): 257.

32. J. Kerr and J. Pender, "Farmers' Perceptions," 264–65.

33. M. Schnepf and C. Cox, *Environmental Benefits of Conservation on Cropland.*

34. J. Kerr, "The Economics of Soil Degradation: From National Policy to Farmers' Fields," in *Assessing Soil Erosion at Multiple Scales*, ed. F. P. de Vries, F. Augus, and J. Kerr (Wallingford, UK: CAB International, 1997), 28–29.

35. J. Kerr, "The Economics of Soil Degradation," 28–29.

36. T. Reardon and S. Vosti, "Links between Rural Poverty and Environment in Developing Countries: Asset Categories and 'Investment Poverty,'" *World Development* 23, no. 9 (1995): 1495–1506.

37. A. Clark, *Managing Cover Crops Profitably*, 3rd ed. (Beltsville, MD: Sustainable Agriculture Network, 2007).

38. J. Kerr, "The Economics of Soil Degradation," 32–34.

39. J. Pretty and P. Shah, "Making Soil and Water Conservation Sustainable: From Coercion and Control to Partnerships and Participation," *Land Degradation and Development* 8, no. 1 (1997): 40–44.

40. *Woodbury County Soil Conservation District v. Ortner*, 279 N.W. 2d. 276 (1979).

41. See http://www.ers.usda.gov/Briefing/ConservationPolicy/retirement.htm (accessed December 5, 2008).

42. Data are available at http://content.fsa.usda.gov/crpstorpt/rmepegg/MEPEGGR1. HTM (accessed December 5, 2008).

43. R. Reeder and D. Westerman, "Soil Management," 67.

44. Ibid, 7.

45. J. Pretty and P. Shah, "Making Soil and Water Conservation Sustainable," 45.

46. S. Wunder, S. Engel, and S. Pagiola, "Taking Stock: A Comparative Analysis of Payments for Environmental Services Programs in Developed and Developing Countries," *Ecological Economics* 65, no. 4 (2008): 834–52.

47. M. Echavarría et al., *The Impacts of Payments for Watershed Services in Ecuador* (London: International Institute for Environment and Development, 2002).

48. M. Pires, "Watershed Protection for a World City: The Case of New York," *Land Use Policy* 21, no. 2 (2004): 167–68.

49. See http://www.chicagoclimateexchange.com/content.jsf?id=781 (accessed December 5, 2008).

50. See http://www.iowafarmbureau.com/special/carbon/pdf/Carbon%20Brochure% 20051109.pdf (accessed December 5, 2008).

51. See http://www.worldagroforestrycentre.org/Sea/Networks/RUPES/index.asp (accessed December 5, 2008).

52. T. Dietz et al., "The Drama of the Commons," in *The Drama of the Commons,* ed. E. Ostrom et al. (Washington, DC: National Academy Press, 2002), 25.

53. S. J. Scherr, *Soil Degradation*, 3.

RESOURCE GUIDE

Suggested Reading

Clark, A. *Managing Cover Crops Profitably*, 3rd ed. Beltsville, MD: Sustainable Agriculture Network, 2007.

Lal, R., ed. *Integrated Watershed Management in the Global Ecosystem*. Boca Raton, FL: CRC Press, 2000.

Ostrom, E., T. Dietz, N. Dlsak, P. C. Stern, S. Stonich, and E. U. Weber, eds. *The Drama of the Commons*. Washington, DC: National Academy Press, 2002.

Schnepf, M., and C. Cox, eds. *Environmental Benefits of Conservation on Cropland: The Status of Our Knowledge*. Ankeny, IA: Soil and Water Conservation Society, 2006.

Web Sites

Chicago Climate Exchange, http://www.chicagoclimateexchange.com.

Conservation Technology Information Center, http://www.ctic.purdue.edu/.

Leopold Center for Sustainable Agriculture, Cover Crop Resources, http://www. leopold.iastate.edu/research/eco_files/cover_crops.htm.

Office of Water and Watersheds, U.S. Environmental Protection Agency, http://www. epa.gov/owow/watershed/.

Soil and Water Conservation Society, http://www.swcs.org.

USDA Economic Research Service, *Agricultural Resources and Environmental Indicators*, http://www.ers.usda.gov/publications/arei/eib16/.

USDA Natural Resources Conservation Service, http://www.nrcs.usda.gov/.

3

Integrated Pest Management, Sustainability, and Risk: Linking Principles, Policy, and Practice

Michael J. Brewer and Marcia Ishii-Eiteman

INTEGRATED PEST MANAGEMENT CONCEPTS AND APPROACHES

Pest occurrence and outbreaks have become more frequent and severe, coincident to anthropomorphic-driven changes in cropping patterns, transportation, pesticide use, and climate. It is broadly recognized that alternatives to broad-spectrum pesticides are needed, given concerns over their environmental and human health risk profiles.[1] Confronting these challenges, integrated pest management (IPM) practitioners have taken advantage of recent advances in both ecologically based (e.g., biological control, cultural control) and input-based approaches (e.g., reduced-risk pesticides, genetically modified crops) in developing IPM tactics.[2] The sustainability and risk of individual IPM tactics differ within these classifications, however, and thus raise questions regarding the underlying goals and appropriate balance required to integrate individual tactics within IPM systems. Indeed, this contemporary issue mirrors the traditional dilemma of balancing pesticide use with biological control within an IPM program.[3]

IPM concepts have been in development since the 1950s, driven in part by challenges of pesticide-induced resistance, pest resurgence and secondary pest outbreaks, and emerging evidence of adverse environmental and human health impacts linked to chemical pesticide use. Early constructs emphasized judicious use of pesticides to suppress pests below "economic" thresholds and reduce adverse effects.[4] Regulatory and policy-based solutions to prevent or reduce harmful effects gained momentum through the turn of the twenty-first century.[5] More recently, biotechnology has advanced the development of genetically modified crops to address key pest control problems.[6] Meanwhile, agro-ecological sciences and innovations have contributed numerous ecologically based IPM strategies.[7] In this chapter, we assess a range of promising IPM approaches and policies well situated to address sustainable pest management requirements in food systems.

Foundations in Building IPM Systems

The Food and Agriculture Organization of the United Nations (FAO) definition for IPM focuses on

> the careful consideration of a number of pest control techniques that discourage the development of pest populations and keep pesticides and other interventions to levels that are economically justified and safe for human health and the environment. IPM emphasizes the growth of a healthy crop with the least possible disruption of agroecosystems, thereby encouraging natural pest control mechanisms.[8]

We emphasize characterization of sustainability and risk of IPM tactics to augment the more traditional approach of classification of IPM tactics by the nature of their development and deployment.[9] IPM tactics within any descriptive category may differ in sustainability and risks associated with their use (see Table 3.1). For example, generalizing sustainability and risk profiles of genetically modified crops and organic-compliant IPM tactics can be controversial and misleading. Assertions include that all genetically modified crops pose no risk and all organic IPM approaches are sustainable. Biotechnology has produced four major transgenic crops (maize, soy, cotton, and canola) resistant to certain insects and herbicides (thereby allowing the use of herbicides that would kill the unmodified crop). These crops pose a lower risk of poisoning agricultural workers and consumers relative to many chemical pesticides. But this human health risk profile does not necessarily extend to ecological and socioeconomic risk—for example, concern has been increasing regarding the following: (1) cross-pollination with nonmodified plants; (2) an increase in herbicide-resistant weeds; (3) the effects on biodiversity and nontarget organisms, including pest predators; and (4) the impacts on small-scale farmers' livelihoods, economic stability of the farm enterprise, culturally and economically important practices (e.g., women's seed-saving), and farmers' legal rights.[10] In the case of organic-compliant IPM tactics, some may be highly sustainable, such as managing noncrop vegetation to promote natural pest control, while others may rely on inputs that are not sustainable with long-term ecosystem functions, such as sulfur for disease control. As with traditional pesticides, patterns of sustainability and risk emerge only when appropriate attributes of the tactics are known (e.g., pesticide toxicity range, reproductive capability, and host range of biological control agents) and when ecological, health, social, and economic assessments are conducted over time.

Through this lens, sustainability of an IPM tactic can be measured by its (1) compatibility when using multiple tactics to synergize performance and forestall pest resistance; (2) regenerative capability or ability to be integrated into ongoing farm activities to reduce system inputs and expenditure of nonrenewable energy; (3) beneficial effects on ecosystem functioning, including the nurturing and enhancing of natural pest control; and (4) strengthening societal arrangements in its support.[11] Likewise, risk assessment of an IPM tactic should consider its (1) environmental effects, (2) human health risks,[12] and (3) societal consequences associated with their availability and use[13] (see Table 3.1).

IPM tactics grounded in ecological principles have had a renaissance in research and are likely to attain high levels of sustainability and moderate to low risk. Examples of ecological sustainability include regenerative tactics such as use

Table 3.1.
Common Classifications of IPM Tactics and Associated Sustainability and Risk

Classification	Definition	Sustainability[a, c]	Risk[b, c]
Subclassification			
Biological control (biocontrol)	Action of natural enemies (e.g., parasitoids, predators, phytophagous species [weed feeders]) that result in the death or suppression of pests	See subclassifications	See subclassifications
Applied biocontrol: classical approach	Natural enemies added to system that provide long-lasting control	Compatibility: Mod/Hi Regenerative: Hi Ecosystem: Low/Mod/Hi	Environ: Low/Mod/Hi Human: Low Social: Low
Applied biocontrol: augmentation and inundation	Natural enemies added to system that require repeated additions, unable to establish	Compatibility: Mod Regenerative: Low/Mod Ecosystem: Mod/Hi	Environ: Low/Mod/Hi Human: Low Social: Low
Naturally occurring biocontrol	Background mortality from naturally occurring organisms	Compatibility: Mod/Hi Regenerative: Hi Ecosystem: Mod/Hi	Environ: Low Human: Low Social: Low
Conservation biocontrol	Efforts to enhance the effectiveness of naturally occurring biocontrol	Compatibility: Mod/Hi Regenerative: Hi Ecosystem: Hi	Environ: Low/Mod Human: Low Social: Low
Chemical control (pesticides)	Chemical compounds used for pest control	See subclassifications	See subclassifications
Broad-spectrum pesticides	Compounds that kill a wide range of pests and nontarget organisms	Compatibility: Low Regenerative: Low Ecosystem: Low	Environ: Hi Human: Low/Mod/Hi Social: Mod/Hi

(Continued)

35

Table 3.1. (Continued)

Classification	Definition	Sustainability[a, c]	Risk[b, c]
Narrow-spectrum pesticides	Compounds that kill a narrow range of pests and nontarget organisms	Compatibility: Low/Mod Regenerative: Low Ecosystem: Low	Environ: Low/Mod Human: Low/Mod Social: Low/Mod/Hi
Reduced-risk pesticides	Compounds that have reduced human health or environmental risk	Compatibility: Low/Mod Regenerative: Low Ecosystem: Low/Mod	Environ: Low Human: Low Social: Low/Mod/Hi
Cultural control	Reduction of pests by practices associated with standard farm practices	See subclassifications	See subclassifications
Host plant resistance	Classical plant breeding for pest resistance	Compatibility: Low/Mod/Hi Regenerative: Low/Mod Ecosystem: Mod/Hi	Environ: Low/Mod Human: Low Social: Low/Mod
Planting strategies	Plant strategies to disrupt pest cycle, such as crop rotations and time of planting	Compatibility: Low/Mod/Hi Regenerative: Mod Ecosystem: Mod/Hi	Environ: Low Human: Low Social: Low/Mod
Mechanical	Disruption to pest with farm implements, such as tillage	Compatibility: Low/Mod/Hi Regenerative: Low/Mod Ecosystem: Low/Mod	Environ: Low/Mod/Hi Human: Low Social: Low/Mod
Noncrop vegetation management	Disruption of pest, such as removing plant hosts, or enhancement of natural control, such as flowers for natural enemies	Compatibility: Mod/Hi Regenerative: Mod Ecosystem: Mod/Hi	Environ: Low Human: Low Social: Low/Mod
Genetic (biotechnology) control	Pest control through action of modifying genes or gene expression in the pest or the protected plant	See subclassifications	See subclassifications

Sterile insect technique	Mass production and release of sexually sterile pest to disrupt mating	Compatibility: Low/Mod Regenerative: Low Ecosystem: Low	Environ: Low Human: Low Social: Low/Mod
Genetically modified crops	Modified crop expresses new form of pest resistance or resistance to herbicides	Compatibility: Low/Mod Regenerative: Low/Mod Ecosystem: Low	Environ: Low/Mod/Hi Human: Low Social: Low/Mod/Hi
Organic control	Organic-derived control options, including most biocontrol, selected pesticides, and most cultural controls	Compatibility: Low/Mod/Hi Regenerative: Low/Mod/Hi Ecosystem: Low/Mod/Hi	Environ: Low/Mod/Hi Human: Low/Mod Social: Low/Mod

Sources: K. M. Maredia, D. Dakuou, and D. Mota-Sanchez, *Integrated Pest Management in the Global Arena* (Wallingford, UK: CABI Publishing, 2003); G. W. Norton, E. A. Heinrichs, G. C. Luther, and M. E. Irwin, *Globalizing Integrated Pest Management: A Participatory Process* (Ames, IA: Blackwell Publishing); R. G. Van Driesche, and T. S. Bellows. *Biological Control* (New York: Chapman & Hall, 1996), 156–157.

Note:

a. Sustainability attributes: Compatibility, when using multiple tactics, performance is synergized and pest resistance forestalled; Regenerative, capability to reduce system inputs and expenditure of nonrenewable energy; Ecosystem, potential for beneficial effects on ecosystem functioning.

b. Risk attributes: it is desirable to emphasize IPM tactics that minimize environmental (Environ) and human health (Human) risks, and potential societal inequities (Social).

c. Hi, Mod, and Low indicate high, moderate, and low degree of sustainability of the IPM tactic, as based on literature review. Multiple indicators reflect the range of sustainability based on nature of individual IPM tactics and differences in perspective.

of biological control agents that successfully establish in the system[14] or integrative tactics such as managing field border vegetation to promote flowers for natural enemies.[15] IPM techniques attaining moderate to low levels of sustainability include spatially and temporally heterogeneous crop rotations,[16] varieties resistant to pests,[17] and biological control agents that require repeated application to achieve the desired level of pest control.[18] Human health risks tend to be very low, while environmental and socioeconomic risks depend on the nature of the interactions (e.g., does the biological control agent reduce native species' vigor?) and how the tactic affects the food system (e.g., are fields rotated with crops appropriate to local use and food distribution networks?).

Modern input-based tactics such as genetically modified crops and reduced-risk pesticides tend to be less sustainable (requiring repeated "application") and vary considerably in risk. Modest sustainability may be achieved through alternating pesticides with different modes of action and integrating their use with other control tactics.[19] Genetically modified crops can reduce insecticide use, although herbicide use typically increases with the use of herbicide-ready modified crops, and the impacts of herbicides and transgenic crops on biological control agents are of concern.[20] These technologies are often developed to optimize use in large-scale agrifood systems that focus on commodity crops and multinational distribution networks, and less so on specialty crops for local consumption and distribution and local production of seed.[21]

Lastly, IPM support services are important building blocks in establishing IPM systems with desirable sustainability and risk profiles. An IPM system should utilize IPM and environmental monitoring to gauge pest status and agricultural and environmental outcomes of deployed IPM tactics.[22] IPM monitoring tools are critical in IPM deployment to identify and monitor pests (or signs of presence), plant response (damage) in reaction to pest herbivory, and the effectiveness of control strategies. Use of environmental monitoring tools may complement IPM monitoring tools (e.g., weather information)[23] or may be developed to assess the effects of pest management tactics on environmental quality (e.g., pesticide effects on water quality).[24] Essential IPM support services also include establishment of educational, regulatory, financial, and community support structures through policy and market mechanisms.

Broadly and consistent with the principles promoted in the FAO definition of IPM, a sustainability and risk focus is valuable in building an IPM system to meet twenty-first-century challenges. An IPM system should be composed of multiple ecologically based tactics that maximize sustainability within a healthy agro-ecosystem, while allowing short-term strategic insertion of low-sustainability, high-input-based tactics to address severe pest problems until more extensive system adjustments can be made. Risks of introducing low-sustainability tactics should be minimized through open, transparent participatory assessment and monitoring of human, environmental, and socioeconomic health.

POLICY OPTIONS FOR SUPPORTING IPM

Public policy can guide the development, delivery, and societal acceptance of IPM. Effective public policies establish regulatory and incentive frameworks to safeguard health and public goods, support good governance over resource allocation and investment decisions, utilize innovative market mechanisms, and ensure private and public sector accountability. A conceptual framework to guide policy and investment options toward IPM systems with high sustainability and low risk can be broadly conceived as consisting of three transitional stages: (1) minimizing environmental and human health harms by decreasing reliance on hazardous chemical inputs; (2) maximizing environmental and health benefits by investing in and encouraging adoption of primarily ecologically based and more effective IPM tactics and strategies; and (3) transforming agrifood systems to achieve broader equitable and sustainable development goals—the latter are necessary to ensure the social sustainability of desired IPM systems. Consistent with this view, the United Nations–led International Assessment of Agricultural Knowledge, Science and Technology for Development (IAASTD) 2009 report presented policy options for a paradigm shift toward agro-ecologically based biodiverse farming that addresses the multiple functions of agriculture (i.e., its social, economic, and cultural dimensions as well as its productive, landscape, and ecosystem functions); the establishment and enforcement of effective regional and international agreements; new and equitable trade arrangements; integration of local and indigenous knowledge with formal scientific efforts; and institutional mechanisms to increase local participation in agricultural policymaking and decision-making processes.[25]

Stage 1. Minimizing Environmental and Public Health Harms

Policy options well suited to reducing reliance on hazardous pesticides have taken the form of regulatory frameworks on pesticide use and distribution, worker protection standards, regional and international treaties and agreements, and economic policy measures such as the removal of pesticide subsidies, levying environmental taxes on pesticide use and importation (i.e., the "polluter pays" principle), and carbon and energy taxes based on integrated analysis of greenhouse gas emissions and energy costs associated with high versus low pesticide-use systems. For example, several European countries (Denmark, Germany, Italy, the Netherlands, and Sweden) and Canada have implemented pesticide-reduction programs with measurable benchmarks for use reduction,[26] and the European Commission requires members to do the same.[27] A growing number of developing countries (including Costa Rica, Ecuador, Paraguay, Thailand, and Vietnam) and China have banned pesticides classified by the World Health Organization (WHO) as "extremely hazardous," and the FAO now advocates a progressive ban on highly toxic (WHO Class 2) pesticides.[28] Numerous national and international protocols, agreements, and treaties that address the use, distribution, management, clean-up, and phase-out of chemical pesticides have been ratified and implemented (see Table 3.2).

A current challenge for many developing countries is the lack of institutional capacity and financial resources to monitor and comply with both phytosanitary and maximum residue level (MRL) standards for pesticides.[29] Tensions in national policy formation around pesticide and pest management practices can arise when countries attempt to meet international phytosanitary requirements of exported produce (which can encourage the overuse of chemical pesticides) and simultaneously not exceed MRLs. Innovative options to overcome these challenges include regional initiatives to harmonize standards, regional pooling of scientific resources

Table 3.2.
Policy Instruments Affecting Pest Management

National level.
- Pesticide registration legislation, pesticide subsidies, use taxes, import duties, and maximum residue levels (MRLs) affect pesticide use and sales.
- Publicly accessible databases on pesticide use, sales, export, residues, environmental effects, and poisonings provide useful information to inform policy-making processes.
- Pesticide Use Reduction programs, Organic Transition Payments, and National IPM extension programs provide farmers with useful guidelines, targets, incentives, and extension assistance to support sustainable pest management decisions.

Regional level.
- *The Organisation for Economic Co-operation and Development (OECD) Guidelines on Pest and Pesticide Management* prioritize IPM and improved pesticide management.
- *The European Commission's "thematic strategy"* provides a policy framework to minimize hazards and risks of pesticide use.
- *The North American Commission on Environmental Cooperation* (NACEC) Sound Management of Chemicals Working Group has action plans to reduce use of specific pesticides.

International level.
- *The Food and Agriculture Organization of the United Nations (FAO) International Code of Conduct on the Distribution and Use of Pesticides* (agreed in 1985 and revised in 2002) promotes ecologically based IPM, provides guidelines on pesticide labelling and advertising, recommends banning extremely hazardous (World Health Organization [WHO] Class 1) pesticides, and provides guidance on developing national pesticide legislation.
- *The Rotterdam Convention on Prior Informed Consent (PIC) Procedure for Certain Hazardous Chemicals and Pesticides in International Trade* (1998) requires that exporting countries provide notification to importing countries of bans and restrictions on listed pesticides.
- *The Stockholm Convention on Persistent Organic Pollutants (POPs)* provides phase-out plans for nine pesticides. The nongovernmental International POPs Elimination Network (IPEN) works alongside the POPs treaty process.
- *The Montréal Protocol (1987)* mandates the phasing out of the ozone-depleting pesticide methyl bromide.
- *The Intergovernmental Forum on Chemical Safety (1994)* is a WHO-sponsored mechanism to develop and promote strategies and partnerships on chemical safety.
- *The United Nations Environment Programme (UNEP) Strategic Approach to International Chemicals Management* articulates global commitments, strategies, and tools for managing chemicals more safely around the world. The agreement emphasizes principles of prevention, polluter pays, substitution for less harmful substances, public participation, precaution, and the public's right to know.
- *The Basel Convention on the Control of Transboundary Movements of Hazardous Wastes and Their Disposal (1992)* focuses on controlling the management, movement, and disposal of hazardous wastes, including pesticides.
- *The Africa Stockpiles Project* brings together diverse stakeholders to clean up and safely dispose of obsolete pesticide stocks in Africa and establish preventive measures to avoid future accumulation.

Source: F. Dreyfus, C. Plencovich, M. Petit, H. Akca, S. Dogheim, M. Ishii-Eiteman et al., "Historical Analysis of the Effectiveness of AKST Systems in Promoting Innovation," *International Assessment of Agricultural Knowledge Science and Technology for Development: Global Report,* ed. B. D. McIntyre, H. R. Herren, J. Wakhungu, and R. T. Watson, 104 (Washington, DC: Island Press, 2009).

and surveillance data, and establishment of regional regulatory programs to spread costs.[30]

The need for increased investment in capacity to prevent, assess risk, and control or manage invasive pest species is also gaining attention at local, national, and international levels. Full eradication requires significant resources and is difficult to achieve in most cases, whereas management plans that utilize low-risk and high-sustainability tactics are more socially acceptable and likely to succeed over the long term.[31]

Stage 2. Maximizing Environmental and Social Benefit through a Focus on High Sustainability and Low Risk

Reducing reliance on pesticides with high risk is most effective when ecologically-based pest management options are provided. An increasing number of developing countries in Asia, Africa, and Latin America have national IPM research, extension, and farmer education training programs.[32] FAO's Global IPM Facility and bilateral donors (e.g., Germany, the Netherlands, Sweden, IPM Europe, and the United States) have promoted IPM in their technical assistance and development aid programs,[33] while international institutes such as *icipe* (the African Insect Science for Food and Health, formerly known as International Centre of Insect Physiology and Ecology) and others have led effective research efforts in IPM and affiliated crop management practices. Some governments have adopted incentive-based programs that include direct payments to farmers for the provision of environmental services associated with high-sustainability pest management (e.g., pollinator conservation, improved water quality, increased biodiversity) and other financial support measures (e.g., special credit lines, crop insurance, profit and income tax exemptions for farmers adopting environmentally beneficial pest management practices).[34]

Public sector investment in higher education and appropriate skills training of both public and private sector agriculturalists enable innovations in ecologically based IPM systems, small-scale diversified farming practices, and the pest management practices of local and indigenous communities.[35] The place-based characteristics of successful IPM systems have a social and cultural dimension as well. This requires a commitment to supporting social science research that recognizes and learns from diverse knowledge systems and alternate ontologies (i.e., conceptualizations of being). Promoting IPM systems with high levels of sustainability and low risk requires the integration of the biological and social sciences in multidisciplinary and interactive research, extension, and education.

Hindrances to a Focus on High Sustainability and Low Risk

With so many options available, what is hindering more rapid progress toward the adoption of ecologically based IPM systems with high-sustainability and low-risk profiles, and what can be done to accelerate the transition to such systems? Establishment and enforcement of pesticide regulatory restrictions is often poor.[36] At the same time, most advisory and extension programs, and some lending and development agencies, have little familiarity with or confidence in ecologically based approaches to pest management, and these agencies continue to promote intensification of agriculture designed to maximize short-term production output.[37] Direct and indirect policy supports for chemical pesticides remain in place in many countries, including direct pesticide subsidies and other price-distorting practices such as large donor gifts of pesticides, fixed credit packages of inputs, reductions in or exemptions on import duties, value added tax (VAT) and sales taxes for pesticides, and overvalued local currencies.[38] Policy efforts to reduce pesticide reliance can be further confounded by marketing and sales.[39] Meanwhile, public sector funding for IPM and biocontrol has been reduced[40] and private sector investments in technologically based tools have increased.[41] Finally, inequitable distribution of costs plays a role: except in a few countries, farmers typically bear the upfront transaction costs and risks of conversion to more socially and environmentally beneficial pest management practices.[42] These constraints point to the need to address the social and institutional sustainability requirements of IPM by means of a broader agrifood systems analysis.

Stage 3. Achieving Equitable and Sustainable Development

While concerted action in establishing and enforcing better regulatory frameworks and increasing investment in ecologically based IPM are fundamental conditions of change, the current global agrifood system constrains deeper transformation of pest management. Serious efforts to advance sustainable and low-risk IPM over the long term must eventually grapple with the social, political, ecological, and structural organization of trade, technology, and societal investments in globalized agrifood systems.

Organization of Trade and Technologies

The current global trade system and existing trade agreements tend to favor industrial agricultural production systems that externalize costs. Small-scale farmers and local food production systems are at a significant disadvantage within a structure primarily supporting globalized agrifood systems.[43] Establishment of new and more democratic local, regional, and global trade rules and arrangements, increased transparency regarding the social and environmental impacts of trade in agriculture, and establishment of a fair competition policy are needed to create the necessary space for small-scale farmers to adopt sustainable and low-risk IPM tactics that support ecosystem function, ensure the viability and integrity of local food systems, and benefit the public good.[44] Such a fundamental transformation of existing trade arrangements requires active engagement by the public and informed decision-making around economic, health, and environmental trade-offs associated with these decisions. Government decision-makers, the public, and other stakeholders need to be able to compare the likely or potential distribution of benefits, risks, and costs of emerging and evolving IPM tactics across different stakeholder groups and members of society. Useful mechanisms to stimulate informed debate include gender analysis (i.e., examination of how technologies and policies differentially affect women and men's lives, including issues from health to social and economic equity), comparative assessments of technologies in terms of their immediate and long-term impacts,[45] and strategic impact assessments of agricultural trade agreements as they affect farmers' production decisions, national investment priorities, and industrial and small-scale farming systems.

Societal Investments in Food Systems

An ecological justice approach to governance of agrifood systems invites exploring community or shared governance to address equity issues and conserve ecosystem function and public goods.[46] Natural resource valuation that protects water quality, biodiversity, and ecosystem function can help create the agro-ecosystem conditions conducive to sustainable and low-risk IPM systems, such as when farming systems are reconfigured at the habitat and broader landscape level to optimize natural processes.[47] This requires collective decision-making and implementation beyond individual farm fields as well as societal examination of the use of natural resources and agricultural lands. Policy options to protect natural resources, increase sustainability, and ensure equitable distribution of costs for damages include adoption of the precautionary and polluter-pays principles,[48] as well as incentive programs to encourage growers to adopt techniques like IPM, with joint environmental protection and agricultural value.[49] All policy options should be assessed for their capacity to effectively engage marginalized or vulnerable groups (e.g., women, farmworkers, indigenous peoples) in crafting and implementing high-sustainability solutions.[50]

Scaling up benefits of community governance requires writing new rules to govern—and where necessary, better balance—competing interests in local and global food systems to ensure equitable outcomes. Strong farmers' organizations have, in many countries, been a precondition for development of a commercially viable and effective agricultural sector.[51] Strengthening women's, farmers', and community-based organizations is a historically proven way to advance social equity and foster community action to conserve shared resources. These efforts can be supported through, for example, legal protections, investment, training, and capacity-building in participatory research and extension, accessing credit and markets, and negotiating contracts.[52] Supporting policies should enable small-scale farmers to adopt high-sustainability and low-risk IPM approaches that supply nutritionally and agriculturally diverse local and regional food systems, maintain national and regional surplus food stocks, and contribute to global food distribution systems in ways that do not undermine local food production and livelihood security.

A CASE STUDY: INDONESIA'S NATIONAL IPM PROGRAM

> IPM is an Ecological Approach where agriculture is viewed as a complex, living system in which humans interact with land, water, plants, and other organisms.... Farmers become experts, and the central focus of the agricultural system.... Farmers determine their own needs and create solutions and practices appropriate to specific local conditions.
>
> —Decree of Indonesian Minister of Agriculture on IPM, May 1994[53]

> Never in my Wildest Dreams did I think that a program about "bugs" would bring the dawn of democracy and liberation to Indonesian villages.
>
> —Journalist and author Mochtar Lubis in *The World Paper*[54]

Indonesia provides an illuminating case of policy promotion of ecologically based IPM through the innovative farmer education approach, the "Farmer Field Schools" (FFS).[55] FFS rely on "learning by doing" through participatory ecological field studies in crop and pest management, undertaken by farmers, government extension services, researchers, nongovernmental organizations (NGOs), and community-based organizations working together. Farmers are recognized as experts, trainers, researchers, strategic planners, organizers, and, ultimately, policymakers. First pioneered in Indonesia by the FAO in Indonesia, the FFS approach has been successfully adopted in countries across Asia, Latin America, Africa, and Central and Eastern Europe.[56]

Indonesia introduced its National IPM Program in May 1989, catalyzed by a brown plant-hopper outbreak in 1985–1986 associated with high levels of pesticide use that increased pesticide resistance and decimated the rice ecosystem's complex food web.[57] The Indonesian government declared IPM the national pest control strategy, banned fifty-seven broad-spectrum insecticides for rice, created new government posts for pest observer personnel, and removed the country's 85 percent subsidy on the price of pesticides. After a conventional Transfer of Technology–style IPM training proved unsuccessful, the government began in-depth farmer education using the FFS approach, in which more than 1.2 million farmers and thousands of extension workers have since participated. The main driver for the policy shift was the central Indonesian government and its Finance and Planning Ministries, whose motives were stimulated by evidence supplied by the FAO regarding the high costs of pesticide use in rice and the viability of ecologically based rice IPM.

Implementation

The choice of government agency proved critical to the successful implementation of the new IPM policy: from 1989 to 1992, the planning agency Badan Perencanaan Pembangunan Nasional (BAPPENAS) implemented the program, rather than the Ministry of Agriculture. BAPPENAS worked with a decentralized, locally responsive agricultural training and innovation model, which gave the agency flexibility. Additionally, the agency was able to operate in relative independence from industry influence. The FAO Inter-Country Programme for IPM provided technical support and pedagogical innovations in nonformal education processes. The FAO and U.S. Agency for International Development (USAID) contributed financial support.

Within its first five years, Indonesia saw a 70 percent reduction in pesticide use; rice yields increased by 10 percent; and the government saved between $110 million and $120 million per year from cancellation of insecticide subsidies.[58] Equally striking was the spontaneous manner in which enthusiastic farmer graduates of IPM field schools began to establish new field schools. Often at their own cost and with the support of senior IPM trainers, training expanded and the social drivers and political center of Indonesian IPM moved to the communities.

Subsequently, responsibility for the program was shifted to the Ministry of Agriculture and a "bridging loan" was obtained from the World Bank. During this time, early successes of the IPM program dissipated, under lender-imposed program specifications, budget cuts of key training and social components of the FFS, centralized management, and the use of funds for other activities.[59] Under the Directorate for Plant Protection in the Ministry of Agriculture, project administrators focused on measuring farmers' attendance and calculating economic rates of return to fulfill loan disbursement requirements, rather than on the broader social and development outcomes associated with the dynamic group learning process.[60] The defining tension of Indonesian IPM in the 1990s has been described as, on the one hand, the central government and World Bank's view that institution-building required first strengthening the existing bureaucratic structures, within which carefully defined projects could then operate, and, on the other, the proliferation of community organizations that focused on reintroducing social, political, and agro-ecological complexity and local autonomy into rural political space.[61]

Farmer graduates of the Indonesian FFS program recognized that the long-term sustenance of IPM in Indonesia would require institutionalization at the farm community level. Thus, farmer-led community-based IPM arose, fueled by local commitment to strengthen farmers' organizations and empower farmers as experts and change agents. A wide array of farmer institutions has emerged, from village-level groups that have elected IPM farmers to village head positions, to province-wide "IPM Farmer Congresses" in which thousands participate. Gender analysis has revealed important opportunities to overcome social, cultural, and political barriers to women's participation in IPM.[62] Indonesia's community-based IPM begins with "bugs"—concrete, tangible issues that farmers know intimately—and progresses towards a "sustainable livelihoods" agenda that builds local leadership and enables farmers to engage in key policy debates with decision-makers regarding, for example, trade, intellectual property, genetically modified crops, and strategies to achieve food security.[63] The program quietly challenges conventional agricultural production paradigms; illuminates the complex social, political, economic, and ecological web of relationships in which farmers live; and grapples with the power dynamics deeply embedded in public policy decision-making.

Assessing Impacts and Lessons Learned

Extensive social, economic, health, environmental, and ecological benefits from FFS have been documented.[64] Yet some economists have questioned the fiscal sustainability of FFS.[65] However, these and other studies that use simple rate-of-return analyses do not quantify externalities—that is, the health and environmental costs of higher-risk pesticides and the noneconomic benefits of IPM (e.g., improved ecosystem function, farmers' increased analytical skills, stronger social institutions). More comprehensive integrated impact analyses are needed to provide policymakers with empirical evidence of the savings, cost-effectiveness, sustainability, and reduced risk of farmer participatory IPM.

In Indonesia, the removal of pesticide subsidies and investment in farmers' education and knowledge processes proved a powerful stimulant to adoption of IPM. Direct and indirect pesticide price subsidies and conventional long-chain input-delivery systems can impede the sustainability and efficacy of IPM programs.[66] An important precondition to developing an integrated national IPM policy framework is the identification of interacting and conflicting policy factors through a comprehensive pesticide policy analysis that engages all stakeholders.[67]

"Learning from the positive" has been identified as a powerful stimulant to policy change.[68] For Indonesian cabinet officials, spending a day in a rice paddy with FFS graduates and speaking with Indonesian ecologists about the rice ecosystem proved to be a tipping point for gaining their support for the new approach to farmer education and extension. Indeed, policy formation rarely follows a linear path driven by preestablished targets or provision of factual information alone. More often, policies evolve in response to multiple and changing influences, dependent on the perspectives, interactions, tensions and shifting power dynamics between diverse groups of actors.[69]

Social sustainability of IPM requires institutional commitment and redirection of funds toward high-sustainability, low-risk endeavors. Developing a local network of progressive and influential farmers, ensuring an active leadership role for rural women, and collaborating with scientists and other actors who see the value of ecologically based community-driven IPM can sustain positive results. The emergence of farmer-driven community-based IPM in Indonesia illustrates some of the challenges and successes experienced in pursuit of advanced IPM (i.e., Stage 3) and the transformation of food and farming systems necessary to achieve broader equitable and sustainable development goals.

MOVING FORWARD IN IPM

Contemporary IPM development for food systems has been affected by increasing food disruptions caused by climate change and pests, advances in biotechnology and agro-ecology, and environmental, health, and other socioeconomic equity concerns related to pesticide use and other technologies. IPM systems should encourage a level of agro-ecosystem functioning that results in pest populations maintained at low noneconomic densities while providing negligible disruption and, preferably, benefits to other components of the farm enterprise. Biological, cultural, and regulatory tactics with high-sustainability and low-risk attributes should be emphasized to complement the innate pest-suppressive qualities of well-planned farm systems at the local and regional levels. Reduced-risk pesticides and biotechnology products can be useful components of an IPM system if products are chosen and used selectively to target a key pest problem, while avoiding socioeconomic harm and reducing environmental impact. Increasing sustainability and decreasing risk requires open, transparent, participatory, and comprehensive assessment of economic, social, environmental, and human health impacts over medium- and long-term horizons. A more profound shift toward agro-ecosystem management benefits from focus on productive systems that optimize natural processes and agrobiodiversity supplemented with high sustainable and low-risk pest management approaches, with support from social institutions and policy mechanisms.

NOTES

1. Committee on the Future Role of Pesticides in U.S. Agriculture, *The Future Role of Pesticides in U.S. Agriculture* (Washington, DC: National Academy Press, 2000), 55–89, 186–92; Jules Pretty and Rachel Hine, "Pesticide Use and the Environment," in *The Pesticide Detox: Towards a More Sustainable Agriculture*, ed. Jules Pretty (London, Sterling, VA: Earthscan, 2005), 1–22; Misa Kishi, "The Health Impacts of Pesticides: What Do We Know Now?" in Pretty, *Pesticide Detox*, 22–38.

2. Council for Agricultural Science and Technology, *Integrated Pest Management: Current and Future Strategies* (Ames: Instructional Technology Center, Iowa State University, 2003), 4–5; Robert Norris, Edward Caswell-Chen, and Marcos Kogan, *Concepts in Integrated Pest Management* (Upper Saddle River, NJ: Prentice Hall, 2003), 209–13.

3. Council, *Integrated Pest Management*, 11–12.

4. Norris et al., *Concepts*, 11–13.

5. Committee, *Future*, 55–89; Norris et al., *Concepts*, 298–310.

6. Norris et al., *Concepts*, 443–70.

7. Miguel Altieri, *Biodiversity and Pest Management in Agroecosystems* (New York: Food Products Press, 2004), 185; Pedro Barbosa, *Conservation Biological Control* (London: Academic Press, 1998), 396.

8. Food and Agriculture Organization, "International Code of Conduct on the Distribution and Use of Pesticides" (Rome: Food and Agriculture Organization of the United Nations, 2005), ftp://ftp.fao.org/docrep/fao/009/a0220e/a0220e00.pdf (accessed September 1, 2008).

9. Norris et al., *Concepts*, 209–13; George Bird and Michael J. Brewer, "Innovative Integrated Pest Management for Sustainable Systems," in *New Social Contract: Developing and Extending Sustainable Agriculture*, ed. Charles Francis and George Bird (New York: The Haworth Press Inc., 2006) 25–42.

10. Norris et al., *Concepts*, 459–68; Jack Heinemann et al., "Biotechnology," in *International Assessment of Agricultural Knowledge, Science and Technology for Development: Synthesis Report*, ed. Beverly D. McIntyre, Hans R. Herren, Judi Wakhungu, and Robert T. Watson (Washington, DC: Island Press, 2009), 40–45, http://www.agassessment.org/ (accessed July 30, 2008); Sheldon Krimsky, "Environmental Impacts of the Release of Genetically Modified Organisms," in *Encyclopedia of Pest Management*, ed. David Pimentel (New York: Marcel Dekker, 2002), 243–46; Maria L. Zapiola, C. K. Campbell, M. D. Butler, and C. A. Mallory-Smith, "Escape and Establishment of Transgenic Glyphosate Resistant Creeping Bentgrass *Agrostis stolonifera* in Oregon," *Journal of Applied Ecology* 45 (2008): 486–94.

11. Bird and Brewer, "Innovative," 25–42; Council, *Integrated*, 120–22.

12. Committee, *Future*, 55–89; Norris et al., *Concepts*, 209–13; Roy G. Van Driesche and Thomas S. Bellows, *Biological Control* (New York: Chapman & Hall, 1996), 156–57.

13. Bird and Brewer, "Innovative," 25–42; Council, *Integrated*, 222–24; Sean P. Keenan and Paul A. Burgener, "Social and Economic Aspects of Area-wide Pest Management," in *Area-Wide Pest Management: Theory to Implementation*, ed. Opender Koul, Gerrit W. Cuperus, and Norman C. Elliott (Oxfordshire, UK: CABI Publishing 2008), 97–116.

14. Van Driesche and Bellows, *Biological*, 128–72.

15. David N. Ferro and Jeremy N. McNeil, "Habitat Enhancement and Conservation of Natural Enemies of Insects," in Barbosa, *Conservation*, 123–30; G. M. Gurr, H. F. wan Emden, and S. D. Wratten, "Habitat Manipulation and Natural Enemy Efficiency: Implications for the Control of Pests," in Barbosa, *Conservation*, 155–78.

16. Norris et al., *Concepts*, 422–25; Council, *Integrated*, 34–39.

17. Norris et al., *Concepts*, 451–57.

18. Van Driesche and Bellows, *Biological*, 178–228.

19. Norris et al., *Concepts*, 325–36.

20. Norris et al., *Concepts*, 459–68; Heinemann et al., "Biotechnology" in *International Synthesis Report*, 40–45; S. Krimsky, "Environmental Impacts of the Release of Genetically Modified Organisms," in *Encyclopedia of Pest Management*, ed. David Pimentel (New York: Marcel Dekker, 2002), 243–46; John J. Obryki, J. R. Ruberson

and J. E. Losey, "Interactions between natural enemies and transgenic insecticidal crops," in *Genetics, Evolution and Biological Control*, ed. L. E. Ehler, R. Sforza, and T. Mateille (Wallingford, UK: CABI Publications, 2002), 83–206; Zapiola et al., "Escape."

21. David A. Andow and C. Zwahlen, "Assessing Environmental Risks of Transgenic Plants," *Ecology Letters* 9 (2006): 196–214; C. Borowiak, "Farmers' Rights: Intellectual Property Regimes and the Struggle over Seeds," *Politics and Society* 32 (2004): 511–43; Carl Pray and Anwar Naseem, "Supplying Crop Biotechnology to the Poor: Opportunities and Constraints," *Journal of Developmental Studies* 43 (2007): 192–217.

22. Norris et al., *Concepts*, 172–207; J. D. Carlson and Albert Sutherland, "Environmental Monitoring in Area-wide Pest Management," in Koul et al., *Area-wide*, 117–41.

23. Carlson and Sutherland, "Environmental," in Koul et al., *Area-wide*, 117–41.

24. Council, *Integrated*, 4–5.

25. IAASTD (International Assessment of Agricultural Knowledge, Science and Technology for Development). *IAASTD Global Report: Summary for Decision Makers.* (Washington DC: Island Press, 2009), http://www.agassessment.org (accessed April 14, 2009).

26. G. J. Gallivan, G. A. Surgeoner, and J. Kovach, "Pesticide Risk Reduction on Crops in the Province of Ontario," *Journal of Environmental Quality* 30 (2001): 798–813; J. E. Jensen and P. H. Petersen, "The Danish Pesticide Action Plan II: Obstacles and Opportunities to Meet the Goals," in *British Crop Protection Council*, ed. BCPC Conference on Weeds 2001 (Brighton, UK: Farnham, 2001), 449–54.

27. European Commission, "Thematic Strategy on the Sustainable Use of Pesticides" (Brussels European Commission, 2006), http://ec.europa.eu/environment/ppps/home.htm.

28. Food and Agriculture Organization, "New Initiative for Pesticide Risk Reduction, Committee on Agriculture, 20th Session, 25–28, April 2007," COAG/2007/lnf.14 (Rome: Food and Agriculture Organization, 2007), ftp://ftp.fao.org/docrep/fao/meeting/011/j9387e.pdf.

29. M. Simeon, "Sanitary and Phytosanitary Measures and Food Safety: Challenges and Opportunities for Developing Countries," *Review Scientifique Technique-Office International des Epizooties* 25 (2006): 701–12.

30. Anne-Marie Izac et al., "Options for Enabling Policies and Regulatory Environments," in *International Assessment of Agricultural Knowledge, Science and Technology for Development: Global Report*, ed. Beverly D. McIntyre, Hans R. Herren, Judi Wakhungu and Robert T. Watson (Washington DC: Island Press, 2009), 472–73.

31. Rüdiger Wittenberg and Matthew J. W. Cock, eds., *Invasive Alien Species: A Toolkit of Best Prevention and Management Practices* (Wallingford, UK: CABI Int., 2001), 228.

32. Fabrice Dreyfus et al., "Historical Analysis of the Effectiveness of AKST Systems in Promoting Innovation," in McIntyre et al., *International: Global Report*, 99–107.

33. Dreyfus et al., "Historical," in McIntyre et al., *International: Global*, 99–107.

34. J. Alix-Garcia et al., "An Assessment of Mexico's Payment for Environmental Services Program" (Rome: prepared for FAO by the University of California, Berkeley, 2005), http://are.berkeley.edu/~sadoulet/papers/FAOPES-aug05.pdf; Michael J. Brewer, Robert J. Hoard, Joy N. Landis, and Lawrence E. Elworth, "The Case and Opportunity for Public Supported Financial Incentives to Implement Integrated Pest Management," *Journal of Economic Entomology* 97 (2004): 1782–89; Izac et al., "Options," in McIntyre et al., *International: Global*, 472–73; Dreyfus et al., "Historical," in McIntyre et al., *International*, 99–107.

35. Dreyfus et al., "Historical," in McIntyre et al., *International:Global*, 104, Box 2.9; and Beintema et al., "Agricultural Knowledge, Science and Technology: Investment and Economic Returns," in McIntyre et al., *International: Global*, 520–26.

36. Department for International Development Agriculture and Natural Resources Team, "Concentration in Food and Retail Chains" (working paper, United Kingdom Department for International Development in collaboration with Tom Fox and Bill Vorley of the International Institute for Environment and Development, London, 2004), http://dfid-agriculture-consultation.nri.org/summaries/wp13.pdf; United Nations Conference on Trade and Development, "Tracking the Trend Towards Market Concentration: The Case of the Agricultural Input Industry" (Geneva: UNCTAD, 2006), http://www.unctad.org/en/docs/ditccom200516_en.pdf; Food and Agriculture Organizaton, "The Role of Transnational Corporations," in *Trade Reforms and Food Security: Conceptualizing the Linkages* (Rome: FAO, Commodity Policy and Projections Service, Commodities and Trade Division, 2003), http://www.fao.org/docrep/005/y4671e/y4671e00.htm.

37. Dreyfus et al., "Historical," in McIntyre et al., *International: Global*, 99–107; United Nations Conference on Trade and Development, "Tracking"; Norton et al., "Pesticide and IPM Policy Analysis" in *Globalizing Integrated Pest Management: A Participatory Process*, ed. Norton et al. (Ames, IA: Blackwell Publishing, 2005), 191–210; S. Sherwood et al., "From Pesticides to People: Improving Ecosystem Health in the Northern Andes," in *The Pesticide Detox: Towards a More Sustainable Agriculture*, ed. J. Pretty (London, Sterling, VA: Earthscan, 2005), 147–64; S. Williamson, "Breaking the Barriers to IPM in Africa: Evidence from Benin, Ethiopia, Ghana and Senegal," in Pretty, *Pesticide Detox*, 165–80.

38. G. Fleischer and H. Waibel, "Pesticide Policy and Integrated Pest Management," in *Integrated Pest Management in the Global Arena*, ed. K. M Maredia, D. Dakouo, and D. Mota-Sanchez (Wallingford, UK: CABI Publishing, 2003), 49–64; Norton et al., "Pesticide and IPM," 191–210; Williamson, "Barriers," in Pretty, *Pesticide Detox*, 165–80.

39. Margaret M. Kroma and Cornelia B. Flora, "Greening Pesticides: A Historical Analysis of the Social Construction of Farm Chemical Advertisements," *Agriculture and Human Values* 20 (2003): 21–35; S. Williamson, "Barriers," in Pretty, *Pesticide Detox*, 165–80.

40. Dreyfus et al., "Historical," in McIntyre et al., *International: Global*, 99–107; B. Jennings, "The Killing Fields: Science and Politics Berkeley, California, USA," *Agriculture and Human Values* 14 (1997): 259–71.

41. B. Dinham, "Corporations and Pesticides," in Pretty, *Pesticide Detox*, 55–69.

42. Michael J. Brewer et al., "The Case and Opportunity for Public Supported Financial Incentives to Implement Integrated Pest Management," *Journal of Economic Entomology* 97 (2004): 1782–1789; L. Ehler, "Integrated Pest Management (IPM): Definition, Historical Development and Implementation, and the other IPM," *Pest Management Science* 62 (2006): 787–90.

43. Izac et al., "Options," in McIntyre et al., *International: Global*, 465–66.

44. Bird and Brewer, "Innovative," 25–42; Council, *Integrated*, 120–22; Alix-Garcia et al., "Assessment"; Brewer et al., "Case," 1782–89; Izac et al., "Options," in McIntyre et al., *International: Global*, 472–73; Dreyfus et al., "Historical," in McIntyre et al., *International: Global*, 99–107.

45. Clive George and Colin Kirkpatrick, "Trade and Development: Assessing the Impact of Trade Liberalisation in Sustainable Development," *Journal of World Trade* 38 (2004): 441–69; Elske van de Fliert and J. Proost, eds. *Women and IPM: Crop Protection*

Practices and Strategies (Amsterdam: Royal Tropical Institute and IT Publications, 1999), 11–14.

46. John Byrne, Leigh Glover, and Hugo Alroe, "Globalization and Sustainable Development: A Political Ecology Strategy to Realize Ecological Justice," in *Global Development of Organic Agriculture: Challenges and Prospects*, ed. N. Halberg et al. (Wallingford, UK: CABI Publishing, 2006), 49–74.

47. Michael J. Brewer, Takuji Noma, and Norman C. Elliott, "A Landscape Perspective in Managing Vegetation for Beneficial Plant-Pest-Natural Enemy Interactions: A Foundation for Area-Wide Pest Management," in Koul et al., *Area-wide*, 17–41.

48. European Environmental Agency, eds., *Late Lessons from Early Warnings: The Precautionary Principle 1896– 2000* (Copenhagen: EEA, 2001), http://reports.eea.europa.eu/environmental_issue_report_2001_22/en/Issue_Report_No_22.pdf (accessed September 4, 2008).

49. Alix-Garcia et al., "Assessment"; Michael J. Brewer et al., "The Case and Opportunity for Public Supported Financial Incentives to Implement Integrated Pest Management," *Journal of Economic Entomology* 97 (2004): 1782–89; Izac et al., "Options," in McIntyre et al., *International: Global*, 472–73; Dreyfus et al., "Historical," in McIntyre et al., *International: Global*, 99–107.

50. A. Gana, T. Marina-Hermann, and S. Huyer. "Women in Agriculture," in McIntyre et al., *International: Synthesis Report*, 75–80; S. Bajaj et al., "Traditional and Local Knowledge and Community-Based Innovations," in McIntyre et al., *International: Synthesis*, 71–74; Norris et al., *Concepts*, 459–68; Heinemann et al., "Biotechnology," in McIntyre et al., *International: Synthesis*, 40–45; Sheldon Krimsky, "Environmental Impacts of the Release of Genetically Modified Organisms," in *Encyclopedia of Pest Management*, ed. David Pimentel (New York: Marcel Dekker, 2002), 243–46; Zapiola et al., "Escape."

51. Izac et al., "Options," in McIntyre et al., *International: Global*, 465–66.

52. Izac et al., "Options," in McIntyre et al., *International: Global*, 475–80.

53. Russell Dilts, ed., *Facilitating The Emergence of Local Institutions: Reflections from the Experience of the Community IPM Programme in Indonesia* (Colombo: Report of the APO Study Meeting on the Role of Institutions in Rural Community Development, 1998), http://www.communityipm.org/docs/Dilts%20APO%201998.doc.

54. Quoted in Dilts, *Facilitating*, 3.

55. Niels Röling and Elske van de Fliert, "Introducing Integrated Pest Management in Rice in Indonesia: A Pioneering Attempt to Facilitate Large-Scale Change," in *Facilitating Sustainable Agriculture: Participatory Learning and Adaptive Management in Times of Environmental Uncertainty*, ed. Niels Röling and M. Annemarie Wagemakers (Cambridge: Cambridge University Press, 1998), 153–71; Ida P. G. N. J. Oka, "Integrated Pest Management in Indonesia: IPM by Farmers," in Maredia et al., *Integrated*, 223–38; Gerd Fleischer and Hermann Waibel, "Pesticide Policy and Integrated Pest Management" in Maredia et al., *Integrated*, 49–63; Norton et al., "Pesticide and IPM," 191–210; Williamson, "Barriers," in Pretty, *Pesticide Detox*, 165–80.

56. G. Luther et al., "Developments and Innovations in Farmer Field Schools and Training of Trainers," in Norton et al., *Globalizing Integrated Pest*, 147–80.

57. P. Kenmore et al., "Population Regulation of the Brown Planthopper within Rice Fields in the Philippines," *Journal of Plant Protection in the Tropics* 1 (1984): 19–37; William H. Settle et al., "Managing Tropical Rice Pests through Conservation of Generalist Natural Enemies and Alternative Prey," *Ecology* 77 (1996): 1975–1988.

58. Röling et al., "Introducing," 153–71.

59. J. R. Pincus, "State Simplification and Institution Building in a Bank-Financed Development Project: The Indonesian Integrated Pest Management Training Project,"

in *Reinventing the World Bank*, ed. Jonathan R. Pincus and Jeffrey A. Winters (Ithaca, NY: Cornell University Press, 2002), 85–100.

60. Pincus, "State," in Pincus and Winters, *Reinventing*, 85–100.

61. Pincus, "State," in Pincus and Winters, *Reinventing*, 85–100.

62. Elske van de Fliert, "Women in IPM Training and Implementation in Indonesia," in van de Fliert and Proost, *Women*, 11–14.

63. Dilts, *Facilitating*, http://www.communityipm.org/docs/Dilts%20APO%201998.doc.

64. P. Stemerding, A. Musch, and Y. Diarra, eds., *Social Dimensions of Integrated Production and Pest Management—A Case Study in Mali* (Rome: FAO, People's Participation Series No. 13, 2002), http://www.fao.org/docrep/005/Y3754e/y3754e00.htm; Henk Van den Berg and Janice Jiggins, "Investing in Farmers: The Impacts of Farmer Field Schools in Integrated Pest Management," *World Development* 35 (2007): 663–86.

65. Gershon Feder, Rinku Murgai, and Jaime B. Quizon, "Sending Farmers Back to School: The Impact of Farmer Field Schools in Indonesia," *Review of Agricultural Economics* 26 (2004): 45–62.

66. Fleischer and Waibel, "Pesticide," in Maredia et al., *Integrated*, 49–64; Norton et al., "Pesticide and IPM," 191–210; Williamson, "Barriers," in Pretty, *Pesticide Detox*, 165–80.

67. Fleischer and Waibel, "Pesticide," in Maredia et al., *Integrated*, 49–64; Norton et al., "Pesticide and IPM," 191–210; Williamson, "Barriers," in Pretty, *Pesticide Detox*, 165–80.

68. Stephen Biggs, "Learning from the Positive to Reduce Rural Poverty and Increase Social Justice: Institutional Innovations in Agricultural and Natural Resources Research and Development," *Experimental Agriculture* 44 (2007): 1–24.

69. Stephen Biggs and Sally Smith, "Paradox of Learning in Project Cycle Management and the Role of Organizational Culture," *World Development* 31 (2003): 1743–57.

RESOURCE GUIDE

Suggested Reading

Altieri, Miguel, and Clara Nicholls. *Biodiversity and Pest Management in Agroecosystems*. New York: Food Products Press, 2004.

Barbosa, P., ed. *Conservation Biological Control*. London: Academic Press, 1998.

Halberg, Niels, Hugo F. Alroe, Marie T. Knudsen, and Erik S. Kristensen. *Global Development of Organic Agriculture: Challenges and Prospects*. Wallingford, UK: CABI Publishing, 2006.

Maredia, Karim M., Dona Dakouo, and David Mota-Sanchez. *Integrated Pest Management in the Global Arena*. Wallingford, UK: CABI Publishing, 2003.

McIntyre, Beverly D., Hans R. Herren, Judi Wakhungu, and Robert T. Watson, eds. *International Assessment of Agricultural Knowledge, Science and Technology for Development: Synthesis Report*. Washington, DC: Island Press, 2009.

Norris, Robert F., Edward P. Caswell-Chen, and Marcos Kogan. *Concepts in Integrated Pest Management*. Upper Saddle River, NJ: Prentice Hall, 2003.

Norton, George W., E. A. Heinrichs, Gregory C. Luther, and Michael E. Irwin. *Globalizing Integrated Pest Management: A Participatory Process*. Ames, IA: Blackwell Publishing, 2005.

Pretty, Jules, ed. *The Pesticide Detox: Towards a More Sustainable Agriculture*. London and Sterling, VA: Earthscan, 2005.

Röling, Niels, and Annemarie Wagemakers, eds. *Facilitating Sustainable Agriculture: A Participatory Learning and Adaptive Management in Times of Environmental Uncertainty*. Cambridge: Cambridge University Press, 1998.

Van de Fliert, Elkse, and Jet Proost, eds. *Women and IPM: Crop Protection Practices and Strategies*. Amsterdam: Royal Tropical Institute and IT Publications, 1999.

Web Sites

Community Integrated Pest Management, http://www.communityipm.org/ (accessed September 1, 2008).

The Food and Agriculture Organization of the United Nations, IPM Group, http://www.fao.org/ag/agp/agpp/IPM/Default.htm (accessed September 1, 2008).

Global Farmer Field School, http://www.farmerfieldschool.info/index.php (accessed September 1, 2008).

The Global IPM Facility, http://www.fao.org/ag/AGP/AGPP/IPM/gipmf/index.htm (accessed September 1, 2008).

icipe: African Insect Science for Food and Health, http://www.icipe.org/ (accessed September 1, 2008).

ILEIA, The Center for Information on Low External Input and Sustainable Agriculture, http://www.ileia.org/ (accessed September 1, 2008).

International Assessment of Agricultural Knowledge, Science and Technology for Development (IAASTD), http://www.agassessment.org/ (accessed September 1, 2008).

National Sustainable Agriculture Information Service, "Appropriate Technology Transfer for Rural Areas (ATTRA)," http://www.attra.ncat.org/ (accessed September 1, 2008).

Online Information Service for Non-Chemical Pest Management in the Tropics, http://www.oisat.org/ (accessed September 1, 2008).

Pesticide Action Network International, http://www.pan-international.org/panint/?q=node/33. (accessed September 1, 2008).

4

Agrobiodiversity

Vicki L. Medland

This chapter explores the two types of biodiversity inherent in agro-ecosystems: the "planned" biodiversity of domesticated agricultural species and wild species that facilitate agricultural productivity and the "associated" biodiversity of wild species using agricultural lands.[1] Many methods and strategies to preserve biodiversity are the same as those used to conserve soil, protect water, and promote and preserve local communities and culture (these topics are covered in detail in other chapters). This chapter describes the important components of agrobiodiversity, incorporating examples of strategies that have been used successfully to maintain and increase agrobiodiversity and to promote sustainable agro-ecosytems and agricultural communities.

THE CONCEPT OF AGROBIODIVERSITY

Types of Biodiversity

Biodiversity is a concept popularized by E. O. Wilson[2] to describe biological diversity: the total variety of living systems on our planet. Ecologists generally recognize three levels of biodiversity: genetic, species, and ecosystem-level diversity. Species-level biodiversity is most commonly defined as a tally of all types of organisms living in a particular area. But diversity also depends on the relative numbers of individuals within each species. Genetic biodiversity is the amount of genetic variability in a population and imparts adaptability to environmental stress and change. Ecosystem or landscape-level biodiversity is the variety of habitat types available in a given area.

In agricultural ecosystems, there are two major types of biodiversity. "Planned" biodiversity, which includes domesticated crops and animals, and "associated" biodiversity, which is part of the agro-ecosystem over which humans have less control. Associated biodiversity includes species with positive effects like pollinators, with neutral effects like grassland birds, or negative effects like crop herbivores or disease.[3] Landscape-level biodiversity of an agro-ecosystem is a landscape mosaic that may include crop fields, field margins, pasture and rangelands, adjacent woodlands or fence rows, and ponds and streams that run through fields. The Food and Agriculture Organization of the United Nations (FAO) defines agricultural biodiversity as "the variety and variability of animals, plants and micro-organisms which are necessary to sustain key functions of the agro-ecosystem, its structure and processes for, and in support of, food production and food security."[4]

Obviously, agriculture is impossible without the suite of species that makes up the base of our food system. Of the thirty thousand or so edible plants, only 23 percent have been collected or grown as food, and of these, only twenty plants make up more than 90 percent of the world's food. Maize, wheat, and rice account for more than half of all calories consumed worldwide.[5] The majority of these organisms are domesticated species that are relative newcomers to the planet, developed through artificial selection some ten thousand years ago at most. But equally important are those native species that make agriculture possible, not the native plants and animals that acted as the gene stock for artificial selection, but the host of species that create and sustain fertile soil or pollinate crops. Additionally, many native (and alien) species survive because agriculture provides them with a hospitable habitat.

Biodiversity has several roles to play in successful agricultural ecosystems. Traditional polyculture systems in which different crops are grown together are more economically and ecologically sustainable for small farmers. Higher crop biodiversity leads to ecosystem stability and increased ecosystem services. Studies comparing productivity and biodiversity have repeatedly shown that increased biodiversity leads to increased agricultural productivity.[6] Polyculture systems are less affected by pests and have higher root development, higher soil nutrient pools and soil moisture, and less erosion.[7] Traditional programs in which farmers save and trade seeds increase genetic variability of varieties by creating locally adapted seed populations. Unfortunately, the twentieth century ushered in a trend toward lower, not higher diversity, in the guise of intensified industrial agriculture.

Intensified agriculture relies on high levels of nonrenewable inputs to attain greater productivity. These inputs, which generally include inorganic fertilizers, other agrochemicals and fossil fuels, hybrid and genetically modified seeds, and specialized machinery and other artificial capital, must be purchased. As a whole, intensified agriculture has resulted in decreased biodiversity of all types, including lower genetic variability as local land races of seeds are replaced by single-genotype hybrids; fewer soil-dwelling species and lower soil fertility as lands are degraded; fewer unplanned species as agro-ecosytems become more toxic; and lower landscape-level diversity as ecosystem services are lost and agrochemicals spill into neighboring ecosystems. Agricultural intensification also puts biodiversity at risk through faster and more widespread transmission of pathogens and genetically engineered transgenes across globalized and homogenous landscapes. Already in Mexico, where planting of transgenic maize is limited to research areas, key land races of maize are contaminated with transgenes.[8] Intensified agricultural practices greatly weaken or prevent agro-ecosytems from functioning as sustainable ecosystems.[9] Nutrient cycling, carbon sequestration, water retention, and aquifer recharge are all reduced with intensified agricultural practices, mainly because of changes in soil biodiversity.[10]

Agriculture has traditionally focused on managing productivity as a non-equilibrium-engineered system that ignores the interrelationships of ecosystem processes and organisms. Ecologists, on the other hand, view ecosystems as equilibrium-based systems. How the system responds to change is determined by the interactions of the biotic players and abiotic conditions. Resiliency, the ability to bounce back after change, is an important feature of stable, sustainable ecosystems. Modern agricultural systems have lost resiliency and require repeated inputs of nutrients and chemicals. Traditionally, problems in modern intensified agriculture are viewed in isolation, with only a few proposed alternative strategies. For example, a pest species outbreak is treated with pesticides without considering the causes (or often the effects) of the outbreak or the chemical control measure. The ecologist is more likely to look for a cause of the change and respond with a more benign control that would have minimal negative impacts on the ecosystem.

Traditional farmers often employ responsible sustainable management programs, often as part of a tradition of indigenous knowledge that is passed from generation to generation. For example, hedgerows have been used for centuries in traditional farming as windbreaks, but they also serve as refuges for natural predators that reduce or eliminate the need for chemical pesticides.[11] Farmers also leave plots or strips of native vegetation between crop rows called beetle banks that provide that same service. It is our responsibility to maintain biodiversity in agro-ecosystems not only to preserve our food supply but also to preserve cultural tradition and foster the economic stability that comes from sustainable practices.

Ecosystem Services

Croplands and pasturelands have become the largest terrestrial ecosystem in the world, accounting for more than one-third of the world's terrestrial ice-free surface and 45 percent of the world's net primary productivity.[12] Agricultural landscapes cover 180 million hectares, an area nearly as large as Alaska,[13] whereas the Northern Boreal Coniferous Forests, the largest natural biome, only makes up 12 percent of the world surface.[14] The predicted increase of human population to 9 billion people in the next fifty years[15] is expected to lead to a doubling of irrigated croplands and pasture lands by 2050, resulting in a net loss of nearly a billion hectares of natural ecosystems.[16] Out of seventeen thousand large parks and natural areas dedicated to conserving wild biodiversity, almost half of these areas have at least 30 percent of their land used for agriculture. Most of the rest lie within predominantly agricultural landscapes.[17] As demand for more agricultural land grows, we have an obligation to conserve currently used agricultural lands to minimize the further fragmentation and loss of wild ecosystems. An understanding of the value of ecosystem services is necessary to accomplish sustainable food production.

Functional ecosystems are often undervalued or not recognized as having value because the services they provide are not directly bought and sold. Yet, the indirect economic value of functional ecosystems outweighs direct capital as land or production value, for without them life as we know it would be impossible. A functioning ecosystem is sustainable and provides essential services to itself and surrounding ecosystems. A recent classification by the Millennium Ecosystem Assessment divides services into provisioning services, regulating services, supporting services, and cultural services. Provisioning services include products obtained from ecosystems. The obvious ecosystem services provided by agro-eco-systems are the agricultural products they produce; food, fiber, pharmaceuticals, and other materials like rubbers, dyes, and adhesives; and the biomass used to pro-duce fuels. Regulating services are buffers that control climate, rainfall, and species migration. Crop productivity depends on the regulating services provided by soil and climate, and also on the activities of pollinators, predators, and parasitoids that attack pest species. Supporting services are those necessary for the production of all other ecosystem services, and include nutrient cycling, carbon fixation, and oxygen production.[18] Global supporting services that agro-ecosystems can provide are climate regulation, carbon sequestration, water purity, surface water flow regu-lation, groundwater storage and recharge, and in some cases, waste absorption and breakdown.[19] Cultural services include knowledge, and the aesthetic, social, and spiritual benefits people obtain from ecosystems. In fact, domestication and its influences may be our greatest contribution to human culture.[20] Only by adopting an ecosystem-based perspective will agro-ecosytems be able to contribute this nat-ural capital, and yet farmers are not compensated for the vital nonmarket services they provide.

Such ecosystem services would come at great or even insurmountable cost if humans had to create infrastructure and provide labor to replace them. Consider the ecosystem service of bee and insect pollination critical to the productivity of as much as 30 percent of the world food supply.[21] Worldwide, farmers who use managed colonies of bees depend on fewer than eleven species out of the twenty-to thirty thousand bee species.[22] Of this, about 30 percent of pollination is pro-vided by the domesticated honeybee (*Apis mellifera*). The annual value of domesti-cated honeybee pollination to U.S. agriculture is more than US$14.6 billion.[23]

A number of studies have shown that native wild bees may be as efficient or even better pollinators of domesticated plants than domesticated bees. A Maryland study showed more than 96 percent of bees trapped in agricultural fields were wild.[24] Elsewhere, native wild bees increase coffee production by as much as 50 percent.[25] Both domesticated and wild bees are capable of pollinating domesti-cated fruit and vegetables and, in some cases, native wild bees are more efficient than honeybees. Alfalfa leafcutter bees are more efficient pollinators than honey-bees. One alfalfa leafcutter bee can pollinate the same acreage of alfalfa as one hundred honeybees.[26]

Colony Collapse Disorder was first documented in 2006 when beekeepers began noticing abandoned hives. The United States has lost 50 percent of its honeybee colonies, and additional losses have been reported in Europe, South America, and India.[27] The condition is not well understood, and the extent of its effects have yet to be determined. Numerous theories about the cause have been raised, includ-ing stress, mites, and viral infections, as well as toxicity from agrochemicals. These findings have important economic implications. Farmers without access to wild bees could suffer devastating losses, requiring them to switch to crops that do not require pollinators to ensure fertility. Pollinated crops would increase significantly in price.[28] More important, genetic variability of some crop species could be lost without pollinators to ensure reproduction. It is unknown whether wild bees are affected by the disease. If they are, it would have significant effects on the survival of all bee-pollinated plants.

To hedge their bets against further declines in domesticated bee populations, farmers are using strategies to attract wild pollinators. Polyculture, allowing crops like lettuce to bolt and flower, planting flowering plants in field margins, and creating wild bee nesting habitats improves the biodiversity of pollinators.[29] Flower-insectary plots—interplanted crop strips of nectar flowers for wild insect pollinators and other beneficial insects—are becoming more common, particularly in organic farms. The flower strips attract bees, as well as hover flies, which pollinate flowers as adults and prey on pest insects as larvae, and beneficial parasitic wasps that prey on agricultural insect pests. These strips also provide additional habitat for other beneficial and commensal species, especially when planted for native species like birds and spiders.[30]

The relationship between ecosystem function and biodiversity has been debated. Agricultural ecosystems are less diverse than the ecosystems they replace. Although in general more diverse systems have higher productivity and more stable functioning, some ecosystems with relatively low levels of biodiversity function successfully. In others, just a few dominant species often control ecosystem function.[31] However, all ecosystems have thresholds in which the loss of key species impairs normal function and leads to the loss of ecosystem services (like our colony collapse example). While scientists work to identify critical species and determine necessary levels of biodiversity, we need to maintain the current biodiversity to preserve existing levels of ecosystem services. To secure sustainable management of ecosystem services in agricultural systems, we need to understand the relationship of biodiversity to agricultural land ecology. This information can then inform policies that recognize economic values of the natural capital of ecosystem services. Better economic strategies and environmental policies would ensure continued sustainable production of agricultural products, while protecting agricultural and surrounding ecosystems.[32]

Soil Biodiversity

Most of the biodiversity in agricultural ecosystems is found within the soil. A single gram of soil may contain millions of individuals and several thousand species of bacteria, as well as hundreds of species of invertebrates like mites, nematodes, and insects.[33] Agro-ecosystem soil biodiversity is usually much lower than the biodiversity of the parent ecosystem soil. For example, numbers of nematode and annelid worms in agro-ecosystems are about one-tenth that of an equivalent area of grassland or prairie soils.[34] Oribatid mite communities are much less diverse in Western Australian wheat fields than in soils of neighboring native ecosystems. There are no unique agricultural soil species, because agricultural soils are modified from soils of other ecosystems and differ depending on the original ecosystem. Although much of agricultural interest in soil organisms is focused on pest species, soil organisms have important positive impacts on agricultural productivity and ecological services. These organisms are responsible for the decomposition of organic matter, nitrogen fixation, and transformation of nutrient chemicals like sulfur, iron, and nitrogen compounds into forms that are available to plants, as well as for the breakdown of toxic compounds created as a by-product of plant metabolism and added to the soil as agrochemical pesticides and fertilizers.[35]

Although decomposition and nutrient dynamics have been studied in agro-ecosystems and soil,[36] the importance of soil biodiversity to agro-ecosystems is not well understood. This is mainly because soil biodiversity in most ecosystems is poorly documented, and relationships between soil function and aboveground agrobiodiversity are not governed by straightforward processes.[37] There may be as many as 1.5 million species of soil fungi, but only seventy thousand or so described species. Only 35 percent of oribatid mites have been identified of the 150,000 or so species.[38] Soil biodiversity and biomass is dominated by bacteria and fungi that are responsible for the majority of nutrient and carbon cycling in the soil and are a major food resource for other soil organisms. Algae are an important food resource for soil herbivores, but perhaps more important, they increase water capacity of soils by as much as 10 percent.[39] Symbiotic associations between soil fungi and plant roots greatly increase uptake of important nutrients (phosphorus, nitrogen, sulfur, and micronutrients copper and zinc) by plants. Mycorrhizae can provide the same nutrient availability to soybeans as an application of 191 kilograms per hectare of phosphorus fertilizer in tropical agro-ecosystems. Most agricultural crops have associated mycorrhizae (an exception are the Brassicaceae or mustards). Crops with large roots and few root hairs are so dependent on mycorrhizal fungi they may not develop normally without them.[40]

By its nature, agriculture creates a less diverse, more homogenous ecosystem than the natural system it replaces, and soil biodiversity likewise decreases. Agricultural soils are always less diverse than the parent ecosystem soils from which they were modified.[41] Chemicals and intensified agricultural practices that compact soils create stressors to soil organisms and lower soil biodiversity further, as does soil acidification from nitrogen fertilizers.[42] Pesticides, especially copper-containing fungicides, have lasting negative impacts on soil biodiversity.

Depending on management philosophy, managing for productivity in agro-ecosystems can have either positive or negative effects on soil biodiversity. Many agricultural programs have focused on the view that specific limiting factors affect ecosystem-level productivity. To increase productivity, chemicals are used to increase soil nutrients or decrease pest damage. The misuse of these chemicals reduces soil biodiversity and leads to the loss of soil productivity, surface and groundwater contamination, and soil degradation.[43] A better strategy is to manage agriculture like ecologists manage ecosystems: as complex dynamic systems, in which productivity changes occur as the systems move out of equilibrium.[44] Although more research is needed to achieve optimal management of agro-ecosystems, we already have enough understanding of the ecology of these systems to begin to manage soil biodiversity that maximizes soil fertility and sustainability and ensures optimal crop productivity.[45]

Several examples exist to support this idea. Both natural fertilizer and no-tillage strategies increase the diversity of beneficial soil mites and collembola (springtails) as opposed to chemical fertilizer and plowed fields. Increased soil biodiversity in some cases has provided disease resistance, ecological resilience after disturbance, and increased recycling of organic waste and nutrient cycling.[46] The total annual contribution of nitrogen fixation by soil microorganisms in both agricultural and natural ecosystems has been estimated to be at least seventy million tons of nitrogen, valued at about US$45 billion per year.[47]

No-till and reduced tillage agro-ecosystems, in which 30 percent or more of the crop debris is left on the soil surface, have significant effects on nutrient cycling and biodiversity in agricultural soils. It is generally accepted that crop debris left as litter on the soil surface reduces soil erosion and soil surface temperature and increases soil moisture content. It can significantly reduce the amount of fuel, labor, equipment, and fossil fuels needed. It can also result in greater soil biodiversity that leads to the creation of a long-term nutrient pool.

In a comparison of conventional tillage and no-tillage systems in Georgia, significant changes in nutrient availability were tied to changes in soil biodiversity and nutrient cycling.[48] In conventional till systems where plant residues are plowed under the soil, most of the decomposition is carried out rapidly by bacteria, sometimes leading to nitrate leaching out of the soil and into surface or groundwater. No-till systems are dominated by a fungal food web in which mites, collembola and earthworms are more abundant. Microarthropods and earthworms are important in increasing the fragmentation and decomposition of litter. Increased numbers of microarthropod predators maintain the fungal food web by controlling populations of fungal grazers. These predators decline with intensive application of agrochemicals, and the system shifts back to a bacterial-dominated system.[49] While slower nutrient cycling might seem antagonistic to the needs of aboveground plants, it actually enhances plant growth by limiting nitrogen leaching and spreading out available nitrogen over the growing period and creating long-term nutrient pools that ensure long-term soil fertility.[50]

STRATEGIES TO PRESERVE AGROBIODIVERSITY

Unlike other ecosystems, in which human activity is the greatest threat to biodiversity, agricultural biodiversity prospers and suffers because of human activity. Biodiversity-based agriculture has been studied and practiced for many years. Intercropping, multicropping, cover crops, low- and no-tillage systems, integrated pest management, as well as some organic practices are known to improve or maintain ecosystem services.[51] Some biodiversity-based practices also increase food security. Intercropping is more labor intensive than growing monocultures, but it provides protection against the failure of an individual crop. Intercropping usually ensures improved nutrition when several different crop species are grown for subsistence.[52] Even farmers that seem to plant monocultures, for example, maize farmers in Mexico or rice farmers in Bangladesh, plant several varieties in small adjoining fields to hedge their bets against environmental variability.[53] Historically, farmers have been seen as passive recipients of agricultural technology transfer from government and science, rather than as active knowledgeable participants in agriculture. Rather than a trickle-down process, Michel Pimbert argues that biodiversity-based practices will succeed only as bottom-up participatory programs.[54] Evolution of agricultural technology in indigenous settings adapts the technology to local conditions and cultures.

Enhancing Native Biodiversity

Although agriculture leads inevitably to lower biodiversity, especially when new lands are cleared, agriculture does not have to lead to further losses. Some researchers, like Jeffrey Lockwood, argue that agricultural lands provide a reservoir for native biodiversity that would otherwise be lost in increasingly fragmented landscapes.[55] Other researchers argue that to preserve both agricultural and associated native biodiversity we need to preserve cultural identity within agriculture by encouraging and enriching traditional agricultural systems rather than industrial programs.

An example of managing traditional agricultural practices involves the Monarch butterfly, one of the few truly migratory insects. Monarchs travel between central Mexico and the United States each year. In both countries, the Monarch has become an important cultural symbol representing nature's fragility. In Mexico, Monarchs overwinter in dense colonies in forests close to Mexico City. These forests have become important tourist destinations for local and international visitors. In 1986, in response to international concern, Mexico set aside fifty-six thousand hectares of land as the Monarch Butterfly Biosphere Reserve. However, more than two hundred thousand subsistence farmers lived within the four regions that make up the reserve.[56] Even where the forests are protected, they are under great pressure from logging and agricultural operations. Without the insulating wind protection of surrounding trees, the overwintering butterflies desiccate or freeze. Forests are cleared as a cash crop and for cooking and heating. Logged areas are burned after logging to clear the land for subsistence agriculture, destroying many of the surviving butterflies. The loss of one acre of Monarch overwintering grounds may mean the loss of up to four million butterflies. While it is unlikely that Monarchs as a species will go extinct in the near future, the migration phenomenon is under threat. Some entomologists predict the Monarch migration may be over by 2030.[57]

A new conservation strategy developed by the World Wildlife Fund (WWF) is being developed to incorporate and benefit the local rural community. The program provides payouts to local community members to perform conservation activities. Payments are tied to agreements to forgo logging or land clearing within the preserve areas. The program has been successful in stopping legal logging, but illegal logging continues.[58] Other strategies include donating efficient wood-burning stoves that decrease the need for firewood by half. Organic farming practices, including composting and switching from monoculture corn to polycropping vegetables with corn, have increased local incomes and decreased pressure to clear more forest.[59] A critical piece of these programs is that they include the farmers in dialogues and planning within the reserve. These strategies—spearheaded by the nongovernmental organization Alternare and funded mainly through the U.S. Fish and Wildlife Service (FWS)—are still new, but they may help to create a sustainable agricultural community and preserve an important species.

Preserving Domesticated Biodiversity

Biodiversity in traditional varieties represents an adaptive history to different environmental, social, cultural, and economic conditions. Preserving this biodiversity preserves the ability of our agricultural resources to persist in a rapidly changing world. Sometimes, these adaptations are obvious and valued in local varieties; though more often they are considered inferior by agronomists who promote high-yield varieties. Farmers often prefer the local varieties, because while they are lower in productivity, the trade-offs are great. Local varieties are often more resistant to local pests and diseases, better adapted to local climatic conditions, more resilient to environmental variability, and better able to preserve local food preferences and cultural practices than imports.[60] In many parts of the world, poverty limits farmers from buying pesticides or chemical fertilizers. Using local varieties is their only option. More recently, farmers are gaining added value on the global market by marketing local low-input varieties as organic.

The biodiversity stored in agricultural species has great potential. Although much of the existing genetic variability has already been utilized to improve the yield and nutrition of wheat, significant improvements in corn and rice are still to be had.[61] Changes in the genetic makeup of crop and livestock varieties have been investigated, and in some cases genetic variability has remained stable from the early twentieth century through today.[62] In other cases, genetic variability has been seriously eroded. The FAO states that about 75 percent of global genetic diversity was lost from crop species in the twentieth century. Nearly ten thousand wheat varieties were cultivated in China in 1949, but by the 1970s, only about one thousand varieties remained. While local landraces of maize are still abundant in some parts of Mexico, varietal loss of maize is well documented. Only 20 percent of the maize varieties reported in 1930 are now known in Mexico.[63] Some crops have become marginalized as they were replaced under pressure to focus on a few industrial varieties.[64]

Preservation of domesticated crops and animals requires continued growing and breeding programs. Seeds have only limited viability even under scientifically controlled storage. Although the occasional ancient seed germinates, most seeds will remain viable for only five to twenty years in normal conditions. Wheat seeds remain viable for about thirty years, but most vegetable seeds survive for only about ten years under ideal conditions.[65]

Traditional farmers have long followed sustainable practices to preserve the genetic variability of crop seeds. Central Mexico is the center of origin for the domestication of maize and supports the highest diversity of maize varieties in the world.[66] Farmers develop landraces that are adapted to local conditions, yield needs, and cultural preferences. Some farmers select for a wide range of morphological and agronomic traits.[67] Central Mexican farmers often grow several local and improved varieties of maize in a season. Because they usually eat what they grow, their planting preferences are influenced by both economic gain and by food quality.[68] And because fields are small and near to each other, pollen usually drifts between fields, which increases diversity. Farmers follow strict programs of seed saving that follow local practices, and many farmers save seed from hybrid as well as open pollinated varieties.[69] Farmers in different regions also practice an extensive trade in seed. Farmers may collect seed from other communities to enhance local landraces (recognizably distinct types), or they may need to acquire fresh seed after crop failures. All of these practices increase the diversity and gene flow between populations of maize and ensure that landraces are maintained over many generations.[70] Farmers follow similar practices for other crops, including potatoes, sorghum, rice, beans, and livestock.[71]

Food as culture has been a mainstay of European agricultural systems and recently has gained a following in other industrial countries where people want to preserve foods related to their familial and ethnic ancestry. Food diversity has increased greatly in developed countries as ethnic diversity from immigration has expanded palates and interest in new and traditional foods. Some foods that were unavailable to urban consumers thirty years ago in the industrial world, like mesclun salad greens, are now widely available and often locally grown. It is now possible to buy relatively obscure foods like okra leaves at farmers markets (used in Hmong and African cuisines) that previously were grown only for home consumption. Global markets have reduced costs to transport unusual fruits like durian (although it remains to be seen whether the long-distance transport of foods is a sustainable option). A great number of self-named "foodies" in Europe and the United States have begun experimenting and promoting new foods and renewing a culture of food and agriculture. Inherent in this new genre are promoters of healthful eating cultures and sustainable practices. Some programs like Slow Food's Foundation for Biodiversity are focused solely on preservation of food species.[72] Other organizations like the Seed Savers Exchange trade and sell seeds and plants to the public in an attempt to increase seed populations. Seed fairs and other trading programs are important ways to preserve seed flow and genetic variability in developing countries.[73] In Japan, the International Food and Life Association has employed marketing strategies to reintroduce the public to a healthful traditional staple that has fallen out of favor, millet.[74]

In Africa, demand is increasing in urban areas for indigenous crops, as people from rural areas seek out familiar repasts. Leafy green species like cowpeas (*kunde*), African nightshade (*managu*), and amaranths (*mchicha*) are now in major supermarkets and restaurants. Some of these species were close to extinction before nutrition- and culture-based marketing by nongovernmental organizations helped to increase their production. Most East African farmers cultivated these vegetables for their own use, but did not see them as a cash crop, and instead had switched to growing crops like broccoli and cabbage for export to Europe. In a turnaround farmers are now exporting African indigenous greens to Great Britain and to Asia as demand for unique species increases. Farmers are being encouraged to intercrop these drought-tolerant vegetables to maximize productivity.[75]

Many developed countries have centralized gene bank facilities for the storage of crops and wild plants. For example, the National Plant Germplasm System, coordinated by the Agricultural Research Service (ARS) in the United States, keeps more than 450,000 accessions of cultivated plant material. As part of this effort, the U.S. Department of Agriculture (USDA) maintains more than 2,500 varieties of apples at its Geneva, New York, facility, including many varieties from Eastern Europe and Asia.[76] Although more than fifteen hundred crop gene banks exist throughout the world, the Svalbard Global Seed Vault is perhaps the most ambitious program to preserve agricultural genetic diversity. Seeds are stored 130 meters inside three large caverns built into the permafrost in the Norwegian Arctic island of Svalbard. The vault can hold almost five million seed samples stored at −18° C. All the seeds stored within the vault are duplicate sets from other seed banks throughout the world. Although this facility provides the space to store a huge amount of genetic biodiversity, the material is limited to seeds only.[77]

Not all agricultural biodiversity can be maintained as seeds. The International Potato Center in Lima, Peru, manages the world's largest collection of tubers, comprising forty-five hundred different varieties, including three thousand from Peru. These tubers are grown in test tubes or kept in cold chambers and must be grown out periodically in small field plots to preserve viability.[78]

Maintaining animal gene banks is much more complicated and expensive. Breeding stocks must be maintained in carefully controlled breeding herds, and eggs and sperm must be frozen to preserve unique breeds. The genes from only six breeds of cattle account for more than 90 percent of cattle raised in industrial countries. Many ancestral breeds have been largely abandoned and are at or near extinction. The FAO has estimated that more than 70 percent of the remaining livestock diversity is contained in developing countries where local varieties are still preferred over the higher-maintenance breeds favored in industrial countries.[79]

STRATEGIES FOR THE FUTURE: THE DIVERSITAS PLAN

DIVERSITAS was established in 1991 as a nongovernmental organization that would focus on answering scientific questions about the decline in global biodiversity. Its science agenda embraces strategies based on understanding and valuing ecosystems as natural capital and ecosystem services as interest on that capital. DIVERSITAS recognizes agrobiodiversity as important but understudied and recently formulated a plan specifically designed to promote the science of agricultural biodiversity. Its plan represents a change in traditional agricultural science because it treats agricultural systems as natural capital and values indigenous as well as scientific knowledge of crops and agro-ecosystems as part of proposed solutions.[80] The goals are to quantify economic and ecosystem goods and services provided by agrobiodiversity at all levels of diversity and to determine culturally relevant and socially responsible economic options for the sustainable use of biodiversity in agricultural landscapes. It is working to develop standards to monitor agrobiodiversity and create meaningful biodiversity indicators that can be used and understood by policymakers and that will help scientists to identify those crops and ecosystems that are most in need of conservation to preserve local biodiversity. The plan is unique because it will evaluate the success of differing management strategies and work to create sustainable systems that are socially and economically viable solutions for communities and that preserve aboveground productivity as well as belowground ecosystem function.[81]

To be successful, these plans must include farmers as well as scientists. The International Institute for Environment and Development, working with the Association for Nature and Sustainable Development (ANDES)—an organization based in Cuzco, Peru—and in agreement with the International Potato Center (*Centro Internacional de la Papa*, CIP), has developed a unique biodiversity-based program. This program is the first to include indigenous growers in preserving biodiversity, which is representative of DIVERSITAS and International Association of Agricultural Development (IAAD) strategies. In the program, potato varieties will be "repatriated" back to the Quechua communities whose ancestors were responsible for the original domestication and improvement of the potato. The potatoes will be grown in a conservation "potato park" in southern Peru. The park was created out of the landholdings of six different indigenous communities that will communally grow and manage the varieties. Of the twelve hundred varieties already grown by the communities, more than two hundred varieties have been reestablished through donations from CIP, and the goal is to create a bank of all three thousand open-pollinated varieties of potatoes known to Peru. The program is unique because it allows local farmers to play a role in the maintenance of local biodiversity. In addition to managing the potato park, the local communities are restoring native forest and are eager for the area to become recognized as a protected conservation park.[82]

CONCLUSION

By 2050, the world's farmers will need to feed nine billion people. To meet demand, agricultural yields will need to double and 18 percent more land will need to be converted to agriculture, resulting in a projected loss of ten billion hectares of wild lands. Intensified agriculture, where a small number of specific products have high value, is a threat to agrobiodiversity and its attendant ecosystem services, but it remains the dominant choice made based on traditional economic analyses of markets and the perceptions of increased management efficiency.[83]

Agrobiodiversity is natural capital that should be valued. Sustainable agricultural practices that promote agrobiodiversity provide capital, including more and better quality foods, chemicals, and other products for a growing human population, while protecting biodiversity and ecosystem services of neighboring wild ecosystems. They also promote the social well-being of farming communities and society as a whole. It has been suggested that an investment portfolio strategy is necessary to foster an understanding of the importance of preserving biodiversity in agro-ecosystems.[84] The agroportfolio should include all levels of biodiversity (genetic, species, and landscape) to maintain a sustainable return in the flow of ecosystem services that promotes human well-being and that is resilient to environmental change. The tools to create sustainable agricultural practice exist, and new ecosystem programs can succeed if properly nurtured.

NOTES

1. M. J. Swift et al., "Biodiversity and Agroecosystem Function," in *Functional Roles of Biodiversity: A Global Perspective*, ed. J. H. Cushman et al. (Hoboken, NJ: Wiley Press, 1996), 261–98.

2. E. O. Wilson, ed., *Biodiversity* (Washington, DC: National Academy of Sciences/Smithsonian Institution, 1988), 1–8.

3. M. J. Swift et al., "Biodiversity and Agroecosystem Function," 261–98.

4. FAO, "Agricultural Biodiversity," *Multifunctional Character of Agriculture and Land Conference, Background Paper 1* (Maastricht, Netherlands: FAO Press, 1999), 1–9.

5. E. O. Wilson, *The Diversity of Life* (Harvard, MA: Belknap/Harvard, 1999), 287–88.

6. Judith Thompson et al., "Biodiversity in Agroecosystems," in *Farming with Nature: The Science and Practice of Ecoagriculture*, ed. Sara J. Scherr and Jeffrey A. McNeely (Washington, DC: Island Press, 2007), 46–60.

7. Jon K. Piper, "Natural Systems Agriculture," in *Biodiversity in Agroecosystems*, ed. W. W. Collins and C. O. Qualset (Boca Raton, FL: CRC Press, 1999), 179–83.

8. Mauricio R. Bellon and Julien Berthaud, "Traditional Mexican Agricultural Systems and the Potential Impacts of Transgenic Varieties on Maize Diversity," *Agriculture and Human Values* 23 (2006): 3–14.

9. R. A. Robinson and W. J. Sutherland, "Post-War Changes in Arable Farming and Biodiversity in Great Britain," *Journal of Applied Ecology* 39 (2002): 157–76.

10. David C. Coleman, Deryee A. Crossley Jr., and Paul F. Hendrix, eds., *Fundamentals of Soil Ecology* (Amsterdam: Elsevier Academic Press, 2004), 408.

11. Alan MacLeod, et al., "Beetle Banks as Refuges for Beneficial Arthropods in Farmland: Long-Term Changes in Predator Communities and Habitat," *Agricultural and Forest Entomology* 6 (2004): 147–54.

12. Erle C. Ellis and Navin Ramankutty, "Putting People in the Map: Anthropogenic Biomes of the World," *Frontiers in Ecology* 6 (2008): 439–47.

13. OECD-FAO, "Agricultural Outlook: 2006–2015," *Industry, Services & Trade 2006* (2006): 55–90.

14. Bellon and Berthaud, "Traditional Mexican Agricultural Systems," 3–14.

15. United States Census Bureau, http://www.census.gov/ipc/www/idb/.

16. Charles Perrings et al., "Biodiversity in Agricultural Landscapes: Saving Natural Capital without Losing Interest," *Conservation Biology* 20 (2006): 263–64.

17. Sara J. Scherr and Jeffrey A. McNeely, "Reconciling Agriculture and Wild Biodiversity Conservation: Policy and Research Challenges of 'Ecoagriculture,'" in *Conservation and Sustainable Use of Agricultural Biodiversity* (Manila, Philippines: CIP-UPWARD, 2003), 48.

18. Millennium Ecosystem Assessment, *Ecosystems and Human Well-being: Synthesis* (Washington, DC: Island Press, 2005), 3–9.

19. Scott M. Swinton et al., "Ecosystem Services from Agriculture: Looking Beyond the Usual Suspects," *American Journal of Agricultural Economics* 88 (2006): 1160–1166.

20. Millennium Ecosystem Assessment, *Ecosystems*, 3–9.

21. Edward E. Southwick and J. R. L. Southwick, "Estimating the Economic Value of Honey Bees (Hymenoptera: Apidae) as Agricultural Pollinators in the United States," *Journal of Economic Entomology* 85 (1992): 621–33.

22. A. M. Klein et al., "Importance of Crop Pollinators in Changing Landscapes for World Crops," *Proceedings of the Royal Society of London Series B-Biological Sciences* 274 (2007): 303–13.

23. Roger A. Morse and Nicholas W. Calderone, "The Value of Honey Bees as Pollinators of U.S. Crops in 2000," *Bee Culture*, 128 (2000): special pullout supplement.

24. Annette Meredith, "Conserving Pollinators: An Interdisciplinary Approach to Evaluating the Ecological, Economic and Cultural Value of Native Bees in Mid-Atlantic Sustainable Agriculture" (PhD dissertation, University of Maryland, 2008).

25. David W. Roubik, "Tropical Agriculture: The Value of Bees to the Coffee Harvest," *Nature* 417 (2002): 708.

26. Texas A&M University, "Native Bees Could Fill Pollinator Hole Left By Honeybees," *Agricultural Communications* (College Station: Texas A&M University, 2006).

27. D. Van Engelsdorp et al., "An Estimate of Managed Colony Losses in the Winter of 2006–2007: A Report Commissioned by the Apiary Inspectors of America," *American Bee Journal 147* (2007): 599–603.

28. Edward E. Southwick and Lawrence Southwick Jr., "Economic Value of Honey Bees," *Journal of Economic Entomology* 85 (1992): 621–33

29. Thompson et al., "Biodiversity in Agroecosystems," 46–60.

30. D. A. Landis, S. D. Wratten, and G. M. Gurr, "Habitat Management to Conserve Natural Enemies of Arthropod Pests in Agriculture," *Annual Review of Entomology* 45 (2000): 175–201.

31. John Philip Grime, "Biodiversity and Ecosystem Function: The Debate Deepened," *Science* 277 (1997): 1260–61.

32. Claire Kremen and Richard S. Ostfeld, "A Call to Ecologists: Measuring, Analyzing, and Managing Ecosystem Services," *Frontiers of Ecology and Environment* 3 (2005): 540–48.

33. James B. Nardi, *The World Beneath Our Feet: A Guide to Life in the Soil* (Oxford: Oxford University Press, 2003), 28.

34. Ibid., 19–20.

35. Else K. Bünemann, Graeme D. Schwenke, and Lukas van Zwieten, "Impact of Agricultural Inputs on Soil Organisms—a Review," *Australian Journal of Soil Research* 44 (2006): 379–406.

36. Paul F. Hendrix, David C. Coleman, and Deryee A. Crossley Jr., "Using Knowledge of Soil Nutrient Cycling Processes to Design Sustainable Agriculture," *Journal of Sustainable Agriculture* 2 (1992): 63–82.

37. Lijbert Brussaard, Peter C. de Ruiter, and George G. Brown, "Soil Biodiversity for Agricultural Sustainability," *Agriculture, Ecosystems and Environment* 121 (2007): 233–44.

38. Coleman, Crossley Jr., and Hendrix, *Fundamentals of Soil Ecology*, 408.

39. Nardi, *The World Beneath Our Feet*, 45–46.

40. Rosa M. Muchovej, "Importance of Mycorrhizae for Agricultural Crops," Document SS-AGR-170 (Gainsville: University of Florida, Institute of Food and Agricultural Sciences 2001), 1–5.

41. Brussaard, de Ruiter, and Brown, "Soil Biodiversity," 233–44.

42. Ibid.

43. P. A. Sanchez, et al., "Soil fertility replenishment in Africa: An investment in Natural Resource Capital," in *Replenishing Soil Fertility in Africa*, ed. R. J. Buresh, P. A. Sanchez, and F. Calhoun (Madison, WI: Soil Science Society of America Special Publication No. 51, 1997), 1–46.

44. David C. Coleman, ed., "Ecology, Agroecosystems, and Sustainable Agriculture," *Ecology* 70 (1989): 1590–1602.

45. Paul Hendrix, Deryee A. Crossley Jr., and David C. Coleman, "Soil Biota as Components of Sustainable Agroecosystems," in *Sustainable Agricultural Systems*, ed. C. A. Edwards et al. (Ankeny, IA: Soil and Water Conservation Society, 1990), 637–54.

46. Owen Olfert et al., "Use of Arthropod Diversity and Abundance to Evaluate Cropping Systems," *Agronomy Journal* 94 (2002): 210–16.

47. Brussaard, de Ruiter, and Brown, "Soil biodiversity," 233–44.

48. Ibid.

49. Ibid.

50. Ibid.

51. Thompson et al., "Biodiversity in Agroecosystems," 46–60.

52. Ibid.

53. Ibid.

54. Michel Pimbert, *Towards Food Sovereignty: Reclaiming Autonomous Food Systems*, Program at the International Institute for Environment and Development (London: IIED Press, 2008), 43–54.

55. Jeffrey A. Lockwood, "Agriculture and Biodiversity: Finding our Place in this World," *Agriculture and Human Values* 16 (1999): 365–79.

56. Carlos Galindo Leal and Eduardo Rendón Salinas, *Danaidas: las Maravillosas Mariposas Monarca* (México, D.F., Mexico: WWF México Telcel, 2005), 1–82.

57. Lincoln P. Brower, Linda S. Fink, and Peter Walford, "Fueling the Fall Migration of the Monarch Butterfly," *Integrative and Comparative Biology* 46 (2006): 1123–42.

58. Mónica Missrie and Kristen Nelson, "Direct Payments for Conservation: Lessons from the Monarch Butterfly Conservation Fund" (*working paper, Research Summary Paper* No. 8 College of Natural Resources, University of Minnesota 2005), 1–48.

59. G. del Rio et al., "Participación y Organización Comunitaria, Un Requisitio Indispensable en la Conservación de los Recursos Naturals, El Caso de los Ecosistemas Templados de Montaña," *Alternate White Paper* (2004): 1–38.

60. Thompson et al., "Biodiversity in Agroecosystems," 46–60.

61. OECD-FAO "Agricultural Outlook," 55–90.

62. M. M. Manifestoa et al., "Quantitative Evaluation of Genetic Diversity in Wheat Germplasm Using Molecular Markers," *Crop Science* 41 (2001): 682–90.

63. OECD-FAO "Agricultural Outlook," 55–90.

64. Thompson et al., "Biodiversity in Agroecosystems," 46–60.

65. Forest Preserve District of Cook County, "Viability of Seeds," *Nature Bulletin No. 507* (Chicago, 1973).

66. Bellon and Berthaud, "Traditional Mexican Agricultural Systems," 3–14.

67. B. Edgar Herrera-Cabrera et al., "Diversidad del Maiz Chalqueño," *Agrociencia* 38 (2004): 191–206.

68. Bellon and Berthaud, "Traditional Mexican Agricultural Systems," 3–14.

69. Michael L. Morris, Jean Risopoulos, and David Beck, "Genetic Change in Farmer-Recycled Maize Seed: A Review of the Evidence" (working paper 99–07, CIMMYT Economics, Mexico, 1999).

70. Bellon and Berthaud, "Traditional Mexican Agricultural Systems," 3–14.

71. Thompson et al., "Biodiversity in Agroecosystems," 46–60.

72. The Slow Food Foundation, http://www.slowfoodfoundation.com/.

73. Patrick Mulvany and Rachel Berger, "Agricultural Biodiversity: Farmers Sustaining the Web of Life," in *Conservation and Sustainable Use of Agricultural Biodiversity* (Manila, Philippines: CIP-UPWARD, GTZ, IDRC, IPGRI and SEARICE, 2003), 17.

74. Yumiko Otani, "Revival of Millets as Gourmet Food in Japan: An Approach to Conservation," in *Conservation and Sustainable Use of Agricultural Biodiversity* (Manila, Philippines: CIP-UPWARD, GTZ, IDRC, IPGRI and SEARICE, 2003), 621–26.

75. Africa Science News Service, "African Indigenous Vegetables a Hit in Urban Centres," http://africasciencenews.org/.

76. Cornell University College of Agriculture and Life Sciences New York State Agricultural Experiment Station, http://www.nysaes.cornell.edu/.

77. Svalbard Global Seed Vault, http://www.nordgen.org/sgsv/.

78. International Potato Center, http://www.eseap.cipotato.org/.

79. Barbara Rischkowsky and Dafydd Pilling, eds., "Structured Breeding Programs," in *The State of the World's Animal Genetic Resources for Food and Agriculture* (Rome: Food and Agriculture Organization, 2007), 235–41.

80. DIVERSITAS Science Committee, "DIVERSITAS Science Plan 2002–2003," DIVERSITAS Report No. 1 (Rome: DIVERSITAS, 2003), 1–37.

81. Charles Perrings et al., "Biodiversity in Agricultural Landscapes," *Conservation Biology* 20 (2006): 263–64.

82. Michel Pimbert, "Transforming Knowledge and Ways of Knowing for Food Sovereignty and Bio-Cultural Diversity" (London: International Institute for Environment and Development, 2007) 6–7.

83. Swift et al., "Biodiversity and Agroecosystem Function," 261–98.

84. Perrings et al., "Biodiversity in Agricultural Landscapes," 263–64.

RESOURCE GUIDE

Suggested Reading

Gliessman, Stephen R. *Agroecology: The Ecology of Sustainable Food Systems*. New York: CRC Press, 2006.

Jarvis, D. I., C. Padoch, and H. D. Cooper, eds. *Managing Biodiversity in Agricultural Ecosystems*. New York: Columbia University Press, 2007.

Scherr, Sara J., and Jeffrey A. McNeely. *Farming with Nature: The Science and Practice of Ecoagriculture*. Washington, DC: Island Press, 2007.

Wood, D., and J. M. Lenne, eds. *Agrobiodiversity: Characterization, Utilization and Management*. New York: CABI Publishing, 1999.

Web Sites

DIVERSITAS, http://www.diversitas-international.org/.

Food and Agriculture Organization of the United Nations, FAO Agricultural Biodiversity, http://www.fao.rg/biodiversity/biodiversity-home/en/.

International Treaty on Plant Genetic Resources for Food and Agriculture, http://www.planttreaty.org/.

Monarch Butterfly Biosphere Reserve, http://whc.unesco.org/en/list/1290.

5

Energy Conservation in Agriculture and Food Transport

David Pimentel

Oil, natural gas, and coal provide the United States with nearly all of its energy needs at a cost of $700 billion per year.[1] Since more than 90 percent of its oil deposits have been depleted, the United States now imports more than 66 percent of its oil at an annual cost of $200 billion.[2, 3] The American food supply is driven almost entirely by these nonrenewable energy sources. In total, each American requires approximately two thousand liters per year in oil equivalents to supply their food, which accounts for about 19 percent of the total energy use in the United States. Farming and production, along with food processing and packaging, consume 14 percent, while transportation and preparation use 5 percent of total energy in the United States.[4]

Global usage of oil and natural gas has peaked at a time when oil and gas reserves are predicted to last about forty years.[5, 6] As oil supplies rapidly decline, there will be a greater dependence on coal and gas as energy resources. Currently, coal supplies are capable of providing the United States with fifty to one hundred more years of energy.[7] Yet, the U.S. population is projected to increase from 327 million to 1 billion in about one hundred years, further exacerbating strains on coal and oil supplies.[8] This study will illustrate how an adequate food supply can be maintained, while reducing U.S. food energy transport by 50 percent.

FOOD CONSUMED BY AMERICANS

The average American consumes 1,000 kilograms (2,200 pounds) of food per year containing an estimated 3,747 kilocalories (kcal) per day (see Table 5.1).[9]

A vegetarian diet of an equivalent 3,747 kcal per day requires 33 percent less fossil energy than the average American diet.[10] The Food and Drug Administration (FDA) recommends an average daily consumption of 2,000 to 2,500 kcal a day, much less than provided by the typical American diet. Simply reducing calorie intake to this more reasonable level would reduce the energy used in food production significantly.

Table 5.1.
Current U.S. Food Consumption versus Recommended Food Consumption without Junk Foods in Either Diet

Food	Current Diet (3,747 kcal per day)		Reduced Consumption Diet (2,503 kcal per day)		
	kcal/day	kg/year	% reduction	kcal/day	kg/year
Grains	1,509	157	15	1,283	133
Starchy roots	136	63	15	116	54
Sweeteners	282	140	65	100	49
Nuts	15	2	0	15	2
Fats & oils	581	86	65	203	30
Vegetables	80	131	0	80	131
Fruits	126	124	0	126	124
Meat	526	94	50	263	47
Fish	28	21	50	14	11
Milk	403	241	40	242	145
Eggs	61	17	0	61	17
Total	3,747	1,076		2,503	743

Source: FAOSTAT, "Food Balance Sheets" (Rome, Food and Agriculture Organization of the United Nations, 2004), http://faostat.fao.org/site/554/default.aspx.

LAND

More than 99.7 percent of the global human food supply (calories) comes from the land, while less than 0.3 percent comes from aquatic ecosystems.[11] At present, food production should be increasing to meet human nutrition needs, yet the per capita availability of world cropland declined by 20 percent in the past decade.[12] The production of biofuels, especially corn ethanol, is reducing the amount of cropland required to produce food.[13] This is increasing malnutrition in the world, as well as increasing food prices 10 to 30 percent.

More than ten million hectares of valuable cropland are degraded and lost each year because of wind and water erosion.[14] Another ten million hectares are abandoned annually because of severe salinization, which is a result of irrigation.[15] Approximately 75 billion tons of topsoil erodes each year.[16] Soil erosion occurs on average cropland at rates ranging from ten tons per hectare per year in the United States and Europe up to thirty tons per hectare per year in Africa, South America, and Asia.[17] Loss of soil is insidious; one rain or wind storm can remove one millimeter of topsoil and nearly fourteen tons of total soil per hectare. This one millimeter of erosion can easily go unnoticed by farmers. Available cropland is declining due to rapid population growth as well as the aforementioned impacts of soil erosion and salinization.[18] Numerous reports indicate a loss in cropland caused by soil erosion and salinization totaling twenty million hectares per year.[19, 20]

The world population sixty years from now is projected to have more than twice as many people as it has today (6.7 billion), or about 13 billion. Considering a World Health Organization report, which states that worldwide there are currently more than 3.7 billion malnourished humans, we should expect food shortage problems to continually worsen.[21] This is the largest number of malnourished people ever in the history of the Earth (~60 percent of world population).

While the number of malnourished people increased worldwide over the past two decades, the per capita grain production declined simultaneously.[22] Many factors contributed to this decline in grain production, including the following: a rapidly growing world population,[23] a 20 percent decline in cropland per capita in the last decade,[24] a 10 percent decline in irrigation,[25] and a 17 percent decrease in per capita fertilizer use.[26] Cereal grains make up 80 percent of the world's food supply.

MECHANIZATION AND MACHINERY

Raising corn and most other crops by hand requires about twelve hundred hours of labor per hectare (nearly five hundred hours per acre).[27] With modern mechanization, however, we can raise a hectare of corn with a labor input of only eleven hours, or 109 times less than the on-farm labor for hand-produced crops.[28] Mechanization requires significant energy for the production and repair of machinery (about 333,000 kcal per hectare) plus the diesel and gasoline fuel used for operation (1.4 million kcal per hectare).[29] About one-third of the energy used to produce a hectare of crops is invested in machine operation.[30] Mechanization generally reduces labor significantly, but it does not contribute to increased crop yields.

Organic corn production requires 30 percent less fossil fuel but 30 percent more labor.[31] A similar amount of mechanization is required in organic systems to that of conventional systems.[32] Economies of scale are still possible with more labor and the use of smaller tractors and other implements. Reports suggest that equipment quantity and size is often in excess for the required tasks. Reducing the number and size of tractors will help increase efficiency and conserve energy.[33]

Another proposal has been to return to horses and mules. One horse can contribute to the management of 10 hectares (25 acres) per year.[34] Each horse requires 1 acre of pasture and 1.5 acres of cropland to produce five hundred pounds of corn grain. Another 1.5 acres of hayland is necessary to produce the roughly eight hundred pounds of hay needed to sustain each animal. In addition to the labor required to care for the horses, labor is required to drive the horses during tilling and other farm operations. The farm labor required per hectare probably would increase from eleven hours to between thirty and forty hours per hectare using draft animal power.

TRANSPORT OF FOOD

Food in the United States travels an average of 2,400 kilometers (1,500 miles) before it is consumed (see Table 5.2). This transport of food is energy intensive (see Table 5.3).

A head of lettuce produced in California and shipped to New York demonstrates the energy demand of transportation. For instance, a head of lettuce weighing 1 kilogram has 110 kcal of food energy and is 95 percent water.[35] To produce the head of lettuce in California using irrigation requires about 750 kcal of fossil

Table 5.2.
Annual Energy Inputs for the Transportation of Food within and to the United States

Transport per Year	Energy Input in kcal	Energy Input/Food/kcal
Per person within the United States	2×10^6	1.4
Total United States	6×10^{12}	—
Per person imported food	6,000	4
Total United States	1.8×10^{12}	—

Source: CUESA, "How Far Does Your Food Travel to get to Your Plate?" (Center for Urban Education about Sustainable Agriculture, 2008), http://www.cuesa.org/sustainable_ag/issues/foodtravel.php (accessed May 30, 2008).

Note: — = not available.

Foods transported within the U.S. average 2,400 km (CUESA 2008). Foods transported to the United States from foreign countries average 4,200 km (see Table 5.3; truck transport = 0.32 kcal/kg/km and air transport = 6.36 kcal/kg/km).

energy.[36] To transport the 1 kilogram head of lettuce from California to New York City, using a refrigerated truck (transport costs plus refrigeration costs), requires 4,140 kcal of fuel.[37] This fuel cost is one reason it is expected that the export of vegetables and fruits from the western and southern United States will decline. Fruit and vegetable production will likely shift to the midwestern and eastern United States. The types and varieties of produce also will change.

For example, 1 kilogram head of cabbage produced in New York State requires only 400 kcal to produce.[38] Cabbage has far more nutrients than lettuce, including vitamins A and C and protein.[39] In addition to reducing transportation costs, the cabbage can be stored all winter long (which is not possible with lettuce).

An energy-intensive part of the American diet is the large quantity of fruits and vegetables that are transported by aircraft. The amount of energy required to ship 1 kilogram of food by aircraft is 6.36 kcal per kilometer. Shipping by rail is only 0.15 kcal per kilogram per kilometer.[40]

Additional evidence concerning the large amount of energy used in the transport of food comes from the transport of food from the supermarket. For example, consider a 1-pound (455 grams) can of sweet corn transported from the market

Table 5.3.
Energy Inputs Required to Transport a Kilogram of Food for 1 Kilometer in the United States

Transport Method	kcal/kg/km
Waterway, ship	0.08
Rail	0.15
Truck	0.32
Aircraft	6.36

Source: David Pimentel, "Food Transport Energy Use," unpublished.

home (see Figure 5.1).[41] The average shopper shops twice per week, travels round-trip ten miles each time, and brings home approximately 9 kilograms of food goods.[42] Assuming 14.5 kilometers per liter (twenty miles per gallon), then it takes about 311 kcal to transport the one pound of sweet corn home, or almost as much fossil energy as the food energy in the can. As illustrated in Figure 5.1, 158 kcal of transportation energy also was spent in getting the can to the distributor, after the processing and packaging of the sweet corn. This confirms that significantly more energy was invested in the can of sweet corn than in the sweet-corn food.

REDUCING ENERGY INPUTS IN THE FOOD SYSTEMS BY REDUCING TRANSPORTATION AND OTHER INPUTS

It has been estimated that the amount of fossil energy used in the food system could be reduced by about 50 percent with changes in production, processing, packaging, transport, and consumption.[43] Using corn production as a model crop, it is estimated that total energy in corn production could be reduced by more than 50 percent with the following changes: (1) using smaller machinery in the field and thus less fuel;[44] (2) replacing the commercial nitrogen used with legume cover crops and livestock manure; and (3) reducing soil erosion in corn production through alternative tillage and conservation techniques, which could reduce the phosphorus, potassium, and lime application to 33 percent of current levels.[45]

The average American consumes 3,747 kcal of food per day, and based on preliminary data, the average person consumes 33 percent of their total calories in junk food.[46] Reducing the junk food intake from 33 percent to 10 percent of the

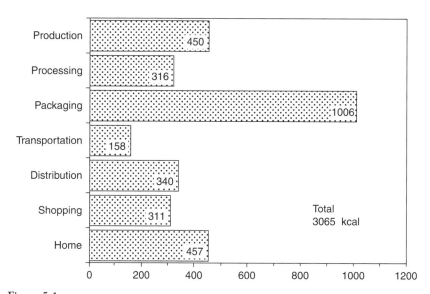

Figure 5.1.
Energy Inputs for a 455 g (375 kcal) Can of Sweet Corn
Source: David Pimentel and Marcia Pimentel, *Food, Energy and Society*, 3rd ed. (Boca Raton, FL: CRC Press, Taylor and Francis Group, 2008), 250.

current level would reduce caloric intake to 2,826 kcal. This would still be 326 kcal above the suggested level for males or 826 kcal for females.

Some of the current foods consumed per person per year are listed in Table 5.1. It is suggested that the amounts of meat and dairy products consumed could be reduced by 50 percent, while still maintaining the necessary quality and quantity of nutrients. This would be especially true if the amounts of cereal grain, fruits, and vegetables were increased.[47] This dietary improvement could reduce the amount of fossil energy input by approximately 50 percent.

Especially important is the long distance that U.S. food is transported. The average distance that food is transported before being consumed by the average American is 2,400 kilometers, which requires about 2 million kcal per year per person. This is 1.4 times the energy in food consumed per person. Although a relatively small percentage of fruits and vegetable are transported by air cargo into the United States, large quantities of fossil energy are required for this transport. The energy input per 1 kcal of fruits and vegetable for transport is 4 kcal. Increased consumption of local foods should be a major goal for energy savings.

CONCLUSION

Energy input in U.S. transport is enormous, representing four times the energy contained in the fruit and vegetable produce being transported. This large amount of energy could be reduced substantially by purchasing more locally produced food items.

ACKNOWLEDGMENT

This research was supported in part by the Podell Emeriti Award at Cornell University.

NOTES

1. United States Census Bureau (USCB), *Statistical Abstracts of the United States* (Washington, DC: Government Printing Office, 2007).

2. Kenneth S. Deffeyes, *Hubbert's Peak: The Impending World Oil Shortage* (Princeton, Oxford: Princeton University Press, 2001).

3. USCB, *Statistical Abstracts*.

4. David Pimentel, Emily Rochon, Jennifer Gardner, Claire Horan, Ximena Garcia, Julie Grufferman, Emily Walling, Julia Schlenker, and Adam Bonnifield, "Energy Efficiency and Conservation for Individual Americans," *Environment Development and Sustainability* (2008), http://www.springerlink.com/content/v153161421265437/ (accessed May 30, 2008).

5. Richard C. Duncan and Walter Youngquist, "Encircling the peak of world oil production," *Natural Resources Research* 8, no. 3 (1999): 219–32.

6. Deffeyes, *Hubbert's Peak*.

7. USCB, *Statistical Abstracts*.

8. Virginia D. Abernethy, "Census Bureau Distortions Hide Immigration Crisis: Real Numbers Much Higher" (Nashville, TN: Vanderbilt University School of Medicine, 2006).

9. U.S. Department of Agriculture, *Agricultural Statistics* (Washington, DC: Government Printing Office, 2007).

10. David Pimentel and Marcia Pimentel, *Food, Energy and Society*, 3rd ed. (Boca Raton, FL: CRC Press, Taylor and Francis Group, 2008), 133–34.

11. FAOSTAT, "Food Balance Sheets" (Rome: Food and Agriculture Organization of the United Nations, 2004), http://faostat.fao.org/site/554/default.aspx (accessed December 15, 2006).

12. Worldwatch Institute, *Vital Signs 2001* (New York: W.W. Norton Company, 2001).

13. David Pimentel and Tad W. Patzek, "Ethanol Production Using Corn, Switchgrass, and Wood; Biodiesel Production Using Soybean and Sunflower," in *Food, Energy and Society*, 3rd ed., ed. D. Pimentel and M. Pimentel (Boca Raton, FL: CRC Press, Taylor and Francis Group, 2008), 319.

14. Rachel F. Preiser, "Living within our Environmental Means. Natural Resources and an Optimum Human Population" (2006), http://dieoff.org/pages50.htm (accessed November 5, 2006).

15. Food and Agriculture Organization of the United Nations, "The Use of Saline Waters for Crop Production" (Rome: FAO Corporate Documentary Repository, 2006).

16. Bruce H. Wilkinson and Brandon J. McElroy, "The Impact of Humans on Continental Erosion and Sedimentation," *Geological Sciences Association Bulletin* 119, no. 1–2 (2007): 140–56.

17. David Pimentel, "Soil Erosion: A Food and Environmental Threat," *Environment, Development and Sustainability* 8, no. 1 (2006): 123–24.

18. Ibid., 132.

19. Preiser, "Living within our Environmental Means."

20. FAO, "The Use of Saline Waters."

21. World Health Organization, "Malnutrition Worldwide" (2005), http://www.mikeschoice.com/reports/malnutrition_worldwide.htm (accessed January 3, 2007).

22. FAOSTAT, "World Cereal Grain Production, Food and Agriculture Organization 1961–2006" (Rome: Food and Agriculture Organization of the United Nations, 2008).

23. Population Reference Bureau, *World Population Datasheet* (Washington, DC: Population Reference Bureau, 2007).

24. David Pimentel and Anne Wilson, "World Population, Agriculture, and Malnutrition," *World Watch* September/October (2004): 22.

25. Sandra Postel, *Last Oasis: Facing Water Scarcity* (New York: W.W. Norton Company, 1997).

26. David Pimentel, Rachel Doughty, Courtney Carothers, Sonja Lamberson, Nirali Bora, and Katherine Lee, "Energy Inputs in Crop Production: Comparison of Developed and Developing Countries," in *Food Security and Environmental Quality in the Developing World*, ed. R. Lal, D. Hansen, N. Uphoff, and S. Slack (Boca Raton, FL: CRC Press, 2002), 145.

27. David Pimentel, "Feeding the World," interview by Jackie May, *Earthbeat*, Radio National, 20 July 2002, http://www.abc.net.au/rn/science/earth/stories/s611400.htm (accessed May 19, 2008).

28. Pimentel et al., "Energy Efficiency for Americans."

29. Pimentel and Patzek, "Ethanol Production," 312–13.

30. Pimentel et al., "Energy Inputs in Crop Production," 129–51.

31. David Pimentel, Paul Hepperly, James Hanson, David Douds, and Rita Seidel, "Environmental, Energetic and Economic Comparisons of Organic and Conventional Farming Systems," *BioScience* 55, no. 7 (2005): 573–82.

32. Ibid., 573–82.

33. Robert Grisso and Robert Pitman, "Gearing Up and Throttle Down – Saving Fuel" (2001), http://www/ext.vy.edu/pubs/bse/442-450/442-450.html (accessed October 25, 2006).

34. F. B. Morrison, *Feeds and Feeding: A Handbook for the Student and Stockman* (Ithaca, NY: The Morrison Publishing Company, 1946).

35. U.S. Department of Agriculture, *Nutritive Value of American Foods, Agricultural Handbook No. 456* (Washington, DC: Agricultural Research Service, 1976).

36. Edward J. Ryder, "Lettuce," in *Handbook of Energy Utilization in Agriculture*, ed. D. Pimentel (Boca Raton, FL: CRC Press, 1980), 191 Radio National 194.

37. Pimentel et al., "Energy Efficiency for Individual Americans."

38. Pimentel et al., "Energy Inputs in Crop Production," 143.

39. USDA, *Nutritive Value of American Foods.*

40. David Pimentel, *Food Transport Energy Use*, unpublished.

41. Pimentel and Pimentel, *Food, Energy and Society*, 250.

42. Chris Muir, "Examining Local Food," (Real Environment, Economic and Scientific Investigations of Environmental Issues, 2008), http://realenvironment.blogspot.com/2006/12/examining-buying-local.html (accessed March 14, 2008).

43. David Pimentel, Sean Williamson, Courtney E. Alexander, Omar Gonzalez-Pagan, Caitlin Kontak, and Steven Mulkey, "Reducing Energy Inputs in the U.S. Food System," *Human Ecology* 36 no. 4, 459–71 (2008).

44. Grisso and Pitman, "Saving Fuel."

45. Pimentel et al., "Reducing Energy in Food System."

46. Sarah Yang, "Nearly One-third of the Calories in the US Diet Come from Junk Food," (UC Berkeley News, 2004), http://berkeley.edu/news/media/releases/2004/06/01_usdiet.shtml (accessed November 3, 2006).

47. Pimentel et al., "Reducing Energy in Food System."

RESOURCE GUIDE

Suggested Reading

Deffeyes, Kenneth S. *Hubbert's Peak: The Impending World Oil Shortage*. Princeton, Oxford: Princeton University Press, 2001.

Duncan, Richard C., and Walter Youngquist. "Encircling the Peak of World Oil Production." *Natural Resources Research* 8, no. 3 (1999): 219–32.

Pimentel, David. "Soil Erosion: a Food and Environmental Threat." *Environment, Development and Sustainability* 8, no. 1 (2006): 123–24.

Pimentel, David, Paul Hepperly, James Hanson, David Douds, and Rita Seidel. "Environmental, Energetic and Economic Comparisons of Organic and Conventional Farming Systems." *BioScience* 55, no. 7 (2005): 573–82.

Pimentel, David, and Marcia Pimentel. *Food, Energy and Society*. 3rd ed. Boca Raton, FL: CRC Press, Taylor and Francis Group, 2008.

Pimentel, David, Emily Rochon, Jennifer Gardner, Claire Horan, Ximena Garcia, Julie Grufferman, Emily Walling, Julia Schlenker, and Adam Bonnifield. 2008. "Energy Efficiency and Conservation for Individual Americans." *Environment, Development and Sustainability* (in press). Available at http://www.springerlink.com/content/v153161421265437/ (accessed May 30, 2008).

Pimentel, David, and Anne Wilson, "World Population, Agriculture, and Malnutrition." *World Watch* (September/October 2004): 22–25.

Wilkinson, Bruce H., and Brandon J. McElroy. "The Impact of Humans on Continental Erosion and Sedimentation." *Geological Sciences Association Bulletin*. 119, no. 1–2 (2007): 140–56.

Web Sites

Leopold.iastate.edu, "Food, Fuel, and Freeways," http://www.leopold.iastate.edu/pubs/staff/ppp/food_mil.pdf.
Globalsubsidies.org, "Biofuels—At What Cost? Government Support for Ethanol and Biodiesel in the United States," http://www.globalsubsidies.org/files/assets/pdf/Brochure_-_US_Report.pdf.
International Forum on Globalization, "False Promise of Biofuels," http://www.ifg.org/pdf/biofuels.pdf.

PART II

Agriculture and Fisheries

6

Sustainable Agricultural Practices in the United States and Other Postindustrial Countries

Daniel A. Cibulka

To forget how to dig the earth and tend the soil is to forget ourselves.
—Mahatma Gandhi[1]

Along with fisheries, agriculture must provide food for 1.30 billion people in industrial countries. A world population of this magnitude places incredible stress on the Earth's natural resources, including arable land. This chapter will examine how the United States and other postindustrial countries may use sustainable agriculture as a way to feed their populations, yet do so in a manner that reduces the stress placed on the natural resources providing their sustenance.

CONVENTIONAL AGRICULTURE

From the moment humans began planting seeds in the Middle East ten thousand years ago until the early 1700s, little changed within the practice of agriculture. Of course, the process of agriculture did evolve. Wood tools turned to stone, and then stone tools to metal. Ox-drawn four-wheeled carts for pulling plows through a field were a familiar sight in northern India in 2,000 B.C.E. New crops became popular over the ages as well, with grapes and wine first mentioned in Egyptian literature around 2,900 B.C.E. In Europe, rye and oats were introduced around 1,000 B.C.E. Irrigation systems evolved in China and the Middle East, which allowed more land to be placed into production. However, it was not until the early 1700s that agriculture experienced a "revolution" of sorts. Agriculture and science then merged to produce more food on less land, while using less labor. And mechanically driven farm machinery, likely the most groundbreaking development to affect agriculture, was introduced during the Industrial Revolution.

Thomas Jefferson once referred to small family farmers as "America's most valuable and most virtuous citizens."[2] In the early 1800s, farmers accounted for 90 percent of the labor force in the country. Today, Jefferson's numerous "cultivators of the earth" and their humble farm homes have been replaced by 530-horsepower tractors and combines, large industrial farms, chemical fertilizers, and harmful pesticides. Colossal agroindustry giants have overtaken the numerous small farms that once dotted the landscape, and U.S. farmers now make up less than 2.5 percent of the population.[3] Unfortunately, with the arrival of conventional (or industrial) agriculture came numerous problems that are beginning to act as roadblocks to this industry's future.

Conventional agriculture primarily uses monoculture (one plant species), as this allows for standardized mechanical planting and harvest. As monoculture crops can create the ideal situation for pests, the need for pesticides increases on these fields. However, the very pesticides that protect our food soon run off into nearby ground and surface waters. From 1992 to 2001, the U.S. Geological Survey (USGS) undertook a nationwide assessment of pollutants in U.S. waters called the National Water-Quality Assessment (NAWQA). The study found that at least one pesticide was detected in water from all streams studied. Even more troubling findings were that agricultural pesticides were detected throughout most of the year in water from streams with agriculture (97 percent of the time), urban (97 percent of the time), or mixed-land-use watersheds (94 percent of the time).[4]

Erosion of topsoil has become another primary issue in modern agriculture. When plants are removed from the land, little residue is left to hold soil particles intact. Large machinery has compacted soils, leaving them less able to absorb rainfall and, consequently, increased runoff. With rainfall, the soil rows between monoculture plots can act as conveyors for soil-laden water, moving the soil from its original position. Ultimately, these forces result in the erosion of fertile soils. Recent studies at Cornell University suggest that U.S. topsoil is being washed off of the landscape ten times faster than it is being replenished.[5] This problem of soil erosion leads to critical losses of water, nutrients, organic matter, and soil biota, as well as to health and aesthetic issues concerning soil and dust particles that are swept into rivers and streams or carried into the air.

Salinization of soils has become a critical issue in many parts of the world. Through "broadcast irrigation," the ground is saturated with more water than plant roots can absorb. The excess water percolates down to layers of salty soil. This continuous column of water allows salts to diffuse upward to the surface or into groundwater to be carried to nearby streams. When vegetation is removed from a landscape, a similar action is seen in which rainwater that was previously sequestered by the plants is allowed to percolate in continuous columns toward the deeper salty soil layers. This is called "dryland salinization." In either scenario, the topsoil becomes too saline to support many crops, or plants in general. In his book *Collapse*, Jared Diamond describes how salinization of soils has rendered 9 percent of all cleared land in Australia useless.[6] Furthermore, several areas within the country have groundwater salt concentrations three times that of the ocean.

Arguably, the most pressing concern for conventional agriculture is that of capital depletion. Investment in conventional agriculture includes massive inputs of water through irrigation, chemical- and often petroleum-based fertilizers, and pesticides to replace depleted soil nutrients and prevent pests, and also includes a reliance on non-renewable fuels such as gas and oil to operate heavy machinery. This heavy reliance on external inputs has created a form of agriculture that cannot sustain itself.

Hirsch, Bezdek, and Wendling explain the future of oil resources by recounting the development of the "Peak Oil" theory.[7] In 1956, petroleum geologist M. King Hubbert created a model to accurately predict when what he termed "Peak Oil" would occur. The resulting "Hubbert Curve" is a bell-shaped curve that shows

U.S. oil production peaking sometime between 1965 and 1970, and then declining due to reduced supply and loss of economic viability of extraction. As it happens, oil production in the continental United States did peak in 1970–1971. Later in life, Hubbert predicted a global oil peak between 1995 and 2000. Although this has yet to be confirmed, fifty-four of the sixty-five largest oil-producing countries in the world have passed their peak production and are now on the decline. Furthermore, many oil experts believe global peak production will occur within twenty years of Hubbert's prediction.[8]

Complicating matters of supply, it is becoming more expensive to mine for oil. To make business more profitable, oil companies have continuously extracted the shallowest oil reserves, the pressurized reserves, and generally the easiest-to-reach reserves first. As supply dwindles, the only oil supplies left eventually will be those located so deep in the Earth (under land or sea) or those so high in by-product (such as sulfur) that it simply will not make financial sense to drill for them.

Modern industrial agriculture is fossil fuel intensive—the machinery requires diesel gasoline and oil, the process to make chemical fertilizer is energy intensive, and many herbicides and pesticides require the use of oil and gas in their production. Walter Youngquist stated in the *Post-Petroleum Paradigm* that "[a]pproximately 90% of the energy in crop production is in oil and natural gas ... 1/3 of this to reduce labor input and 2/3 for production, of which 1/3 of this is for fertilizers alone."[9] What will happen now that we are on the downward slope of the Hubbert Curve, and when our primary energy source becomes too expensive or short in supply to fuel the equipment, produce the fertilizers, and truck the product to feed the people of the industrial world?

Industrial agriculture faces an uphill struggle in assisting the developed world to cope with a booming population and reduce the extent of environmental degradation. The good news, however, is that models of sustainable agriculture are being developed in postindustrial nations. Let us discuss these examples and examine the biological, political, social, and economic context behind the sustainable practices.

SUSTAINABLE AGRICULTURE AS A SYSTEM

An unsustainable system, by definition, is any system that simply cannot continue to operate as it currently does. Agriculture may be thought of as a complex system involving many inputs and outputs, and globally about 6.756 billion people depend on this system. Agriculture's inputs and outputs must be managed in a way that allows future generations to harvest food from the same land to feed the population for generations to come. This is the essence of sustainable agriculture.

In 1990, the U.S. Congress addressed sustainable agriculture in the Farm Bill (Food, Agriculture, Conservation, and Trade Act of 1990).[10] Under the Farm Bill, Congress defined sustainable agriculture as an

integrated system of plant and animal production practices having a site-specific application that will, over the long term:

- satisfy human food and fiber needs;
- enhance environmental quality and the natural resource base upon which the agricultural economy depends;

- make the most efficient use of nonrenewable resources and on-farm resources and integrate, where appropriate, natural biological cycles and controls;
- sustain the economic viability of farm operations; and
- enhance the quality of life for farmers and society as a whole.[11]

Sustainable agriculture has two primary components. The first includes biophysical aspects such as the effects of agricultural management on the soil and crop productivity as well as the ability to produce nutritious food. A truly sustainable plot of land must ensure that the soil will always be rich in nutrients, organic matter, and organisms that break down waste material. The land must be farmed in a way that does not result in the pollution of nearby waters or the air, and the produce coming from the land must be healthy and nutritious. The second component of sustainable agriculture addresses socioeconomic aspects, such as the ability of farmers to obtain system inputs, manage resources, and produce affordable food for the public. Both components must be considered along with the underlying concept of thinking in the long term. To do otherwise, endangers the agricultural system for future generations.

APPROACHES TO SUSTAINABLE AGRICULTURE

With the erosion of fertile topsoil being one of the critical issues in agriculture, much research has been done on agricultural practices, such as intensive tilling, which are responsible for this loss. Historically, fields were tilled to remove weeds, which compete with crops for space, water, and nutrients. Conservation tillage is a more sustainable way of dealing with weeds in a less mechanical manner. The process refers to a number of strategies for establishing crops within the previous crop's residues. Through conservation tillage, soil erosion is reduced, organic matter and moisture content improved, air pollution reduced, and wildlife habitat created. Moreover, tractor use is reduced by half, thus reducing fuel consumption, labor, and maintenance costs.

Conservation tillage is performed in several ways. One popular technique is called ridge tillage. Using this method, permanent ridges are carved into the land on which row crops are grown. A special planter places new seed in the top of the ridge after pushing last year's crop residue out of the way. The ridge-tillage planter is a multipurpose device that not only plants seeds and removes residue, but also rebuilds ridges and removes weeds. This process keeps weeds under control, allowing the farmer to restrict herbicide use.

No-till is another conservation tillage approach. This method utilizes a special planter to place seed directly into the previous year's crop residue, with only a double disc opener to place the seed at the correct depth. No-till offers excellent soil erosion control and greatly reduces the number of tractor trips across the field. In the past, no-till was criticized because in its early stages, chemical herbicides were the only means of weed control with this method. However, newer technology (the "no-till cultivator") permits herbicide to be applied in bands between rows, reducing the overall amount of herbicide used.

Conservation tillage has quickly become one of the most effective methods of retaining soil in the United States, and has slowly been adopted in other industrial nations. In 2004, the number of U.S. acres under conservation tillage broke 40 percent for the first time.[12] American farmers have gained some administrative support for conservation tillage through the Farm Bills of 1985, 1990, and 1996. In more recent installments of the Farm Bill (2002 and 2008), the Environmental Quality Incentives Program (EQIP) was created to offer financial and technical assistance to farmers for using conservation tillage, among other conservation techniques.

Along with the United States, other industrial nations such as Australia and Canada have been steadily increasing the use of conservation tillage, while Europe lags well behind.[13] According to the European Conservation Agriculture Federation, conservation agriculture has been slower to catch on in European countries because of heavy subsidies (less need to take "risks"), a lack of technology and the ability to transfer this technology from scientific researchers to farmers, and a lack of institutional support.[14]

The use of cover crops (or green manure) has also been shown to assist in making agriculture sustainable. A cover crop is a monoculture crop planted to improve soil conditions and prevent soil erosion. The use of legumes (nitrogen-fixing plants such as alfalfa, soybeans, and sweetclover) increases levels of nitrogen, while all cover crops assist in the production of other essential minerals, such as phosphorous, potassium, calcium, magnesium, and sulfur. Other benefits of cover crops include enhancing the organic matter content of soils, soil microbial activity, weed suppression, and water conservation. Following are several types of cover crops:

- Winter cover crops planted in late summer or fall
- Summer cover crops, which occupy the land for a portion of the growing season
- Living mulch, which is interplanted with primary crops
- Catch crops used to fill a niche in a crop rotational schedule
- Forage crops that also allow for pasturage of grazing animals[15]

The sustainability of agricultural land also must address the animals that forage the land. When livestock graze the land without constraint, problems occur. They will likely forage on the tastiest plants first, leaving less desirable species dotting the landscape. If these plants are repeatedly foraged upon, their roots will not have enough time to recover and the result will be a field of only undesirable plants. Given enough time, some herds will clear a landscape of all vegetation. This "overgrazing" can result in serious environmental issues such as soil erosion, increased dust in the air, and desertification of a previously vegetated landscape.

With rotational grazing, livestock are moved from pasture to pasture, which creates rest periods for the plant species. The soil in the fields will also enjoy the rest period from compaction. Additionally, the animal's health will improve with more exercise and constant fresh, preferred food sources. Parasite cycles can also be broken by rotating foraging species in a specific sequence. Finally, nearby waters will benefit when livestock are no longer defecating near water sources and the soil has enough vegetation to reduce erosion of soils. Some carbon sequestration can occur, as has been demonstrated by the Polyface farm.[16]

Rotational grazing can be a relatively inexpensive technique in the growing number of sustainable agricultural strategies. Fencing is the primary requirement for managing animal herds. To make efficient use of water sources, the pasture plan should be designed carefully to reduce piping and portable water container expenses. With a more even distribution of animal manure, rotational grazing can decrease pasture fertilization costs. While livestock are foraging elsewhere, farmers may even allow pastures enough rest so that hay, alfalfa, or other food crops can be grown. These crops may then be harvested and stockpiled, instead of being purchased. Typically, conventional grazing does not allow this opportunity.

LOCAL AND ORGANIC CROPS

A critical part of sustainable agriculture relies on the choices consumers make. The demand for both organic and locally grown foods has increased in the past few years. The U.S. market for organic foods has grown from $1 billion in 1990 to $20 billion in 2008, according to the Organic Trade Association.[17] In 2007, wordsmiths at the *Oxford American Dictionary* gave their support of the local food movement by making "locavore" (n.: a person who attempts to eat only foods grown locally) the word of the year.[18] In London, a recent poll shows two-thirds of consumers are attempting to buy more locally, and seasonally as well.[19]

Organic food is grown according to certain government standards. Australia, Canada, the European Union, Japan, and the United States have all established certification procedures for organic foods. The U.S. Department of Agriculture (USDA) is responsible for certifying organic produce in the United States. Their crop standards include the following:

- Land without prohibited substances applied in the last three years
- Use of conservation tillage and cultivation practices, crop rotations, and cover crops
- Fertilized only with animal and crop waste materials
- Biological and physical or other natural controls for pests only
- Use of genetic engineering, ionizing radiation, and sewage sludge prohibited[20]

Organic foods are often touted for their land conservation ethics and healthy, chemical-free produce. Organic farms typically sustain more diverse ecosystems (with many serving as sanctuaries for wildlife), consume less energy, and produce less waste than conventional farms. While it is true that organic methods of agriculture should be commended as "more sustainable," the origin of the food relative to where it is sold should be considered by people who wish to eat environmentally friendly foods.

The local food movement is gaining attention, partly due to concerns over energy consumption. Food that is trucked in from the far side of the country has more "food miles" than the food grown nearby, and therefore more energy has been used in the transport. When purchasing locally, a consumer also has a better opportunity to understand where their food comes from and how it is produced. Many farmers will conduct tours of their farm to promote closer relationships with customers. Although local food is not always organic, many small farms are likely to include other sustainable growing methods in their operation. The demand for local food also provides economic support as residents learn of its importance to the local economy. When food is purchased from across the nation (or even across seas), local economies do not receive the benefits of that transaction. Spending a dollar with local farmers or businesses reinvests that dollar regionally, in effect keeping economic prosperity in your region.

FARM SIZE

In 1900, there were 5.7 million farms in the United States, with an average farm size of 146 acres; now there are 2.1 million farms averaging 441 acres each. As farmers switched from biologically diverse practices to monocultures, the average number of commodities produced per farm decreased as well, from 5.1 to 1.3.[21] Massive government subsidies have perpetuated this process. In the past five years, the U.S. government has paid $95 billion in agricultural subsidies.[22] In the European Union, agricultural subsidies make up more than 40 percent of the total budget.[23]

Although these governments are allocating funds to large farms and agricultural corporations, studies are beginning to show that large farms are less efficient than smaller ones. Smaller farms that produce polycultures (more than one crop) are actually more productive when compared with monocropping larger farms on a basis of total produce per acre.[24] While smaller farms tend to generate wealth and create jobs in local rural areas, large industrial farms are more mechanistic; they tend to incorporate more large machinery in their processes that takes the place of hard-working farmers. As a result, large industrial farms have been criticized for exporting farm income from the community and offering fewer job opportunities.

The USDA acknowledges the differences between small and large farms. A 1998 report by the National Commission on Small Farms highlighted the fact that small farms were invaluable to vibrant rural communities. The report recommended new regulations that would increase federal funds to small family farms, along with enforcing fair and competitive markets between small farms and their larger counterparts.[25]

SUSTAINABLE AGRICULTURE SYSTEMS

Natural Systems Agriculture

Numerous types of agricultural systems have employed sustainable techniques. Natural systems agriculture is a method of food production in which "nature is mimicked rather than subdued and ignored."[26] Scientists at the Land Institute in Salina, Kansas, believe that agriculture can become resilient, economical, and ecologically sound by examining native biological communities in a region. After years of study, they have discovered that the only communities that persist through evolutionary time are those that achieve the following:

- Maintain or build their ecological capital
- Fix and hold their nutrients
- Adapt to periodic stress, such as drought and fire
- Manage their weed, pest, and pathogen populations[27]

Much of the research that is taking place at the Land Institute focuses on the Great Plains region of the United States. In this region, the dominance of herbaceous perennials had persisted over millennia, until the introduction of annual plants that modern agriculture prefers. Research at the Institute has shown native perennial crops hold and build soil more efficiently, increase plant diversity within a field, promote nutrient recycling, and retard the spread of pathogens and pests. In addition, the harvest of perennials is less energy intensive, as yearly replanting is no longer required.

Since 1976, the Land Institute has enjoyed success with numerous, native perennial grains. It has discovered the potential perennial wheat varieties, intermediate wheatgrass, grain sorghum, and the Illinois bundleflower—a native prairie legume that fixes atmospheric nitrogen and produces protein-rich seed. Besides research, the Land Institute has obtained enough financial support to sponsor short courses on perennial agriculture and also finance student fellowships. In 2009, eighteen graduate students conducted research through its fellowship program.[28] Through continued research, experimentation, and living examples, the Land Institute hopes to revolutionize the way farmers and consumers currently think about agriculture.

Hydroponics

Problems with soil fertility, soil loss, and soil pollution have been a reoccurring theme in this chapter. It was only a matter of time before someone solved these issues by simply not using soil to grow food. Hydroponic systems are a method of growing plants in a mixture of water and fertilizers, requiring no soil whatsoever.

At the Hamakua Springs in Pepe'ekeo, Hawaii, the Ha family grows numerous varieties of fruits and vegetables using a hydroponic system that is powered by an annual average of 130 inches of rainfall.[29] Because they are not using a soil medium to grow their crops, they do not need to worry about many of the weeds or soil-borne pests that traditional farmers experience. As a result they use few pesticides and herbicides. They have eliminated the need for tractors or other harvesting equipment, because they have no soil to till. This reduces energy inputs.

To support the booming tourism industry, Hawaii reduced sugarcane and pineapple production by 70 and 42 percent, respectively.[30] In contrast to these losses, the Ha family farm now has reached its 30th year of business and supplies produce to many restaurants and supermarkets throughout the Hawaiian Islands. For an island chain that currently imports 90 percent of its food and has only a seven-day supply of perishables, local farms such as Hamakua Springs will likely proliferate as it becomes more expensive to import food.[31]

Permaculture and the Philosophies of Masanobu Fukuoka

In 1975, Australian ecologist Bill Mollison and his student David Holmgren developed a sustainable type of agriculture supported by a lifestyle that promotes ecological balance and reduces societal reliance on industrial systems. Permaculture, a term which blends permanent agriculture to permanent culture, has been the focus of numerous books and pamphlets written by these two research scientists.[32] The core concept is the design of an ecological landscape that produces food, but permaculture embraces much more than food production. The holistic design of the landscape incorporates energy-efficient buildings, wastewater treatment, recycling of nutrients and wastes, and land stewardship. Often, societal development is emphasized as well through the process of co-housing projects and ecovillages. Organic practices are encouraged to reduce pesticide and chemical fertilizer use. Permaculture is not a system of mass agricultural production. Rather, it is a land-use and community planning philosophy. And, because it is a site- and culture-specific system, by incorporating flexible ideas and design into its methodology, this form of self-sustaining agriculture can be used in different regions.

Farmer and philosopher Masanobu Fukuoka was another pioneer in the field of permaculture. Trained as a microbiologist and soil scientist in Japan, Fukuoka soon began to doubt what he called "scientific" farming. At age twenty-five he returned to his family's farm to devote his life to developing a unique, small-scale organic farm that operated on four principles: no cultivation, no (engineered) fertilizer, no weeding, and no pesticides. Fukuoka favored the addition of a deep layer of organic matter and incorporation of trees into the garden as opposed to working the soil with tools. He writes:

> [A]s the farmer turns the soil with his hoe, this breaks the soil into smaller particles which acquire an increasingly regular physical arrangement with smaller interstitial spaces.... The result is a harder, denser soil.... With the addition of organic humus and trees, the roots reach down into the earth, and air and water penetrate into the soil with the roots. As these wither and die, many types of microorganisms proliferate. Earthworms appear and moles begin burrowing through the soil. The soil lives of its own accord and plows itself. It needs no help from man.[33]

After years of developing his method, he found he could produce crop yields at least equal to or better than those yields grown under industrial farming. The Fukuoka method utilized only a fraction of the labor and other costs of more intensive farming, and produced no pollution. Additionally, the philosophies of Fukuoka (and permaculture in general) have given agriculture a spiritual basis that is lacking from modern practices. Fukuoka claimed that natural farming proceeds from an individual's spiritual health. "The healing of the land and the purification of human spirit is one process. Natural farming is not just for growing crops, it is for the cultivation and perfection of human beings."[34]

Even after Fukuoka's passing, Japanese farmers still use his methods in their communities. Kiyokazu Shitara oversees the Permaculture Center Japan in the Kanagawa mountain town of Shinobara. With smart design and a garden of biologically symbiotic plants and animals, the Center has become a thriving institute, both agriculturally and educationally. In the courses Shitara teaches at the Center, he explains the intricacies of his system: "The marigolds eliminate microorganisms that cause disease. They also get rid of insects from the eggplants and tomatoes. Onions get rid of kabi (mold)."[35]

The Center uses fruit trees not only for their fruit, but also for their ability to block wind from other crops. Cows are kept upslope so that rain and gravity distributes their natural fertilizers down to the gardens. The slopes are also used to collect excess nutrient-rich water to use later for irrigation. Shitara's chickens and ducks roam free, picking insects off of the crops and eating weeds between the crop rows. The motorized hand plow his neighbors gave him in 1995 still sits next to the chicken shed.

Organizations around the globe have adopted the teachings of permaculture, including some in the industrial world. The Circle School[36] in Richmond, Virginia, is a vegetarian families' cooperative that provides invaluable education for students, as well as work-study opportunities for teaching students from the nearby Virginia Commonwealth University. By working with the local Department of Parks and Recreation, the school developed an area of nearby parkland under the principles of the Fukuoka way of agriculture. Instead of a typical short-grassed park that contains broadleaf weed-killer and wasteful spending on maintenance and labor costs, this section of the park, called Wildflower Walk, is now a beautiful environment in which food is grown, cafeteria spoils are recycled, and students actively participate in observing the biological relationships the park harbors.

Sustainable Agriculture and the Triple Bottom Line

Many people are familiar with the movement to reduce environmental impacts in agriculture, but they do not know where to start to make changes themselves. This offers a ripe opportunity for the entrepreneurial spirit. Kris August saw this and decided to offer expertise on sustainable practices to the farmers who wished to change their ways. The New Zealand Farmsure[37] program now coaches farmers on the principles of food safety, animal welfare, and sustainable resource management, based upon meeting goals of the "Triple Bottom Line (TBL)." The TBL was first discussed in 1994 by John Elkington, and today is a phrase used to capture the values and criteria for measuring organizational success in three areas: economic, ecological, and social.[38] The New Zealand Farmsure program encompasses the ideology of the TBL through three plans. The Animal Management Plan seeks to maximize animal welfare and animal health through sustainable practices. The Land Management Plan provides assistance to farm managers on soil health, water quality, shelter and shade, pasture, biodiversity, biosecurity (from pests and pathogens), and a gas budget to monitor greenhouse-gas emissions. Finally, the Social Responsibility Plan covers issues of training staff, committing to a sustainability pledge, integrating with community, and learning the values of local heritage. Through these plans, Farmsure program farmers have access to knowledgeable professionals to sustainably increase their yields, ensure happy and healthy livestock, keep the land ecologically sound, and create market opportunities within the regional economy.

CONCLUSION

This chapter described a selection of the types of sustainable agriculture approaches taken in the industrial world. Which are most effective? Which will be the most realistic? Is one more sustainable than the other?

Clearly, these approaches demonstrate that sustainable forms of agriculture are being practiced in postindustrial countries. However, public interest to move from conventional agriculture to something more holistic has not gained enough momentum to achieve greater support from national agricultural policies. We have discussed numerous problems with conventional agriculture that will shape and define our transition to a more sustainable way of obtaining food. Environmental degradation, health concerns, and energy consumption will likely be the motivation behind a shift from large-scale, industrial agriculture to smaller, ecologically sound, community-based agricultural structures. We can learn from our ancestors *and* these contemporary trailblazers to select the strategies best suited for our communities. In the meantime, we must *seriously* start to think not only about how we acquire our food, but also about how future generations will acquire theirs.

NOTES

1. John Broomfield, *Other Ways of Knowing: Recharting Our Future with Ageless Wisdom* (Rochester, VT: Inner Traditions, 1997), 204.

2. Paul Thompson, "Agrarianism and the American Philosophical Tradition," *Journal of Agriculture and Human Values* 7, no. 1 (1990): 3–8, 4.

3. M. Grunwald, "Why Our Farm Policy Is Failing," *TIME*, November 2, 2007.

4. U.S. Geological Survey, "Pesticides in the Nation's Streams and Ground Water, 1992–2001—A Summary," NAWQA Fact Sheet 2006–3028 (Washington, DC, 2006).

5. David Pimentel, "Soil Erosion: A Food and Environmental Threat," *Journal of Environment, Development and Sustainability* 8, no. 1 (2006): 119–37.

6. Jared Diamond, *Collapse: How Societies Choose to Fail or Succeed* (New York, Penguin Books, 2006).

7. R. L. Hirsch, R. Bezdek, and R. Wendling, *Peaking of World Oil Production: Impacts, Mitigation, & Risk Management* (Washington, DC: Department of Energy-National Energy and Technology Laboratory, 2005).

8. Ibid.

9. W. Youngquist, "The Post-Petroleum Paradigm—and Population," *Population and Environment: A Journal of Interdisciplinary Studies* 20, no. 4 (1999): 297–315.

10. *Food, Agriculture, Conservation, and Trade Act of 1990*, Public Law 101—624, Title XVI, Subtitle A, Section 1603. Subchapter I: Findings, Purposes, and Definitions, *U.S. Code*, Title 7, Chapter 64, Agricultural Research, Extension and Teaching (1990).

11. Ibid.

12. D. Peterson, "Land & Water: Conserving Natural Resources in Illinois," *University of Illinois Extension Bulletin* 6 (2005), 1.

13. CIRAD—Agricultural Research for Developing Countries, "Conservation for greater sustainability," http://www.cirad.fr/en/actualite/communique.php?id=472. (Accessed April 19, 2009).

14. Garcia-Torres, L., Martinez-Vilela, A., Holgado-Cabrera, A., and E. Gónzalez-Sánchez, "Conservation agriculture, environmental and economic benefits," Workshop on Soil Protection and Sustainable Agriculture Summary (Soria Spain 15–17 May 2002): 5–6.

15. Appropriate Technology Transfer for Rural Areas (ATTRA), "Overview of Cover Crops and Green Manures," http://attra.ncat.org/attra-pub/PDF/covercrop.pdf (accessed January 20, 2009).

16. Polyface Farm, http://www.polyfacefarms.com (accessed January 29, 2009).

17. Organic Industry Overview Fact Sheet (Organic Trade Association, 2008).

18. M. Nizza, "Oxford's Word of the Year, and Runners-Up," *The New York Times*, November 13, 2007.

19. Sustain Web, "The Value of Seasonal Food," http://www.sustainweb.org/page.php?id=360 (accessed January 29, 2009).

20. USDA, "Organic Production and Handling Standards," *Agricultural Marketing Service Factsheet-2008* (Washington, DC: U.S. Department of Agriculture, 2008).

21. C. Dimitri and A. Effland, "Milestones in U.S. Farming and Farm Policy," USDA pamphlet, *Amber Waves*, 3, no. 3 (2005).

22. D. Morgan, G. Gaul, and S. Cohen, "How to Spend an Extra $15 Billion," *The Washington Post*, http://www.washingtonpost.com/wp-srv/nation/interactives/farmaid/ (accessed January 29, 2009).

23. European Commission, "Financial Programming and Budget," http://ec.europa.eu/budget/budget_glance/what_for_en.htm (accessed January 29, 2009).

24. B. Halweil, "Where Have all the Farmers Gone?" *Worldwatch Institute* (September/October 2000): 11–28.

25. USDA, "Small Farms: A Time to Act," http://www.csrees.usda.gov/nea/ag_systems/in_focus/smallfarms_if_time.html (accessed January 28, 2009).

26. Quote used by Land Institute and their publications, http://www.landinstitute.org/ (accessed January 27, 2009).

27. The Land Institute, http://www.landinstitute.org/ (accessed January 27, 2009).

28. Ibid.

29. Alternative Hawaii, http://www.alternative-hawaii.com/agriculture/index.htm (accessed January 30, 2009).

30. Ibid.

31. Ibid.

32. Bill Mollison and Reny Mia Slay, *Permaculture: A Designer's Manual* (Tasmania: Tagari Publications, 1997).

33. The Fukuoka Farming Web site, http://fukuokafarmingol.info/fover.html#toc (accessed January 28, 2009).

34. Ibid.

35. Ibid.

36. The Circle School, http://fukuokafarmingol.info/fglist.html (accessed January 28, 2009).

37. The Farmsure Program, http://www.nzfarmsure.co.nz/ (accessed January 28, 2009).

38. Elkington, J. "Towards the sustainable corporation: win-win-win business strategies for sustainable development," *California Management Review*, 36, no. 2 (1994): 90–100.

RESOURCE GUIDE

Suggested Readings

Heinberg, Richard. *Peak Everything: Waking up to the Century of Declines*. British Columbia, Canada: New Society Press, 2008.

Mollison, Bill. *Introduction to Permaculture*. 2nd ed. Tasmania: Tagari Publications, 1994.

Pollan, Michael. *The Omnivore's Dilemma*. New York: Penguin Books, 2007.

Saroja Raman. *Agricultural Sustainability: Principles, Processes, and Prospects*. Philadelphia: Haworth Press, 2006.

Web Sites

Center for Agroecology and Sustainable Food Systems, http://casfs.ucsc.edu.

National Sustainable Agriculture Information Service, http://attra.ncat.org/.

New Zealand Farmsure, http://www.nzfarmsure.co.nz/index.html.
Sustainable Table, http://sustainabletable.org.
The Land Institute, http://www.landinstitute.org/.
The Meatrix, http://www.themeatrix.com/inside/.
Polyface Farms, http://www.polyfacefarms.com/.
U.S. Department of Agriculture, http://www.usda.gov.

7

Sustainable Agricultural Development in Developing Countries

Richard H. Bernsten and Sieglinde Snapp

Since the early 1970s, the international community has recognized the limitations of conventional development strategies and the need to promote sustainable development, encompassing three interrelated themes: sustainable economic, environment, and community development. Since the convening of the United Nations Environmental Summit (Stockholm, 1972), many meetings and reports have focused on sustainable development-related issues—including the Brundtland Commission Report (1987), the United Nations Conference on Environment and Development (Rio de Janeiro, 1992), the World Summit on Social Development (Copenhagen, 1995), the United Nations Millennium Summit (2000), and the World Summit on Sustainable Development (Johannesburg, 2002). Although these forums focused broadly on sustainable development, in most instances, the agenda included agricultural sustainability, given agriculture's key role in the economies of developing countries.

Today, it is widely recognized that the world's food system, especially in poor countries, is facing a crisis. Several trends illustrate the magnitude of the crisis. First, while most Asian and Latin American countries have dramatically increased food production, in many African countries, food production per capita is below the 1960 level. Second, despite the worldwide decline in the fertility rate (i.e., number of children a woman has in her lifetime), in many African countries, the population continues to grow—forcing farmers to cultivate marginal land, resulting in soil degradation. Third, success in increasing food production—especially in Asia—has been due to farmers' adoption of high-yield rice and wheat varieties and the application of high levels of chemical fertilizers and pesticides. However, intensive use of these inputs has polluted water supplies, and the misuse of pesticides has led to insect resistance and now threatens farmers' health. Fourth, as a result of the HIV/AIDS pandemic, many families in eastern and southern Africa no longer have sufficient labor to cultivate their farms. Fifth, recent evidence indicates that global warming will have a major impact on agricultural production. According to the United Nations, by "2025, Africa could lose as much as two-thirds of its arable land, compared with 1990,"[1] and low-lying areas in Asia will increasingly be threatened by flooding, due to rising sea level and increasingly intense typhoons. Sixth, with growing urban and agricultural demand for water, many countries are projected to face severe water shortages in the near future. Seventh, the rapid increase in energy costs has raised the price of fertilizer. According to the International Fertilizer Development Center (IFDC), world fertilizer prices doubled in 2007 and continued to soar in 2008[2]—making it too expensive for poor farmers, especially those in Africa, to purchase fertilizer. Finally, as a result of the increase in oil prices, the United States has sought to achieve energy independence by producing ethanol from corn. In response, farmers have converted land previously planted with wheat and soybeans to corn fields—thereby contributing to record-level wheat, soybean, and corn prices. In developing countries that rely heavily on food imports to meet shortfalls in domestic production, these price increases are having a severe impact on the food security of the poor.

Recognizing that these problems must be addressed for poor countries to ensure the food security of future generations and protect the environment from degradation, development specialists, agricultural scientists, donor agencies, nongovernmental organizations (NGOs), and government policymakers in both rich and poor countries are beginning to place high priority on identifying strategies to promote sustainable agricultural development.

WHAT IS SUSTAINABLE AGRICULTURAL DEVELOPMENT?

Agricultural development is broadly defined as a process that takes place over time and leads to the transformation of the agricultural sector, resulting in a decline in the relative contribution of agriculture to a country's gross national product and the sector's percentage share of employment. For example, in the United States, only approximately 3 percent of the population live on a farm. In developed countries, this transformation has been achieved by investments in public and private sector–funded research to develop new technologies that have increased yields (e.g., higher-yielding crop varieties, chemical fertilizers, pesticides), reduced labor costs (e.g., using energy-intensive farm machinery), and increased infrastructural investments (e.g., dams, transportation, communications, marketing systems). In addition, developed countries have invested heavily in farmer education through extension systems that introduce new technologies to farmers and help them to diagnose problems and identify appropriate solutions. Until the recent rise in oil prices, these investments enabled the United States and other rich countries to produce more food on less land and deliver it to consumers at an increasingly lower cost. Drawing on the success of developed countries, conventional wisdom suggested that to modernize their agriculture, developing countries should follow the example of developed countries. Until recently, little attention was paid to the negative impacts of this input-intensive, high-energy-based agricultural development strategy, including its impact on the environment and its sustainability over time.

While there is widespread agreement as to the need to develop more sustainable agricultural systems, there is considerable debate regarding the definition of and approaches for achieving this agricultural sustainability. Furthermore, definitions of sustainable agriculture are heavily value laden and generic. Paul Thompson argues that "current usage reveals two substantive approaches, resource sufficiency and functional integrity, as well as the widespread non-substantive usages intended to promote social action."[3] The resource sufficiency paradigm focuses (1) on measuring the "rate at which a given production or consumption practice deletes or utilizes resources," (2) estimating the "stock or store of resources available," and (3) assessing the relative sustainability of a practice "by predicting how long it may be continued, given the existing stock of resources." The functional integrity paradigm defines a practice as unsustainable if it "creates a threat to the system's capacity to reproduce itself over time." Finally, nonsubstantive sustainability refers to its use as a mild "way of conveying approval or disapproval in an inoffensive way" or using sustainability as a banner "to unify political and social causes."

Both the U.S. Congress and the Consultative Group for International Agricultural Research (CGIAR) have proposed complementary definitions of sustainable agriculture. In the 1990 Farm Bill,[4]

the term sustainable agriculture means an integrated system of plant and animal production practices having a site-specific application that will, over the long term:

- satisfy human food and fiber needs,
- enhance environmental quality and the natural resource base upon which the agricultural economy depends,
- make the most efficient use of nonrenewable resources and on-farm resources and integrate, where appropriate, natural, biological cycles, and controls,
- sustain the economic viability of farm operations, and
- enhance the quality of life for farmers and society as a whole.

The CGIAR[5] is a leading player in international agricultural research. In recent years, the CGIAR's research agenda has evolved from a commodity (crop) focus to incorporating concepts of sustainability, the ecoregion, and integrated natural resource management. In 1988, the CGIAR recognized sustainability as a part of its research portfolio, describing it as a dynamic concept: "Sustainable agriculture would involve the successful management of resources for agriculture to satisfy changing human needs while maintaining or enhancing the quality of the environment and conserving natural resources."[6] Recognizing that the ecoregion, which combines the physical, biological, and socioeconomic dimensions of the production environment, represents a more logical level of hierarchy of systems to deal effectively with resource management problems than the farm level, in the early 1990s several CGIAR centers introduced the ecoregional approach as a means of integrating resource management with productivity concerns (i.e., the production of biological and economic goods and ecosystem/ecological services per unit of resources used). Finally, in 1997, the CGIAR System Review recommended that the Consultative Group (CG) adopt an integrated natural resource management approach "as a way of doing development-oriented research that aims to simultaneously reduce poverty, increase food security, and achieve environmental protection."[7]

SUSTAINABLE AGRICULTURE: EVOLUTION OF THE CONCEPT

The rich history of sustainable agriculture has two discernable threads in the evolution of the term: (1) ecological agriculture and (2) stability of agricultural systems. An ecologically informed agriculture, which has also been termed biological or regenerative agriculture, has close links with the history of organic agriculture and started with a focus on holism (as opposed to reductionism). A detailed history of ecologically based agriculture is presented by Harwood.[8] Initially, in the 1930s and 1940s, connections between soil health and biologically robust farm systems were made by such thinkers as Lady Eve Balfour, Sir Albert Howard, and J. I. Rodale. Compost making, the "humus farming" concept, and an integrated approach to promoting health in soil, plants, animals, and human were central tenets during this period. Principles of ecological agriculture were developed based on observations about natural systems and drew on examples from traditional systems of farming. In recent decades, theory and practice in ecological agriculture have been furthered by the works of such authors as Miguel Alteri and Steve Gliessman, building on examples from traditional farming systems of Central America and innovations by North American alternative farmers.

A second view of sustainable agriculture has emerged in the second half of this century with a focus on longevity of practice, environmental impact, and resilience. This view grew out of and in response to the Green Revolution of the 1960s. The Green Revolution research approach targeted specific technologies that improved productivity (notably, new wheat and rice genotypes that markedly improved irrigated production systems under high input management) and focused on practices that could be linked to market incentives. In most cases, this strategy relied heavily on large doses of external inputs. In the early 1970s with the emergence of the first energy shortage caused by the Organization of Petroleum Exporting Countries (OPEC) embargo, this narrow focus on productivity at any cost was questioned. A shift occurred toward improving efficiency of input use and understanding the long-term consequences of agricultural production practices. A vision of sustainable agriculture evolved that explicitly considered externalities (e.g., the impact on the environment from pesticides and other agricultural chemicals) and the stability of production over a long time period. In keeping with the sustainable development movement, efficiency of conversion between input and output, the stability of return over the long term, and resource-intensive requirements also were considered.[9]

In the 1970s, an integrated pest management (IPM) approach developed out of this second sustainable agriculture theme and has continued to evolve. IPM initially focused on mitigation and economic threshold approaches to address the virulent environmental problems associated with pesticide use and abuse, as publicized by Rachel Carson and others. However, an important aspect of IPM from its inception has been attention to biology and promotion of knowledge-based management, substituting for reliance on inputs. Promotion of farmer experimentation and learning about natural systems has been fostered by the Farmer Field School (FFS) movement, which successfully taught ecology-based IPM and integrated crop management to millions of farmers in Southeast Asia. Recently, FFSs have been instrumental in promoting experimentation for sustainable agriculture and have improved understanding of ecological management among smallholder farmers in Africa.[10]

A recent theme in sustainable agriculture has been to broaden the scope of sustainable management, optimize ecosystem services across rural landscapes, and take into account diverse livelihood strategies.[11] Sustainable practices are essential to ensure such ecosystem services as climate regulation, regeneration of clean air and water, disease regulation, and soil protection, in addition to the provisioning of food, energy, and foraged products. The foundation for agricultural development in a sustainable manner is the science of agro-ecology. That is, the study of agricultural ecosystems and their components, as they function within themselves and in the context of the landscapes that contain them. Application of this knowledge can lead to the development of more sustainable agricultural ecosystems in relationship to the larger ecosystem, ecoregion, and social and political context.

Ecological principles of particular relevance to understanding sustainable systems are the concepts of system stability, resistance, and resilience. Resistance describes the likelihood that a system will not be affected by a disturbance, such as climate change or pest outbreaks. Conversely, resilience relates to the ability of an agricultural system to compensate rapidly for a disturbance or major stress. For a system to exhibit stability over the long term, both resistance and resilience are important attributes.

A whole-systems approach to sustainable agriculture considers all of the products of agriculture, including the food, feed, and fiber production, and considers these in the balance with environmental soundness, social equity, and economic viability. An even broader view is that sustainability is a concept that extends not only over space, but also indefinitely in time, and to all living organisms including humans.

For a wide range of production systems and approaches, farmers and agricultural advisors aim to meet goals of stewardship and profitability, as well as quality of life for current and future generations. One well-known approach, but by no means the only one, is the system of farming called organic farming, which follows specific recommended practices that recently have been codified through an organic certification program in the United States and abroad.

STRATEGIES

Definitions of sustainable agriculture articulate concepts and principles that give direction to research, agricultural development projects, training and extension efforts, and national policies that are designed to achieve a variety of sustainability-related goals, such as increasing production, increasing productivity, insuring food security, protecting the environment, insuring gender equity, and increasing farmers' income.

The limitations of conventional agriculture and the goals of sustainable agriculture have been articulated by many, but it is far less clear how to achieve these goals. Thus, to date, efforts to develop more sustainable agricultural systems that can be adopted by farmers and communities in developing countries have focused on conducting research. This research would be used to identify possible strategies and interventions for relaxing constraints to agricultural sustainability and promoting their use in developing countries.

As discussed previously, scientists associated with the CGIAR's agricultural research centers are now using an integrated natural resource management approach to develop sustainable agricultural systems that are appropriate for priority ecosystems. Since the early 1970s, the U.S. government has supported agricultural research and capacity building in developing countries through the Collaborative Research Support Programs (CRSPs).[12] Administered by the U.S. Agency for International Development (USAID), these programs are designed to strengthen the capacity of U.S. land-grant universities to carry out agricultural research, in collaboration with partners in developing countries, and strengthen the capacity of scientists in developing countries. As was the case of the CGIAR, in the early years, the CRSPs followed a commodity approach, focusing on a variety of crops and animal species (e.g., sorghum, millet, common beans, cowpeas, peanuts, small ruminants). Subsequently, additional CRSPs were created that focused on soil management, global livestock, aquaculture and fisheries, broadening access and strengthening input systems, integrated pest management (IPM CRSP), and sustainable agriculture and resource management (SANREM CRSP). While all of the CRSP now include sustainable agricultural development as a goal, the research agendas of the IPM CRSP and SANREM CRSP focus most explicitly on sustainable agricultural development. The IPM CRSP utilize a

> systems approach to reducing damage caused by pests to an acceptable level without harming the environment. IPM includes the adoption of pest-resistant varieties of crops; biological and physical control methods; environmental modification; biopesticides; and when absolutely necessary, non-residual, environmentally-friendly and low mammalian-toxic chemical pesticides.[13]

The SANREM CRSP utilizes a "nested landscape systems approach beginning with field level systems, building through farm, enterprise, and watershed systems nested in broader ecological, governance and policy systems."[14]

The Food and Agriculture Organization of the United Nations (FAO) also supports efforts to improve the sustainability of agriculture in developing countries. "Recognizing that responsible natural resource management is key to attaining sustainable agricultural and rural development," in 2007 FAO strengthened its commitment to this goal by creating a new Natural Resources Management and Environment Department, which replaces it Sustainable Development Department.[15] The new department focuses on

> supporting environmental services, to promote sustainable management and use of land, water, and genetic resources, and to strengthen agricultural research and extension services and take the lead in the areas of bioenergy, climate change issues, land and water management, land tenure issues, biodiversity for food and agriculture, and research and extension.

STATE-OF-THE-ART SOLUTIONS

Many technologies exist (e.g., IPM, contour plowing, terracing, crop rotations, animal manure and compost as a substitute for inorganic fertilizer, rotating grains and legumes, pest- and disease-resistant crop varieties) that have the potential to increase the sustainability of agricultural systems in poor countries and increase farmers' incomes. To date, many of these technologies have been adopted by some farmers in some countries in some ecosystems. Whether or not farmers throughout the developing world will adopt these technologies depends on many factors, including their performance in a given ecosystem, their profitability, labor requirements, the availability of the required inputs, access to extension services, and government policies. Thus, "adaptive research" is required to determine how a given technology must be fine-tuned to fit the ecological, socioeconomic, and policy environment of a specific watershed, community, and country.

Approaches to promoting sustainable agriculture include research-driven, market-driven, and extension-driven strategies. Research-driven strategies first carry out technical and socioeconomic diagnostic studies to identify constraints to sustainability, after which research is conducted to assess various interventions for relaxing these constraints. Interventions are assessed with respect to sustainability goals (e.g., improve food security, reduce poverty, support gender equity, enhance biodiversity, and reduce resource degradation). Lessons learned are incorporated into methodological guidelines to conduct similar research in other locations and to scale up and promote the uptake of the technologies to other communities. Research-driven strategies typically utilize participatory methods, draw on indigenous knowledge, and are implemented in collaboration with international and local partners, including NGOs, national agricultural research systems, universities, farmers, communities, and government officials. At each stage, priority is given to building capacity among farmers, communities, and local researchers through, for example, FFSs, workshops, farmer associations, training guides, and extension brochures. In addition, research-driven strategies identify changes in government policies that are needed to facilitate the adoption of promising interventions. In contrast, extension-driven strategies are most commonly utilized by NGOs, which draw on available research results to identify technologies that they can extend to farmers and communities. Finally, market-driven strategies provide small farmers an opportunity to receive premium prices by exporting to industrial countries crops certified as fair trade, organic, or produced using sustainable agricultural practices.

CGIAR Strategies

Research-driven strategies being implemented at CGIAR centers are documented in a recent report, which describes seven promising broad-based natural resource management approaches.[16] In Asia, a project led by the International Water Management Institute (IWMI), in collaboration with its partners in six countries (Indonesia, the People's Democratic Republic of Laos, Nepal, Philippines, Thailand, and Vietnam), focused on identifying sustainable integrated land and water management interventions. Recognizing that land degradation, including soil erosion, is driven by socioeconomic factors, the project involved farmers and other stakeholders in developing and promoting sustainable and socially acceptable community-based land management options that conserve resources and improve food security. Promising land management options for reducing soil erosion in marginal upland catchments included hedgerow cropping technology (natural vegetative strips), fodder banks combined with livestock production, cover crops, crop rotations, and improved fallows.

In Latin America, the International Center for Tropical Agriculture (CIAT) and its partners in Colombia, Peru, and Central America developed decision-support tools that considered the opinions of local stakeholders and were geared toward informing decision-making processes at the local level. These tools enable poor communities to improve hillside production systems, maintain more sustainable landscapes, strengthen organizational processes for natural resource management, and enable communities to better assess options for managing hillside watersheds.

In East Africa, the sustainability of Lake Victoria is threatened by eutrophication, due to soil erosion and nutrient runoff. The World Agroforestry Center (ICRAF) and its partners around the Lake Victoria basin (Kenya, Tanzania, Uganda, and Rwanda) provided new information, methods, technologies, and approaches for improving land productivity while enhancing the environment. Several improved land management techniques (e.g., agroforestry, water management, improved fallows, striga [a parasitic weed of corn] control, grazing exclusion) have been identified that reduce soil erosion and nutrient runoff and improve the farm resource base and household food security.

In East Kalimantan, Indonesia, the Center for International Forestry Research (CIFOR) and its partners developed strategies to reduce forest loss—due to inappropriate harvesting, which reduces biodiversity, regrowth of valuable species, and water quality. While the project demonstrated the cost-effectiveness of reduced-impact logging, various factors limited implementation of the innovation, including the diversity of stakeholders, their overlapping interests, and policies of the Indonesian government.

In low-rainfall areas of the Near East, the International Center for Agricultural Research in the Dry Areas (ICARDA), the International Food Policy Research Institute (IFPRI), and their partners in eight countries improved the barley-livestock production systems in marginal areas through the development of technological, institutional, and policy options for farmers and communities. Successful technologies included improved barley varieties, multinutritional feed blocks, forage legume-barley rotations, improved sheep fertility and reproduction, and the rehabilitation of degraded rangelands.

In the Andean high plateau between Peru and Bolivia, the International Potato Center (CIP) and its partners implemented an action plan that increased farmers' incomes and protected the environment through the introduction of value-added products, improved marketing, supervised credit, and new technologies (e.g., methods to conserve soil and water, legume crops to improve fallow, improved potato varieties, the reintroduction of virus-free local varieties, improved pasture management practices).

Finally, in India's Adasha watershed, the International Crops Research Institute for the Semi-Arid Tropics (ICRISAT) and its partners reduced water runoff and soil loss, improved productivity, and increased farmers' income by introducing cost-effective soil-water-nutrient practices (e.g., the construction of water storage structures, contour plowing, planting a leguminous tree on a field bund [a soil mound to trap soil and water and encourage water infiltration] as a source of nitrogen-rich organic matter, afforestation, vermicomposting as a microenterprise to generate incomes for poor women, biological pest control measures, pest-tolerant crop varieties).

SANREM CRSP's Strategies

Similar to the CGIAR centers, SANREM CRSP's research-driven strategies focus broadly on sustainable agriculture and natural resource issues in five projects in Africa, Asia, and Latin America.[17] Initiated in 2006, these five-year projects are in the early stages of implementation.

In many countries, recent decentralization and property rights reforms are having a major impact on the forestry sector. Failure to consider the impact of these policies at the farm, field, and forest levels often results in policies that do not promote sustainable natural resource management or improve local livelihoods. In Bolivia, Kenya, Mexico, and Uganda, the SANREM CRSP and its partners are assessing the motivation for decentralization and its implications for various groups (including women and the poor) and the implications of forest decentralization policies for resource conservation, biodiversity, and ecological stability. In addition, the project will identify public policies that will improve both the ecological sustainability of the forests and the livelihood of communities that depend on them.

In Zambia, the SANREM CRSP is working to preserve biodiversity and improve food security in partnership with Community Markets for Conservation (COMACO), a local NGO that has established community trading centers and food-processing facilities in the Luangwa Valley. The project focuses on evaluating the economic sustainability of COMACO's agribusiness model, the potential for integrating new technologies, and the extent to which the model provides self-sustaining institutions and meaningful roles for participants. In addition, the project is evaluating the impact of the model on biodiversity and watershed conservation. Initiatives to increase villagers' income include expanding the trade centers' potential for selling crops in domestic and export markets, training local staff in food-processing practices required to earn export certification, and training villagers in poultry and goat production. The introduction of more sustainable production methods should lead to wiser use of natural resources, and reduced deforestation should improve soil retention and reduce downstream flooding.

In Ecuador and Bolivia, the SANREM CRSP and its partners are working to "improve farm families' lives and incomes by finding alternatives, identifying constraints to adopting these alternatives, and encouraging genetic diversity in crop selection." Project initiatives include evaluating soil conservation techniques (e.g., contour plowing), assessing IPM techniques, and testing alternative crops for their potential to increase a family's income. Interventions found to have high economic returns and protect the environment include low-cost soil conservation methods, reduced agrochemical application (especially IPM for potatoes), and growing medicinal plants.

In the Andean highland communities of Bolivia and Peru, smallholder production systems are threatened by climate, economic, and social changes. The SANREM CRSP and its partners are working to strengthen the capacity of local farmers, communities, and institutions to conduct research and develop strategies to adapt to change, reduce vulnerability, and enhance biodiversity in highland agro-ecological systems. Interventions being assessed include in situ conservation of cultivars and crops, new opportunities for marketing traditional crops, the introduction of technologies and new crop varieties to mitigate weather-related risks, and strategies to enhance soil organic matter.

In Southeast Asia, the forest, soil, and water resources in many forest and vegetable-producing watersheds are being degraded. The SANREM CRSP and its partners are working to improve the quality of life of small-scale farmers by developing "economically viable and ecologically sound vegetable-agroforestry systems and to quantify the economic and environmental benefits of these systems." In Vietnam, Indonesia, and the Philippines, the project is evaluating several interventions, including high-value medicinal plants and vegetables, cash-crop trees, drip irrigation, reduced tilling methods, pest management, the reintroduction of indigenous vegetables, and soil enhancement.

IPM CRSP's Strategies

Research-driven strategies supported by the IPM CRSP are directed at improving the sustainability of cropping systems.[18] Because the IPM CRSP global mandate is limited to pest and disease management, these efforts focus on controlling specific pests and diseases that threaten important food and cash crops.

In Jamaica, where the tobacco Etch virus greatly reduces hot pepper yields, the IPM CRSP and its partners have introduced methods for controlling the insect-transmitted virus that reduce or eliminate the need to apply pesticides.

In Asia, the IPM CRSP and its partners in India are developing strategies for controlling thrips, a major vector for diseases that reduce vegetable yields. In Bangladesh, women farmers have been trained to graft high-yielding eggplant varieties onto wilt-resistant rootstock—thereby reducing pesticide use and increasing farmers' yields and incomes.

Farmers in Mali grow mangos, tomatoes, and green beans that are exported to the European Union. To ensure that these exports meet the European Union's stringent standards for pesticide residuals, the IPM CRSP and its partners have trained Mali scientists how to use a new, effective, and inexpensive method for analyzing pesticide residuals on fruits and vegetables and have hosted FFSs to teach farmers how to safely use pesticides.

In Honduras, mites greatly reduce strawberry yields. The IPM CRSP and its partners have developed techniques for controlling mites, which eliminate the need to apply pesticides. In Ecuador, the CRSP developed IPM-based techniques for controlling pests and diseases that reduce potato yield—which increased farmers' yield and greatly reduced their pesticide and fungicide costs.

Finally, in Albania, olives are a major export crop, but weed, disease, and pest are major constraints to higher yields. The introduction of IPM-based technologies has enabled farmers to reduce the use of chemicals and increase their yields and income. In addition, farmers are now able to grow olives organically and export organic extra virgin olive oil to Europe.

Extension-Driven Strategies

Extension-driven strategies include FFSs and NGO-led training initiatives. For new agricultural technologies and resource management strategies to have widespread impact, they must be adopted by farmers and communities. Historically, national extension services have had the mandate to introduce new technologies to farmers. However, in many poor countries, public extension systems are either ineffective or have been disbanded because of a lack of funds to support them. In 1989, FAO introduced FFSs as a strategy to promote rice IPM in Indonesia. FFSs represent an alternative to the tradition extension approach, which "expected farmers to adopt generalized recommendations that had been formulated by experts from outside the community."[19] In contrast, FFSs utilize a "group learning process that brings together concepts and methods from agro-ecology, experiential education, and community development." Since the early 1990s, many governments, NGOs, and international agencies adapted the FFS approach to other crops and utilized it as a strategy to introduce new technologies to farmers.

In Latin America, a similar strategy is being used to empower farmers and help them identify appropriate technologies to address various production constraints. With the assistance of NGOs and supported by agricultural scientists, farmers form community-based associations (CIALs), which identify research themes, conduct adaptive research, and analyze the results.

In addition, many grassroots NGO-led initiatives are working with farmers and communities to promote sustainable agricultural development and protect the environment. When established in 1977 by Wangari Maathai, the Greenbelt Movement focused on encouraging communities in Kenya to plant trees. Today, the Greenbelt Movement is active in many African countries and has broadened its agenda from planting trees to include "environment conservation, community development, and capacity building."[20] Since 1977, the movement has been responsible for "planting over 30 million trees and training 30,000 women in forestry, food processing and bee-keeping, and other trades that help them earn income while preserving their lands and resources."

A "push-pull" approach to promoting sustainable development is illustrated by the soil, food, and healthy communities project in Northern Malawi.[21] This NGO-led, long-term education effort on family nutrition has generated a "push"— that is, empowering farmers to improve their situation by experimenting with legume intercrops, improved integrated crop management practices, and recipes to promote incorporation into local diets. Over time the "pull" has grown—that is, supporting new markets for selling legume products and increasing demand for legumes to feed children and other members of the family. More than four thousand smallholder families are now growing crops following more sustainable practices, and more than seventy thousand families are reached through the project's outreach efforts. This type of integrated approach holds promise, as it pays simultaneous attention to local capacity building, education, and experimentation in agro-ecology, building the conditions that promote agroinnovation. Taking projects such as this to the next level, scaling up and reaching the majority of smallholders, remains the biggest challenge in sustainable agriculture.[22]

Market-Driven Strategies

Market-driven strategies based on third-party certification provide an opportunity for farmers to increase their income and reduce the impact of agriculture on the environment. Since the late-1990s, the Rainforest Alliance, "under the auspices of the Sustainable Agricultural Network (SAN), has worked with farmers to ensure compliance with SAN standards for protecting wildlife, wild land, workers' rights and local communities."[23] These standards require farmers to implement practices to reduce water pollution, soil erosion, threats to environmental and human health, destruction of wildlife habitat, waste, and water use; and to improve efficient farm management and working conditions for farm labor. Farms that comply with SAN standards are awarded the Rainforest Alliance Certified Seal. Farmers awarded certification can sell their crops to markets in industrial countries at premium prices. While the program currently focuses on forest products and cash crops (including coffee, cocoa, bananas, mango, pineapple, and tea), it is being extended to include staple food crops. Similarly, the growing demand for fair trade and organic products in industrial countries has been a catalyst for small-scale farmers to adopt environmentally friendly farming practices and receive premium prices. Farmers wishing to sell their crops as fair trade or organic products must first obtain certification by a third party, typically a local or international NGO that has been authorized to certify the product. Fair trade certification assures consumers that these products (e.g., coffee, cocoa, rice) are produced by small-scale farmers who are members of democratically organized associations and are marketed with minimal reliance on intermediaries. Organic certification assures consumers that these products comply with the U.S. Department of Agriculture organic standards, which prohibit the use of chemical fertilizers and inorganic pesticides. Farmers whose products are certified as fair trade or organic receive a premium price when exported to markets in industrial countries. In recent years, several major U.S. food retailers have responded to the preferences of ethical consumers by offering certified food products. For example, Wal-Mart/ Sam's Club is now the largest U.S. retailer of fair trade (Rainforest Alliance certified) coffee. Recently, Whole Foods Market established its Whole Trade™ Program, which provides market access to small farmers in developing countries who meet the program's stringent food quality, environmental, and labor standards.

PROSPECTS FOR ACHIEVING SUSTAINABLE AGRICULTURAL DEVELOPMENT

The challenge of developing more sustainable agricultural systems is daunting. Clearly, the international community finally recognizes the threats posed by failures to address these challenges. After decades of reductions in international funding for agricultural research, it appears that this trend will be reversed. Recognizing the importance of agriculture in developing countries, the theme of the World Bank's annual Development Report in 2007 was agriculture for development.[24] Considerable progress has been made in conceptualizing the problems and developing potential technologies and strategies for creating more sustainable agricultural systems. However, much more remains to be done to develop additional new strategies and technologies, further refine interventions that have already been developed, and scale up successful technologies and strategies to reach the billions of smallholders in developing countries.

Context is key to envisioning new sustainable production systems. The environment involves both biophysical and social dimensions that constrain the resources available to maintain fertility and that provide incentives. Human capacity building can address constraints to an extent, as knowledge of processes can increase efficiency and substitute for some external inputs. However, biophysical constraints such as temperature and moisture regimes will determine the length of the growing season and the condition and quality of soil and water resources, as well as the options available for maintaining soil fertility. This in turn will define sustainable options for agricultural production. In a similar manner, access and connectivity to markets for both inputs and outputs will condition production options and long-term sustainability. In mesic climates, where rainfall and temperature are moderate most of the year, soil resources can be regenerated through biological processes, such as growing green manure plants; in turn, this will support rapid plant and animal growth, and efficient use of inputs such as fertilizer. By contrast, in more extreme environments there are limited windows in which life can be harnessed for agriculture. Thus, large energy inputs, such as fixed nitrogen in fertilizer or extensive systems that utilize large areas of land, are necessary preconditions for maintaining productive agriculture. An upcoming challenge is that a large proportion of arable land is predicted to be subjected to extreme weather events with global warming under way.

NOTES

1. Brad Knickerbocker, "Global Warming May Uproot Millions," *The Christian Science Monitor*, June 21, 2007.

2. IFDC, "World Fertilizer Prices Soar As Food and Fuel Economies Merge," http://www.ifdc.org/i-wfp021908.pdf.

3. Paul B. Thompson, "Agricultural Sustainability: What It Is and What It Is Not," *International Journal of Agricultural Sustainability* 5 (2007): 5–16.

4. *Food, Agriculture, Conservation, and Trade Act of 1990 (FACTA)*, Public Law 101–624, Title XVI, Subtitle A, Section 1603, 16 U.S.C. (1990).

5. Established in 1971, the CGIAR is a strategic partnership with sixty-four members, including twenty-one developing and twenty-six industrial countries, four co-sponsors, and thirteen other international organizations. It supports fifteen international agricultural research centers, which work in collaboration with many hundreds of governments, civil society organizations, and private businesses around the world. CGIAR, http://www.cgiar.org/.

6. R. H. Harwood, A. H. Kassame, H. M. Gregersen, and E. Fereres, "Natural Resource Management Research in the CGIAR: The Role of the Technical Advisory Committee," *Experimental Agriculture* 41 (2005): 1–19.

7. R. R. Harwood and A. H. Kassam, eds., *Research towards Integrated Natural Resource Management: Examples of Research Problems, Approaches and Partnerships in Action in the CGIAR* (Rome: Interim Science Council, Centre Committee on Integrated Natural Resources Management, 2003).

8. R. R. Harwood, "A History of Sustainable Agriculture," in *Sustainable Agricultural Systems*, ed. C. A. Edwards, R. Lai, P. Madden, R. H. Miller, and G. House (Ankeny, IA: Soil and Water Conservation Society, 1990).

9. M. Dover and L. M. Talbot, *To Feed the Earth: Agro-ecology for Sustainable Development.* (Washington, DC: World Resources Institute, 1987).

10. V. Morrone, "Outreach to Support Rural Innovation," in *Agricultural Systems: Agroecology and Rural Innovation for Development*, ed. S. S. Snapp and B. Pound (Burlington, MA: Academic Press, 2008).

11. S. S. Snapp, "Designing for the Long Term: Sustainable Agriculture," in *Agricultural Systems: Agroecology and Rural Innovation for Development*, ed. S. S. Snapp and B. Pound (Burlington, MA: Academic Press, 2008).

12. Collaborative Research Support Programs (CRSPs), http://crsps.org/crspdirs.htm.

13. Integrated Pest Management, http://www.oired.vt.edu/ipmcrsp/IPM_2008/draft_home.htm.

14. Virginia Tech Office of International Research Education and Development, "SANREM CRSP," http://www.oired.vt.edu/sanremcrsp/.

15. FAO, http://www.fao.org/.

16. R. R. Harwood and A. H. Kassam, eds., *Research Towards Integrated Natural Resource Management: Examples of Research Problems, Approaches and Partnerships in Action in the CGIAR* (Rome: Interim Science Council, Centre Committee on Integrated Natural Resources Management, 2003).

17. Virginia Tech Office of International Research Education and Development, "SANREM CRSP," http://www.oired.vt.edu/sanremcrsp/.

18. Virginia Tech Office of International Research Education and Development, "Integrated Pest Management," http://www.oired.vt.edu/ipmcrsp/IPM_2008/draft_home.htm.

19. Wikipedia, "Farmer Field Schools," http://en.wikipedia.org/wiki/Farmer_Field_Schools.

20. Wikipedia, "The Green Belt Movement," http://en.wikipedia.org/wiki/Green_Belt_Movement.

21. Soils, Food and Healthy Communities, http://soilandfood.org/.

22. R. Tripp, *Self-sufficient Agriculture: Labor and Knowledge in Small-Scale Farming* (London: Earthscan, 2006).

23. Rainforest Alliance, http://www.rainforest-alliance.org/.

24. World Bank, *World Bank Development Report 2008: Agriculture for Development* (Washington, DC: World Bank, 2007).

RESOURCE GUIDE

Suggested Reading

Conway, G. *The Doubly Green Revolution: Food for All in the 21st Century*. Ithaca, NY: Cornell University Press, 1997.

Harwood, Richard R. "A History of Sustainable Agriculture." In *Sustainable Agricultural Systems*, ed. Clive A. Edwards, Rattan Lai, Patrick Madden, Robert H. Miller, and Gar House. Ankeny, IA: Soil and Water Conservation Society, 1997.

Harwood, Richard, and Amir H. Kassam, eds. *Research Towards Integrated Natural Resource Management: Examples of Research Problems, Approaches and Partnerships in Action in the CGIAR*. Rome: Interim Science Council, Centre Committee on Integrated Natural Resources Management, 2003.

Snapp, S. S., and B. Pound, eds. *Agricultural Systems: Agroecology and Rural Innovation for Development*. Burlington, MA: Academic Press, 2008.

Tripp, Robert. *Self-Sufficient Agriculture: Labor and Knowledge in Small-Scale Farming*. London: Earthscan, 2006.

Web Sites

Center for Information on Low External Input and Sustainable Agriculture, http://www.leisa.info/index.php?url=index.tpl.

8

Urban Agriculture

Jim Bingen, Kathryn Colasanti, Margaret Fitzpatrick, and Katherine Nault

It is forbidden to live in a town which has no garden or greenery.

—Persian Proverb[1]

For the first time in history, the world's urban population exceeds that of rural areas, and the United Nations projects that in fewer than twenty-five years two-thirds of the world's people will live in cities. The urban farming campaign, Food for the Cities, launched by the Food and Agriculture Organization of the United Nations (FAO) in early 2007, testifies to both the immediacy of the need to supply these rapidly urbanizing populations with fresh food and to the growth of the urban and peri-urban agriculture movement.[2]

In the 1970s and 1980s, the back-to-the-land and alternative agrifood movements in North America and Europe stimulated wide-ranging debates over the structure and sustainability of farming and food distribution in industrialized societies.[3] Similarly, today's twenty-first-century "quiet revolution"[4] of urban farmers, marketers, and their supporters may be generating similar shifts in thinking about the relationships among farming, food, and cities around the world. This chapter seeks to contribute to this rethinking by discussing critical issues in urban agriculture as well as the strategies and solutions to address these issues.

Urban agriculture refers to the production, processing, marketing, and distribution of fresh food and other products by individuals, families, groups, cooperatives, or commercial enterprises on private or public land in and around cities. To frame and identify the critical issues surrounding farming and marketing in cities, we start with the observation that urban agriculture is first and foremost distinguished from rural agriculture by being embedded in an urban or largely built ecology, and is closely tied to the public and private institutions, culture, history, and economy of specific urban places.[5] This observation draws our attention to three sets of questions that arise in discussions of the issues in urban agriculture.

First, the history of urban agriculture shows that city farms and gardens have not been subject to the same process of increasing capital intensity that characterizes most of rural farming in industrial countries.[6] On the contrary, city farming and gardening tends to be labor intensive, even while benefiting from specific but small-scale capital investments such as unheated greenhouses (hoop houses) to extend the growing season, or water tanks and facilities for aquaculture. Nevertheless, many of the issues confronted by urban farmers and gardeners, marketers, and their supporters arise directly from the consequences of capital investment or disinvestment in our cities. Capital flight from cities created the vacant lots, as well as both the challenges and opportunities for many urban agriculture programs, and today's headlines remind us that new capital investments back into cities may now threaten the viability of some of these agriculture initiatives. How, then, are urban farm and garden activities both shaped by, and active in shaping, instances of disinvestment or investment in cities?

Second, urban agriculture involves a range of government, corporate, and social actors who have focused historically on the functioning of cities. As these actors add urban agriculture to policy, program, and planning agendas, will there be opportunities for city farmers, marketers, and other urban agriculture actors to sit at the policy tables and contribute to the urban agendas for urban food and farming activities? Do urban agriculture activities and programs create the conditions for grassroots and neighborhood groups and coalitions to emerge in defense of urban agriculture in public policymaking and planning?

Third, urban agriculture, like its rural counterpart, is place based. Specific urban farming and gardening activities are defined by particular vacant lots, housing developments, public plots, and schools where farms and gardens are located. But these places are more than simply spaces. They carry their own history and memories and become part of the history and culture of the people that continue to define these places. This singular distinct identity, or "autonomy of diversity,"[7] represents an important source of strength for each urban garden or farm. How might these individual programs create alliances, coalitions, or networks to address shared concerns or issues without compromising their particular identities? Can such collective relationships become part of political strategies for defining a politics of place, for empowerment and for change in the structure of food and farming in cities?

With these questions in mind, this chapter discusses three sets of closely related topics in urban agriculture: the where and how of city farms and gardens; policy, planning, and politics; and valuing multiple agendas. The chapter concludes with a brief note on next steps for broadening the urban agriculture policy agenda.

THE WHERE AND HOW OF CITY FARMS AND GARDENS

> If you have control over the land and the water, if you can feed yourself, you can really transform society.... But these communities don't have any of those things, so how can you have a just society?
>
> —Erika Allen, *Growing Power*[8]

Michael Ableman's observation about urban agriculture as a "revolution ... taking place in small gardens, under railroad tracks and power lines, on rooftops, in farmers' markets, and in the most unlikely of places"[9] captures a distinguishing feature of farming and gardening in cities: it depends in part on the availability of land,

and in part on the ability to "create land" or places to grow crops in pots, boxes, rooftops, and parking lots.

Land Availability

Many North American cities have documented the number of vacant lots that could be available for urban agriculture. In 2000 Martin Bailkey and Joe Nasr referred to "the large inventories of vacant land in American cities" and observed that urban agriculture might be "a viable, albeit partial solution to the vacant land problem."[10] Outside of North America, the United Nations Development Program (UNDP) reported "there is seldom a lack of space [or] land ... to farm in urban areas. The problem lies in gaining legal access and secure tenure to farm this land."[11]

Growing Power in Wisconsin and Fairview Gardens in Southern California illustrate how private ownership of land is one option. A more common practice involves various city and nonprofit programs or individuals that seek permission to use vacant lots or other public spaces. These programs represent a significant portion of the U.S. Department of Agriculture (USDA) Community Food Projects Program.[12]

Nevertheless, government, nonprofit, or foundation-funded urban agriculture projects do not necessarily protect the tenure rights of urban farmers and gardeners. Capital reinvestment in cities often trumps policies that support urban gardening. Witness the destruction of the Esperanza Garden, once one of the six hundred gardens in New York City's Green Thumb Program, or the politically contested community gardens in Loisaida on the Lower East Side of Manhattan.[13] More dramatically, the East London Manor Garden Allotments was bulldozed in late 2007 to make way for the 2012 Olympic games, despite the fact that it had been cultivated for more than one hundred years.[14] In short, even with long-standing government commitments, urban agriculture remains vulnerable to changing capital investment opportunities in the world's cities.

National and local nonprofit land trusts offer one strategy to provide public access to, and sometimes tenure of, vacant and unused land in cities by offering the means to purchase land. The Madison Area Community Land Trust's support of Troy Gardens in Madison, Wisconsin,[15] and the Neighborhood Gardens Association/Philadelphia Land Trust's work to preserve community-managed gardens illustrate two cases of successful land trust programs.[16] Public land banks can purchase, hold, or develop vacant land instead of allowing tax-foreclosed land to be purchased at public auctions or default to municipal ownership. The Adopt-A-Lot Program in Flint, Michigan, through the Genesee County Land Bank allows continued access without tax or other financial burdens for community groups who were gardening on vacant lots, as well as the option to purchase the property.

Creating the Land

Because of past industrial use or other types of pollution, many vacant lots, or brownfields, that might be available for urban agriculture are unsafe for growing food and require some type of soil remediation. While the extent and type of soil pollution is site specific, experience shows that most physical or biological remediation requires significant and multiple public and private sources of capital and technical support that exceeds the organizational capacity of most neighborhood or community groups.[17] The U.S. Environmental Protection Agency's Brownfields Federal Partnership Action Program can help communities leverage the resources needed to clean up and reuse brownfields for urban agriculture.[18]

The small-scale and intense production practices that characterize urban agriculture encourage the use and adaptation of several technologies that are within reach of both individual and collective or neighborhood-level investments. In fact, one of the broader policy promises of urban agriculture may lie in showing how small-scale, grassroots capital investments, and not large-scale investments, are the key to fostering the technological innovations needed to address the ecological challenges of growing in cities. In doing so, such investments may transform the way we think about urban food production.

In 1998, Greensgrow Farm Inc. pioneered with such an investment to create a brownfield urban farm using hydroponics to grow lettuce on the site of a former galvanized steel plant in Philadelphia.[19] More recently, the youth group Added Value worked with the New York City Parks Department to establish Red Hook Farm in 2003 on an abandoned three-acre asphalt ball field by using raised beds and an acre of compost two feet deep on top of the asphalt.[20]

In addition to these biointensive efforts to overcome specific types of urban ecological challenges, other initiatives adapt gardening to uniquely urban spaces. Mole Hill Lane in Vancouver landscapes with food as part of the growing attack on urban front lawns,[21] and rooftop gardens are literally sprouting in cities around the world. Chicago has planted or negotiated the construction of more than two million square feet of rooftop gardens, and Beijing's urban plan calls for gardens on three million square meters of roof space over the next ten years.[22]

Two other technologies, vermicomposting and aquaculture, offer additional opportunities for grassroots investments to connect urban agriculture to the life of a city by recycling food waste into valuable agricultural resources.[23] Vermicomposting, or using worms to compost food waste, is an increasingly popular, low-cost technology to reduce urban waste flows and enhance garden soils.[24] The City of Vancouver has offered worm bins and composting instructions to residents since 1991,[25] and vermicomposting has become integral to other publicly sponsored urban agriculture programs such as those in Buenos Aires and Havana. Growing Power in Milwaukee, Wisconsin, is nationally recognized for its program to source food wastes from local grocery stores and restaurants to produce worm compost for farm fertilization and to sell in dried compost tea bags. In collaboration with Heifer International, Growing Power has also led the way in urban aquaculture, routing water from hydroponic production through tilapia fish tanks, and then into a filtering system for farm irrigation.[26] This recycling process is now used to raise tilapia for sale.

Urban Livestock

The incorporation of aquaculture into urban agriculture raises the question about (re)incorporating livestock into cities. Outside of North America and Europe, livestock are integral parts of city life.[27] Several U.S. cities—Ann Arbor, Spokane, Boise, Portland, Seattle, and Missoula—now permit residents to keep small numbers of backyard chickens.[28] Heifer Project International was a pioneer in diversifying urban agriculture through several projects, such as East New York Farms! and the Field to Table's Urban Bees Project in Toronto. Based on these initiatives and others, the emerging urban livestock movement may represent a major opportunity for urban agriculturalists to revitalize and diversify urban farming.

Grassroots Capital Investment

In stark contrast to these grassroots investments, models of vertical farms, or "living towers," incorporate crop production into the design and functioning of city buildings. As a twenty-first-century version of the hanging gardens of Babylon, it is suggested that a thirty-story "tower of food" could feed fifty thousand people.[29] Such visions remind us that only our imagination limits the ways to connect fresh food production and the layout and design of our cities. But beyond the architectural possibilities and the debate over the real estate realities of such farms, these plans raise two important socioeconomic and political questions. First, do these ideas represent a path toward a more capital intensive urban agriculture that will mirror the industrialized structure of agriculture around the world? Second, do these architectural visions for urban agriculture allow for grassroots capital investments, and would they generate the kind of neighborhood revitalization that urban agriculture now promises?

POLICY, PLANNING, AND POLITICS

From the ancient cities in the Middle East, China, and pre-Columbian America through the biointensive steam-heated greenhouses in nineteenth-century Paris, we've always farmed in cities.[30] But as our societies industrialized, cities throughout Europe and North America dissociated food production from city planning and life. Changes in sewage systems precluded the use of wastewater for agricultural irrigation, and health regulations made urban livestock production illegal. As a result, our concept of urban became defined in opposition to agriculture.[31] With the notable exception of the Garden City Movement,[32] the ideals of city planning left out productive landscapes.

However, after a "seven-year odyssey," urban food and farming is back on the planning table in North America.[33] The 2007 American Planning Association (APA) Policy Guide on Community and Regional Planning identifies urban agriculture as one of several efforts to build more self-reliant and sustainable community and regional food systems.[34] The guide encourages mixed-use neighborhood design and redevelopment, including community gardens and small farms, the development of vegetable gardens, and edible landscaping on publicly owned lands.[35]

This policy guide represents an important step in creating and strengthening a North American urban agricultural movement. First, the guide acknowledges the increasing breadth and depth of urban agriculture in many of the world's cities. Cuba's eight thousand urban gardens, for example, provide a significant source of fresh produce to the country's urban and suburban populations.[36] More than 40 percent of the residents of Vancouver, British Columbia, have some type of garden plot, and in May 2006 the Vancouver City Council adopted a motion to increase the number of food-producing garden plots to 2,010 by 2010. The city also suggests that developers should include 30 percent shared gardening space in high-density residential developments without access to private garden spaces.[37]

A growing number of North American cities now make urban agriculture part of their development policy. In Braddock, Pennsylvania, urban agriculture, including biofuel production, represents one approach to revitalize the "rust belt city's" economy and integrate farming with urban development. Somerton Tanks Farm also illustrates the importance of political commitment and partnership between a public utility, the Philadelphia Water Department, and the nonprofit Institute for Innovations in Local Farming to model the economic viability of "environmentally sound sub-acre farming" within a major U.S. city.[38] Other cities around the country are revising their planning documents and zoning ordinances to establish, maintain, or preserve community gardens.[39] In Rhode Island, the Providence Urban Agriculture Policy Task Force recognizes the diversity of urban farming types and recommends planning that matches the types and scales of agriculture to different zoning areas as well as the development of model regulations to facilitate mutual benefits between hand-tended farms and urban neighborhoods.[40]

Second, at least two conferences in 2008 provided an opportunity for diverse public, private, and professional actors in urban planning and agriculture to address issues raised in the guide. A symposium at Ryerson University (Toronto) brought together architects, landscape architects, designers, and engineers with other actors in urban food and agriculture systems to examine the physical aspects of urban food provision and distribution, and urban design and architecture.[41] Similarly, the Urban Agriculture Conference in Milwaukee convened "a wide range of often disconnected stakeholders ... to address the most important and controversial issues of poverty alleviation, environmental and waste management, local economic, social and community development, and global warming."[42]

Third, the orientation of the APA policy guide toward community and regional food planning and the strengthening of local and regional economies stimulates new conversations and initiatives that (re)link our towns and cities with the livelihoods of surrounding small family farms. This renewed attention to city-farm connections echoes Kropotkin's call for new relationships between the cities and the peasantry[43] as well as Wendell Berry's reminder that cities "exist within agriculture."[44] The regionalized perspective in the policy guide appeals to diverse groups concerned about local food, eating seasonally, maintaining viable family farms and the full range of alternatives to our global and industrialized food system. The guide encourages discussions about sites for farmers' markets and farm stands, the development of more regional food-processing facilities, regionalized food distribution centers, incentives for reinvestments in neighborhood groceries that carry fresh produce, and the kind of infrastructure and transportation needed to support these initiatives. The "Food and Agriculture Precinct" concept proposed by the Southlands Community Planning Team from the South Delta in the Vancouver region provides one example in which citizens have articulated this type of broad vision for urban agriculture.[45]

As urban agriculture becomes a legitimate part of city political and planning agendas, it will be critical for city planners and local government agencies to facilitate dialogue, mediate divergent interests, empower residents, and champion established practices and resource networks.[46] Just as the technological appeal of "food towers" overlooks the contribution of grassroots economic, social, and political investments, new agriculture agendas may easily, but mistakenly, assume that the politically mobilized citizen groups, who successfully promoted and protected urban agriculture gardens, are no longer needed.[47]

Continuing reports of "guerrilla" initiatives confirm that in the absence of deliberate and open public policy discussions, city residents are willing to take "garden action" into their own hands. From freeway off-ramp plantings to vacant lot gardens in Los Angeles, San Francisco, Toronto, Montreal, or London, a new generation of activist gardeners brings to mind a level of political engagement reminiscent of an earlier era.[48] Guerrilla gardeners are replacing "flower power" with the call of "Let's fight the filth with forks and flowers."[49]

VALUING MULTIPLE AGENDAS

The day is coming when a single carrot, freshly observed, will set off a revolution.

—Paul Cézanne[50]

The United States has a long history of relying on urban agriculture in response to social and economic crises. From the Potato Patches in the late 1800s, through the Liberty, Relief, and Victory Gardens spanning the period from World War I, through the Great Depression and World War II, community gardening has carried numerous banners and reflected multiple socioeconomic agendas. Detroit Mayor Pingree's allotment gardening following the Panic of 1893 sought to assimilate immigrants and provide them with a healthful occupation. Urban reformers from the early 1900s through the 1920s promoted school gardens to help young people reestablish contact with nature while inculcating work habits. During World War I, the National War Garden Commission organized a U.S. School Garden Army and called for "soldiers of the soil" to dig in vacant lots.[51] The objectives of the World War II–era National Victory Garden Program are easily adapted to our current concerns with energy use, climate change, and safe food, which explains the renewed references to this program found regularly in today's popular press.[52]

Multifunctional agendas continue to characterize the growing number of urban gardening and farming initiatives involving a wide diversity of public, private, and nonprofit actors in the United States. The USDA Community Food Project grant program represents the premier federal source of funding, but support from numerous private foundations, nonprofit groups, and local agencies has created an "extensive but largely disjointed patchwork of individuals, organizations and institutions" in urban agriculture.[53] For a wide variety of political and economic reasons it may be neither feasible nor desirable to create a national urban agriculture program or office to give more attention to this multiplicity of grassroots efforts. As environmentalist and entrepreneur Paul Hawken might argue, the creation of such a governance structure would be looking to the past and would jeopardize the opportunity to stimulate discussions leading to new forms of democratic governance.[54] Perhaps the new North American Urban and Peri-Urban Agriculture (UPA) Alliance may provide an opportunity to encompass and give voice to the wide and culturally diverse actors in urban agriculture.[55] Such an alliance should address at least three broad sets of sociocultural and economic agendas: (1) preserving and enhancing cultural heritages, and creating community;

(2) promoting food security; and (3) improving the health of and offering educational opportunities to urban residents.

Celebrating Cultural Heritage and Creating Community

Many urban gardens in North America are inspired by the rich agricultural traditions brought by immigrants to once-booming cities. By growing their own food, they helped to preserve important cultural practices. For older generations as well as today's generation of immigrants, these gardens offer a place to revive or recreate cultural heritage through celebrations, events, and intergenerational knowledge sharing.[56] Klindienst's stories[57] of fifteen gardens across the United States illustrate the ways in which these gardens preserve ethnic heritages, embody a restorative ecology, and offer an ongoing process of cultural exchange and evolution.[58] Hynes' chronicle shows how gardening can restore America's inner cities by bringing nature and hope back to communities in environmentally degraded urban neighborhoods.[59] As the stories of gardeners in Flint, Michigan, reveal, community garden involvement creates new opportunities to participate in positive community change.[60]

Promoting Food Security, Health, and Education

Under a broad food security umbrella, most urban agriculture projects throughout North America address the interrelated themes of health and education, while seeking to promote "access to culturally acceptable, nutritionally adequate food through local, non-emergency sources at all times."[61]

Many of these projects (e.g., the Food Project in Boston, City Sprouts in Omaha, Our Roots in Holyoke, Green Guerrillas in New York City, or the Capuchin Soup Kitchen in Detroit, to name just a few) have gained national attention. The innovative People's Grocery in West Oakland promotes enterprise development to create meaningful and healthful jobs and develop fresh food distribution channels to address the reality of those living in urban food deserts.[62] Others, such as urban youth garden and school garden programs, focus more on influencing dietary behaviors and enhancing environmental awareness and appreciation. The Edible Schoolyard program represents one high-profile program "to create and sustain an organic garden ... wholly integrated into the school's curriculum and lunch program."[63]

An increasing number of studies argue convincingly for stronger public policies in support of urban gardening to improve public health. Lautenschlager and Smith's study in Minneapolis-St. Paul found that garden participants were more willing to eat nutritious food and try ethnic and unfamiliar food than those not in the program.[64] Based on their review of trends in urban agriculture in the United States, Brown and Jameton suggest that urban gardening offers one means to integrate three important elements of twenty-first-century urban public health policy: food security through local sources, urban greening, and environmentally efficient employment. They conclude that while the urban public health achievements of the twentieth century were based on water and sewer systems, the twenty-first-century achievements "will depend on our ability to coordinate complex, materially modest networks of human activity such as gardening to support simple and healthy ways of life."[65] The California Healthy Cities and Communities (CHCC) programs may offer one such approach to incorporating gardens into urban public health policy.[66]

In contrast to these relatively recent public health concerns, school gardens have been a part of the urban agriculture agenda since the early 1900s. Gardens as cultivated ecosystems offer a way to understand ecological processes and the practical techniques of growing food.[67] Gardens reintroduce nature into cities and thereby contribute to the healthy development of children. They represent an accessible way to strike a balance between our built city environments and natural processes.[68] Equally important, a school garden in which students, teachers and parents participate "becomes not only a dynamic and participatory tool, but also a highly cooperative social unit in which people of all ages can work together toward practical ends."[69] Gardens can serve as outdoor laboratories to enhance academic performance in terms of meeting standard, state-mandated learning objectives.[70] They may also create learning communities that emerge from the practice of science in the garden.[71]

These diverse projects raise three broad issues that are critical to the future of the North American urban agriculture movement. First, it will be important to identify and discuss how these types of projects are being framed and incorporated into broader sets of urban agriculture and food policy agendas. The Toronto Food Policy Council's multipronged action program embodied in the city's Food Charter[72] provides one such approach to framing and supporting discrete, yet related, activities. The philosophy of Toronto's FoodShare aptly summarizes the move from a project focus to a broader policy orientation toward food production, distribution, and consumption.[73] Similarly, the new W. K. Kellogg Foundation Food and Fitness Initiative seeks to link healthy eating with locally grown food and living in an environment that supports family and community health.[74]

Second, networking across multiple community and neighborhood groups as well as government agencies creates the foundation for moving from a project-specific orientation to one in which projects are integral and related parts of a broader urban and food policy perspective and program. Connecting and networking needs to come front and center as both a strategy for building urban community gardens and for building community through gardens. Grassroots networks, such as From Our Roots (in Spanish, Nuestras Raíces) in Holyoke, Massachusetts, and the "neighborhood cluster groups" at the base of The Garden Resource Program Collaborative in Detroit, are important organizational tools and also form the base for a broader collaborative alliance among several urban programs.

Third, to advance an urban agriculture agenda, it will be important to examine how urban agriculture projects shape new political spaces and opportunities. Do these projects create the conditions for city farmers and garden activists to influence urban food and agriculture policy? Will these projects generate a new generation in defense of urban agriculture in public policymaking and planning? As Antonio Roman-Alcala, a former garden guerrilla in San Francisco, says, "approach [urban farming] to win, not to cause a ruckus."[75]

NEXT STEPS

Urban agriculture still needs conceptual maturity,[76] but this is more than an ivory tower academic exercise. It is fundamental to creating a grassroots national collaborative movement for reshaping the political landscape of our cities and our food system. The new North American UPA Alliance captures what is required to create such a collaborative movement. By forming an alliance of culturally diverse actors and stakeholders involved in urban and peri-urban agriculture in North America, we may see the beginnings of what Paul Hawken calls a new form of community that ultimately changes how we govern and organize ourselves.

NOTES

1. Cited in Santosh Ghosh, "Food Production in Cities," *Acta Horticulturae* 643 (2004): 233–39, 237.

2. "Urban Farming Against Hunger," http://www.fao.org/newsroom/en/news/2007/1000484/index.html (accessed June 20, 2008).

3. Patricia Allen, *Together at the Table: Sustainability and Sustenance in the American Agrifood System* (University Park: The Pennsylvania State University Press, published in cooperation with the Rural Sociological Society, 2004).

4. M. Ableman cited in Katherine H. Brown, "Urban Agriculture and Community Food Security in the United States: Farming from the City Center to the Urban Fringe. Prepared by the Urban Agriculture Committee of Community Food Security Coalition" (Venice, CA: Report from Community Food Security Coalition, 2002), 3.

5. Henk de Zeeuw, "Introduction," in *Annotated Bibliography on Urban Agriculture*, ed. SIDA and ETC Urban Agriculture Programme (Leusden, The Netherlands: ETC - Urban Agriculture Programme, 2001), 7–20; Luc J. A Mougeot, "Urban Agriculture: Definition, Presence, Potentials and Risks," in *Growing Cities, Growing Food. Urban Agriculture on the Policy Agenda*, ed. Nico Bakker, Mariëlle Dubbeling, Sabine Gündel, Ulrich Sabel-Koschella, and Henk de Zeeuw (Feldafing, Germany: DSE, German Foundation for International Development, 2000), 1–42.

6. David Goodman, Bernardo Sorj, and John Wilkinson, *From Farming to Biotechnology: A Theory of Agro-Industrial Development* (Oxford: Blackwell, 1987).

7. Paul Hawken, *Blessed Unrest. How the Largest Movement in the World Came into Being and Why No One Saw It Coming* (New York: The Penguin Group, 2007), 18.

8. Erika Allen cited in Phoebe Connelly and Chelsea Ross, "Farming the Concrete Jungle," *In These Times* (2007): 20–24, 24.

9. Ableman cited in Brown, "Urban Agriculture," 3.

10. Martin Bailkey and Joe Nasr, "From Brownfields to Greenfields: Producing Food in North American Cities," *Community Food Security News* (Fall 1999/Winter 2000), Special Issue, Growing Food in Cities: Urban Agriculture in North America (2000): 7.

11. UNDP, *Urban Agriculture. Food, Jobs and Sustainable Cities* (New York: United Nations Development Program, 1996), 104.

12. Tracie McMillan, "Urban Farmers' Crops Go from Vacant Lot to Market," *New York Times*, Dining & Wine, May 7, 2008, http://www.nytimes.com/2008/05/07/dining/07urban.html?_r=2&oref=slogin&oref=slogin (accessed May 7, 2008).

13. Karen Schmelzkopf, "Urban Community Gardens as Contested Space," *Geographical Review* 85, no. 3 (1995): 364–81.

14. See National Public Radio, "London's Gardens: Allotment for the People," http://www.npr.org/templates/story/story.php?storyId=91805611 (accessed July 18, 2008).

15. Martin Bailkey, "Combining Agriculture, Nature and Housing: Madison's Troy Gardens" (paper presented at Symposium on the Role of Food and Agriculture in the Design and Planning of Buildings and Cities, Ryerson University, Toronto, 2008).

16. See Neighborhood Gardens Association, http://ngalandtrust.org/ (accessed July 24, 2008).

17. Physical remediation methods include excavation, geotextiles, soil washing, and soil vapor extraction; biological remediation techniques involve microbial remediation, phytoremediation, fungal remediation, and composting.

18. See Brown Fields and Land Revitalization, http://www.epa.gov/brownfields/index.html.

19. See Greensgrow Farms, http://www.greensgrow.org/.

20. McMillan, "Urban Farmers."

21. See Edible Estates Regional Prototype Gardens, http://www.edibleestates.org.

22. Brian Halweil and Danielle Nierenberg, "Farming the Cities," in *2007 State of the World. Our Urban Future*, ed. Molly O'Meara Sheehan (New York, London: W. W. Norton & Company, 2007), 48–65; See a partial list of these cities at City Farmer, "Urban Agriculture Notes, Rooftops and Urban Agriculture," http://www.cityfarmer.org/subrooftops.html.

23. Alexandra Woodsworth, "Urban Agriculture and Sustainable Cities" (*Urban Agriculture Notes*, 2001), http://www.cityfarmer.org/alexandraUA.html.

24. Luc J. A. Mougeot, *Agropolis. The Social, Political and Environmental Dimensions of Urban Agriculture* (Ottawa, London: International Development Research Centre and Earthscan, 2005).

25. See Urban Composting, Garbage Delight, http://www.garbagedelight.com/.

26. See Growing Power, http://www.growingpower.org; Heifer Project International has been instrumental in supporting aquaculture in a wide variety of urban agriculture projects in the U.S. See http://www.heifer.org/site/c.edJRKQNiFiG/b.734899/.

27. FAO, "Livestock Keeping in Urban Areas. A Review of Traditional Technologies Based on Literature and Field Experience" (Rome: Food and Agriculture Organization of the United Nations, 2001).

28. See The New West, "Urban Livestock: A Tender Issue," http://www.newwest.net/magazine/article/urban_livestock_a_tender_issue/C555/L555/ (accessed July 10, 2008).

29. Bina Venkataraman, "Country, the City Version: Farms in the Sky Gain New Interest," *New York Times*, July 15, 2008; Also see the recent discussion of a SkyFarm in Toronto, *The Toronto Star*, http://www.thestar.com/News/Ideas/article/468023 (accessed July 28, 2008).

30. Mougeot, *Agropolis*.

31. Kameshwari Pothukuchi and Jerome L. Kaufman, "Placing the Food System on the Urban Agenda: The Role of Municipal Institutions in Food Systems Planning," *Agriculture and Human Values* 16, no. 2 (2000): 212–24.

32. In the late 1890s, Ebenezer Howard published "Garden Cities of Tomorrow" presenting his vision of small garden cities that would be planned for the "convenience of the community as a whole," preserve natural beauties, and embody the "utmost degree of healthfulness." Cited in Ewart G. Culpin, *The Garden City Movement Up-to-Date* (London: The Garden Cities and Town Planning Association, 1913), 1.

33. Jerry Kaufman, "Food in Planning: A Seven Year Odyssey from Off the Planning Table to On the Planning Table" (paper presented at the Symposium on the Role of Food and Agriculture in the Design and Planning of Buildings and Cities, Ryerson University, Toronto, 2008).

34. American Planning Association, "Policy Guide on Community and Regional Food Planning" (report from the American Planning Association, 2007).

35. In 2007, the U.S. Conference of Mayors acknowledged the contribution of green roofs and green spaces to climate protection strategies (The U.S. Conference of Mayors, 2007).

36. Miguel A. Altieri, Nelso Companioni, Kristina Cañizares, Catherine Murphy, Peter Rosset, Martin Bourque, and Clara I. Nicholls, "The Greening of the 'Barrios': Urban Agriculture for Food Security in Cuba," *Agriculture and Human Values* 16, no. 2 (1999): 131–40.

37. See City Farmer, "Urban Agricultural Notes," http://www.cityfarmer.org (accessed July 25, 2008).

38. See Somerton Tanks Farm, http://www.somertontanksfarm.org/about/pwd_iilf. shtml (accessed June 30, 2008).

39. Richard D Felsing, "How Community Gardens Are Treated in the Planning Documents and Zoning Ordinances of Selected Cities" (report from The Madison Ad-Hoc Committee on Community Gardens, Department of Urban and Regional Planning, University of Wisconsin, Madison, 2001).

40. Benjamin Morton, "Planning for Appropriately Scaled Agriculture in Providence" (report from Providence Urban Agriculture Policy Task Force, Providence, RI, 2006).

41. This symposium built on work started in 1996 by the Community Food Security Coalition to broaden the debate about the contribution of urban agriculture to community economic development, neighborhood revitalization, public health, and ecological sustainability. The authors thank Kami Pothukuchi for bringing this to our attention. "The Role of Food & Agriculture in the Design & Planning of Buildings & Cities" (report from symposium, Department of Architectural Science, Ryerson University, Toronto, Ontario, May 2–4, 2008), http://architecturefood.googlepages.com/home (accessed July 18, 2008).

42. See Pollinating Our Future, Urban Agriculture Conference, http://growurban. org/about.shtml (accessed June 30, 2008).

43. Peter Kropotkin, *The Conquest of Bread* (New York: Vanguard Press, 1926).

44. Wendell Berry, "When Cities and Farms Come Together," in *Radical Agriculture*, ed. Richard Merrill (New York: New York University Press, 1976), 14–25, 18.

45. Southlands Community Planning Team, "Southlands: A Vision for Agricultural Urbanism" (report from the Southlands Community Planning Team, 2008), 10.

46. Kameshwari Pothukuchi and Jerome L. Kaufman, "The Food System—a Stranger to the Planning Field," *Journal of the American Planning Association* 66, no. 2 (2000): 113–24.

47. Gail Feenstra, Sharyl McGrew, and David Campbell, "Entrepreneurial Community Gardens. Growing Food, Skills, Jobs and Communities" (report from the University of California Agriculture and Natural Resources, Davis, 1999).

48. Deena Kamel, "Guerrilla Gardening," *Toronto Star*, June 2, 2008; Joe Robinson, "Guerrilla Gardeners Dig In," *Los Angeles Times*, May 29, 2008.

49. See Guerilla Gardening, http://www.guerrillagardening.org (accessed May 20, 2008).

50. Cited on the home page of The Edible Schoolyard, http://www.edibleschoolyard. org.

51. Thomas J. Bassett, "A Brief History of Community Gardening in America," *Brooklyn Botanic Garden Record Plants and Gardens* 35, no. 1 (1979): 4–6.

52. Ibid.

53. Joe Nasr, James Kuhns, and Martin Bailkey, "The North American Urban and Peri-Urban Agriculture Alliance" (report from Toronto and Madison, November, 2007).

54. Hawken, *Blessed Unrest*.

55. Nasr, et al., "The North American Urban."

56. Laura Saldivar-Tanaka and Marianne E. Krasny, "Culturing Community Development, Neighborhood Open Space, and Civic Agriculture: The Case of Latino Community Gardens in New York City," *Agriculture and Human Values* 21, no. 4 (2004): 399–412.

57. Patricia Klindienst, *The Earth Knows My Name. Food, Culture, and Sustainability in the Gardens of Ethnic Americans* (Boston: Beacon Press, 2006).

58. Sam Bass Warner, *To Dwell Is to Garden. A History of Boston's Community Gardens* (Boston: Northeastern University Press, 1987).

59. Patricia H. Hynes, *A Patch of Eden: America's Inner-City Gardeners* (White River Junction, VT: Chelsea Green Publishing Company, 1996).

60. Katherine Alaimo and David Hassler, eds., *From Seeds to Stories, the Community Garden Storytelling Project of Flint* (Flint: Prevention Research Center of Michigan, University of Michigan School of Public Health, 2003); also see Ruth Landman, *Creating Community in the City. Cooperatives and Community Gardens in Washington, DC* (Westport, CT: Bergin & Garvey, 1993).

61. Katherine H. Brown and Anne Carter, "Urban Agriculture and Community Food Security in the United States: Farming from the City Center to the Urban Fringe" (a primer prepared by the CFSC's North American Urban Agriculture Committee, Venice, CA, 2003), 4.

62. Samina Raja, Changxing Ma, and Pavan Yadav, "Beyond Food Deserts," *Journal of Planning Education and Research* 27, no. 4 (2008): 469–482; Anne Short, Julie Guthman, and Samuel Raskin, "Food Deserts, Oases, or Mirages?" *Journal of Planning Education and Research* 26, no. 3 (2007): 352–64.

63. Cited on the home page of The Edible Schoolyard, http://www.edibleschoolyard.org/mission.html (accessed July 15, 2008).

64. Lauren Lautenschlager and Chery Smith, "Beliefs, Knowledge, and Values Held by Inner-City Youth About Gardening, Nutrition, and Cooking," *Agriculture and Human Values* 24, no. 2 (2007): 245–58.

65. Katherine H. Brown and Andrew L. Jameton, "Public Health Implications of Urban Agriculture," *Journal of Public Health Policy* 21, no. 1 (2000): 20–39, 36.

66. Joan Twiss, Joy Dickinson, Shirley Duma, Tanya Kleinman, Heather Paulsen, and Liz Rilveria, "Community Gardens: Lessons Learned from California Healthy Cities and Communities," *American Public Health Association* 93, no. 9 (2003): 1435–38.

67. Warren Pierce, "Polyculture Farming in the Cities," in *Radical Agriculture*, ed. Richard Merrill (New York: New York University Press, 1976), 224–56.

68. Richard Louv, *Last Child in the Woods: Saving Our Children from Nature-Deficit Disorder* (Chapel Hill, NC: Algonquin Books of Chapel Hill, 2005).

69. Pierce, "Polyculture," 225.

70. Emily J. Ozer, "The Effects of School Gardens on Students and Schools: Conceptualization and Considerations for Maximizing Healthy Development," *Health Education & Behavior* 34, no. 6 (2007): 846–63.

71. Dana Fusco, "Creating Relevant Science through Urban Planning and Gardening," *Journal of Research in Science Teaching* 38, no. 8 (2001): 860–77.

72. Toronto's Food Charter, http://www.toronto.ca/food_hunger/pdf/food_charter.pdf; For the Toronto Food Policy Council, see http://www.toronto.ca/health/tfpc_index.htm.

73. See FoodShare, http://www.foodshare.net/whoweare05.htm.

74. See W. K. Kellogg Foundation, "Overview: Food and Fitness," http://www.wkkf.org/default.aspx?tabid=75&CID=383&NID=61&LanguageID=0 (accessed July 28, 2008).

75. Matthew Green, "Guerrilla Gardeners: When Push Comes to Shovel," *San Francisco Chronicle*, March 29, 2008.

76. Mougeot, "Urban Agriculture."

RESOURCE GUIDE

Suggested Reading

American Planning Association. "Policy Guide on Community and Regional Food Planning." 2007.

Bakker, Nico, Mariëlle Dubbeling, Sabine Gündel, Ulrich Sabel-Koschella, and Henk de Zeeuw, eds. *Growing Cities, Growing Food. Urban Agriculture on the Policy Agenda.* Feldafing, Germany: DSE, German Foundation for International Development, 2000.

Brown, Katherine H., and Anne Carter. *Urban Agriculture and Community Food Security in the United States: Farming from the City Center to the Urban Fringe.* A Primer Prepared by the Community Food Security Coalition's North American Urban Agriculture Committee. Venice, CA: Community Food Security Coalition, 2003.

Halweil, Brian, and Danielle Nierenberg. "Farming the Cities." In *2007 State of the World. Our Urban Future.* Edited by Molly O'Meara Sheehan New York & London: W. W. Norton & Company, 2007, 48–65.

Hynes, H. Patricia. *A Patch of Eden: America's Inner-City Gardeners.* White River Junction, VT: Chelsea Green Publishing Company, 1996.

Klindienst, Patricia. *The Earth Knows My Name. Food, Culture, and Sustainability in the Gardens of Ethnic Americans.* Boston, MA: Beacon Press, 2006.

Mougeot, Luc J. A., ed. *Agropolis. The Social, Political and Environmental Dimensions of Urban Agriculture.* Ottawa and London: International Development Research Centre and Earthscan, 2005.

SIDA, and ETC. "Annotated Bibliography on Urban Agriculture." Leusden, The Netherlands: Swedish International Development Agency; ETC-Urban Agriculture Programme, 2001 (2003).

UNDP. *Urban Agriculture. Food, Jobs and Sustainable Cities.* New York, NY: United Nations Development Program, 1996.

Van Veenhuizen, René. "Introduction." In *Cities Farming for the Future—Urban Agriculture for Green and Productive Cities.* Edited by René van Veenhuizen. RUAF Foundation, IDRC & IIRR, 2006.

Web Sites

Michael Levenston, Executive Director of City Farmer, "Urban Agriculture Notes," City Farmer, http://www.cityfarmer.info/.

Community Food Security Coalition, http://www.foodsecurity.org/.

Genesee County Land Bank, "Adopt-A-Lot Program," Genesee County Land Bank, http://www.thelandbank.org/default.asp.

Growing Power, Inc., http://www.growingpower.org/.

Grow Pittsburgh, http://www.growpittsburgh.org/growpittsburgh/.

Oakland Based Urban Gardens (O.B.U.G.S.), http://www.obugs.org/#Home.

People's Grocery, http://www.peoplesgrocery.org.

The Edible Schoolyard, http://www.edibleschoolyard.org/homepage.html.

Earthworks Boston, "Outdoor Classroom Overview," Earthworks Projects Inc., http://earthworksboston.org/page/outdoor.

The Youth Farm and Market Project, http://www.youthfarm.net.

9

Achieving Sustainable Fisheries: All Hands On Deck!

Tracy Dobson

Fish and other aquatic living resources hold a critical position in human nutrition, livelihoods, local and national economies, and ecosystem health. They also provide recreation through fishing and fish viewing. Consequently, reduction and loss of fish stocks has gained increasing attention as a significant public policy concern. This chapter provides readers with a brief overview of global fisheries and critical issues related to their management. The remainder of the chapter highlights a representative sample of the broad array of approaches that have been pursued by those either responsible in some way for fisheries management or who are otherwise concerned enough to take action to halt and reverse the downward trends of the past few decades. In addition to identifying salient Web sites and readings, this information provides encouragement to those who would like to participate in the quest for sustainable fisheries.

Key fish stocks have been in precipitous decline in many fisheries. Recent studies of fisheries abundance indicate that this is a global and not merely a local issue.[1] Indeed, many marine species are now considered threatened.[2] As one species is fished beyond commercial viability, another takes its place, only to be similarly depleted.[3] A frequently cited example from North America is the commercially important Atlantic cod for which commercial fishing was closed in Canada in 1992.[4] Ransom Myers and Boris Worm report that 90 percent of large predatory fish are gone from the oceans.[5] In 2006, Worm and colleagues reported in *Science* that unless appropriate action is taken soon, the nation's marine fisheries may face collapse by 2050.[6]

These losses can be attributed to two main causes: overfishing and habitat degradation and loss. At the same time that these trends escalate, growing human populations demand more fish for food and other purposes, causing more and more fishing pressure on decreasing stocks. Alien species invasions are a significant driving force in fish stock decline. This chapter will discuss the causes in some detail.

The right set of management tools, including stock assessments and other relevant scientific information, fishing quotas of one type or another guided by "optimum sustainable yield," fishing gear restrictions, written management plans, and sufficient staff can result in sustainable fisheries. Unfortunately, these critical management tools are missing in many fisheries, contributing to stock decline, damaged habitats, and inequities in allocation of fishing opportunities. Among many examples is the Indian Ocean, where only 50 percent of fisheries are considered "managed in some way," and for most of these, no formal management documents exist.[7] It should be noted, however, that stocks are decreasing even where management resources are relatively plentiful.

Historically, the majority of fish catches came from oceans. Today, aquaculture production, both land-based and within aquatic habitats, is overtaking annual marine catch quantities that in the 1980s reached and stabilized at their peak, in terms of tons caught (although which species make up the catch shifts over time). Fish harvests from rivers and lakes continue to grow, but reduced catches from overfishing, loss of critical habitat through development, global warming, and exotic species invasions loom on the horizon. At the same time, contamination of fish through agricultural runoff and toxic chemicals diminishes fish quality and suitability for human consumption.

Fish trade is an important component of global fisheries. According to the Food and Agriculture Organization of the United Nations (FAO), fish and fish products account for the most traded food in the world.[8] Roughly 38 percent of fish production, including live and processed fish and fish meal, was exported from developing and industrial countries in 2004. For developing nations, fish trade is a significant source of foreign currency earnings, along with providing employment and enhancing food security.[9]

In response to concerns about fisheries in decline in a context of increasing human demand for fish and fish products, a variety of organizations have developed strategies aimed at creating sustainable fisheries. International organizations, governments, and nongovernmental organizations (NGOs) have developed a number of approaches that it is hoped will maintain capture (as opposed to farmed) fisheries harvests (both marine and inland), preserve ecosystems, and improve aquaculture's safety and environmental record to provide sufficient quantities of fish for human consumption.

FISH STOCKS DECLINE: CAUSES AND IMPACTS

Habitat change plays a key role in the loss of fish species and populations. Focusing on changes in the United States as a case study, the Pew Oceans Commission[10] reports that more than half of U.S. citizens reside in the coastal zone, and it projects that twenty-seven million more will live in this zone before 2020. Coastal zone population density is five times that of the country's interior. Typically wealthier, residents in coastal areas consume more land, boat more, drive more, and generally consume at a higher level than other citizens, imposing greater burdens on fish habitat. Densely populated and rapidly expanding U.S. urban areas also contribute significantly to aquatic habitat change. In addition to the obvious direct impact through alteration or removal (such as filling wetlands), growth in impervious surface area has repeatedly been implicated in aquatic habitat decline. Once that surface achieves 10 percent of a watershed's acreage, aquatic system health begins to deteriorate.[11]

Economic activity can cause significant water quality damage, with the side effect of negatively affecting fish. Runoff of agricultural chemicals and animal waste from large-scale animal farming has been a major factor and continues to degrade fish habitat. For example, phosphorous overload in the 1960s brought about the eutrophication of Lake Erie, wreaking havoc with commercial and recreational fish stocks there.[12] More recently, an 18,000-square-kilometer hypoxic (oxygen-depleted) region in the Gulf of Mexico developed through the increased input of nitrogen-bearing chemicals in the Mississippi River watershed.[13] Deprived of oxygen, fish cannot survive in this large area.

Another example of critical fish habitat shrinking and suffering degradation through expansion and intensification of human activities is the once most productive estuary in North America. Chesapeake Bay has experienced extensive eutrophication and explosive growth of toxic microbe populations primarily from suburban and agricultural runoff,[14] as well as a loss of commercially important seafood species. In response, many of the multijurisdictional government, business, NGO, and other stakeholders joined together to rescue this significant resource, and remediation is under way.[15] A recent report suggests that this complicated effort has made little progress over its twenty-five-year history.[16]

Dams have had serious negative effects on fisheries while providing hydropower and flood control for businesses and homes and irrigation for agriculture. In the United States, some small dams have been removed in part to promote fisheries, but in general dam construction continues to expand worldwide.[17] While dams provide these important services, they also kill fish and act as obstacles to their passage to spawning grounds. Dams in China, for example, have caused the extirpation of important fish species whose habitat has been altered and whose access to upstream breeding waters is forever blocked.[18]

Manufacturing and transportation-caused air pollution also brings about significant fish habitat degradation. Airborne pollutants from car and truck exhaust and utility power plants pollute aquatic habitats around the globe. In the Laurentian Great Lakes, rain-borne mercury and PCBs (polychlorinated biphenyls) have so contaminated fish that government-issued advisories urge consumers to limit fish consumption (especially children and pregnant women and women of childbearing age). Moreover, studies showed children's fish consumption there resulted in reduced intelligence and other neurological damage.[19]

Introductions of exotic fish species come in two varieties, intended and incidental. Both types can result in problems for ecosystems, including negative impacts on indigenous fish species. Predation and competition, genetic contamination through interbreeding, disease transmission, and habitat alteration are the primary negative effects. The FAO database on Introductions of Aquatic Species contains information on more than four thousand introductions and yet is incomplete.[20] The arrival of the sea lamprey through the Welland Canal early in the twentieth century led to the near demise of the top predator and highly desirable food fish, lake trout, in the Laurentian Great Lakes.[21] One hundred years later, the Great Lakes Fishery Commission continues efforts to thwart its ongoing negative impacts. In Lake Victoria, bordering Uganda, Kenya, and Tanzania, the intentional introduction of the Nile perch in the 1960s to provide an export commodity caused the collapse of the food web as the perch consumed the indigenous cichlids on which local people depended for their food and livelihoods.[22]

A key and well-documented cause of reduced fish stocks globally is unsustainable fish harvesting. Fisheries scientists have published and written extensively on the grim state of fish and fishing around the world.[23] Constant and systematic overharvesting is driven primarily by too many boats chasing a diminishing stock of fish.[24] The International Commission for the Conservation of Atlantic Tunas estimates that western North Atlantic blue fin tuna populations, for example, have been reduced by 97 percent since 1960 (and the size and age of those caught has concomitantly reduced), much of it by Japanese long line fishing.[25] In Malawi, loss of the prized chambo from Lake Malombe due to overfishing in the 1980s and early 1990s[26] led the Fisheries Department to revamp its management strategy.

Along with overcapitalization, many modern fishing methods that in effect scour the ocean, lake, river, or pond clean of fish have contributed to the fisheries crisis. Most significant in this category are the enormous factory ships that can catch and process tons of fish while at sea,[27] but even at the artisanal fishing level, small mesh nets that drag the bottom leave no room for fish to escape and also degrade the benthic habitat. The relentless quest for more and more fish is motivated by desires and needs for food and profit, and it ignores the long-term consequences of this behavior.

Some intensive fishing impacts are only now coming to light. Christian Anderson and colleagues recently provided "strong evidence" for the idea that selective stock harvesting may result in population booms and busts that "can precede systematic declines in stock levels."[28] In addition, removal of older, larger fish leaves younger fish that may not yet be ready to reproduce or, if they do reproduce, the survival rates of their offspring are lower than offspring of larger fish.[29] Thus, the long-employed strategy of harvesting the most mature fish does not augur well for species strength and survival. Also, variability in a particular species caused by fishing may be caused by the effects of fishing on linear dynamics (which are rapidly reversible) or on nonlinear dynamics (which are only slowly reversible or irreversible) in cases in which a species is susceptible to the latter. The nonlinear kind can predispose to extreme booms and busts in the abundance of such a species. Species with particular kinds of population dynamics may be susceptible to nonlinear fluctuations.[30]

LOSS OF BIODIVERSITY

Overwhelming fishing pressure and habitat degradation ultimately results in smaller and fewer fish to feed humans, shrinking biological diversity, and reduced ecosystem vitality and resilience. This is true in the fishing communities of the eastern United States as well as the lakeshores of Malawi, where fish historically accounted for 70 percent of dietary animal protein. That percentage diminished to 30 percent in 2005. FAO reports widespread concern about this worrying trend. Other outcomes include shifting human consumption down the food chain to prey fish as top predators disappear, exacerbating the problem by reducing prey fish populations on which the remaining predators depend.

THE CURRENT STATUS OF FISHERIES

The information presented in this section of the chapter is the best available and yet is incomplete. The contributions of subsistence fishing, for example, are not taken into account. Additionally, one-third of African countries did not supply data for the FAO report that provides much of the statistical information relied on here. Furthermore, the data are used generally in the aggregate to keep the discussion reasonably brief. This necessarily ignores significant variations across local areas and larger regions.

Capture Fisheries

According to the FAO's 2006 report, recent world capture fisheries stand between eighty-five million and ninety-five million tons per year, fluctuating because of periodic variations in the quantity of Peruvian anchoveta caught.[31] Inland fishing accounted for a little over nine million tons in 2004, with nearly 95 percent coming from China[32] and other developing countries.[33] Fifty-two percent of fisheries are fully exploited, while 25 percent are overexploited, depleted, or recovering from depletion. The remaining 23 percent could be expanded, according to the FAO.[34] Many high-value species stand precariously among those that are the most depleted, while a number of those for which additional exploitation might occur are less valuable for human consumption. Furthermore, those exploitable fish species may be important prey for species of use to humans, creating potential problems for the aquatic food chain if their harvest is expanded.

To complete the picture of capture fisheries production and its impact on stocks, issues such as bycatch (nontarget species) and other discards, border losses, and illegal, unregulated, and unreported (IUU) fishing must also be taken into account. Capture of nontarget species that are discarded, or catch of juveniles or quantities beyond the allowed amount that are discarded, lay waste to large quantities of fish as they are removed and killed but not used. Moreover, while they may not be of interest to the capturing vessel, they are likely ecologically important.[35] FAO reported, for example, that bycatch for the Bangladesh finfish industry amounted to 80 percent.[36] Shipments of fish that are delayed at international borders account for another significant quantity of fish that are wasted when they spoil before border disputes can be resolved.[37] Good data for the amount of fish and other captured marine resources falling within the IUU category do not exist, but the number is believed to be large.[38] Moreover, IUU fishing stands as one of the most significant threats to the future of fisheries globally.[39]

Aquaculture's Contribution

The other main component of global fisheries production is aquaculture (farming of fish). Large scale and widespread by 2008, aquaculture has been promoted to meet escalating demand for fish, and it has seen dramatic expansion over the last half century. Fish are farmed primarily in ponds, lakes, and increasingly in ocean pens. Production grew from less than one million tons in 1950 to more than 59 million tons in 2004,[40] providing 43 percent of fish for human consumption.[41] In that year, 91.5 percent of quantity and 80.5 percent of aquaculture value came from the Asia Pacific region.[42] Thus, as capture fisheries have leveled off, aquaculture production is experiencing a rapid rate of growth. This additional production may help to meet the increasing demand for fish that is mostly associated with human population growth and increased affluence pushing up demand.

Aquaculture offers opportunities for developing countries to expand protein pro-duction through integrated farming and fish production systems.

Accompanying its remarkable expansion, however, aquaculture faces numerous challenges because of its negative impacts on wild fish and the environment. Rebecca Bratspies succinctly summarizes the many issues plaguing, most notably, industrial fish farming in coastal waters.[43] Seen as a replacement for capture fisheries, they in fact put additional pressure on stressed fisheries because high-market-value farmed species consume two to five kilograms of wild fish as food to produce one kilogram of farmed fish. Seemingly, this is an inefficient and unsustainable system. Farming also modifies coastal habitats to the detriment of threatened species such as Atlantic salmon. It can negatively affect humans when mangroves are removed to further shrimp aquaculture. Indian communities where mangroves were removed sustained significant damage from the catastrophic 2004 tsunami. Where the mangroves had not been cut down, damage was significantly less.[44]

Another concern is fish escaping their pens. The inevitable escapes of farmed fish can overwhelm wild populations. In short, their reduced suitability for the wild does not translate to a lack of breeding success, so that in the future, if they replace wild populations, they may not thrive, resulting in no populations in the longer term. Other threats from industrial aquaculture include the rapid spread of disease in large, crowded populations, and the introduction in water bodies of waste streams from the farmed fish and the pharmaceuticals used to keep them healthy. In the United States, standards regulating these aquaculture operations are not rigorous and not well enforced.[45] Finally, transgenic fish, species "improved" through transfer of genetic material from other organisms to grow more quickly and larger, are not well regulated. Escape of these organisms poses environ-mental risks to ecosystems and wild populations that at this point are little under-stood.[46] An additional good source of information on aquaculture is the World Resources Institute Report, "Environmental Impacts of Aquaculture."[47]

Another necessary component of any overview of global fisheries is its impor-tance as a human food source. Seventy-five percent of fish harvested are used for food, and 25 percent for other purposes.[48] Generalizing, fish provide about 20 percent of per capita dietary protein,[49] highlighting their significance for human subsistence around the globe. In contrast to a trend of increasing fish consumption in many countries, however, the amount has shrunk significantly in some developing countries in Sub-Saharan Africa, from 9.9 kilograms per capita in 1982 to an estimated 7.6 kilograms in 2006. This trend may reflect the failure of aquaculture to gain recognition and the consequences of overfishing, while human population continues to expand, even taking into account the HIV/AIDS pandemic.[50]

Fisheries are a significant source of employment. Forty-one million people (thir-teen million in China) work in the capture and aquaculture industries. This num-ber includes those engaged in fishing, fish processing, gear manufacture, fish trade, and other support areas. It does not take into account the less-well-documented number of people engaged in subsistence fishing.[51] In 1994 in Malawi, a govern-ment report estimated this number to be forty-two thousand,[52] suggesting that it is likely a significant sector, especially in developing nations. Although this impor-tant source of employment is shrinking where fisheries have collapsed (e.g., the U.S. Atlantic cod fishery, which closed in the late 1970s and again in 1994, and then reopened in 2001), it is expanding in aquaculture, so that fishing and fish product production remain significant livelihood activities.[53]

Equity among fishing sector participants, in fishing and elsewhere in employment related to the fishing industry, presents significant issues at all levels of governance that need resolution to bring about food security and fisheries sustainability. These issues are critical because, without fundamental fairness in which ethical behavior is preferred and encouraged, widespread poverty and unsustainable fisheries (and other food systems) will persist globally. To create a world in which all people have an abundant, nutritionally adequate, and safe food supply, achieving equity in the fisheries domain is essential.

In fisheries sector employment, equity can be addressed so that all participants have the opportunity to provide for themselves and their families. In fact, sustainability will not be achieved in the absence of a fair production system. IUU fishing, for example, will continue among those excluded from allocations sufficient to meet their basic needs. Regarding U.S. coastal fishing, for instance, problems of fairness in fishing opportunity allocation have risen as significant political issues addressed in 2006 amendments to the Magnuson-Stevens Fisheries Conservation and Management Act. This is a global issue, as large corporate fleets compete with small-scale fishers, especially in coastal waters but also on the high seas, with the more marginal operators typically losing out.[54] As these small-scale fishers suffer the loss of livelihood or sustenance, they are pushed into engaging in IUU activities.

The seemingly never-ending bounty of the seas led to the expansion of fishing fleets of many nations after World War II, to levels that the fisheries ultimately could not support. In the end, they reached a state of "overcapitalization,"[55] and many countries instituted regulations on fleet growth. Such restrictions may have led to a reduction in the number of vessels. However, this restriction pushed producers to employ fewer but larger ships, resulting in no reduction in fish catches.[56] Recent fuel price increases may help control fishing efforts. Even as more energy-efficient ships are built, skyrocketing petroleum costs nonetheless could dampen fishing activity.[57]

Rights distribution systems vary around the globe, but those that seem to work well are based on long-lasting, divisible, transferable, and exclusive fisheries rights. Also, full community participation in deliberations and decisions on rights allocation principles and allocation is more likely to result in durable and accepted arrangements.[58] Dialogue at all levels that engages all affected and interested parties is essential to successful rights systems, including marginalized groups such as women and the poor. And, because fisheries resources are inadequate to meet demand, policymaking must create alternative systems that meet everyone's needs, whether they include compensation for reduced fishing opportunities, training for new livelihood pursuits, or other options.

Certain marginalized groups are particularly vulnerable to exclusion and loss in natural resources allocation schemes. Women typically fall into the marginalized category. Millions of women play key roles primarily in small-scale fishing operations in near-shore waters, fishing, processing, and trading fish. They are also wage laborers in large-scale processing operations. In addition, they labor in all phases of aquaculture activity, principally outside of industrial operations.[59] Unfortunately, available statistics do not permit a complete description of the number of women participants, but it is clear that when new policies and institutions are proposed, these women often are left out of planning discussions and programs developed to address allocation issues. For example, increasing exports from developing to industrial countries for processing have resulted in a reduction in employment for women, typically middle-age women with little education, in the exporting nation.[60]

With little power in typically patriarchal communities, women are most often victimized by the HIV/AIDS crisis. The prevalence rates in fishing communities are four to fourteen times greater than the national average for adults ages fifteen to forty-nine.[61] With limited options, they may be forced to provide sex for food (in this case, fish), resulting in disease transmission from mobile fishers who sustain high rates of infection. In addition, as caregivers in the home, their essential livelihood activities may be curtailed as they are needed to care for dying relatives. Thus, the pandemic results in less food, fodder, fuel, and water for the household and reduced fish industry participation. This unfortunate disease expansion has been slowed and even halted in situations in which women achieve greater societal equity, permitting them life choices beyond childbearing.[62]

This brief overview of global fisheries highlights several key issues:

- Unsustainable overfishing and bycatch result in the loss of significant fish stocks in many locations around the globe
- Significant damage to fish habitat results in additional losses for fisheries
- Some aquaculture production practices are unsustainable and incompatible with wild fisheries' survival
- Better management arrangements that lead to sustainability are needed
- Greater fishing rights equity, including the right to food security and livelihood access, and policies fair to marginalized populations are needed

Although the discussion and analysis of the problem of global fish stock decline and fish habitat degradation has recently intensified, much remains to be learned.

RESPONDING TO PROBLEMS AND AIMING FOR SUSTAINABILITY

Bringing science, including risk assessment, into the policy process should contribute to fish conservation. But, science must be made more accessible if it is to gain wider acceptance. Moreover, calls are increasingly made to strengthen the knowledge-creation process through greater transparency.[63] Despite these concerns, scientists are hard at work learning about the state of the stocks and evaluating conservation measures, including promising data regarding the use of individual tradable quotas (ITQs) as a way to limit catch.[64]

Many actions have been taken by international organizations, national governments, NGOs, and others to respond to concerns about past, present, and future decreases in capture fisheries and aquaculture. Once research data revealed the dimensions and configurations of the key issues, strategies creating new governance policies and institutions began to emerge. These policies and institutions often offer opportunities for participation and input; thus, an understanding of the overall scheme of organizations and approaches will be useful to those who want to affect a transformation to sustainable fisheries. And, these opportunities are abundant. Such opportunities are described below.

International Organizations

Individuals and NGOs can and do participate in international forums and the work of international agencies, principally by attempting to influence government actors or by working with participating NGOs.

The FAO and its many subsidiary fisheries-focused bodies are important actors in international arenas. Along with its Committee on Fisheries (COFI), the FAO has established a number of regional commissions, with subcommissions focused on particular fishery issues. For example, the European Inland Fisheries Advisory Commission oversees four subgroups that in turn are composed of a number of "working parties" focused on such issues as introductions and stocking, fish disease, aquaculture, and recreational fishing.[65]

The FAO also operates in the realm of fishery policy development. In 1995, it issued its Code of Conduct for Responsible Fisheries.[66] The Code sets out a framework for a regulatory approach and guiding principles that are designed to bring about fisheries sustainability. It calls on countries to establish and enforce rules emphasizing a precautionary approach and to engage in extensive public education so that all citizens will be enabled to participate in appropriate fish and fish habitat conservation while continuing to enjoy the multiple benefits of fish harvest and production. Studies undertaken to gauge awareness of the Code, however, indicate that further dissemination is needed.[67] Moreover, a number of developing country governments reported that they have inadequate resources to implement the Code's provisions.[68] As IUU activity continues to pose an enormous threat to fisheries, in 2007, 131 FAO member nations agreed to the creation of a legally binding instrument to force countries with ports to take stronger action.[69] The agreement is now in preparation.

The 1982 United Nations Law of the Sea Treaty (LOS)[70] requires participating coastal nations to negotiate in good faith regarding the management of shared transboundary fish stocks. It rapidly became clear to policymakers that this provision of the LOS was ineffective in managing stocks as negotiations did not result in agreements. Discussions launched at the Earth Summit in 1992 culminated in the 1995 agreement for management of straddling and highly migratory fish stocks, which went into force in 2001.[71] This agreement called for creation of regional fisheries management organizations (RFMOs) to bring about collaborative management of transboundary fish stocks. Assessments had shown (unsurprisingly) that management without cross-border collaboration was largely ineffective. To date, several RFMOs have been formed to share management across global regions, with varying degrees of success.[72] As they continue their efforts to operationalize the 1995 agreement, they are striving to employ the precautionary approach. Another major issue for these organizations is determining how to allocate fishing opportunities to new entrants while reducing overall effort. Failure to resolve this issue will likely result in increased IUU activity.[73]

Regional Bodies

Regional bodies responding to more localized concerns are also working to address fish stock declines. In North America, the Great Lakes Fishery Commission (GLFC), founded jointly by the United States and Canada in 1955, promotes research and collaborative management as well as control of the invasive sea lamprey.[74] It was created in response to the crash of the lake trout in 1948, which was brought about primarily by overexploitation and sea lamprey predation. In response to slumping trout populations, much of the lakes' commercial fishing industry was replaced with recreational fisheries supported by stocking.

The commission operates with a small staff, an advisory board of technical experts, and management and technical committees for each of the five lakes in the basin. Funded by the two countries, the GLFC annually makes grants for pertinent research. Because of the dispersed nature of management authority in considering issues of biological and policy concern, the commission not only must work through issues of joint governance between two nations, but also must deal with eight states, two provinces, and a number of Native American tribes and First Nations. The nonbinding 1981 Joint Strategic Management Plan for Great Lakes Fisheries, signed by all entities with legal management authority, guides governance activities in the basin.[75] The Commission is advised by a large panel of knowledgeable members of the public (appointed "citizen advisors"), especially on issues of quota recommendations.

National Politics

In response to key wild fish stocks plummeting, many nations also created new policies and institutions designed to rein in overharvesting. Within a particular country, it is possible to participate in fisheries policymaking and implementation through available political avenues such as voting, contacting lawmakers and regulators, and affiliating with appropriate NGOs.

In Malawi, for example, important inland fish stocks were overexploited, threatening livelihoods and food security.[76] Recognizing the insufficiency of government regulatory resources and the detrimental effect of the uncooperative relationship between the Fisheries Department and fishing peoples, Parliament enacted a new approach in the Fisheries Conservation and Management Act of 1997, which had been tried on a pilot basis beginning in 1993.[77] The act authorizes the creation of management partnerships between local fishing communities and the government.[78] Beach Village Committees (BVCs) may be organized to manage local fisheries, ideally establishing a sense of ownership and hence an enhanced desire to conserve fisheries for the future.[79] To date, the BVCs have not fulfilled this promise.[80]

Operating on a larger scale in the United States, the Magnuson-Stevens Fishery Conservation and Management Act created eight regional fishery management councils to better manage stocks within the country's exclusive economic zone (EEZ).[81] Once the United States closed its EEZ in 1991, it was believed that pressure on stocks would be reduced with the exclusion of foreign fishers. Fishing in U.S. waters is now limited to vessels constructed in the United States.[82] Data indicate that this regulation has not appreciably reduced harvests, however, as U.S. fishers replaced those excluded.[83]

Critics have claimed that, since their creation, the councils—dominated by industry—disregarded relevant scientific information, authorized overfishing, and ignored warning signs of fishery decline, resulting in more fishing and less conservation.[84] In fact, U.S. coastal fisheries have faced growing challenges as stocks diminished. In an effort to reverse downward fish stock trends, 2006 statutory amendments were passed specifically to strengthen the role of science in manage-ment.[85] They require the government to attack IUU fishing in a more forceful manner, to advocate the creation of vessel databases for monitoring and enforce-ment, and to address the issue with all international organizations to which the United States belongs. The legislation mandates greater sharing of fishing opportu-nity allocation, especially among small operators who previously had limited opportunities.[86]

In a promising new development, The North Pacific Fishery Management Council, with a jurisdiction over nine hundred thousand square miles of water off Alaska, in agreement with fishers, concluded an unprecedented agreement to close expanding Arctic waters to commercial fishing. Thawing sea ice could have pro-vided substantial new fishing grounds. Following a precautionary approach, the sig-natories agreed to protect the Arctic's abundant fisheries.[87]

Special Interests

The fishing industry, environmental groups, and consumer groups have also taken action to conserve. Consumer product labeling is one approach employed to achieve sustainability. Working in cooperation, the World Wide Fund for Nature (WWF) and Unilever established the Marine Stewardship Council (MSC) in 1997 (it became independent in 1999). MSC promotes fisheries sustainability by the use of its blue ecolabel. Only those products that meet rigorous standards for fishing in a sustainable manner, without significant impact on the marine environ-ment, and employing a sustainable management system, will be rewarded with the MSC's mark of environmental stewardship. Independent bodies approved by MSC certify fisheries under the MSC standards.[88] Retailers, restaurants, and consumers participate by limiting their purchases to ecolabeled products. Traceability via the blue label thus facilitates the protection of threatened fisheries and ecosystems. MSC offers other sustainability-focused services such as its education Web site for children.[89]

The Monterey Bay Aquarium's Seafood WATCH offers another way for indi-viduals to exert influence through their purchasing power. Seafood WATCH pro-vides widely distributed regional guides that alert U.S. consumers to sustainable choices for fish consumption. Downloadable guides list those fish found to be "best choices" because they come from sustainable capture fisheries or aquaculture farms. Fish fall on their "avoid" list if they belong to overfished stocks or are caught or farmed in ways that harm the environment.[90]

NGOs AND POLICY ENGAGEMENT

The International Union for Conservation of Nature (IUCN) is a large inter-national NGO focused broadly on biological diversity conservation.[91] Some of its extensive advocacy and policy development activity focuses on fisheries globally and in particular countries. It typically works in partnership with other interna-tional and local NGOs in promoting its conservation agenda.

Engaging in research, fisheries project development, and partnership building, the World Fish Center (WFC), formerly International Centre for Living Aquatic

Resources Management (ICLARM), operates in twenty-five nations in Asia, Africa, and the Pacific. One WFC focus is vulnerable populations. In Malawi, working with World Vision, they are assisting HIV/AIDS-afflicted women and orphan-headed families to establish agriculture and aquaculture operations. This approach has increased family protein intake and provided income to purchase antiretroviral drugs.[92]

Greenpeace's reputation for confrontational marine-living resource advocacy is well known, but the organization is also gaining a reputation as a policy advocate. Greenpeace's 1996 "Principles for Ecologically Responsible Fisheries" emphasize low-impact, ecologically sound fisheries that employ a precautionary approach.[93] It has mounted an education campaign on the subject of the devastation caused by trawl fishing on delicate, species-rich seamount habitats.[94] Like coal mining via mountaintop removal in Appalachia, the damage caused to these habitats by trawling is presumed to be long-lived, driving indigenous species to extinction. Reducing or banning altogether harmful fishing gear is yet another approach that can make a significant contribution to fisheries conservation and sustainability. Initiatives led by Greenpeace and other NGOs are targeting trawling and long lines.[95] For example, gear mesh size restrictions preserve juvenile fish by enabling them to pass through fishing nets.

The NGO Project Seahorse, housed at the University of British Columbia, is taking a different approach. As its name suggests, the organization's initial concern and activity was focused on the overharvest of some species of seahorse, especially as bycatch, and on habitat destruction that threatened the existence of these place-based animals.[96] More recently, the project has broadened its scope to include issues of bycatch, marine protected areas, sustainable livelihoods, and community-based management, to name a few. While working in communities, conducting research, and providing volunteer opportunities,[97] its staff team and its volunteers strive for marine conservation.

A number of scientific societies focus on fish resources. The American Fisheries Society (AFS), for example, encourages scientific exchange on topics of importance to fisheries scientists and managers. AFS publishes a monthly journal and organizes annual meetings, providing a forum for discussion and debate. Its Web site offers information and access to experts as well as its extensive list of publications.

Local NGOs also play important roles in fisheries conservation. For example, as a dispute between fishers and a sugar company simmered, an official of the Malawi Wildlife and Environment Society[98] stepped in to facilitate the creation of the Dwangwa fish sanctuary that not only reserved most of the company-owned lakeshore, but also permitted fishing (and siting of fishing villages) on either end of the sanctuary. Although this is a recent development, thus far it appears to have provided a promising resolution for the company while simultaneously promoting fisheries sustainability.

No discussion of fisheries sustainability initiatives would be complete without mention of aquatic protected areas. The Convention for Biological Diversity, an international treaty, calls for 10 percent of oceans being reserved in Marine Protected Areas.[99] These protected areas also are used in lakes such as the Laurentian Great Lakes. Where they are honored by fishers, reports indicate that protected areas are effective in rebuilding stocks by protecting breeding and nursery grounds.[100] These areas typically are established by governments, but NGO advocacy often is a crucial factor in their creation. Some protected areas have been created by fishers. Early reports suggest that Malawi's new fish sanctuaries, created by local fishers in response to plummeting stocks, have met with success.[101]

Concerns about the potential threats of aquaculture to wild species have stimulated research, commentary, and activism as described by Bratspies.[102] COFI reported a 1997 initiative of twenty-five conservation NGOs requesting governments to take steps to eliminate unsustainable aquaculture.[103]

CONCLUSION

In addition to their ecological significance, fisheries provide critical food resources to humans. Currently, capture fisheries everywhere are in peril. Aquaculture, if pursued in an environmentally sustainable manner, may continue to replace a significant portion of capture fisheries, allowing them the time and space to recover from human harvesting. The threats to fisheries are widely recognized by governments, scientists, and environmental NGOs, but wider citizen support will be necessary to overcome the political might of industrial fishing operations. Aid to subsistence fishers must be provided to allow them to reduce their fishing effort. Also essential is education to alert the citizenry to the fisheries crisis and its implications for food and ecological sustainability. As they say in a boating emergency, we need all hands on deck.

NOTES

1. Daniel Pauly and Maria-Lourdes Palomeres, "Fishing down Marine Food Web: It Is Far More Pervasive Than We Thought," *Bulletin of Marine Science* 76 (2005): 197–211; Ransom A. Myers and Boris Worm, "Rapid Worldwide Depletion of Predatory Fish Communities," *Nature* 423 (2003): 280.

2. World Conservation Union, *2003 IUCN Red List of Threatened Species* (Gland, Switzerland: IUCN, 2003).

3. Pauly and Palomeres, "Fishing down."

4. C. T. Taggart et al., "Overview of Cod Stocks, Biology, and Environment in the Northwest Atlantic Region of Newfoundland, with Emphasis on Northern Cod" (publication from International Council for the Exploration of the Sea, Marine Science Symposium 198, St. John's, NF, Canada, 1994): 140–57.

5. Myers and Worm, "Rapid Worldwide."

6. Boris Worm et al., "Impacts of Biodiversity Loss of Ocean Ecosystem Services," *Science* 314 (2006): 787–90.

7. Food and Agriculture Organization of the United Nations, *The State of World Fisheries and Aquaculture* (Rome: FAO, 2006), 127.

8. Ibid., 88.

9. Ibid., 44.

10. Pew Oceans Commission, *American's Living Oceans: Charting a Course for Sea Change* (Philadelphia, PA: Pew Charitable Trust, 2003).

11. Ibid., 56.

12. Margaret Beatty Bogue, *Fishing the Great Lakes: An Environmental History 1783–1933* (Madison: University of Wisconsin Press, 2000).

13. Gregory F. McIsaac et al., "Nitrate Flux in the Mississippi River," *Nature* 414 (2001): 166–67.

14. Daniel Pauly and Jay MacLean, *In a Perfect Ocean* (Washington, DC: Island Press, 2003), 19.

15. Chesapeake Bay Commission, "Policy for the Bay," http://www.chesbay.state.va. us/history.html (accessed June 28, 2008).

16. Tom Horton, "Growing! Growing! Gone! The Chesapeake Bay and the Myth of Endless Growth" (prepared on a grant from The Abell Foundation, 2008), http://www. abell.org/pubsitems/env_Growing_808.pdf.

17. FAO, *World Fisheries* 34 (2006): 110–11. See also Jessica Seares et al., "Effects of Globalization on Freshwater Systems and Strategies for Conservation," in *Globalization: Effects on Fisheries Resources*, ed. William W. Taylor, Michael S. Schechter, and Lois G. Wolfson (New York: Cambridge University Press, 2007), 81–83.

18. Songguang Xie et al., "Fisheries of the Yangtze River Show Immediate Impacts of the Three Gorges Dam," *Fisheries* 32, no. 7 (2007): 343–44.

19. Chris Bright, "The Nemesis Effect," *World?Watch* May/June (1999): 12–23.

20. FAO, *World Fisheries*, 82.

21. Gerald R. Smith, *Fishes of the Great Lakes Region*, rev. ed. (Ann Arbor: University of Michigan Press, 2007), 56.

22. Tony J. Pitcher and Paul J. B. Hart, *Impact of Species Changes on African Lakes* (London, New York: Chapman and Hall, 1995); F. Witte, J. H. Wanink, M. Kishe-Machumu, "Species Distinction and the Biodiversity Crisis in Lake Victoria," *Transactions of the American Fisheries Society* 136 (2007): 1146–59.

23. Christian N. K. Anderson et al., "Why Fishing Magnifies Fluctuations in Fish Abundance," *Nature* 457 (2008): 835–39; See also, Pauly and MacLean, *In A Perfect Ocean*; In addition, numerous scholarly articles can be found via the University of British Columbia Fisheries Centre Web site, http://www.fisheries.ubc.ca.

24. FAO, *World Fisheries*, 29–37 (overharvesting), 5–6, 25–26 (overcapitalization).

25. National Geographic News, http://news.nationalgeographic.com/news/2006/07/ 060724-bluefin-tuna.html (accessed October 10, 2008).

26. Simon J. Bland and Steve Donda, *Management Initiatives for the Fisheries of Malawi*. Fisheries Department Report (Lilongwe: Government of Malawi, 1994).

27. Dag Standal, "The Rise and Fall of Factory Trawlers: An Eclectic Approach," *Marine Policy* 32 (2008): 326–32; David Helvarg, "Full Nets—Empty Seas," *The Progressive Magazine*, November (1997), http://www.thirdworldtraveler.com/Environment/Full-Nets_EmptySeas.html (accessed on October 10, 2008).

28. Anderson et al., "Fluctuations in Fish Abundance," 835–39.

29. S. J. Rowland, "Overview of the History, Fishery, Biology and Aquaculture of Murray Cod (*Maccullochella peelii peelii*)" (statements, recommendations, and supporting papers from workshop on Management of Murray Cod in the Murray Darling Basin by MDB Commission, Canberra, Australia, June 3–4, 2005), http://www.mdbc.gov.au/data/page/ 641/5 Stuart J. Rowland.pdf (accessed on December 20, 2008); Steven A. Berkeley, Colin Chapman, and Susan M. Sogard, "Maternal Age as a Determinant of Larlval Growth and Survival in a Marine Fish, *Sebastes melanops*," *Ecology* 85, no. 5 (2004): 1258–64.

30. "Linearity" refers to quantitative aspects of particular processes or dynamics of some systemic entity that can be described reasonably accurately using old-fashioned mathematics, such as arithmetic in particularly simplistic cases. "Nonlinearity" refers to other systemic processes or dynamics for which old-fashioned mathematics don't work; electronic computer methods may be helpful as in trial-and-error iteration of

hypothetical solutions with models that incorporate feedbacks, bifurcations, or systemic flips, and so on.

31. FAO, *World Fisheries*, 8.

32. Many scientists question the accuracy of Chinese fishing data, for example, Daniel Pauly, in his talk, "Maritime Biodiversity: Evaluation of Major Threats," July 19, 2005, Brasilia. A more oblique reference to this issue is found in FAO, *World Fisheries*, 5.

33. FAO, *World Fisheries*, 15.

34. Ibid., 34.

35. Ibid., 119.

36. Ibid., 120.

37. Ibid., 136.

38. Ibid., 75.

39. Ibid., 75.

40. Ibid., 16.

41. Ibid., 38.

42. Ibid., 16.

43. Rebecca M. Bratspies, "Can Transgenic Fish Save Fisheries?" in *Globalization: Effects on Fishery Resources*, ed. William W. Taylor, Michael S. Schechter, and Lois G. Wolfson (New York: Cambridge University Press, 2007), 472–80.

44. F. Dahdouh et al., "How Effective Were Mangroves as a Defence against the Recent Tsunami?" *Current Biology* 15, no. 14 (2005): 1337–38.

45. Bratspies, "Can Transgenic," 479.

46. Ibid., 485–86.

47. United Nations Atlas of the Oceans, "Environmental Impacts of Aquaculture," http://www.oceansatlas.org/world_fisheries_and_aquaculture/html/issues/ecosys/envimpactfi/aqua.htm (accessed May 27, 2008).

48. FAO, *World Fisheries*, 34.

49. Ibid., 38.

50. Ibid., 154.

51. Ibid., 22.

52. Simon J. R. Bland and Steven J. Donda, Common Property and Poverty: Fisheries Co-Management in Malawi, Fisheries Bulletin no. 3 (1995): 3.

53. FAO, *World Fisheries*, 22–24.

54. Ibid.

55. Ibid., 26; Susan Hanna, et al., *Fishing Ground: Defining a New Era for American Fisheries Management* (Washington, DC: Island Press, 2000), 53.

56. FAO, *World Fisheries*, 26.

57. Ibid., 133.

58. John S. Hammond, Ralph L. Keeney, and Howard Raiffa, *Smart Choices: A Practical Guide to Making Better Decisions* (Boston: Harvard Business School Press, 1999).

59. FAO, *World Fisheries*, 25.

60. Ibid., 114.

61. Ibid., 94.

62. See e.g., Amartya Sen, "Population: Delusion and Reality," in *The Gender Sexuality Reader: Culture, History, Political Economy*, ed. Roger Lancaster and Michaela di Leonardo (New York: Routledge, 1997), 91–106.

63. Sheila Jasanoff, "Technologies of Humility," *Nature* 450 (2007): 33.

64. Geoffrey Heal and Wolfram Schlenker, "Sustainable Fisheries," *Nature* 455 (2008): 1044–45.

65. Food and Agriculture Organization of the United Nations, description of its organization may be found at http://www.fao.org/unfao/govbodies/statbod_en.htm (accessed May 25, 2008).

66. Food and Agriculture Organization of the United Nations, "Code of Conduct for Responsible Fisheries" (Rome: Food and Agriculture Organization, 1995).

67. S. M. Nazmul Alam et al., "Compliance of Bangladesh Shrimp Culture with FAO Code of Conduct for Responsible Fisheries: A Development Challenge," *Ocean & Coastal Management* 48 (2005): 2, 177–88.

68. FAO/COFI, *Progress Report on the Code of Conduct for Responsible Fisheries and Related International Plans of Action*, FAO Fisheries Report No. 665 (Rome: FAO, 2001); Janet G. Webster and Jean Collins, *Fisheries Information in Developing Countries: Support to the Implementation of the 1995 Code of Conduct for Responsible Fisheries*, FAO Fisheries Circular No. 1006 (Rome: FAO, 2005).

69. FAO, *Committee on Fisheries, Subcommittee on Fish Trade* (Rome: FAO, 2008).

70. 1833 UNTS 3; 21 ILM 126, 1982.

71. "1995 Fish Stock Agreement, The United Nations Agreement for the Implementation of the Provisions of the United Nations Convention on the Law of the Sea Relating to the Conservation and Management of Straddling Fish Stocks and Highly Migratory Fish Stocks," December 10, 1982 (in force as of December 11, 2001).

72. FAO, *World Fisheries*, 52–57.

73. Ibid., 54–55.

74. Great Lakes Fishery Commission, *Joint Strategic Plan for the Management of Great Lakes Fisheries*, rev. ed. (Ann Arbor, MI: GLFC, 1997).

75. Great Lakes Fishery Commission, *Strategic Vision of the Great Lakes Fishery Commission for the First Decade of the New Millennium* (Ann Arbor, MI: GLFC, 2001).

76. Tracy A. Dobson and Kristine D. Lynch, "As Nearshore Stocks Drop, Malawi Begins a Return to Local Fisheries Management," *Journal of Great Lakes Research* 29, no. 2 (2003): 232–42, 236.

77. Ibid., 239.

78. *Fisheries Conservation and Management Act*, Government of Malawi, 1997.

79. Ibid., Part III, Local Community Participation.

80. Aaron J. M. Russell, Tracy Dobson, and John G. M. Wilson, "Fisheries Management in Malawi: A Patchwork of Traditional, Modern, and Post-Modern Regimes Unfolds." in *International Governance of Fisheries Ecosystems*, ed. William W. Taylor, Michael S. Schechter, and Nancy Leonard (Bethesda, MD: American Fisheries Society, 2008).

81. Title III, Sec. 302 and 90 Stat. 347.

82. Hanna et al., *Fishing Ground*, 30.

83. FAO, *World Fisheries*, 26.

84. Hanna et al., *Fishing Ground*, 87–98.

85. Fisheries Office of International Affairs, National Oceanographic and Atmospheric Administration, "Overview of International Provisions in the Magnuson-Stevens Act Reauthorization Act Fact Sheet" (Silver Spring, MD: NOAA, 2007).

86. Ibid.

87. Janet Raloff, "Arctic Warming Chills Interest in Fishing," *Science News* October (2008), http://www.sciencenews.org/view/generic/id/37352/title/Arctic_warming_chills_interest_in_fishing.

88. Marine Stewardship Council, http://eng.msc.org/ (accessed May 24, 2008).

89. Fish and Kids, http://www.fishandkids.org (accessed May 26, 2008).

90. Monterey Bay Aquarium, http://www.mbayaq.org/cr/SeafoodWatch/web/sfw_regional.aspx?region_id=6 (accessed May 24, 2008).

91. International Union for Conservation of Nature (IUCN), http://www.iucn.org (accessed May 26, 2008).

92. "Relief for HIV Victims Through Integrated Agriculture-Aquaculture," http://www.worldfishcenter.org/v2/ourwork-health-hiv-aq.html (accessed June 26, 2008).

93. Greenpeace, "Principles for Ecologically Responsible Fisheries," http://www.greenpeace.org/usa/news/principles-for-ecologically-re (accessed May 20, 2003).

94. Greenpeace, "Seamount Protection Campaign," http://www.greenpeace.org.uk/oceans/solutions/saving-the-mountains-under-the-sea (accessed November 17, 2008).

95. FAO Committee on Fisheries, "Initiatives of Non-Governmental Organizations Regarding Sustainable Resource Use and Environmental Protection in Fisheries" (paper from Rome, Italy, March 17–20, 1997).

96. Amanda C. J. Vincent, A. D. Marsden, and U. R. Sumaila, "Possible Contributions of Globalization in Creating and Addressing Sea Horse Conservation Problems," in *Globalization: Effects on Fisheries Resources*, ed. William W. Taylor, Michael G. Schechter, and Lois G. Wolfson (New York: Cambridge University Press, 2007), 191.

97. Project Seahorse, http://seahorse.fisheries.ubc.ca/index.html (accessed May 24, 2008).

98. Russell et al., "Fisheries Management," 81–82.

99. 1760 UNTS 79; 31 ILM 818, 1992.

100. Craig Leisher, Pieter van Beukering, and Lea M. Scherf, *Nature's Investment Bank: How Marine Protected Areas Contribute to Poverty Reduction* (Canberra, ACT, Australia, The Nature Conservancy, 2007); P. Christie, A. White, and E. Deguit, "Starting Point or Solution? Community-Based Marine Protected Areas on the Philippines," *Journal of Environmental Management* 66 (2002): 441–54.

101. Russell et al., "Fisheries management," 82–83.

102. Bratspies, "Can Transgenic."

103. FAO Committee on Fisheries, "Initiatives of Non-Governmental Organizations Regarding Sustainable Resource Use and Environmental Protection in Fisheries and Urging Governments to Ban Unsustainable Aquaculture" (report from the 22nd Session, Rome, Italy, 17–20 March, 1997).

RESOURCE GUIDE

Suggested Reading

Food and Agriculture Organization of the United Nations. *The State of World Fisheries and Aquaculture*. Rome: FAO, 2006.

Food and Agriculture Organization of the United Nations. *Code of Conduct for Responsible Fisheries*. Rome: FAO, 1995.

Goldburg, R. J., M. S. Elliott, and R. L. Naylor. *Marine Aquaculture in the United States: Environmental Impacts and Policy Options*. Arlington, VA: Pew Oceans Commission, 2001.

Hollister, David C. *Public Policy Primer: How to Get Off the Sidelines and Into the Game*. East Lansing, MI: Institute for Educational Leadership, 2007. Available at http://www.iel.org/pubs/publicpolicy.pdf.

National Research Council. *Sustaining Marine Fisheries*. Washington, DC: National Academy Press, 1999.

Ostrom, Elinor, et al. eds. *The Drama of the Commons*. Washington, DC: National Academy Press, 2002.

Pauly, Daniel, and Jay Maclean. *In a Perfect Ocean: The State of Fisheries and Ecosystems in the North Atlantic Ocean*. Washington, DC: Island Press, 2003.

Pew Oceans Commission report, 2003.

Taylor, William T., Michael S. Schechter, and Lois G. Wolfson, eds. *Globalization: Effects on Fishery Resources*. New York: Cambridge University Press, 2007.

Webster, D. G., and Oran R. Young. *Adaptive Governance: The Dynamics of Atlantic Fisheries Management*. Cambridge, MA: MIT Press, 2008.

Web Sites

American Fisheries Society, http://www.fisheries.org.

Fisheries and Aquaculture Department, Food and Agriculture Organization of the United Nations, http://www.fao.org/fisheries.

Fisheries Centre, University of British Columbia, http://www.fisheries.ubc.ca.

Great Lakes Fishery Commission, http://www.glfc.org.

Indigenous Peoples Restoration Network, http://www.ser.org/iprn/default.asp.

Marine Stewardship Council, http://www.msc.org.

Greenpeace International, http://www.greenpeace.org/international/campaigns/oceans.

National Marine Fisheries Service, National Oceanographic and Atmospheric Administration, http://www.nmfs.noaa.gov/ia/intlagree/.

World Fish Center, http://www.worldfishcenter.org.

World Resources Institute, http://www.wri.org.

PART III

Health

10

Food Security and Food Insecurity in the United States and Their Consequences for Child Health

John T. Cook

Food is at the foundation of what psychologist Abraham Maslow called the "hierarchy of human needs."[1] Along with oxygen, water, and regulated body temperature, it is a basic necessity for human survival. But food is much more than the nutrients it contains, and its availability and consumption affect human health and well-being in ways far beyond its nutritional characteristics. Food is also at the heart of humans' conceptions of nurturance and abundance. Moreover, food is the focus of many social activities, from sharing a drink or cup of tea, to celebrating important life-cycle passages such as weddings, or major holidays like Thanksgiving, Passover, Ramadan, or Christmas.

Food security—access by all people at all times to enough food for an active, healthy life—is one of several conditions necessary for a population to be healthy and well nourished. Food insecurity, in turn, refers to the limited or uncertain availability of nutritionally adequate and safe foods, or to limited or uncertain ability to acquire food in socially acceptable ways.[2] Food security can be measured at many different levels, including individual, household, community, regional, national, and even global. This chapter deals primarily with household-level food security in the United States.

MEASURING FOOD SECURITY

The conceptual framework on which U.S. food security measures are based is part of a broader framework for nutritional indicators laid out by an Expert Panel convened by the Life Sciences Research Office (LSRO) of the Federation of American Societies for Experimental Biology (FASEB) in 1990.[3] Three dimensions of food security were articulated by the Expert Panel as amenable to measurement: (1) the quantity and quality of food that is available, (2) its accessibility, such as physical accessibility in terms of grocery store location and transportation systems, and (3) affordability or price relative to community residents' resources.[4]

Lack of access to adequate food by U.S. households resulting from constrained household financial resources has been measured by questions assessing "hunger," "risk of hunger," "food insufficiency," and most recently "food insecurity."[5] In 1990, the LSRO Expert Panel developed the following conceptual definitions of food security, food insecurity, and hunger:[6]

- **Food security:** "Access by all people at all times to enough food for an active, healthy life. Food security includes at a minimum: (1) the ready availability of nutritionally adequate and safe foods, and (2) an assured ability to acquire acceptable foods in socially acceptable ways (e.g., without resorting to emergency food supplies, scavenging, stealing, or other coping strategies)."
- **Food insecurity:** "Limited or uncertain availability of nutritionally adequate and safe foods or limited or uncertain ability to acquire acceptable foods in socially acceptable ways."
- **Hunger:** "The uneasy or painful sensation caused by a lack of food. The recurrent and involuntary lack of access to food. Hunger may produce malnutrition over time.... Hunger ... is a potential, although not necessary, consequence of food insecurity."

The Expert Panel approved these conceptual definitions, and an interdisciplinary research team developed a scale to measure these operational conditions at the household level in the U.S. population.[7] Consisting of eighteen questions, the U.S. Food Security Scale (FSS) is administered annually by the Census Bureau in its Current Population Survey (CPS) with results reported by the USDA's Economic Research Service.[8] These recurring administrations of the FSS provided a twelve-year time-series of data on food security, food insecurity, and hunger in the U.S. population for 1995–2007.[9]

Recently, a Children's Food Security Scale (CFSS) consisting of the eight child-referenced items in the larger eighteen-item FSS was validated by the U.S. Department of Agriculture (USDA) Economic Research Service (ERS).[10] The CFSS can be scored and scaled to more directly depict the food security status of children in a household, and yields higher prevalence of child hunger when administered separately than is obtained from the FSS.[11] The eighteen-question FSS is shown in Table 10.1, with the eight items that make up the CFSS in the lower section. Thresholds for the various household and child food security categories are also indicated.

USDA's ERS implemented recent changes in FSS report terminology used to label the most severe levels of deprivation measured by the household and children's scales, replacing the term "hunger" with "very low food security."[12] Because this change is relatively recent, and not uniformly accepted by either scientists or advocates, this chapter uses the term "hunger," where appropriate.

RELATIONSHIP OF FOOD INSECURITY TO POVERTY

Food insecurity and hunger, as measured by the FSS, are specifically related to limited household resources. Thus, they are referred to as "resource-constrained" or "poverty-related" conditions. The official definition of poverty for the U.S. population is based on historical estimates of the portion of an average household's

Table 10.1.
Questions Comprising the U.S. Food Security Scale with Child Food Security Scale
Questions in the Lower Section

1. "We worried whether our food would run out before we got money to buy more." Was that often, sometimes, or never true for you in the last 12 months?	
2. "The food that we bought just didn't last and we didn't have money to get more." Was that often, sometimes, or never true for you in the last 12 months?	Household Food Secure
3. "We couldn't afford to eat balanced meals." Was that often, sometimes, or never true for you in the last 12 months?	
4. In the last 12 months, did you or other adults in the household ever cut the size of your meals or skip meals because there wasn't enough money for food? (Yes/No)	
5. (If yes to Question 4) How often did this happen— almost every month, some months but not every month, or in only 1 or 2 months?	Household Food Insecure _without_ Hunger
6. In the last 12 months, did you ever eat less than you felt you should because there wasn't enough money for food? (Yes/No)	
7. In the last 12 months, were you ever hungry, but didn't eat, because you couldn't afford enough food? (Yes/No)	
8. In the last 12 months, did you lose weight because you didn't have enough money for food? (Yes/No)	
9. In the last 12 months, did you or other adults in your household ever not eat for a whole day because there wasn't enough money for food? (Yes/No)	Household Food Insecure _with_ Hunger
10. (If yes to Question 9) How often did this happen— almost every month, some months but not every month, or in only 1 or 2 months?	

(Questions 11–18 are asked only if the household included children age 0–18)

11. "We relied on only a few kinds of low-cost food to feed our children because we were running out of money to buy food." Was that often, sometimes, or never true for you in the last 12 months?	Child Marginally Food Secure
12. "We couldn't feed our children a balanced meal, because we couldn't afford that." Was that often, sometimes, or never true for you in the last 12 months?	
13. "The children were not eating enough because we just couldn't afford enough food." Was that often, sometimes, or never true for you in the last 12 months?	Child Food Insecure _without_ Hunger
14. In the last 12 months, did you ever cut the size of any of the children's meals because there wasn't enough money for food? (Yes/No)	
15. In the last 12 months, were the children ever hungry but you just couldn't afford more food? (Yes/No)	Child Food Insecure _with_ Hunger
16. In the last 12 months, did any of the children ever skip a meal because there wasn't enough money for food? (Yes/No)	

(Continued)

145

Table 10.1. (*Continued*)

17. (If yes to Question 16) How often did this happen—
     almost every month, some months but not every month,
     or in only 1 or 2 months?
18. In the last 12 months, did any of the children ever not
     eat for a whole day because there wasn't enough money
     for food? (Yes/No)

Source: Nord, M., Andrews, M., Carlson, S. Household Food Security in the United States, 2007. ERR-66, USDA Economic Research Service. November 2008.

income required to purchase a "minimally nutritious diet" (about 30 percent in the early 1960s). Poverty thresholds—set at three times the amount needed to buy such a diet on the basis of the 1960s' overall average proportion of income spent on food—represent the amounts of money estimated by the government to approximate levels of necessity for families of different size and composition (i.e., number of people in the household, and number of children or elderly).

Although the cost of living (especially housing and food costs) varies from state to state and region to region, the official government poverty thresholds do not vary geographically. They are updated annually for inflation using the Consumer Price Index (CPI), a broad national index of overall increases in aggregate consumer prices.[13] However, although an average U.S. family currently spends only about 12 percent of its total annual expenditures on food, implying a poverty threshold closer to eight times (100 percent ÷ 12 percent) the cost of a minimally nutritious diet instead of three times, this "multiplier" has not been updated since its conception in the early 1960s. The official 2007 (the latest year for which data are available) poverty threshold for families of four people, two adults and two children, was $21,027.[14]

Both the definition of poverty and the poverty thresholds have been criticized on grounds that they do not accurately reflect families' true financial resources, nor the amount of money families actually need to be economically self-sufficient.[15] Empirical estimates of minimum income levels required for families to achieve basic economic self-sufficiency range from two to three times the official federal poverty thresholds.[16]

Based on these official poverty definitions, in 2007, 37.3 million people (12.5 percent) lived in households with incomes below the poverty thresholds in the United States. Of these, 13.3 million were children under eighteen years old, and 5.1 million were children under six years old. Subpopulations with highest prevalence of poverty (see Figure 10.1) are people in female-headed households with no spouse present (28.3 percent), blacks (24.5 percent), Latinos (21.5 percent), and children under age six years old (20.8 percent).[17] From 2000 to 2004, the poverty rates for all major ethnic groups increased steadily, although they declined slightly from 2005 to 2006 and increased in 2007.

Although the populations affected by poverty and food insecurity in the United States overlap, they are not identical. Not all poor people are food insecure, and food insecurity extends to people with incomes above the federal poverty level. In 2007, 36.2 million people in the United States (12.2 percent) lived in food-insecure households, 24.3 million lived in households without hunger, and

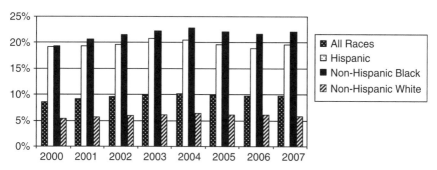

Figure 10.1.
Proportion of U.S. Families with Incomes Below Poverty by Race and Ethnicity, 2000–2007[a]
Source: U.S. Census Bureau, Current Population Survey, various years.
Note: a. Includes households with and without children.

11.9 million lived with hunger (see Figure 10.2). Of the 36.2 million food-insecure people in the United States in 2006, 12.4 million were children under age eighteen. As with poverty, subpopulations with the highest prevalence of household food insecurity (HFI) are blacks (22 percent), Latinos (22.3 percent), people in households with children under six years old (17.7 percent), and single-mother households (30.4 percent). In 2007, 39.9 percent of all people in the United States with incomes below the poverty thresholds were food insecure.

Averaging data over the years 2005–2007, USDA ERS calculated state-level estimates of the proportion of food insecure households in each state over this period. The lowest state-level HFI prevalence was 6.5 percent in North Dakota; the highest was 17.4 percent in Mississippi. In 34 states, more than 10 percent of all households were food insecure. The prevalence of food insecurity with hunger was lowest in North Dakota at 2.2 percent and highest in Mississippi at 7 percent.

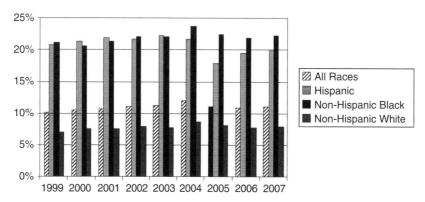

Figure 10.2.
Proportion of U.S. Households That Are Food Insecure by Race/Ethnicity: 1999–2007*
*Includes households with and without children.
Source: U.S. Census Bureau, Current Population Survey, various years.

Seven states had an average prevalence of food insecurity with hunger at 5 percent or higher over this period.[18]

In 2008, state-level child food insecurity prevalence estimates (at any severity level, both with and without hunger) were produced using a similar averaging approach with state-level FSS microdata from the CPS for children living in food-insecure households during 2004–2006. Those estimates are reproduced in Table 10.2.[19]

FOOD INSECURITY, CHILD HEALTH, AND DEVELOPMENT

Food insecurity influences health and development through its impacts on nutrition and as a component of overall family stress. The condition of food insecurity includes both inadequate quantities and quality of nutrients. At less severe levels of food insecurity, household food managers (usually mothers) trade off food quality for quantity to prevent household members, especially children, from feeling persistently hungry.

Overall, less-expensive, more filling foods are more energy-dense and nutrient-sparse, and often contain large amounts of starches, sugar, salt, and fats. Nutrient-dense, energy-sparse foods, by contrast, are usually more expensive. This inverse relationship between food prices and food quality has implications for micronutrient deficiencies at all ages and could be a potential factor in the widespread emergence of obesity in adults and possibly in older children.[20]

Early Childhood: Birth to Three Years

A relatively large number of studies have examined associations between food insecurity and child health and development in the birth to three age-group, many conducted by the Children's HealthWatch (previously the Children's Sentinel Nutrition Assessment Program, C-SNAP) at Boston Medical Center. C-SNAP has conducted household-level surveys and medical record audits at seven central-city medical centers since 1998. Primary adult caregivers accompanying children from birth to three years old seeking care are interviewed by trained interviewers in private settings at primary-care clinics or emergency departments during waiting periods. This age-group was chosen for sampling because its special vulnerability makes it a sentinel population for adverse health outcomes in pediatric populations that are related to constrained household resources and changes in social policies and economic conditions. Children's weight and, if possible, length are recorded at the time of the interview. The C-SNAP survey instrument is composed of questions on household characteristics, children's health and hospitalization history, maternal health, maternal depressive symptoms, participation in federal assistance programs, energy insecurity, and changes in benefit levels. In addition, the interview includes the U.S. FSS and the Parent's Evaluation of Developmental Status (PEDS) scales.[21]

Food Insecurity and Adverse Health Outcomes in Young Children

By 2003, studies examined adverse health and development outcomes associated with malnutrition in young children, and food insufficiency (a precursor to

Table 10.2.
Estimated Number and Percent of Children Food Insecure by State, Based on
Three-Year Average of Estimates from the Current Population Survey Food
Security Scale for 2004–2006

	Average Number of Children in State 2004-2006	Average Number of Children Food Insecure 2004–2006	Average Percent of Children Food Insecure 2004–2006
US	77,550,276	13,527,196	17.4%
AK	195,221	33,662	17.2%
AL	1,144,315	171,469	15.0%
AR	725,629	115,520	15.9%
AZ	1,674,152	364,482	21.8%
CA	10,030,581	1,823,347	18.2%
CO	1,220,103	217,391	17.8%
CT	880,688	100,500	11.4%
DC	114,489	23,104	20.2%
DE	212,323	29,227	13.7%
FL	4,274,726	666,087	15.6%
GA	2,468,824	471,338	19.0%
HI	317,372	38,391	12.2%
IA	732,707	119,432	16.3%
ID	406,187	77,132	19.0%
IL	3,391,496	521,628	15.4%
IN	1,683,883	245,452	14.6%
KS	730,193	121,487	16.7%
KY	1,044,097	197,643	18.9%
LA	1,120,289	211,221	19.0%
MA	1,565,732	167,670	10.7%
MD	1,443,002	220,837	15.3%
ME	304,274	60,393	19.8%
MI	2,684,870	471,912	17.5%
MN	1,324,281	163,564	12.3%
MO	1,485,531	257,533	17.3%
MS	797,328	182,006	22.8%
MT	218,828	32,493	14.7%
NC	2,235,404	448,696	20.1%
ND	155,573	16,076	10.4%
NE	465,002	64,311	13.8%
NH	314,572	27,947	8.9%
NJ	2,285,425	277,169	12.1%
NM	528,632	115,004	21.8%
NV	661,357	106,763	16.1%
NY	4,779,467	720,401	15.1%
OH	2,944,382	594,647	20.2%
OK	912,948	192,808	21.2%
OR	910,481	183,448	20.2%
PA	2,998,420	509,341	17.0%

(Continued)

Table 10.2. (*Continued*)

	Average Number of Children in State 2004-2006	Average Number of Children Food Insecure 2004-2006	Average Percent of Children Food Insecure 2004-2006
RI	261,980	40,984	15.6%
SC	1,094,884	219,838	20.1%
SD	197,926	29,573	14.9%
TN	1,487,628	307,825	20.7%
TX	6,723,289	1,584,266	23.6%
UT	795,714	157,425	19.8%
VA	1,964,741	216,631	11.0%
VT	137,438	19,500	14.2%
WA	1,586,338	286,664	18.1%
WI	1,370,207	217,633	15.9%
WV	421,182	63,296	15.1%
WY	126,164	22,030	17.4%

Source: Census Bureau, Current Population Survey, Food Security Supplement, 2004, 2005, 2006. Data accessed via the Federal Datanet using Data Ferret.

the food security measures), hunger, and risk of hunger related to poor health in children (less than eighteen years old), but none had yet focused on birth to three years old using the new FSS. A C-SNAP study found food-insecure children more likely to have fair or poor health and be hospitalized more often than similar children in food-secure households.[22] Also, higher odds of "fair or poor" health correlated with higher food insecurity. Receipt of food stamps was found to attenuate the effects of food insecurity on this outcome, but did not eliminate it.

Child Food Insecurity Intensifies Adverse Effects of Household Food Insecurity

If households with children are categorized by the FSS as food insecure at the household level, this does not show specific evidence of *child* food insecurity *per se.* Typically, adult caregivers in food-insecure U.S. households ration food to spare children from suffering the feeling of hunger, although this often results in detrimental overall reductions in the quality and variety of foods available in the household.[23]

A C-SNAP study[24] found that out of 17,158 caregiver-child dyads interviewed over six years, 10 percent reported HFI only, and 12 percent reported household *and* child food insecurity (H&CFI), with child food insecurity measured by the CFSS (see Table 10.1). Compared with food-secure children, those with only HFI had significantly higher odds of fair or poor health and being hospitalized, while those with both H&CFI experienced even more extraordinary adverse effects (100 percent greater odds of fair or poor health and 23 percent higher odds of hospitalization respectively).

Food Stamp Program (FSP, recently renamed the Supplemental Nutrition Assistance Program or SNAP) participation modified the effects of food insecurity on child health status (odds of fair or poor health), reducing, but not eliminating, them. In these cases, children in HFI households had odds of experiencing fair or poor health 24 percent lower than those in similar non-FSP households, while children in H&CFI households had adjusted odds of experiencing fair or poor health 42 percent lower than those in non-FSP households.

These results, like previous ones, indicate the adverse effects of food insecurity worsen as its severity increases. They also suggest that food stamps, like a therapeutic drug prescribed in inadequate doses, appear to attenuate but not fully reverse this association.

Child Food Insecurity and Iron Deficiency

Iron deficiency, and iron deficiency anemia (IDA), are the most prevalent nutritional deficiencies in the United States and worldwide. Iron deficiency in early life has been linked to concurrent and persistent deficits in cognition, attention, and behavior even after treatment. There is a higher prevalence of IDA in children of high-risk subpopulations in the United States. One study found that joint or separate participation in the Special Supplemental Nutrition Program for Women, Infants, and Children (WIC) and FSP reduced the risk of iron deficiency.[25] The link between these child nutrition programs and iron deficiency confirms a recent study examining associations between food insecurity and IDA in children ages six months to three years.[26] Children in food-insecure households had adjusted odds of having IDA 140 percent greater than food secure children.[27]

Food Insecurity, Maternal Depression, and Child Health

Maternal depression can affect child development in a variety of ways, including reduced ability to provide needed care, impaired mother-child interaction and attachment, and child neglect and abuse.[28]

A recent study examined associations among mothers' positive depressive symptoms (PDS), food insecurity, and changes in benefits from federal assistance programs.[29] Out of 5,306 mother-child dyads, mothers with PDS had odds of reporting household food insecurity 169 percent greater, fair or poor child health 58 percent greater, and child hospitalizations 20 percent greater than mothers without PDS. In addition, mothers with PDS had odds of reporting decreased welfare support 52 percent greater and odds of reporting loss of food stamp benefits 56 percent greater than mothers without PDS.[30] These results suggest that maternal depression may be an indirect pathway by which household food insecurity exerts a negative influence on child health and development.

School-Age Children and Adolescence

The past decade's research has examined the influence of food insecurity on physical and mental health and academic, behavioral, and psychosocial functioning of preschool and school-age children. Using different measures, these studies find adverse effects of food insecurity on physical and mental health, academic performance, and behavioral and psychosocial problems in preschool and school-age children.

Examining associations between household food sufficiency and children's health, school performance, and psychosocial functioning, one study found food insufficiency associated with higher prevalence of fair or poor health and iron deficiency, and with greater likelihood of experiencing stomachaches, headaches, and colds in children one to five years old.[31] Another found that six- to eleven-year-old children in food-insufficient families had lower arithmetic scores, were more likely to have repeated a grade, to have seen a psychologist, and to have had more difficulty getting along with other children, than similar children whose families were food sufficient. This study also found teenagers from food-insufficient families more likely than food-sufficient peers to have seen a psychologist, been suspended from school, and had difficulty getting along with other children.[32] A third study showed that fifteen- to sixteen-year-olds from food-insufficient households were significantly more likely to have had dysthymia (a form of depression), thoughts of death, and a desire to die, and to have attempted suicide.[33]

Another set of studies examined associations between hunger and physical and mental health in school-age children. The first study found children under twelve years old categorized as hungry or at-risk of hunger were twice as likely as not-hungry children to be reported as having impaired functioning by either a parent or the child themselves. Teachers reported significantly higher levels of hyperactivity, absenteeism, and tardiness among children categorized as hungry or at-risk of hunger.[34]

A second study had parents of children ages six to twelve years complete a Pediatric Symptom Checklist (PSC). This study found children categorized as hungry by the Community Childhood Hunger Identification Project (CCHIP) scale more likely to have clinical levels of psychosocial dysfunction on the PSC than either at-risk or not-hungry children. Analysis of individual items from the PSC found most behavioral, emotional, and academic problems more prevalent in hungry children, and that aggression and anxiety had the strongest degree of association with hunger.[35]

The third study found that severe hunger was a significant predictor of chronic illness among both preschool-age and school-age children, and significantly associated with internalizing behavior problems, while moderate hunger was a significant predictor of health conditions in preschool children. Severe hunger was associated with higher reported anxiety and depression among school-age children.[36]

Finally, some studies examined associations of food insecurity with health, growth, and development after the first three years of life. A recent study from the Early Childhood Longitudinal Study (ECLS) included data from the kindergarten and third-grade administrations in a longitudinal assessment of how food insecurity over time is related to changes in reading and mathematics test performance, weight and body mass index (BMI), and social skills in children.[37] This longitudinal study found food insecurity in kindergarten associated with lower mathematics scores, increased BMI and weight gain, and lower social skills in girls at third grade, but not in boys. The authors found that children from persistently food-insecure households (food insecure at both kindergarten and third grade) had greater gains in BMI and weight than children in persistently food-secure households, although these effects were only significant for girls in stratified analysis. Also among girls, but not boys, persistent food insecurity was associated with smaller increases in reading scores over the period than for persistently food-secure girls.[38]

For households that transitioned from food security to food insecurity between kindergarten and third grade (i.e., became food insecure), dynamic models showed that the transition was associated with significantly smaller increases in reading scores for both boys and girls compared with children from households remaining food secure between kindergarten and third grade. For children transitioning from food insecurity to food security (i.e., becoming food secure), the transition was associated with larger increases in social skills scores for girls, but not for boys. Similarly, in difference models when children from households that became food insecure were compared with children who became food secure, becoming food insecure was associated with smaller increases in reading scores for both boys and girls, although they were significant only for girls.[39]

In gender-stratified difference models examining BMI, weight, and social skills, becoming food insecure was associated with significantly greater weight and BMI gains for boys, but not for girls. Becoming food insecure was also associated with greater declines in social skills scores for girls, but not for boys.[40]

These results provide the strongest empirical evidence to date that food insecurity is linked to developmental consequences for girls and boys, although these consequences are not identical across gender groups. Particularly strong associations are found between food insecurity and impaired social skills development, reading performance, and increased BMI and weight gain for girls. The effects on BMI and weight gain, however, appear to differ depending on whether the girls are persistently food insecure or their status changes over time. Food insecurity in the early elementary years thus has developmental consequences that may be both nutritional and nonnutritional.[41]

CONCLUSION

Taken together, the studies summarized in this chapter offer solid evidence that food insecurity is associated with a range of adverse health, growth, and development outcomes in children from birth to eighteen years old, although these relationships are complex and vary from study to study. Age, ethnicity, gender, and other factors all contribute to this variability.

Food insecurity, even at the least severe household levels, is a highly prevalent risk to growth, health, cognitive, and behavioral potential in America's poor and near-poor children. Threshold levels of severity for adverse effects of food insecurity on health and development in young children occur before the appearance of readily identifiable clinical markers, such as being underweight. Research indicates that the effects of food insecurity worsen as its severity worsens, and that child food insecurity and hunger are associated with more severe consequences than household food insecurity alone. Even at the lowest levels of severity, however, data suggest that, for babies, household food insecurity is an established risk factor for health and development. This leads to the troubling conclusion that for infants and toddlers food insecurity is an "invisible epidemic" of a widely prevalent and serious condition known to pose serious risks to child health and development. Although the remedy to this food insecurity is well understood and cost effective, it is being withheld from those at greatest risk.

Food insecurity can occur and inflict harm at any or all phases of the life cycle. However, the particular vulnerability of infants and toddlers from birth to three years who are undergoing especially rapid physical growth and neurocognitive development provides a special opportunity for protecting and positively influencing the remainder of the life cycle. Moreover, the apparent heightened susceptibility of older girls to the negative impacts of food insecurity in multiple domains suggests that it is particularly urgent to decrease this risk among those who will become mothers of the next generation of children.

Of the many interlocking forms of deprivation experienced by poor and near-poor children in the United States, food insecurity is one of the most readily measured as well as one of the most rapidly remediable by policy changes. The United States, unlike many other nations, is clearly capable of producing and distributing sufficient healthful food to all its inhabitants, constrained only by political will.

NOTES

1. A. H. Maslow, *Motivation and Personality*, 2nd ed. (New York: Harper & Row, 1970).

2. M. Nord, M. Andrews, and S. Carlson, *Measuring Food Security in the United States: Household Food Security in the United States, 2007* (Economic Research Report No. 66, USDA Economic Research Service, Washington, DC, November 2008), http://www.ers.usda.gov/publications/err66/ (accessed December 6, 2008).

3. S. A. Anderson, ed., "Core Indicators of Nutritional State for Difficult-to-Sample Populations," *Journal of Nutrition* 120, no. 11S (1990): 1557–1600.

4. Ibid.

5. Nord, Andrews, and Carlson, *Measuring Food Security in the United States: Household Food Security in the United States, 2007*; S. A. Anderson, ed., "Core Indicators of Nutritional State for Difficult-to-Sample Populations" 1557–1600; W. L. Hamilton et al., "Household Food Security in the United States in 1995: Technical Report," (Alexandria, VA: prepared by Abt Associates, Inc., for U.S. Department of Agriculture, Food and Consumer Service, 1997); G. W. Bickel, M. S. Andrews, and B. W. Klein, "Measuring Food Security in the United States: A Supplement to the CPS," in *Nutrition and Food Security in the Food Stamp Program*, ed. D. Hall and M. Stavrianos (Alexandria, VA: U.S. Department of Agriculture, Food and Consumer Service, 1996).

6. S. A. Anderson, ed., "Core Indicators of Nutritional State for Difficult-to-Sample Populations."

7. W. L. Hamilton et al., "Household Food Security in the United States in 1995: Technical Report"; Bickel, Andrews, and Klein, "Measuring Food Security in the United States: A Supplement to the CPS."

8. Nord, Andrews, and Carlson, *Measuring Food Security in the United States: Household Food Security in the United States, 2007*; W. L. Hamilton et al., "Household Food Security in the United States in 1995: Technical Report."

9. Nord, Andrews, and Carlson, *Measuring Food Security*.

10. M. Nord and H. Hopwood, "Recent Advances Provide Improved Tools for Measuring Children's Food Security," *Journal of Nutrition* 137 (2007): 533–36.

11. Ibid.

12. Bickel, Andrews, and Klein, "Measuring Food Security in the United States: A Supplement to the CPS."

13. U.S. Census Bureau, "How the Census Bureau Measures Poverty—Official Measures," http://www.census.gov/hhes/www/poverty/povdef.html#1 (accessed June 25, 2007).

14. U.S. Census Bureau, "Poverty Thresholds," http://www.census.gov/hhes/www/poverty/threshld.html (accessed June 25, 2007.)

15. Constance F. Citro and Robert T. Michael, eds., *Measuring Poverty: A New Approach* (Washington, D.C., National Academy Press, 1995).

16. Women's Educational and Industrial Union, *Defining Success in the New Economy: Self-Sufficiency as a Benchmark for Workforce Programs* (Boston, MA: prepared for the Commonwealth Corporation, 2001).

17. C. DeNavas-Walt, B. D. Proctor, and J. C. Smith, *Income, Poverty and Health Insurance Coverage in the United States: 2007*, U.S. Census Bureau, Current Population Reports, P60-235 (Washington, DC: Government Printing Office, 2008).

18. Nord, Andrews, and Carlson, *Measuring Food Security in the United States: Household Food Security in the United States, 2007*.

19. J. T. Cook, *Child Food Insecurity in the United States: 2004–2006* (Chicago, IL: Feeding America–formerly America's Second Harvest, The Nation's Food Bank Network, 2008).

20. A. Drewnowski and S. E. Specter, "Poverty and Obesity: The Role of Energy Density and Energy Costs," *American Journal of Clinical Nutrition* 79 (2004): 6–16; W. H. Dietz, "Does Hunger Cause Obesity?" *Pediatrics* 95, no. 5 (1995): 766–767; C. M. Olson, "Nutrition and Health Outcomes Associated with Food Insecurity and Hunger," *Journal of Nutrition* 129 (1999): 521S–524S; M. S. Townsend et al., "Food Insecurity is Positively Related to Overweight in Women," *Journal of Nutrition* 131 (2001): 1738–45; E. J. Adams, L. Grummer-Strawn, and G. Chavez, "Food Insecurity is Associated with Increased Risk of Obesity in California Women," *Journal of Nutrition* 133 (2003): 1070–74.

21. G. Bickel et al., *Measuring Food Security in the United States: Guide To Measuring Household Food Security*, rev. ed. (Alexandria, VA: USDA, Food and Nutrition Service, Office of Analysis, 2000); F. P. Glascoe, *Collaborating with Parents: Using Parents' Evaluation of Developmental Status to Detect and Address Developmental and Behavioral Problems* (Nashville, TN: Ellsworth and Vandermeer Press, Ltd., 1998).

22. J. T. Cook et al., "Food Insecurity Is Associated With Adverse Health Outcomes Among Human Infants and Toddlers," *Journal of Nutrition* 134, no. 6 (2004): 1432–38.

23. S. A. Anderson, ed., "Core Indicators of Nutritional State for Difficult-to-Sample Populations"; DeNavas-Walt, Proctor, and Smith, *Income, Poverty and Health Insurance Coverage in the United States: 2007*; U.S. Census Bureau, *Current Population Reports*, P60–235 (Washington, DC: Government Printing Office, 2008); J. T. Cook, *Child Food Insecurity in the United States: 2004–2006* (Chicago, IL: Feeding America–formerly America's Second Harvest, The Nation's Food Bank Network, 2008); A. Drewnowski and S. E. Specter, "Poverty and Obesity: The Role of Energy Density and Energy Costs," *American Journal of Clinical Nutrition* 79 (2004): 6–16; W. H. Dietz, "Does Hunger Cause Obesity?" *Pediatrics* 95, no. 5 (1995): 766–67; C. M. Olson, "Nutrition and Health Outcomes Associated with Food Insecurity and Hunger," *Journal of Nutrition* 129 (1999): 521S–524S.

24. J. T. Cook et al., "Child Food Insecurity Increases Risks Posed by Household Food Insecurity to Young Children's Health," *Journal of Nutrition* 136 (2006): 1073–76.

25. B. J. Lee, L. Mackey-Bilaver, and M. Chin, *Effects of WIC and Food Stamp Program Participation on Child Outcomes* (Contractor and Cooperator Report No. 27, USDA Economic Research Service, Washington, DC, December 2006).

26. A. Skalicky, A. F. Meyers, W. G. Adams, Z. Yang, J. T. Cook, and D. A. Frank, "Child Food Insecurity and Iron Deficiency Anemia in Low-Income Infants and Toddlers in the United States", *Maternal and Child Health Journal* 10, No. 2 (March 2006).

27. Ibid.

28. M. C. Lovejoy et al., "Maternal Depression and Parenting: A Meta-Analytic Review," *Clinical Psychology Review* 20, no. 5 (2000): 561–92.

29. P. Casey et al., "Children's Sentinel Nutritional Assessment Program Study Group: Maternal Depression, Changing Public Assistance, Food Security, and Child Health Status," *Pediatrics* 113, no. 2 (2004): 298–304.

30. Ibid.

31. K. Alaimo et al., "Food Insufficiency, Family Income, and Health in U.S. Preschool and School-Aged Children," *American Journal of Public Health* 91, no. 5 (2001): 781–86.

32. K. Alaimo, C. M. Olson, and E. A. Frongillo Jr., "Food Insufficiency and American School-Aged Children's Cognitive, Academic, and Psychosocial Development," *Pediatrics* 108, no. 1 (2001): 44–53.

33. K. Alaimo, C. M. Olson, and E. A. Frongillo Jr., "Family Food Insufficiency, but Not Low Family Income, Is Positively Associated with Dysthymia and Suicide Symptoms in Adolescents," *Journal of Nutrition* 132, no. 4 (2002): 719–25.

34. J. M. Murphy et al., "Relationship Between Hunger and Psychosocial Functioning in Low-Income American Children," *Journal of the American Academy of Child & Adolescent Psychiatry* 37, no. 2 (1998): 163–70.

35. R. E. Kleinman et al., "Hunger in Children in the United States: Potential Behavioral and Emotional Correlates," *Pediatrics* 101, no. 1 (1998): E3.

36. L. Weinreb et al., "Hunger: Its Impact on Children's Health and Mental Health," *Pediatrics* 110, no. 4 (2002): E41.

37. D. F. Jyoti, E. A. Frongillo, and S. J. Jones, "Food Insecurity Affects School Children's Academic Performance, Weight Gain, and Social Skills," *Journal of Nutrition* 135 (2005): 2831–39.

38. Ibid.

39. Ibid.

40. Ibid.

41. Ibid.

RESOURCE GUIDE

Suggested Reading

Cook, J. T. et al. "Food Insecurity Is Associated with Adverse Health Outcomes among Human Infants and Toddlers." *Journal of Nutrition* 134, no. 6 (2004): 1432–38.

Jyoti, D. F., E. A. Frongillo, and S. J. Jones. "Food Insecurity Affects School Children's Academic Performance, Weight Gain, and Social Skills." *Journal of Nutrition* 135 (2005): 2831–39.

Web Site

Children's HealthWatch, http://www.childrenshealthwatch.org/.

11

Food Security in Developing Countries

John M. Staatz, Duncan H. Boughton, and Cynthia Donovan

The term "food security" is like a blank screen. Each author seems to project her own meaning on the term, despite the efforts of such organizations as the Food and Agriculture Organization of the United Nations (FAO) and the U.S. Department of Agriculture (USDA) to develop standard definitions. For some, food security means national or local food self-sufficiency—an argument to protect local farmers against outside competition and an argument against production of cash-crops for export; for others, it is equated with emergency famine relief. With its multitude of meanings, "food security" is invoked to justify all sorts of actions, some of which are detrimental to the well-being of the hungry.

The purposes of this chapter are to provide a systematic definition of food security, focusing on its different dimensions; examine the nature and magnitude of the different dimensions of food insecurity in developing countries; discuss the difficult trade-offs that policymakers face in trying to address food security's multiple dimensions simultaneously; and explore promising new approaches to address food insecurity. The geographic focus is on Sub-Saharan Africa and South Asia, where the majority of the world's food-insecure people live.

DEFINING FOOD SECURITY

The FAO defines food security as follows: "Food security exists when all people, at all times, have access to sufficient, safe and nutritious food to meet their dietary needs and food preferences for an active and healthy life." Definitions used by the USDA, the World Bank, and the U.S. Agency for International Development are similar.[1] This definition, while seemingly straightforward, has several important implications.

The authors acknowledge with gratitude the financial support of the United States Agency for International Development, Bureau of Economic Growth, Agriculture and Trade, through the Food Security III Cooperative Agreement (award number GDG-A-0-02-0000021-00) with Michigan State University. The view expressed are solely those of the authors.

Access and Availability

First, food security requires that all people have *access* to sufficient food. Having access to food requires that the food be available, but availability does not guarantee access. Thus, a focus on trying to ensure food security simply through increasing food production is incomplete at best, and in some circumstances, actually can worsen access to food by pricing the poor out of the market if local production takes place at high cost.

Access involves having both *physical access* to a place where food is available and *economic access*—that is, having a socially legitimate claim to that food—what Amartya Sen calls an "entitlement to food."[2] This entitlement can come about through owning the food a person has produced himself, having the purchasing power to buy it in the market, or having some other recognized claim to the food, such as being a family member entitled to a share of household resources or being included in a relief agency's list of those qualifying for food aid.

Sen notes that at a most fundamental level, people are hungry because they do not own enough food; thus, to understand hunger, one needs to study the structure of ownership in society.[3] Food security in a given locale is thus inextricably linked to the fundamental rules of that society—everything from land tenure to gender roles to where international borders are drawn. The food insecure are hungry ultimately not because their villages or countries produce too little food, but because the hungry do not own enough rights in society to command that an adequate diet be produced (either through their own efforts or those of others) and ceded to them. In this fundamental sense, food insecurity is a question of poverty.

For the majority of the people in the world, including the majority in low-income countries, access to food comes at least partially through the market—through having the income necessary to purchase an adequate diet rather than produce it entirely oneself.[4] Having sufficient income to purchase an adequate diet depends not only on the amount of money one earns but also on the price of food. Here is where the *availability* and the *access* dimensions of food security become inextricably linked. Availability reflects the supply side of the food security equation, while access reflects effective demand, with *food prices* linking the two sides of the equation.[5] In low-income countries, where the poor may spend up to 70 percent of their cash incomes on food, the price of food determines in large part the poor's real income (i.e., what goods they can obtain with their earnings) as well as wage rates for unskilled labor, and thus nonfarm employment opportunities.

The price of food, in turn, depends on the *cost* at which the food can be made available, either through local production, commercial imports, or aid. It is the cost of food to the consumer relative to her income, not the physical availability per se, that is crucial in determining food security. Mountains of high-priced food do little to help the poor who have no claim on that food. For example, the Bangladesh famine of 1974, in which between twenty-six thousand and one hundred thousand people perished, occurred in a year in which food grain availability per capita actually was higher than it had been in any of the preceding three "normal" years. The famine was triggered by floods that destroyed the earning opportunities of landless rural workers, so that even though food was available, it was too "expensive" relative to their very low incomes.[6]

The real cost of food to consumers depends not only on farm-level productivity (which determines farm-level cost of production), but also on productivity throughout the *food system*—the set of activities that runs from "seed to table," including agricultural input markets, assembly markets, processing, wholesaling, and retailing. Frequently, in poor countries, postharvest operations account for more than 50 percent of the cost to the consumer of even relatively unprocessed products, such as grains, particularly in Sub-Saharan Africa, where transport costs are high. *Productivity* is the key concept here rather than *production*. Productivity refers to the efficiency with which resources (e.g., farm labor, fertilizer, and seeds) are converted to desired outputs (e.g., food). Production simply refers to the level of output, which can be raised in many ways. Some ways can be costly, such as the heavy use of subsidies; these drain resources from other productive uses in society, for example, the financing of health care, agricultural research, and expanded education, many of which are critical inputs to long-term food security. Thus, initiatives that simply seek to increase food production with little regard to improving the productivity of the food system ultimately contribute little if anything to food security.

Because the food system is a major employer of the poor in South Asia and Sub-Saharan Africa (either as farmers, farm laborers, or in marketing and processing activities), increasing productivity of this system (an aspect of "food availability") is linked in another important way to food access. Increasing productivity in the food system increases incomes of these workers, improving their ability to access food through the market. Broad-based growth of agriculture and the rest of the food system is thus critical to improving food security, but its impact on raising the incomes of the food insecure is at least as important as its impact on increasing local food availability.

Utilization

The FAO definition of food security speaks of "sufficient, safe and nutritious food for an active and healthy life." An active and healthy life requires, at the cellular level, that the person's body be able to extract and use the nutrients in the food consumed. Thus, how the food is prepared (which affects its nutritional value) and the state of health of an individual (which affects the body's ability to absorb and use the nutrients) affect food security. Diarrhea, intestinal parasites, and a host of diseases can compromise the body's ability to benefit from the food ingested.[7] Efforts to provide safe drinking water; control, treat, and prevent disease (e.g., through vaccinations and oral rehydration therapy); and offer improved nutrition education all contribute to food security through improving food utilization, and, in some cases, may contribute more to food security than increasing local food production.

Transitory versus Chronic Food Insecurity

People become food insecure when the availability of food, their access to it, or their ability to utilize it are disrupted, either on a transitory or a chronic basis. For example, hurricanes or wars can wipe out crops, livestock, and roads, temporarily disrupting both food availability and access, leading to transitory food insecurity. The most extreme example of transitory food insecurity is *famine*, in which thousands or millions of people are pushed to starvation by such disruptions. Given the great improvements in emergency relief procedures in the second half of the twentieth century, no major famines since the late 1970s have been caused by natural disasters, such as droughts, alone. All the major famines since the 1980s have had human disruptions, typically war and civil strife, as major contributors.

Famine is the most visible manifestation of food insecurity. As real and as painful as images of famine are, however, it represents just the tip of the iceberg of food insecurity. In a given year, famine may affect a few million people worldwide. Yet *chronic* food insecurity, reflecting long-term inadequate access to food and the ability to utilize it (due to poor health) affects nearly one billion people per year.[8] This chronic food insecurity is a silent killer that increases morbidity and mortality (especially among children), saps the energy of large elements of the population, reduces the cognitive ability of malnourished children, and slows economic growth. Its root causes are poverty (which results in inadequate access to food), slow productivity growth throughout the food system (which affects both the real cost of food to consumers and the incomes of those working in the food system), and poor health and nutritional knowledge (which affect the body's ability to utilize the food consumed). Addressing the problem of chronic food security represents one of the most important yet stubborn challenges of the twenty-first century.

Just as food access and food availability are linked and cannot be analyzed independently, so too are transitory and chronic food insecurity. *Coping strategies* provide the conceptual link between the two. As poor households attempt to cope with transitory food insecurity, they frequently sell off assets (farm equipment, draft animals, and in the extreme, their seed for next year's planting), compromising their ability to produce food or income in subsequent periods, plunging them into chronic food insecurity. Such a transition is referred to as a *poverty trap*.[9] One of the challenges in responding to acute food insecurity crises, particularly when relief responses are limited, is how to target relief to those households that absent assistance are most likely to fall into such poverty traps.

Magnitude and Location of Food Insecurity in the World

The FAO estimates that as of early 2009, 963 million people suffered from undernourishment, which it defines as chronic hunger.[10] While the number of undernourished in the world grew by eighty million between 1990–1992 and 2008, the percentage of the population in developing countries suffering from undernourishment fell steadily from 1990–1992 through 2006, from 20 to 16 percent, reflecting impressive progress in poverty reduction in Asia over the period, particularly in China and India. During the period 1997–2006, the rate of undernourishment fell by more than 3 percent per year in East Asia and by 1.7 percent in South Asia.[11] But the global incidence of undernourishment, or chronic food insecurity, reversed its long-term decline in 2007–2008, as the worldwide food price increases reduced the poor's economic access to food.

As shown in Table 11.1, South Asia is home to the largest number of the food insecure (314 million in 2003–2005; 21 percent of the region's population), but Sub-Saharan Africa has the largest incidence of undernourishment (30 percent of the population, for a total of 212 million people). Sub-Saharan Africa remains the part of the world where food insecurity seems most intractable, as evidenced by high, and in some cases increasing, rates of undernourishment. These high rates are

Table 11.1.
Prevalence of Undernourishment in the World, 2003–2005

Region	Total Population (millions)	Undernourished Population (millions)	Percent of Total Malnourished
World	6,406.0	848.0	13
Developing Countries	5,141.0	832.2	16
Asia and the Pacific	3,478.6	541.9	16
East Asia	1,930.6	218.7	11
China	1,312.4	122.7	9
Southeast Asia	544.5	86.9	16
South Asia	1,468.4	313.6	21
India	1,117.0	230.5	21
Latin America and Caribbean	544.2	45.2	8
Near East and North Africa	420.0	33.0	8
Sub-Saharan Africa	698.6	212.1	30
Central Africa	93.1	53.3	57
East Africa	242.4	86.0	35
Southern Africa	99.2	36.8	37
West Africa	263.7	36.0	14

Source: Food and Agriculture Organization of the United Nations, *The State of Food Insecurity in the World 2008* (Rome: FAO, 2008), 48–49.

frequently associated with disruption of the food system and collapse of incomes caused by current or recent wars (e.g., the rate of undernourishment in 2003–2005 was 76 percent in the Democratic Republic of the Congo and 68 percent in Eritrea). Yet even in Africa, as shown in Table 11.1, the rates are highly variable by region, with the countries of West Africa that were not involved in civil strife generally having the subcontinent's lowest rates of chronic food insecurity.

Ironically, even though food in developing countries is overwhelmingly produced in rural areas, a disproportionate share of the food insecure live in these areas, where incomes, and hence economic access to food, are much lower than in urban areas.[12] Yet with rapid urbanization in most developing countries, urban food insecurity is a growing problem. A common feature of many of the food insecure in both urban and rural areas is their reliance on markets to obtain most of their food. While the urban poor's reliance on food markets is widely recognized, it is less well known that the majority of the rural food insecure, including not only the landless but frequently the majority of small farmers, are net buyers of basic staples.[13] Thus, improving the efficiency of both urban *and* rural food markets to drive down the real cost of food to poor consumers needs to be a central element of any strategy to reduce chronic food insecurity.

Approaches to Improving Food Security

Given the broad definition of food security, covering food availability, access, and utilization, it is not surprising that a wide range of projects and programs claim to improve either transitory or chronic food security. Efforts aimed at dealing with transitory food insecurity have focused on all three dimensions of food insecurity: availability (e.g., through the creation of food reserve stocks), access (e.g., through distribution of emergency rations), and utilization (e.g., through distribution of oral rehydration kits to control diarrhea). Efforts to reduce chronic food insecurity have focused mainly on improving food availability. These efforts have included (1) development of improved agricultural technologies through conventional and transgenic plant and animal breeding and better farm equipment; (2) improved postharvest handling, processing, and marketing technologies; (3) expansion of the quantity and quality of farmland available, including expansion of irrigation; and (4) access to agricultural inputs such as fertilizers and improved seeds.

On a global level, increases in agricultural productivity are essential to allow food availability to grow apace with demand, which is driven by population growth, higher incomes, and increasing demands for nonfood uses of the products (e.g., biofuels). Yet on a country and local level, a single-minded focus on the availability side of food security may be counterproductive for three reasons: (1) local food self-sufficiency may be a costly way of achieving food security, (2) the *pattern* of resource use to achieve agricultural growth is at least equally important for improving food security as the *rate* of agricultural growth, and (3) some efforts to expand food availability through increased production may hurt food utilization.

Self-Sufficiency as a Costly Path to Food Security

Self-sufficiency refers to producing most or all of the food one consumes oneself—at the household, national, or regional level. Advocates of a "food first" approach[14] argue that food-insecure countries should give first priority to producing staple foods for their own populations and eschew production of export crops, which is seen as using the resources of the poor to feed rich overseas consumers (or fill the fuel tanks of the rich with biofuels). The shortcoming of this approach is that it focuses only on the impact of agricultural production on food *availability* and ignores economic access to that food. *If* the poor can participate in a remunerative way in the production of export commodities (either through producing the products themselves, as is the case in smallholder cocoa and coffee production in West Africa; or through employment elsewhere in the value chain), and *if* staple food markets work well, the poor may be able to assure themselves much greater access to food by participating in the export production and using their earnings to buy food produced by others (e.g., rice farmers in Vietnam). A self-sufficiency approach foregoes the potential gains from comparative advantage and trade, which historically have been major factors in improving the welfare of the poor in much of the world.[15] However, lack of access by the poor to remunerative participation in export production (e.g., due to insecure land tenure, highly stringent grades and standards, and weak labor laws) and poorly functioning international and local food markets can undermine these potential gains from a trade-based approach to food security. For example, export restrictions imposed by many Asian and African food-exporting countries during the food crisis of 2007–2008 led many countries to move away from trade-based approaches to food security, seeking instead either to increase their food self-sufficiency or to acquire access to overseas land where they could produce food to export to their own countries.[16] These developments highlight the need for international agreements aimed at ensuring reliable, open international markets for food if countries are to avoid costly second-best approaches to ensuring food security.

The Pattern of Agricultural Growth

Efforts to expand agricultural production through large-scale mechanized farming in low-income areas of Asia and Sub-Saharan Africa fall into the same trap as the Food First approaches—they focus solely on increasing food availability, with little attention to whether the projects generate the broad-based income growth essential to improving the poor's access to food. Frequently, such large-scale approaches use capital-intensive, labor-saving equipment such as large tractors and combines that are economically efficient in high-income countries where labor is expensive and capital is relatively cheap but that are not efficient in the low-wage economies of South Asia and Sub-Saharan Africa. Few such projects for the production of staple foods have been sustainable in these areas without substantial subsidies.[17] Moreover, such approaches, by concentrating the returns to farming in a few hands of large landowners, fail to generate the broad-based mass of purchasing power necessary for sustained growth of both agricultural and nonagricultural incomes that are at the core of ensuring improved access to food.[18]

Potential Conflicts between Agricultural Expansion and Other Contributors to Food Security

Poorly designed efforts to expand agricultural production can lead to unintended negative effects on food security by compromising food utilization. For example, expanded agricultural production may increase demands on women's time for agricultural tasks, which can lead mothers to devote less time to child care (resulting in poorer child health). Irrigation schemes may result in more standing water and consequently growing populations of disease vectors, such as mosquitoes and schistosomiasis-bearing snails, and agricultural workers may face greater exposure to pesticides. In each case, the resulting poorer health can lead to poorer food utilization and hence greater malnutrition. The solution is not to eschew agricultural growth, but to recognize that food security is determined by factors broader than just agricultural production; consequently, efforts to expand agricultural production need to consider these other factors.

These considerations notwithstanding, increasing broad-based agricultural production *is* critical to improving long-term food security in most low-income countries, not only to increase food availability, but also to increase incomes of the poor (both in agriculture and related nonagricultural enterprises) in order to increase their economic access to food and to provide the economic growth necessary to finance the education and health services critical to improving food utilization.[19] The central challenge is to do so in a way that fosters improved food access, availability, and utilization in the long run and is consistent with responding to short-run crises of food insecurity.

The Central Challenge: Designing Approaches That Simultaneously Address Transitory and Chronic Food Insecurity

The central challenge in dealing with food insecurity is to design approaches that deal with short-term (transitory) food crises in ways that do not undermine the long-term productivity growth that is critical to overcoming chronic food insecurity. Many traditional ways of dealing with food crises, such as distribution of emergency food aid, imposition of price controls, and bans on food exports, depress food prices and thereby undermine incentives for farmers, traders, and processors to invest in the types of productivity-enhancing innovations critical to reducing chronic food insecurity. The challenge arises because of what Timmer, Falcon, and Pearson have termed the *food price dilemma*.[20] The dilemma arises because food prices play a dual role in the economy: they create incentives for farmers, traders, and processors to invest in productivity-enhancing innovations in the food system (the higher the prices, the greater the incentive); and they are major determinants of the real income of the poor, and hence their access to food (the lower the prices, the greater the access). This dual role of food prices makes "getting prices right" to promote food security a complex task, as one needs to ask "right for whom and over what time period?"

The long-term solution to the food price dilemma is increased productivity throughout the food system, which allows food to be produced and delivered to consumers at lower real prices (by lowering costs), while maintaining sufficient profitability in the system to induce ongoing private investment. The problem is that in the short run, many people still face food insecurity, and their coping strategies may lead them to disinvest (sell off or eat their assets, such as livestock), which undermines productivity growth. Thus, efforts to spur productivity growth over the longer term must be accompanied by shorter-term measures to protect those most vulnerable to both transitory and chronic food insecurity. Timmer, Falcon, and Pearson's recommended solution for transitory food insecurity is *targeted* food subsidies to the poor. The notion of targeting is crucial because the cost to a country of generalized subsidies (either explicit budgetary subsidies to reduce the price of food, or implicit subsidies, such as those that result from price controls) is high. The cost is high in terms of budgetary outlays or in terms of the opportunity cost of resources that could be used either to increase productivity in the food system or invest in other activities, such as improved health systems or nutrition-education programs. Ideally, what one seeks are targeted subsidies that actually enhance rather than discourage the long-term investments necessary to improve productivity throughout the food system. Examples include food-for-work programs that build infrastructure that reduces marketing costs for food, and child feeding programs that keep children in school, thereby expanding investment in the human capital needed to spur broad-based income growth. Targeting such assistance is difficult, however, in economies characterized by pervasive poverty and where the administrative capacity to identify "the deserving poor" from the "undeserving" is weak. We now turn to operational approaches to address the food-price dilemma, focusing on ways to increase productivity in the food system and reduce transitory food insecurity in ways that are mutually reinforcing.

WAYS FORWARD: OPERATIONAL APPROACHES

Improving Food System Productivity

Increases in productivity of the food system require increases in productivity on the farm (as well as off the farm so that agricultural inputs can reach the farm) and require farm produce be delivered to consumers more cheaply. Increases in the productivity of food systems require capital investments. And given two decades of underinvestment in agriculture in food-insecure countries, there is a lot of catching up to do.[21] Bonnen identifies four types of capital necessary for rural development: physical, biological, human, and institutional. The mix of these types of capital will vary over time and space according to the natural and economic endowments of a particular food system, but all four types of capital must be engaged.[22]

Physical capital investments lower the cost of food by increasing the productivity of labor and management in both the on- and off-farm parts of the food system. Massive investments in irrigation were the foundation of Asia's Green Revolution. With water control established, modern varieties could express their full yield potential with little risk of crop failure. The higher financial profitability of irrigated production led to a second round of investments in equipment, such as mechanical threshers and power tillers. Physical capital investments also took place off the farm, in primary and secondary road networks, and crop storage and marketing facilities. While capital investments like irrigation may contribute to reducing food insecurity, they are not a panacea. They are costly investments and require high levels of management and expensive maintenance, and water is also becoming an increasingly scarce resource. For example, only 3.5 percent of Sub-Saharan Africa's arable land is irrigated, less than a fourth that of India in 1961, at the dawn of its Green Revolution. Increasing the percentage of irrigated land up to the level India had in 1960 would cost approximately US$114 billion, more than fifty-five times the annual official development assistance allocated to African agricultural development in the early 2000s.[23]

Biological capital refers to ecosystem resources, such as soil, plant life, forests, aquifers, and wildlife, as well as investments in genetic modification to increase the biological and economic productivity of plants and animals. The importance of biological capital is receiving greater attention because of concerns about loss of biodiversity, as well as the potential to earn income through trading carbon credits. In many food insecure countries, particularly in Africa, soil biological capital has become severely degraded.[24] The increased real cost of chemical fertilizers makes investment in improved, biologically sustainable production systems— together with conservation farming techniques that make better use of limited rainfall—a high priority. Genetically modified organisms (GMOs), often painted as a threat to biodiversity in industrial countries where they were developed to tolerate specific herbicides or resist pests, may have a key role to play in achieving food security in the future. Examples of GMOs include varieties of drought-resistant corn, parasitic weed-resistant sorghum, vitamin A–enriched rice and cassava, aflatoxin-resistant peanuts, and insect-resistant pulses.

Human capital investment is essential for increased productivity on the farm, for diversification into nonfarm income sources, and for making the transition to full-time employment in nonagricultural sectors.[25] Human capital investment involves, primarily, education and improved health. Indeed, the effectiveness of investment in education requires complementary investments in health and nutrition. On the farm, education in literacy and numeracy provides the foundation for learning about improved production and storage technologies. It also facilitates membership in farming organizations and the ability to use market information. Education is also correlated with the ability to diversify into nonfarm activities that use off-season labor.[26] Nonfarm activities both increase total households income and provide an important shock absorber when farm income is reduced by climatic or disease problems. Education is essential to the transition from employment in the agricultural to nonagricultural sectors, which often is accompanied by migration from rural to urban areas. When migration takes place without adequate investment in education, the result can simply be a transfer of rural food insecurity to urban food insecurity, and even greater levels of political instability.

Institutional capital is the "invisible hand" that enables markets to work. Institutions define ownership of resources and the rules by which they can be exchanged. In addition to laws concerning property rights, and the mechanisms to enforce them, a broad range of institutional "software" is needed to enable food systems to function effectively, such as food policies (including trade policy), grades and standards, rules governing commodity exchanges, biosafety frameworks for the development and testing of GMOs, and agricultural statistics and market information systems. The creation and maintenance of this economic software is costly, involving investments such as the development and retention of trained researchers and analysts, and investment in land-titling programs to enable assets to be used as collateral. An important subset of institutions relates to the management of production and exchange risks at different levels of the food system—household, community, national, and global.

While the specific mix and form of each type of capital will vary, all are needed to achieve improvements in food security. Two key issues for development policy are (1) who should be responsible for identifying and making the investments (public versus private versus community investments), and (2) what policy framework will best facilitate private investment? There is high degree of interdependence between public, private, and community investments in the four types of capital necessary for the promotion of food security over time. A particular challenge to policymakers is the high degree of heterogeneity in capital resource endowments within rural communities, as well as across communities (i.e., spatially). For example, the majority of smallholders in Africa are net buyers of food staples; and even among those with a surplus, the majority of sales come from just a small minority of households.[27] Thus, trade policy and marketing investments that lead to higher prices for sellers in a given location may hurt net buyers in the same location (even if net buyers somewhere else are better off as a result). Recognizing and understanding heterogeneity in resource endowments is essential to developing strategies and programs with the appropriate mix and form of capital investments to avoid "robbing Peter to pay Paul." Decentralized approaches to local food security planning, such as those adopted recently in Mali, where local communities develop their own priorities, which then guide public (including local) and nongovernmental organization (NGO) investments to improve food security, are one way to address such heterogeneity.[28]

Addressing Transitory Food Insecurity in a Way That Reduces Chronic Food Insecurity

When evaluating ways to address transitory food insecurity, a critical step is to seek solutions that address short-term food needs of the vulnerable and simultaneously support (or at least do not damage) long-term improvements in food security. Selecting food aid commodities and distribution systems that do not undermine local production incentives is one of the key decisions highlighted in the literature, but there are many other areas in which interventions to meet short-term needs actually can support long-term improvements.

Saving lives by improving transitory food security, especially during emergencies with the risk of famine, has been the focus of international organizations such as the United Nations World Food Programme (WFP), as well as nongovernmental organizations and national governments. While past emergency response efforts have not always been closely coordinated with long-term development programs, new approaches seek to meet immediate food needs while building assets and improving future prospects for achieving long-term food security, at individual, household, community, and market levels. These interventions may address food availability issues, such as improving agricultural production or lowering transport costs, or they may improve access by increasing incomes of food-insecure households.

Food-for-work and cash-for-work programs have been in use for decades, including during the Great Depression of the 1930s in the United States and during crises in India since the 1960s and in Bangladesh in 1975 and 2000–2001, helping to build infrastructure while providing income to impoverished workers. In these programs, participants receive much-needed income in the form of cash or food, while the roads built or forests planted contribute to long-term growth or sustainability for society as a whole. For success in meeting the short-term needs, there must be labor availability in the households with greatest need. For example, if the most food-insecure households are made up of the aged and infirm, such programs will not be effective in raising their incomes. Also, the program must be designed to attract those households with the greatest need and not draw labor from other productive activities. In food-for-work programs, the selection of foods used to pay the workers can mean the difference between households eating the food or selling the food to obtain other types of food, pay debts, or use the receipts in other ways.

Cash transfers, whether conditional (e.g., in exchange for sending children to school) or unconditional (given simply as payments to those deemed most food-insecure) are one type of intervention being used more frequently in recent years as an alternative to delivery of food aid directly to households. As with the food- and cash-for-work schemes, the design of the programs and the targeting aspects are essential to ensure that the needs of the food insecure can be met.

Unconditional cash transfers to food-insecure households or individuals are designed to help provide the means to purchase the food in local markets. As an alternative to free food distribution, this approach aims to (1) give the household greater choice in the type of food obtained and (2) rely on the private marketing system, rather than relief agencies, to deliver the food, thereby increasing incentives to local farmers and traders to invest in food production and distribution. Since cash is fungible, however, cash transfers enable households to make their own decisions on the use of the funds, whether for health needs, food, school fees, or other needs. Although some may see use of the money on nonfood items as a "leakage" of a food-security program, funds spent on health care, for example, may increase food security by improving food utilization. Although donors have expressed concern about how the funds will be used, program monitoring in several pilot schemes indicates that the fears of misuse by recipients (to buy alcohol or "luxury" items) may be exaggerated.[29]

Many safety-net programs use cash transfers, especially in urban environments where the markets for consumer staples are functioning and can respond to increased demand caused by the income transfer. Key to this intervention is the idea that the cash inflow will assist the household in retaining productive assets (including human health) that enable the household to survive and avoid falling into a poverty trap. Such programs are not, however, suitable for emergency situations in which markets have been severely disrupted and in which the injection of increased purchasing power by the poor will likely lead to increased food price inflation. In such situations (which are usually temporary), direct distribution of food is frequently more effective in addressing transitory food insecurity.

Conditional cash transfers are funds that are available to an individual or a household if specific actions are taken. For example, households may be given cash if their daughters attend school. The current income supplement encourages building the human capital of girls, which is known to bring about improvements in health and welfare over time in rural communities where girls are not attending school.[30] Another example is vouchers that have value when used for the purchase of seeds or other agricultural inputs. In this case, the transfer encourages agricultural investments that are designed to increase incomes within a cropping cycle, while also enabling farmers to select new technologies with less financial risk. In contrast to unconditional cash transfers, investment decisions resulting from conditional cash transfers are made by a third party that sets the conditions for the grant (e.g., a local government or an NGO), with a specific view on what will make a long-term difference while meeting the immediate food need.

Innovations on the food-availability (supply) side are currently being tested. With the encouragement of several donors, the WFP is increasingly purchasing food for aid distributions within the country or region of the distributions. For example, in 2001–2005, WFP purchased maize and beans in Mozambique to distribute within Mozambique to victims of flood and drought, as well as to chronically food-insecure populations. The three key goals with this approach are (1) to meet the food needs of vulnerable populations with locally appropriate foods; (2) to lower the costs of procurement and distribution of food aid by buying locally; and (3) to increase the producer incentives for production within the country to meet those needs now and in the future. Tschirley and del Castillo evaluated WFP local and regional purchase operations and found that the first and second objectives are usually met.[31] Additional research is needed to fully assess the third objective. Local and regional purchases work best when food shortages are localized or when food insecurity is primarily caused by low incomes (poor access). Purchasing relief supplies locally in the context of a widespread production shortfall can lead to further food price inflation.

Related to the local and regional purchase are the efforts to increase food staple stocks in rural areas, which can be achieved by improving on-farm storage, community grain banks, or market storage incentives. In Mozambique, community development funds have been used as seasonal stocking loans for private traders, such that maize, a major staple, can be sold by local farmers, and then those stocks are available for the local markets later in the year when farm stocks run low. Community cereal banks have been promoted based on the same idea, although management of such cereal banks frequently remains problematic.

Food-aid decision-makers may also look to commodity selection as a key supply-side consideration. Research in southern Africa has demonstrated that by distributing maize grain rather than flour, there is increased use of local small-scale maize milling facilities in rural and urban areas, providing a low-cost staple, which is an inferior good in economic terms, but more nutritious than industrially refined flours.[32] Thus, the self-targeting commodity (maize grain for whole-grain maize flour) is useful in developing local processing, while avoiding leakage of the product to nontarget populations. Local knowledge is needed to identify commodities that are self-targeting and least likely to cause problems for local producers and in local markets (e.g., rice with high percentage of broken grains, whole-grain maize meal, or cassava).

ROLES OF DIFFERENT ACTORS: WHO SHOULD DO WHAT?

We now turn to the issue of organizational roles (i.e., who does what) with regard to the implementation of food-security measures. Major factors affecting the success or failure of food security initiatives are (1) the degree of organizational capacity to undertake identified roles, and (2) the ability to coordinate among organizations over time, space, and levels of aggregation. We focus primarily on Sub-Saharan Africa (SSA) because of its very high incidence of food insecurity.

The World Food Summit of 1996 recognized that national governments have primary responsibility for ensuring the food security of their populations.[33] Indeed, the most severe food insecurity crises occur when national government fails or is overwhelmed. Governments are primarily responsible for providing the public goods to enable households to pursue food security through their economic activities. The most essential public goods are security of life and property and the rule of law. Governments are also responsible, in most cases, for ensuring the provision of investments, such as road and communication infrastructure, education, health services, crop and livestock pest and disease prevention, information services, and policy frameworks to govern resource use, markets, and trade (despite moves in recent years to support some of these services through user fees). The provision of public goods affecting food security is a complex proposition, involving multiple line ministries and multiple levels of government (local, regional, and national). The coordination challenge, even within government, let alone between government and other actors, is real and daunting.

SSA nations, in particular, have found it difficult to put in place effectively coordinated national food security strategies. A 2008 U.S. Government Accountability Office report on international food security noted that fewer than half of national poverty reduction strategies in SSA adequately articulate food security as a priority despite high rates of malnutrition, and that in 2006 only seventeen of forty-eight SSA countries provided a report to the FAO office responsible for monitoring the World Food Summit plan of action.[34] A recent review of government responses to food crises in southern and eastern Africa found that interventions in national and regional food markets further aggravated the situation.[35] As a consequence of the failure to make adequate, coordinated investments in food security, development assistance expenditure on food aid for African countries has risen dramatically over the last fifteen years, crowding out resources for investment in long-term food production growth.

To encourage African governments to take greater responsibility for agriculture and food security, the Africa Union (AU) endorsed in 2003 the Comprehensive African Agricultural Development Program (CAADP). CAADP encourages countries to adopt annual targets for agriculture's share of total public investment and agricultural growth of 10 percent and 6 percent, respectively, focusing on investment programs for land and water use, markets and agribusiness, food security, and agricultural technology. In 2008, the AU Ministers of Agriculture approved the Framework for African Food Security (FAFS), which provides guidance to countries on the development of national food security strategies and investment plans to improve food security risk management, increase food supply, improve dietary quality, and expand economic opportunities for vulnerable populations.

While African governments, as well as governments in some smaller, very poor Asian countries such as Laos People's Democratic Republic and Cambodia, are gradually taking more leadership for national food security policy, they clearly face major capacity constraints in terms of trained analytical capacity. As a result, functions that normally would be carried out by governments are often shared with (and in cases duplicated by) international donors and international NGOs and their local counterparts. As international prices for wheat and rice began to rise dramatically in early 2008, the WFP and FAO rapidly deployed country assessment teams in conjunction with country food-security thematic groups to assess the degree of vulnerability and response options. In some cases, the governments established their own response working groups, but without any regular consultation mechanism in place with the donor group. The role of international NGOs has expanded considerably over the past two decades from a primary focus on emergency food, medical, and disaster relief to include the delivery of a broad range of agricultural development services, including agricultural research, agricultural extension, seed multiplication and input delivery, and farmer association development. NGOs are facilitating the participation of smallholder farmers in commercial crop and livestock value chain development in partnership with private sector companies. Inevitably, the lines of responsibility between government, donors, and NGOs are blurred by government capacity constraints, and governments often find themselves in a catch-22 situation of being unable to compete with international organizations in recruitment and retention of qualified national personnel.

For the vast majority of countries that adopt a market-based approach to food security, the private sector is the locomotive, and well-functioning food markets need to serve as the first line of defense against food insecurity. The private sector involves a broad range of actors, including farmers, farm organizations, input suppliers, traders at many levels, food processors and preparers, transporters, and banks. The private sector needs the support of government to provide public goods such as infrastructure, as well as transparent regulatory frameworks that safeguard consumers and enable fair competition. It also needs the state to create "space" for civil society, including professional organizations for farmers and traders, which can undertake collective action to reduce transaction costs and lobby for policies to promote broad-based economic growth. Critical to effective coordination among government, the private sector, and civil society is trust, built on a foundation of understanding each other's roles and constraints. All too often that understanding is missing, with government (and sometimes NGOs) perceiving the private sector as exploitative of farmers or consumers, or trust breaks down because regulations become a means to rent-seeking or bribery. When governments try to take over some of the functions of the private sector in response to food crises, the private sector can become "paralyzed" and the crisis becomes worse.[36] Market information systems can provide a valuable communication bridge between the government and private sectors, and provide both with information needed to undertake their respective roles. Unfortunately, the rapid rise of prices on international markets in 2008, accompanied by temporary export bans, has undermined many governments' confidence in the role of markets to achieve food security. Restoring that confidence will require careful analysis of international food market risks and risk management tools, as well as upgrading national market information systems to be able to analyze the likely impacts of international markets on domestic prices.

CONCLUSION

Despite enormous progress in reducing poverty over the past twenty years, particularly in Asia, one out of every six people in the developing world suffers chronic hunger, a number that increases to one in three in SSA countries. Superimposed upon this landscape of chronic food insecurity are episodes of transitory food insecurity—crises caused by temporary disruptions of local food availability, vulnerable populations' access to food, and their ability to utilize it. At its base, food insecurity in its different dimensions is rooted in poverty—of individuals, families, communities, and governments, as well as in a poverty of ideas and institutions. These ideas and institutions are needed to simultaneously foster the broad-based productivity growth in the food system needed to reduce chronic food insecurity in the long run and to build reliable and affordable social safety nets for both the chronically and temporarily destitute.

If the various dimensions of food security—availability, access, and utilization, as well as transitory and chronic—could each be addressed independently, solutions would be much easier. But the various dimensions are inextricably linked through food prices and household coping strategies. For example, ensuring food security involves much more than just producing more food, and in some cases, concentrating single mindedly on local food production may actually undermine food security. The key challenge remains understanding how to design financially and socially sustainable strategies, policies, and programs that address the poverty and low productivity in the food system that lie at the heart of chronic food insecurity, while simultaneously addressing the very real needs of victims of transitory food crises. Improved technologies, policies, and institutions are all needed to address the challenge. All three can contribute, among other things, to making food markets work better in both rural and urban areas. Such improvement needs to be a central part of any such strategy, given the huge reliance of the food insecure on such markets. But markets, by their very nature, do not serve the destitute, so complementary public policies are needed to reach those whom markets cannot serve, while not undermining the capacity of the markets to serve those who do have purchasing power. Such approaches require collaboration of the public sector, the private sector, and civil society. Building such approaches will remain one of humanity's key challenges during the first half of the twenty-first century.

NOTES

1. FAO (Food and Agriculture Organization of the United Nations), "Special Programme for Food Security," http://www.fao.org/spfs/en/ (accessed December 22, 2008); U.S. Department of Agriculture and Economic Research Service, "Food Security in the United States: Measuring Household Food Security," http://www.ers.usda.gov/Briefing/FoodSecurity/measurement.htm (accessed December 22, 2008); U.S. Agency for International Development and Bureau for Program and Policy Coordination, "Food Aid and Food Security Policy Paper" (Washington, DC: USAID, 1995), 7; Shlomo Reutlinger, "Policy Options for Food Security" (working paper, World Bank Agricultural Research Unit, Washington, DC, 1985).

2. Amartya Kumar Sen, *Poverty and Famines: An Essay on Entitlement and Deprivation* (New York: Clarendon Press, 1982).

3. Ibid., 154–56.

4. Although the majority of the poor and malnourished in Sub-Saharan Africa still live in rural areas and are engaged in producing a significant portion of their own food, numerous surveys have shown that a very large number of these farmers, in some cases the majority, are net buyers of basic staples. Thus, the price of these staples in rural markets has a large impact on their food security. For details, see Michael T. Weber et al., "Informing Food Security Decisions in Africa: Empirical Analysis and Policy Dialogue," *American Journal of Agricultural Economics* 70, no. 5 (1988).

5. Effective demand is need backed up by purchasing power. For a discussion of the role of food prices in linking access and availability, see C. Peter Timmer, Walter P. Falcon, and Scott R. Pearson, *Food Policy Analysis* (Baltimore, MD: Published for the World Bank by Johns Hopkins University Press, 1983).

6. Sen, *Poverty and Famines*, 137–38.

7. The utilization of the food also depends on the *safety* of the food—it being free of chemicals and pathogens that could cause illness. Issues of food safety, while very important, are beyond the scope of this chapter.

8. The Food and Agriculture Organization of the United Nations (FAO) estimates that soaring food prices in 2007 and the first half of 2008 increased the number of food-insecure people in the world from 848 million in 2003–2005 to 963 million in 2009. This illustrates how food prices critically affect the poor's access to food and hence their food security. See FAO, "FAO Newsroom: Number of Hungry People Rises to 963 Million," http://www.fao.org/news/story/en/item/8836/icode/ (accessed January 10, 2009); FAO, *The State of Food Insecurity in the World 2008* (Rome: FAO, 2008).

9. Michael R. Carter and Christopher B. Barrett, "The Economics of Poverty Traps and Persistent Poverty: An Asset-Based Approach," *Journal of Development Studies* 42, no. 2 (2006): 178–199.

10. FAO, "FAO Newsroom." Unless otherwise indicated, the figures cited in this and the following paragraph draw from this document and from the FAO's *State of Food Insecurity in the World 2008*.

11. World Bank, *World Development Report 2008: Agriculture for Development* (Washington, DC: World Bank, 2007), 47, 94.

12. World Bank, *World Development Report 2008*, 96.

13. FAO, *State of Food Insecurity in the World 2008*, 24–25; Weber et al., "Informing Food Security Policy"; T. S. Jayne, D. Mather, and E. Mghenyi, "Smallholder Farming under Increasingly Difficult Circumstances: Policy and Public Investment Priorities for Africa" (working paper no. 86, ed. Carl Liedholm and Michael T. Weber, MSU International Development, Departments of Agricultural Economics and Economics, Michigan State University, East Lansing, 2006), http://aec.msu.edu/fs2/papers/idwp86.pdf.

14. See, for example, Frances Moore Lappe, Joseph Collins, and Cary Fowler, *Food First: Beyond the Myth of Scarcity* (Boston: Houghton-Mifflin, 1977).

15. John M. Staatz, "Conceptual Issues in Analyzing the Economics of Agricultural and Food Self-Sufficiency," in *National and Regional Self-Sufficiency Goals: Implications for International Agriculture*, ed. Fred J. Ruppel and Earl D. Kellogg (Boulder, CO: Lynne Rienner Publishers, 1991).

16. John M. Staatz et al., "Agricultural Globalization in Reverse: The Impact of the Food Crisis in West Africa" (paper presented at the Geneva Trade and Development Forum, Crans-Montana, Switzerland, 2008), http://www.gtdforum.org/download/Agricultural%20Globalization%20in%20Reverse_MSU_Crans-Montana%20paper.final.pdf; GRAIN, "Seized! The 2008 Land Grab for Food and Financial Security" (Barcelona: GRAIN, 2008), http://www.grain.org/briefings_files/landgrab-2008-en.pdf. The efforts of countries like the Republic of Korea and some of the Gulf States to acquire huge tracts of land in Sub-Saharan Africa to produce food for export back to these countries raises serious concerns about the impact of such projects on the food security of the African countries involved—particularly for the indigenous populations currently living in the areas to be ceded to the outside investors.

17. For a recent analysis of this issue for Sub-Saharan Africa, see World Bank, Africa Regional Office, Agriculture and Rural Development Unit, *Awakening Africa's Sleeping Giant: Prospects for Commercial Agriculture in the Guinea Savannah Zone and Beyond* (Washington, DC: World Bank, forthcoming).

18. Bruce F. Johnston and Peter Kilby, *Agriculture and Structural Transformation: Economic Strategies in Late-Developing Countries* (New York: Oxford University Press, 1975).

19. For a full discussion of the role of broad-based agricultural growth in stimulating income growth for the poor and generating a tax base for social services, see World Bank, *World Development Report 2008*.

20. Timmer, Falcon, and Pearson, *Food Policy Analysis*. The following paragraphs draw heavily on and expand some of the ideas developed in this classic book.

21. Joachim von Braun, "The World Food Situation: New Driving Forces and Required Actions," *Food Policy Report* (Washington, DC: International Food Policy Research Institute, 2007).

22. James T. Bonnen, "Agricultural Development: Transforming Human Capital, Technology, and Institutions," in *International Agricultural Development*, ed. Carl K. Eicher and John M. Staatz (Baltimore, MD: Johns Hopkins University Press, 1998).

23. John M. Staatz and Niama Nango Dembélé, "Agriculture for Development in Sub-Saharan Africa," *Background Paper for the World Development Report 2008* (Washington, DC: World Bank, 2007), 32.

24. Pedro A. Sanchez, "Soil Fertility and Hunger in Africa," *Science* 295 (2002): 2019–2020; David Weight and Valerie Kelly, "Fertilizer Impacts on Soils and Crops of Sub-Saharan Africa" (working paper no. 21, Michigan State University International Development, Department of Agricultural Economics, Michigan State University, East Lansing, 1999), http://aec.msu.edu/fs2/papers/idp21textonly.pdf.

25. A significant portion, perhaps between one-third and one-half, of small farmers in developing countries, lack enough land and other assets to "farm their way out of poverty" and will likely need, over a generation, to move out of agriculture into other professions if they are to escape poverty. For an analysis of this issue, see World Bank, *World Development Report 2008*, 72–93.

26. Steven Haggblade, Peter Hazell, and Thomas Reardon, *Transforming the Rural Nonfarm Economy: Opportunities and Threats in the Developing World* (Baltimore, MD: Johns Hopkins University Press, 2007).

27. Jayne, Mather, and Mghenyi, "Smallholder Farming;" Weber et al., "Informing Food Security Policy."

28. John Staatz et al., "PROMISAM (Project to Mobilize Food Security Initiatives in Mali): Final Technical Report," *Report to USAID/Mali* (Bamako, Mali: Michigan State University, 2008), http://aec.msu.edu/fs2/mali_fd_strtgy/PROMISAM_final_technical_report_2008.pdf.

29. Hanna Mattinen and Kate Ogden, "Cash-Based Interventions: Lessons from Southern Somalia," *Disasters* 30, no. 3 (2006).

30. For an example from Mozambique, see Claudio Massingarela and Virgilio Nhate, "The Politics of What Works: A Case Study of Food Subsidies and the Bolsa-Escola in Mozambique" (background paper for the *Chronic Poverty Report 2008–2009*, Chronic Poverty Research Center, Manchester, UK, 2006).

31. David Tschirley and Anne Marie del Castillo, "Local and Regional Food Aid Procurement: An Assessment of Experience in Africa and Elements of Good Donor Practice" (working paper no. 91, MSU International Development, Departments of Agricultural Economics and Economics, Michigan State University, East Lansing, 2007), http://aec.msu.edu/fs2/papers/idwp91.pdf.

32. In economics, a good is defined as an "inferior good" if it has a negative income-elasticity of demand—that is, if, as an individual's income rises, she chooses to buy less of the good (substituting a preferred good—perceived as "higher quality" to the "inferior good"). For example, in many low-income countries, whole-grain flour is perceived as an inferior good; as incomes rise, consumers tend to shift toward more highly refined flour. "Inferior good" in this sense does not refer to nutritional quality, for the whole-grain product may be superior nutritionally. Inferior goods are important in addressing food insecurity because if they exist in a particular setting, they can serve as a "self-targeting food" that can be subsidized to reach the poor, while the rich choose not to consume it.

33. FAO, FAO Corporate Document Depository, "Rome Declaration on World Food Security and World Food Summit Plan of Action," http://www.fao.org/wfs/index_en.htm (accessed January 15, 2009).

34. U.S. Government Accountability Office, "International Food Security: Insufficient Efforts by Host Governments and Donors Threaten Progress to Halve Hunger in Sub-Saharan Africa by 2015," Report to Congressional Requesters (Washington, DC: GAO, 2008).

35. David Tschirley and T. S. Jayne, "Food Crises and Food Markets: Implications for Emergency Response in Southern Africa" (working paper no. 94, Michigan State University International Development, Department of Agricultural, Food and Resource

Economics, Michigan State University, East Lansing, 2008), http://aec.msu.edu/fs2/papers/idwp94.pdf.
   36. Ibid.

RESOURCE GUIDE

Suggested Reading

Donovan, Cynthia, Megan McGlinchy, John Staatz, and David Tschirley. *Emergency Needs Assessments and the Impact of Food Aid on Local Markets*. Rome: World Food Programme, Emergency Needs Assessment Branch, 2005. http://documents.wfp. org/stellent/groups/public/documents/ena/wfp086537.pdf.
Food and Agriculture Organization of the United Nations. *The State of Food Insecurity in the World 2008*. Rome: FAO, 2008. (This is an annual publication; check for the latest issue.)
Sen, Amartya Kumar. *Poverty and Famines: An Essay on Entitlement and Deprivation*. New York: Clarendon Press, 1982.
Timmer, C. Peter, Walter P. Falcon, and Scott R. Pearson. *Food Policy Analysis*. Baltimore, MD: Published for the World Bank by Johns Hopkins University Press, 1983.
World Bank. *World Development Report 2008*. Washington, DC: World Bank, 2008. Available at http://www.worldbank.org/wdr2008.

Web Sites

Development Gateway Foundation, dgCommunities, Food Security Portal, http://food security.developmentgateway.org/.
ELDIS, "Food Security Resource Guide," http://www.eldis.org/go/topics/resource-guides/food-security.
Food and Agriculture Organization of the United Nations, Special Programme on Food Security, www.fao.org/spfs/en/.
Food and Agriculture Organization of the United Nations, Committee on World Food Security, Food Security Statistics, http://www.fao.org/unfao/govbodies/cfs/indicators_en.htm.
International Food Policy Research Institute, http://www.ifpri.org/.
Michigan State University, Department of Agricultural, Food and Resource Economics, Food Security Group, http://www.aec.msu.edu/fs2/.
U.S. Department of Agriculture, Economic Research Service, "Food Security in the United States: Measuring Household Food Security," http://www.ers.usda.gov/Briefing/FoodSecurity/measurement.htm.
World Bank, Food Crisis, http://www.worldbank.org/html/extdr/foodprices/.
World Bank, *World Development 2008: Agriculture for Development*, www.worldbank.org/wdr2008.
World Food Programme of the United Nations, www.wfp.org.

12

The Effect of Agricultural Practices on Nutrient Profiles of Foods

Debra Pearson

There is no disputing the fact that food has undergone a profound transformation, particularly in industrial countries. We've gone from *Leave it to Beaver* family dinners—a slab of meat, steamed vegetables, and mashed potatoes that June Cleaver prepared and delightfully served her family night after night—to heat-up-in-the-microwave dinner Hot Pockets™, drive-up McDonalds Happy Meals™ or "chicken" nuggets for a quick family meal. While one can voice serious concern over the "heavy on the meat, light on the vegetables" family dinners, I am particularly hoping these images conjure up a time when one could easily recognize the animals and plants from which the dinner plate items were derived in contrast to many present-day foods that bear virtually no resemblance to that from which they came. Many of us know that this shift in our diets to more and more processed, pre-prepared, and fast foods means that our diets contain larger amounts of added salt, sugars, and fats but less fiber. We can collectively refer to these changes in our food supply as postharvest changes or to the modifications made to foods after their growth and harvest or butchering. Many of us also know that these changes combined with our sedentary lifestyles play an important role in the prevalence of diseases such as cardiovascular disease, type 2 diabetes, and cancer in industrial countries, as well as their rising prevalence in the developing world. Yet on a less obvious level, the very nature of our food has undergone another transformation that is problematic. Over the past century and in particular the last fifty years, what we grow and the way we grow food has dramatically changed and consequently changed the nutrient content of our crops. Techniques of plant breeding, selection, and genetic modification; fertilizer, pesticide, and herbicide practices; and crop and livestock management have all altered the nutrient profiles of these crops and the livestock that eat them. We refer to this these collective changes as preharvest changes. It is these preharvest changes and their effect on the nutrient profiles of foods that will be the focus of this chapter.

The Centers for Disease Control and Prevention estimate that approximately 73 percent of all deaths in the United States are due to diseases that are largely

diet and lifestyle driven. Increasingly, in developing countries, we see a rising incidence of Western Hemisphere diseases for certain segments of the population
alongside serious, pervasive malnutrition in other segments of these populations.
Meaningful, sustainable progress in preventing these diseases will require a careful
examination of the quality of food that current industrial agricultural systems
deliver. In industrial countries, populations are paradoxically overfed yet undernourished. The continuing prevalence of the major diet- and lifestyle-related diseases combined with the epidemic of obesity[1] makes obvious the fact that the last
thing Westerners need is more "empty calories" or low-nutrient-density foods. In
fact, more nutrients in fewer calories are needed. In developing countries where
populations experience considerable severe micronutrient deficiencies, the need
for a variety of nutrient-dense crops is important to successfully combating malnutrition. At a time when there is a need for healthy, nutrient-rich foods globally,
our most common agricultural practices have been delivering the opposite—that
is, foods with declining nutrient content.

Research is accumulating that indicates that some aspects of modern farming
techniques creating improvements in farming efficiency come at the expense of
nutritional quality. This is causing many to rethink how we grow food. A careful
look at how current agricultural practices have affected the nutritional quality of
the world's food supply is critical if we are to effectively modify agricultural systems to better meet the nutritional needs of humans.

THE NUTRIENT CONTENT OF EDIBLE PLANTS

During the past century, several farming practices have dramatically altered the
agricultural landscape and the food on our table as well. For some time, concern
has been voiced over whether (1) these agricultural changes are adversely affecting
the nutritional quality of the food supply and, if so, (2) what foods are being
affected, (3) what specific nutrients are being affected, and (4) what specific farming practices are causing the change in the nutrient profiles of foods? Trying to
reliably answer these questions has proven difficult. The difficulty lies in part with
the fact that several aspects of conventional farming may be exerting an effect on
the nutrient profiles of foods. Conventional farming (i.e., "modern agriculture" or
"industrial farming") has become the dominant farming system, particularly since
World War II. Numerous practices come under the umbrella of conventional farming, but some key aspects include the intensive use of synthetic fertilizers, synthetic pesticides and herbicides, and the growing of monocultures that may be
genetically modified to be pest or herbicide resistant and selected for high yields,
or for hardy handling, storage, and transport characteristics. While an in-depth
discussion of all the permutations of conventional farming is beyond the scope of
this chapter, we will say a few things about certain common conventional farming
practices as they relate to the nutrient content of the crops grown using these
methods. This will be contrasted with what is known about the effects of organic
farming on the nutritional quality of foods. Where possible, other types of sustainable farming practices will be discussed, but research is limited on practices other
than that of organic farming.

WHICH PLANTS ARE WE GROWING?

When one compares the agricultural landscape before the 1950s to that of the present we see that what is grown has changed in several ways. Two of the important changes are that (1) farming has moved from a more diverse variety of crops to monocultures, and (2) the specific varieties (cultivars) of any given crop that are grown have changed considerably over time. The crops that have come to dominate the landscape have largely been bred for one or more of the following traits: (1) high yield, (2) faster growth, (3) pest resistance, (4) herbicide tolerance, (5) postharvest handling qualities, (6) cosmetic appeal, and (7) suitability for the conventional methods of agriculture. What is conspicuously missing from this list is selection for nutritional quality. Oddly enough, up until very recently the nutrient and phytochemical profile of a food item has decidedly not been the goal of crop breeding and selection. Increasingly, researchers are identifying several aspects of the current system of cultivar selection that have inadvertently compromised the nutritional quality of our food supply.

Monoculture farming fundamentally violates one of the basic tenets of nutrition: variety. Any decrease in the variety of foods consumed increases the likelihood of nutrient deficiencies.[2] The Green Revolution successfully increased availability of calories from high-yielding grains. This increase in grain consumption also triggered a decrease in the diversity of plant consumption in some regions. As per capita grain consumption has increased, consumption of legumes, root crops, and other vegetables that characterized a more diverse food supply has dropped off considerably in some regions of the world,[3] and this has been associated with a rise in the incidence of micronutrient deficiencies.[4] Thus, international, multidisciplinary initiatives are under way with the goal of refocusing plant-breeding techniques toward selecting for nutrient density traits, not only yield, as part of a more sustainable, diverse food-based approach to combating malnutrition in developing countries.[5]

The U.S. Department of Agriculture (USDA) maintains and updates a nutrient composition database of foods available and eaten in the United States, and the same is done in many other countries. A recent systematic review of the 1950 and 1999 USDA databases was completed in which the content of thirteen nutrients in forty-three vegetables and fruits was compared to determine whether any significant changes occurred over this approximate fifty-year period.[6] Significant decreases in six nutrients (protein, calcium, phosphorus, iron, vitamin B_2, and vitamin C) were found over this time period. Reductions in several nutrients were also reported in a study done on the United Kingdom food databases from the 1930s to the 1980s.[7] A third, more recent report also examined the historical variation of the mineral content of vegetables, fruits, and nuts in the United States and the United Kingdom using these food composition databases from the 1930s to the 1980s or later.[8] They, too, found significant decreases of copper, magnesium, and sodium in vegetables and decreases of copper, iron, and potassium for fruits in the United Kingdom. For the United States, they noted significant decreases of calcium, copper, and iron in vegetables and decreases of copper, iron, and potassium in fruits. What was conspicuously not seen in these three reports were significant increases in mineral or vitamin content. These reports cite several limitations to their findings, and possible reasons for the apparent decline in nutrient content. A widely cited reason for the apparent decline in some nutrients involves the processes agronomists, seed companies, federal agencies, and farmers employ in plant breeding and selection. In selecting for certain traits (i.e., high yield, faster growth), we have inadvertently selected against nutrient density.

The dilution effect is one explanation of what may have occurred as plants have been bred for certain traits.[9] This refers to the idea that selection for one resource-requiring trait such as yield may divert plant resources away from other jobs, such as the acquisition of minerals or the synthesis of vitamins and phytochemicals. There are several examples for which higher yield is associated with lower nutrient density. Nearly all broccoli varieties currently consumed in the United States are hybrid, with the Marathon variety the industry standard and dominant since the 1990s. These commercial hybrids tend to have high head density (higher yield). In an analysis of twenty-seven commercial hybrids of broccoli a significant inverse relationship was found between calcium and magnesium content and head density (yield).[10] In addition, a comparison of the calcium and magnesium levels of broccoli as reported in the USDA food composition databases since the 1950s and the newer high-yield Marathon variety indicate a trend of declining calcium levels. The researchers suggest that the ability of the plant to acquire more calcium and magnesium does not keep pace with the growth of denser broccoli heads.

Wheat has been bred successfully for increased yield. From approximately 1873 to 2000, wheat harvested per acre more than tripled on a typical American farm. A recent study demonstrated a significant inverse association between yield and seed content of iron, zinc, and selenium among fourteen U.S. hard red winter wheat varieties that have spanned this time period.[11] In addition, for many cereal grains, a negative relationship exists between yield and protein concentration.[12]

Beyond the dilution effect, there appear to be other factors that in part explain the nutrient declines in some foods. Murphy and colleagues recently compared sixty-three spring wheat varieties.[13] Fifty-six of these were historical cultivars commonly grown in the Pacific Northwest from 1842 to about 1965, and the other seven were modern varieties that currently make up 69 percent of that region's spring wheat crops. These sixty-three varieties were grown in controlled conditions and evaluated for their yield and concentration of eight minerals. The modern wheat cultivars had significantly higher yields than the historic varieties; and for seven of the eight minerals, the historical cultivars had significantly higher mineral concentrations. Given these mineral differences between the historical and modern cultivars, the researchers estimated that significantly more bread slices made from modern wheat cultivars would have to be consumed to meet a person's minerals requirements compared with bread made from historical wheat cultivars. Although these data indicate an overall trade-off between high-yield and mineral concentration (dilution effect), the researchers also highlighted the tremendous variation in mineral concentration among the sixty-three varieties. They found some wheat varieties that had both high yield and relatively high mineral levels. They concluded that given the tremendous variability in mineral levels among wheat cultivars, "it should be possible to improve mineral concentrations in modern cultivars without negatively affecting yield."[14] Simply put, in selecting for traits such as yield, or fast growth, while ignoring nutrient profiles, agronomists have inadvertently passed over varieties with relatively high nutrient density and relatively high yield.

Numerous, additional examples are available of the considerable genetic variability in mineral and vitamin content among varieties of any given crop. For instance, potatoes are an important source of vitamin C in the U.S. diet and also in many developing countries where potatoes make up a large part of the subsistence diet. The range of vitamin C in potato cultivars can vary considerably. Among seventy-five North American potato cultivars, vitamin C varied by nearly threefold.[15] Other studies demonstrated a more than fourfold variance in vitamin C (7.9 to 36.1 milligrams per 100 grams fresh weight).[16] Only relatively recently have researchers taken steps to select potato cultivars based on their higher concentrations of vitamins such as vitamin C. Among fifty varieties of broccoli, vitamin C varied by twice as much, α-tocopherol and γ-tocopherol varied by nine-fold and by sixteen-fold, respectively (α-tocopherol and γ-tocopherol are two forms of vitamin E), and β-carotene and α-carotene varied by five and six times as much, respectively (these two carotenes are precursors to vitamin A).[17] The authors state that "the public perceives all broccoli as a good source of vitamins and anticarcinogens. This diversity indicates that potential health benefits depend greatly on the genotype consumed."

There are also considerable genetic variations in the ability of many plants to accumulate minerals.[18] Among eight potato cultivars copper concentrations differed by more than four times, and among six strawberry varieties copper concentrations differed by twice as much.[19] Among five varieties of cranberries, copper differed by sixteen-fold and iron differed by nineteen-fold.[20] Iron differed by eight-fold among eleven varieties of plums.[21] With a reorientation of plant breeding priorities combined with the genetic diversity among varieties, agronomists and farmers should be able to select for nutrient profiles that help meet human nutrition needs without severely affecting yield. In addition, a reorientation away from monocultures and toward agricultural biodiversity could ensure the availability of the wide array of nutrients necessary for human health.

The preceding paragraphs have dealt with studies assessing specific vitamin or mineral levels in various foods. In fact, for several decades the focus has been largely on variability of vitamin, mineral, and protein levels depending on plant genetics and farming methods (i.e., conventional versus organic methods). As indicated above, monocultures and the high-yield plant-breeding goals that are hallmarks of conventional farming have resulted in undesirable vitamin, mineral, and protein declines in various crops. But the nutritional value of food goes well beyond its mineral, vitamin, and macronutrient content (macronutrients are the protein, carbohydrate, and fat components of foods). In comparison to the approximate forty essential nutrients (vitamins, minerals, essential amino acids, and fatty acids) that are found in food, edible plants have more than eight thousand phytochemicals. Phytochemicals are substances synthesized by plants with many exhibiting physiologic health effects. Some common phytochemicals are polyphenols, flavonoids, and anthocyanins; phytochemicals are also known as secondary plant metabolites. A growing body of research indicates that these phytochemicals play pivotal roles in human health.[22] Nutrition experts have claimed for a long time that food is much more than the sum of its vitamin and mineral content. Just as vitamin and mineral content varies considerably among varieties of a given crop, so does the phytochemical content. Furthermore, researchers increasingly understand that it is the complex interactions of several components in food that produce their health benefits, and these health effects are not duplicated with isolated nutrients from the food.[23]

Examples of the genetic variability of phytochemicals among varieties of a given crop are numerous. Intake of cruciferous vegetables (i.e., broccoli, brussels sprouts, cabbage, cauliflower, kale) is associated with reduced risk for a number of cancers.[24] The group of phytochemicals referred to as glucosinolates are concentrated in cruciferous vegetables and exhibit anticancer properties.[25] Among fifty varieties of broccoli grown under controlled conditions, glucoraphanin (the predominant glucosinolate in broccoli) varied by more than twenty-seven times.[26] In the same study, the level of sinigrin varied by two- to fivefold among the varieties of brussels sprouts, cabbage, cauliflower, and kale tested (sinigrin is the predominant glucosinolate in these cruciferous vegetables). This study demonstrates not only the tremendous variation in phytochemical content among varieties within one crop, but also the variability in phytochemical profiles (i.e., the different glucosinolate profiles) among the different cruciferous vegetables. This latter point highlights the value of agricultural diversity to enhance dietary diversity in obtaining a wide array of phytochemicals.

Eleven varieties of blackberries varied in both their total phenolic and total anthocyanin contents by approximately twofold.[27] When looking at individual anthocyanins and phenolics, the blackberry varieties varied ninefold in cyanidin 3-rutinoside (the second most abundant anthocyanin in these blackberries) and eightfold in catechin (one of the phenolics). Current agricultural practices are not taking advantage of this knowledge, as some of the blackberry varieties that have been tested are higher in anthocyanin and phenolic content than the common commercial varieties. Significant genetic variations in phytochemical content among varieties of other crops, such as pears, blueberries, and tomatoes, also have been documented.[28]

In general, phytochemicals tend to be concentrated in the skins and rinds of many fruits. Another goal of plant breeders has been to breed for larger varieties of fruits, and this trend has inadvertently decreased the phytochemicals. For instance, a one hundred-gram serving of large strawberries means fewer numbers of strawberries than a one hundred-gram serving of small strawberries. The smaller strawberries give more surface area and thus more total phytochemicals than the serving of larger strawberries.

Recent research on cranberries illustrates a number of issues raised in the preceding paragraphs. There are more than four hundred varieties of cranberries, yet a very small number make up the vast majority of the commercial cranberries sold. Traditional medicine has touted cranberry juice for the prevention and treatment of urinary tract infections, but with no empirical proof of its efficacy. A study published in the New England Journal of Medicine demonstrated that proanthocyanidins isolated from cranberries inhibit the adherence of E. coli from uroepithelial cells.[29] The adherence of bacteria to mucosal surfaces, such as the lining of the bladder (uroepithelial cells), is a prerequisite to the development of most infections. A recent systematic review of clinical trials indicated that cranberry juice is indeed effective in reducing the incidence of urinary tract infections.[30] In addition, research in the areas of cancer and cardiovascular disease suggests that phytochemicals in cranberries may have additional beneficial effects. The phytochemical profile varies substantially among the numerous varieties of cranberries. Indeed, for many crops, the nutrient and phytochemical contents vary considerably among the varieties of any one crop. Modern agriculture has all but ignored this fact in the selection for plant varieties that have come to dominate our monoculture system of farming and the commercial market. Researchers at Rutgers University and elsewhere are now focusing their plant-breeding and selection activities on selecting for cranberry varieties with optimal phytochemical and nutrient profiles in terms of human health.

The substantial variation in nutrient and phytochemical profiles that exists among all the varieties of any given crop provides a promising and as yet largely untapped resource for making wiser choices in what is grown. Nutritionists, public health officials, plant breeders, agronomists, and farmers are beginning to work cooperatively in screening the sometimes hundreds of native heirloom varieties of crops and also are breeding plants with a focus on the nutrient content of plants. Also, these specialists are reconsidering the practice of monocultures as they come to understand the nutritional value of agricultural biodiversity. These changes are already being seen at the local level with the increase in the number of farmers' markets at which a greater variety of heirloom produce are available for sale. On the global level, international projects are trying to reestablish and increase the variety of local and traditional foods to attain agricultural biodiversity, dietary diversity, and improved health.[31]

HOW ARE WE GROWING OUR PLANTS?

Conventional farming practices differ from sustainable practices in several aspects. Organic farming techniques are the most heavily studied among the types of sustainable practices and will be focused on in this section. Differences in these systems include the types of fertilizers used, soil management practices, and techniques used for pest and weed management. Conventional farming utilizes synthetic fertilizers, particularly fossil-fuel-derived nitrogen fertilizers, and synthetic pesticides and herbicides. These techniques particularly help to increase yield per acre and create more rapid growth, but over time they tend to compromise soil fertility. In contrast, organic farming is characterized by its use of green manure, compost, crop rotation, biological pest control, mechanical cultivation, and the exclusion or minimal use of synthetic fertilizers, herbicides, and pesticides and plant growth regulators. An important goal of organic farming is its use of techniques to maintain and improve soil fertility (i.e., a high level of soil organic matter and a rich, diverse microbial population) so that the soil will yield nutrient-rich produce, now and in the future. In addition, organic farming seeks to respect and promote biodiversity and biological cycles while growing crops for human or animal consumption. These characteristics and goals of organic farming are summed up in the commonly used phrase, "healthy soils equals healthy foods equals healthy people." In-depth discussion of all these farming practices is beyond the scope of this section, but we will explore some of these practices as they relate to their effects on the nutrient profiles of crops grown with these methods.

For decades, the nutrient differences of produce grown organically versus conventionally have been contentiously debated. Yet, relatively few well-controlled studies give clarity to this debate.[32] Part of the difficulty lies with the numerous challenges inherent in this type of research. Many factors, if not controlled, make reliable comparisons suspect or invalid. The following factors substantially influence the nutrient profiles of produce: (1) different varieties of a crop (as detailed in the previous section); (2) the macro- and microenvironment (i.e., climate, rainfall, sunlight intensity, temperature, and so on, and insect and disease pressures); (3) year-to-year variability; (4) soil type; (5) method and timing of harvest; (6) storage and transport conditions of the crop; (7) the experience of the farmer; and (8) the length of time a field has been in organic cultivation. To reliably determine whether specific farming techniques causally affect nutrient and phytochemical profiles in crops, these factors must be matched and controlled. In addition, the level of soil organic matter and the amount and types of microorganisms change substantially over time in organically managed fields,[33] and these changes in the quality of the soil over time are associated with nutrient changes in the crop.[34] Thus, ideally, comparisons should be made with produce grown on fields that have been organic for a period of time. While numerous studies are inconclusive because of the lack of control of one or more of these factors, there are enough well-designed studies to suggest that indeed some nutrient differences exist between certain crops grown conventionally compared with those grown organically or sustainably.

Thus far, well-designed studies indicate that the nutrient profiles of some crops may be more heavily influenced by different farming techniques than others. Organic versus conventional cultivation techniques significantly influenced phytochemical and vitamin C content in two varieties of tomatoes, but these nutrients in two varieties of bell peppers were not influenced by the farming technique.[35] In this same study, three years worth of data were collected and the high year-to-year variability in the nutrient levels, which is common, highlights the need for multiple-year comparisons.

For many years, minerals, a relatively small number of vitamins, and nitrates were tested in organically versus conventionally grown produce. In more recent years, several phytochemicals have also been analyzed. In the earlier research, particularly in studies in which at least some of the above-mentioned methodological problems were controlled, the most consistent findings were higher vitamin C levels and lower nitrate levels in organically produced food crops versus those conventionally grown.[36]

Lower nitrate levels in organically grown produce are particularly seen in leafy, root, and tuber vegetables (i.e., lettuce, spinach, cabbage, beetroot, radish, potato). The higher nitrate levels in conventionally grown produce appear to be linked to the higher availability of nitrogen from synthetic fertilizers.[37] Nitrates are a negative nutrient attribute, as they are a potential precursor to the formation of carcinogenic nitroso-compounds (i.e., nitrosoamines) within the digestive tract.[38] Thus, the lower nitrate levels seen in organically produced crops is a positive nutritional attribute.

Synthetic nitrogen fertilizers are readily available for uptake by plants, whereas the nitrogen from organic systems is more slowly released to plants. This difference in the availability of nitrogen not only affects the nitrate content of the plant, but also may influence certain nutrient levels. The carbon-nutrient balance theory and the growth-differentiation balance theory[39] suggest that the availability (or lack thereof) of nutrients (i.e., ample to excess available nitrogen in conventional systems) influences where a plant will direct its resources. Ample nitrogen shunts a plant's resources toward rapid growth and nitrogen-containing compounds, such as proteins, and away from carbon-containing compounds, such as some vitamins and phytochemicals. Organic fertilizers, such as manure and cover crops, release nutrients such as nitrogen more slowly. This may encourage a more robust, deeper root system that has greater capacity to absorb nutrients from the soil.

Numerous studies of varying quality have assessed vitamin C status as a function of cultivation techniques. Although many of these studies are inconclusive, the vast majority of studies analyzing for vitamin C have either found higher levels in the organically grown produce or no difference,[40] whereas only a very small number of studies have found higher vitamin C in conventionally grown produce. A well-designed study using multiple-year comparisons of organic and conventionally grown tomatoes found 14 to 26 percent higher vitamin C in the two varieties tested.[41] Likewise, three varieties of organic potatoes averaged 30 percent higher vitamin C.[42] Organically grown produce does appear to have higher vitamin C, but the specific organic techniques matter as well. A study in which plums were grown with three different organic techniques as well as conventionally found that, while two of the organic techniques resulted in higher vitamin C, the third organic technique resulted in lower vitamin C as compared with the conventional method.[43]

Studies that have examined the mineral content of crops grown with different farming techniques have been inconclusive in part due to inadequate control of confounding factors.[44] Here, too, more studies have either found higher mineral levels in the organically produced crops or no difference between organic and conventional crops, and only a small number of studies report higher minerals in conventional crops. More research is needed to clarify the effect of farming practices on mineral content, especially because certain soil constituents do influence mineral uptake, and these constituents are affected by cultivation techniques. For instance, arbuscular mycorrhizal fungi, one of the most common microorganisms in many soils, form a symbiotic relationship with a large number of plants. Arbuscular mycorrhizae assist the plant with mineral—copper, zinc, calcium, and particularly phosphorus—uptake from the soil.[45] Some cover crops enhance and maintain the mycorrhizae content of the soil; and while cover cropping is not exclusive to organic and sustainable farming, it is more commonly used in these methods of farming. Soluble phosphorus fertilizers used in conventional farming reduce these arbuscular micorrhizae in the soil. In a recent study in Australia, wheat was grown over a few years either organically (with insoluble phosphorus fertilizer) or conventionally (with soluble phosphorus fertilizer, nitrogen fertilizer, and herbicides).[46] The organically produced wheat had higher zinc (25 to 56 percent higher) and copper (16 to 58 percent higher) than the conventional wheat. The conventionally managed system had reduced soil mycorrhizal fungi. Another study correlated increased zinc uptake with increased mycorrhizal fungi in wheat and field pea crops.[47]

Another important aspect regarding the mineral status of produce is not only the amount of a mineral present in the plant, but also its bioavailability for the organism that eats the plant. Bioavailability refers to the ability of an organism (i.e., humans) to digest and absorb the mineral from the food for its own use. The phytate level of a plant-based food is one factor that can decrease the bioavailability of a number of minerals. By forming insoluble complexes with minerals such as calcium, copper, zinc, and iron, phytate can render these minerals less bioavailable.[48]

This phytate-mediated decrease in mineral availability appears to be partly responsible for the widespread micronutrient deficiencies in populations subsisting largely on grains and other plant-based foods, particularly in developing countries. A study examined the mineral and phytate level of sorghum grown with conventional fertilizers and herbicides or with traditional methods (no fertilizers or herbicides) in Somalia.[49] The conventionally grown sorghum had 76 to 80 percent higher phytate, whereas zinc was only 37 to 41 percent higher. This creates a higher (less desirable) phytate-to-zinc ratio, which indicates less zinc bioavailability. Furthermore, when young rats were fed either the traditionally or conventionally grown sorghum, results indicated that the iron and zinc were less bioavailable to the rats. Rats fed the conventional sorghum had significantly lower iron in their tibia (leg bones) than the control rats. Zinc levels in the tibia were highest in the control rats, whereas rats fed the traditional sorghum had the next highest zinc tibia levels, and those fed the conventional sorghum had lower zinc levels. Similarly, millet grown with superphosphate fertilizer had 25 to 29 percent higher phytate and 6 to 11 percent lower zinc—a worse phytate-to-zinc ratio—than millet fertilized with crop residue.[50] These studies indicate that the absolute amount of a nutrient in a crop is not the only important measure. Future research needs to consider other components in a plant that may enhance or decrease the bioavailability of a given nutrient.

Perhaps the most exciting area of research is that of phytochemicals and how agronomic practices influence their synthesis in crops. Plants produce thousands of phytochemicals, and our full understanding of the health effects of these myriad plant metabolites is in its early stages. Studies increasingly suggest that it is the complex sum total of phytochemicals, vitamins, and minerals in plant-rich diets that correlate with reduced disease incidence.[51] Phytochemicals (also called secondary plant metabolites) are synthesized at varying stages in a plant's life and in response to a number of factors. They are largely responsible for the color of plants and their fruits, which is important for attracting pollinators and animals to help disperse the plant's seeds. Numerous phytochemicals function in plant defense against pathogens, herbivores, ultraviolet-B radiation, oxidative stress, and wounding. Plants increase their synthesis in response to these stressors.[52] A current theory is that the intensive use of pesticides and herbicides in conventional farming may inadvertently "make life easier for the plants," such that plants have less stimulus to synthesize phytochemicals.[53]

Of the thousands of phytochemicals that plants produce, only a relatively small number have been studied relative to different farming techniques. A majority of these studies, especially well-designed studies, indicate higher phytochemical content in organic produce compared with conventional produce.[54] The same variety of blueberries were grown on five organic farms and five conventional farms in New Jersey with similar soil and environmental conditions.[55] Organic blueberries averaged significantly higher total and individual phenolics (68 percent higher total phenolics) and anthocyanins (59 percent higher total anthocyanins) than the conventional blueberries. Even with this difference in anthocyanin content, there was substantial variation among the organic farms. Variation in phytochemical content among different conventional farms and among organic farms is commonly seen. Thus, further research must better identify specific practices that optimize phytochemical profiles.

One of the more extensive studies of phytochemical profiles has come out of the Long-Term Research on Agricultural Systems (LTRAS) project at the University of California–Davis. The LTRAS project was started in 1993 and is designed to run one hundred years. Various farming systems, including organic and conventional systems, are being compared while carefully controlling for the numerous confounding factors that have plagued past research. The LTRAS project will generate numerous insights into the relationship between various farming inputs and the sustainability and quality of the agricultural products, including the nutrient content of crops.[56] Tomatoes produced organically or conventionally at the LTRAS over a ten-year period were evaluated for their content of the three main flavonoids found in tomatoes: quercetin, naringenin, and kaempferol (flavonoids are one category of phytochemicals).[57] Quercetin and kaempferol were significantly higher in the organic tomatoes as compared with conventional tomatoes, averaging 79 and 97 percent higher levels, respectively. Over the ten-year period, nitrogen application rates, in the form of N-P-K starter fertilizer and ammonium nitrate, remained stable in the conventional system. In the organic system, winter legume cover crops and composted manure were used for nitrogen. In the first three years, higher amounts of manure were added to the organic plots, but as the soil organic matter increased to a steady state, the amount of manure was decreased. Over the ten-year period, the quercetin and kaempferol content of tomatoes from both systems increased, with a greater rate of increase in the organic tomatoes. This coincided with a decrease in the total amount of nitrogen application on the organic field and higher soil organic matter. The form and amount of nitrogen application remained constant over the ten years on the conventional fields, and they had a consistently low level of soil organic matter. The authors contend that either the total amount of nitrogen or the behavior of different forms of nitrogen in these two systems may be influencing the flavonoid content. The tomato yields were not significantly different between these two systems over the ten-year period. In support of different forms of nitrogen (slow-release nitrogen in organic systems) affecting phytochemical synthesis, another study found that tomatoes fertilized with chicken manure or grass-clover mulch had 17 percent higher total phenolics and 29 percent higher vitamin C than tomatoes fertilized with inorganic nitrogen fertilizer.[58]

In the final analysis, an important reason for shifting to more sustainable or organic farming strategies is whether or not animals and humans consuming sustainably produced foods are healthier. Only a handful of studies have looked at this, with conflicting results, and a definitive answer is experimentally daunting.[59] A well-designed three-generation rat study compared the effect of organic versus conventional feed on fertility.[60] Pregnancy rates, birth weight, and the weight gain of offspring were not significantly different between the two groups, but there were significantly fewer stillborn offspring in the first litter and a lower number of perinatal deaths in the organically fed group.

A recent study examined the effects of five varieties of strawberries on the proliferation of two human cancer cell lines—a breast cancer and colon cancer cell line.[61] Extracts from the organically grown strawberries inhibited cancer cell proliferation to a greater degree than their conventional counterparts at two of the concentrations tested. In addition, this study analyzed the reduced and oxidized forms of vitamin C, ascorbic acid and dehydroascorbate, respectively, and a small number of phytochemicals in the strawberries. The phytochemicals assayed were not consistently higher in the varieties of organic strawberries. In two of the organic strawberry varieties, the ascorbic acid to dehydroascorbate ratio was two times and eight times higher than their conventional counterparts. This difference in the ratio of ascorbic acid to dehydroascorbate between the organic and conventional strawberries brings up another important point. It is not enough to only assess the total amount of a nutrient. It is also important to look at the relative amounts of the various forms of the nutrient. It is the reduced form of vitamin C, ascorbic acid, that acts as a protective antioxidant. Thus, a high ascorbic acid to dehydroascorbate ratio is desirable. Another study found that two varieties of strawberries grown in soil with added compost had higher vitamin C, a higher ascorbate to dehydroascorbate ratio, and a higher reduced-to-oxidized glutathione ratio (glutathione also functions as an antioxidant).[62] Although the question of the human health effects resulting from the consumption of organically versus conventionally grown produce is far from answered, the few studies to date are intriguing, suggest that there may be a difference, and strongly argue for further research.

Harvesting numerous crops well before their peak ripeness is a common practice in conventional agriculture, largely because of the time and distance between farm and the dinner table that the average food item travels. It is well known that many nutrients and phytochemicals reach their maximum concentration in a plant at the fully ripe stage. For instance, total anthocyanins in two varieties of blackberries vary considerably from the underripe to the ripe to overripe stages[63] (74.7 to 317 milligrams per 100 grams fresh weight and 69.9 to 164, respectively). Similarly, in raspberries, strawberries, and blueberries, the total anthocyanin and phenolic content increases with maturity.[64] While not always the case, organically and sustainably grown produce is more frequently picked closer to full maturity, and the time from harvesting to consumption tends to be shorter. These factors typically favor higher overall nutrient content.

The complex factors that govern mineral uptake, and vitamin and phytochemical synthesis in plants are incompletely understood, making determination of the role of various agricultural practices challenging. The evidence thus far, however, suggests a more favorable level of some nutrients in organically grown foods. With more sensitive analytical tools and a better grasp of the variables that must be accounted for, researchers more thoroughly understand the effects of agricultural practices on nutrient profiles. Indeed, a number of ongoing studies, including those at the LTRAS project, should provide more conclusive data in the near future. This area of research will benefit from being driven less by ideology and more by desired, holistic outcomes. These outcomes need to include optimizing nutrient profiles of foods, while adhering to sustainable principles regarding the environment and the social and economic health of communities on a local and global level. As research moves forward, it is important to determine which specific types of organic or sustainable soil, fertilizer, pest-management practices, and varieties optimally influence the nutrient profile of crops.

CONCLUSION

The nation is on the verge of a profound paradigm shift in how we grow, harvest, process, and consume food. Growers and breeders are shifting away from the largely single-minded idea of increased crop yield to a broader view of growing plants that includes as a very high priority the need to improve nutrient density. All stakeholders, from farmers, crop breeders and geneticists, and agricultural scientists, to consumers are recognizing that the overarching goal in the food system must be shifted to a focus of improving the nutritional quality of the food supply and doing so in a way that sustains the natural and human environment, both locally and globally.

NOTES

1. Physical Activity and Obesity Division of Nutrition, National Center for Chronic Disease Prevention and Health Promotion, *U. S. Obesity Trends 1985–2007*, http://www.cdc.gov/nccdphp/dnpa/obesity/trend/maps/index.htm (accessed July 24, 2008).

2. Emile A. Frison et al., "Agricultural Biodiversity, Nutrition, and Health: Making a Difference to Hunger and Nutrition in the Developing World," *Food and Nutrition Bulletin* 27 (2006): 167–79.

3. FAO (Food and Agriculture Organization of the United Nations), FAOSTAT Statistical Database, http://www.faostat.fao.org (object Agriculture/Production/Core Production Data, 2007).

4. Robin D. Graham, R. M. Welch, and H. E. Bouis, "Addressing Micronutrient Malnutrition through Enhancing the Nutritional Quality of Staple Foods: Principles, Perspectives and Knowledge Gaps," *Advances in Agronomy* 70 (2001): 77–142; Ross M. Welch, "The Impact of Mineral Nutrients in Food Crops on Global Human Health," *Plant Soil* 247 (2002): 83–90.

5. Howarth E. Bouis, "Plant Breeding: A New Tool for Fighting Micronutrient Malnutrition," *Journal of Nutrition* 132 (2002): 491S–494S.

6. Donald R. Davis, M. D. Epp, and H. D. Riordan, "Changes in USDA Food Composition Data for 43 Garden Crops, 1950 to 1999," *Journal of the American College of Nutrition* 23 (2004): 669–82.

7. Anne-Marie Mayer, "Historical Changes in the Mineral Content of Fruits and Vegetables," *British Food Journal* 99 (1997): 207–11.

8. Philip J. White and M. R. Broadley, "Historical Variation in the Mineral Composition of Edible Horticultural Products," *The Journal of Horticultural Science and Biotechnology* 80 (2005): 660–67.

9. W. M. Jarrell and R. B. Beverly, eds., *The Dilution Effect in Plant Nutrition Studies*, ed. N. C. Brady, vol. 34, *Advances in Agronomy* (New York: Academic Press, 1981).

10. Mark W. Farnham, M. A. Grusak, and M. Wang, "Calcium and Magnesium Concentration of Inbred and Hybrid Broccoli Heads," *Journal of the American Society for Horticultural Science* 125 (2000): 344–49.

11. D. F. Garvin, R. M. Welch, and J. W. Finley, "Historical Shifts in the Seed Mineral Micronutrient Concentration of US Hard Red Winter Wheat Germplasm," *Journal of the Science of Food and Agriculture* 86 (2006): 2213–20.

12. N. W. Simmonds, "The Relation between Yield and Protein in Cereal Grain," *Journal of the Science of Food and Agriculture* 67 (1995): 309–15.

13. Kevin M. Murphy, Philip G. Reeves, and Stephen S. Jones, "Relationship between Yield and Mineral Nutrient Concentration in Historical and Modern Spring Wheat Cultivars," *Euphytica* 163 (2008): 381–90.

14. Ibid., 381.

15. Stephen L. Love et al., "Stability of Expression and Concentration of Ascorbic Acid in North American Potato Germplasm," *Horticulture Science* 39 (2004): 1456–60.

16. P. Kemp and T. C. Kemp, "The Ascorbic Acid Content of Thirteen Varieties of Potato," *Proceedings of the Nutrition Society* 41 (1982): 6A; J. Augustin et al., "Vitamin Composition of Freshly Harvested and Stored Potatoes," *Journal of Food Science* 43 (1978): 1566–74.

17. Anne C. Kurilich et al., "Carotene, Tocopherol and Ascorbate Contents in Subspecies of Brassica Oleracea," *Journal of Agricultural and Food Chemistry* 47 (1999): 1576–81, 1580.

18. Martin Broadley et al., "Phylogenetic Variation in Heavy Metal Accumulation in Angiosperms," *New Phytologist* 152 (2001): 9–27.

19. Mari Hakala et al., "Effects of Varieties and Cultivation Conditions on the Composition of Strawberries," *Journal of Food Composition and Analysis* 16 (2003): 67–80.

20. J. R. Davenport and J. Provost, "Cranberry Tissue Nutrient Levels as Impacted by Three Levels of Nitrogen Fertilizer and Their Relationship to Fruit Yield and Quality," *Journal of Plant Nutrition* 17 (1994): 1625–34.

21. Cevdet Nergiz and Hasan Yildiz, "Research on Chemical Composition of Some Varieties of European Plums (*Prunus Domestica*) Adapted to the Aegean District of Turkey," *Journal of Agricultural and Food Chemistry* 45 (1997): 2820–23.

22. Johanna W. Lampe, "Health Effect of Vegetables and Fruit: Assessing Mechanisms of Action in Human Experimental Studies," *American Journal of Clinical Nutrition* 70 (1999): 475S–90S; Paul Knekt et al., "Flavonoid Intake and Risk of Chronic Disease," *American Journal of Clinical Nutrition* 76 (2002): 560–568; Penny Kris-Etherton et al., "Bioactive Compounds in Foods: Their Role in the Prevention of Cardiovascular Disease and Cancer," *American Journal of Medicine* 113 (2002): 71S–88S.

23. Rui H. Liu, "Health Benefits of Fruit and Vegetables Are from Additive and Synergistic Combinations of Phytochemicals," *American Journal of Clinical Nutrition* 78, supplement (2003): 517S–520S; David R. Jacobs and Lynn M. Steffen, "Nutrients, Foods and Dietary Patterns as Exposures in Research: A Framework for Food Synergy," *American Journal of Clinical Nutrition* 78, supplement (2003): 508S–513S.

24. L. Kohlmeier and L. Su, "Cruciferous Vegetable Consumption and Colorectal Cancer Risk: Meta-Analysis of the Epidemiological Evidence," *The Journal of the Federation of American Societies for Experimental Biology* 11 (1997): 369.

25. K. Faulkner, R. Mithen, and G. Williamson, "Selective Increase of the Potential Anticarcinogen 4-Methylsulfphinylbutyl Glucosinolate in Broccoli," *Carcinogenesis* 19 (1998): 605–9.

26. Mosbah Kushad et al., "Variation of Glucosinolates in Vegetable Crops of Brassica Oleracea," *Journal of Agricultural and Food Chemistry* 47 (1999): 1541–48.

27. T. Siriwoharn et al., "Influence of Cultivar, Maturity, and Sampling on Blackberry (*Rubus L.* Hybrids) Anthocyanins, Polyphenolics, and Antioxidant Properties," *Journal of Agricultural and Food Chemistry* 52 (2004): 8021–30.

28. A. C. G. Sanchez, A. Gil-Izquierdo, and M. I. Gil, "Comparative Study of Six Pear Cultivars in Terms of Their Phenolic and Vitamin C Contents and Antioxidant Capacity," *Journal of the Science of Food and Agriculture* 83 (2003): 995–1003; L. Howard, J. Clark, and C. Brownmiller, "Antioxidant Capacity and Phenolic Content in Blueberries as Affected by Genotype and Growing Season," *Journal of the Science of Food and Agriculture* 83 (2003): 1238–47; I. Martinez-Valverde et al., "Phenolic Compounds, Lycopene and Antioxidant Activity in Commercial Varieties of Tomato (*Lycopersicum Esculentum*)," *Journal of the Science of Food and Agriculture* 82 (2002): 323–30.

29. Amy B. Howell et al., "Inhibition of the Adherence of P-Fimbriated Escherichia Coli to Uroephithelial-Cell Surfaces by Proanthocyanidin Extracts from Cranberries," *New England Journal of Medicine* 339 (1998): 1085–86.

30. Ruth G. Jepson and J. C. Craig, "A Systematic Review of the Evidence for Cranberries and Blueberries in Uti," *Molecular Nutrition and Food Research* 51 (2007): 738–45.

31. Frison, "Agricultural Biodiversity."

32. Katrin Woese et al., "A Comparison of Organically and Conventionally Grown Foods - Results of a Review of the Relevant Literature," *Journal of the Science of Food and Agriculture* 74 (1997): 281–93; Virginia Worthington, "Nutritional Quality of Organic Versus Conventional Fruits, Vegetables, and Grains," *Journal of Alternative and Complementary Medicine* 7, no. 2 (2001): 161–73; Diane Bourn and John Prescott, "A Comparison of the Nutritional Value, Sensory Qualities and Food Safety of Organically and Conventionally Produced Foods," *Critical Reviews in Food Science and Nutrition* 42, no. 1 (2002): 1–34; Ewa Rembialkowska, "Review: Quality of Plant Products from Organic Agriculture," *Journal of the Science of Food and Agriculture* 87 (2007): 2757–62; Charles Benbrook et al., "New Evidence Confirms the Nutritional Superiority of Plant-Based Organic Foods," The Organic Center, http://www.organiccenter.org/reportfiles/5367_Nutrient_Content_SSR_FINAL_V2.pdf (accessed May 15, 2008).

33. R. Ford Denison, Dennis Bryant, C. Kearney, and T. E. Kearney, "Crop Yields over the First Nine Years of LTRAS, a Long-Term Comparison of Field Crop Systems in a Mediterranean Climate," *Field Crops Research* 86 (2004): 267–77.

34. Alyson E. Mitchell et al., "Ten-Year Comparison of the Influence of Organic and Conventional Crop Management Practices on the Content of Flavonoids in Tomatoes," *Journal of Agricultural and Food Chemistry* 55 (2007): 6154–59.

35. Alexander W. Chassy et al., "Three-Year Comparison of the Content of Antioxidant Microconstituents and Several Quality Characteristics in Organic and Conventionally Managed Tomatoes and Bell Peppers," *Journal of Agricultural and Food Chemistry* 54 (2006): 8244–52.

36. Bourn and Prescott, "Comparison of Organic and Conventional"; Benbrook et al., "Nutritional Superiority."

37. Ewa Rembialkowska, "Comparison of the Contents of Nitrates, Nitrites, Lead, Cadmium and Vitamin C in Potatoes from Conventional and Ecological Farms," *Polish Journal of Food and Nutrition Science* 8, no. 49 (1999): 17–26.

38. C. Oldreive and C. Rice-Evans, "The Mechanisms for Nitration and Nitrotyrosine Formation in Vitro and in Vivo: Impact of Diet," *Free Radical Research* 35 (2001): 215–31.

39. Nancy Stamp, "Out of the Quagmire of Plant Defense Hypotheses," *The Quarterly Review of Biology* 78 (2003): 23–55.

40. Worthington, "Nutritional Quality of Organic."

41. Chassy, "Three-Year Comparison."

42. Jana Hajslova et al., "Quality of Organically and Conventionally Grown Potatoes: Four-Year Study of Micronutrients, Metals, Secondary Metabolites, Enzymic Browning and Organoleptic Properties," *Food Additives and Contaminants* 22, no. 6 (2005): 514–34.

43. Ginerva Lombardi-Boccia et al., "Nutrients and Antioxidant Molecules in Yellow Plums (*Prunus Domestica L.*) from Conventional and Organic Productions: A Comparative Study," *Journal of Agricultural and Food Chemistry* 52 (2004): 90–94.

44. Bourn and Prescott, "Comparison of Organic and Conventional"; Worthington, "Nutritional Quality of Organic."

45. H. Marschner and B. Dell, "Nutrient Uptake in Mycorrhizal Symbiosis," *Plant Soil* 159 (1994): 89–102.

46. Megan H. Ryan, J. W. Derrick, and P. R. Dann, "Grain Mineral Concentrations and Yield of Wheat Grown under Organic and Conventional Management," *Journal of the Science of Food and Agriculture* 84 (2004): 207–16.

47. Megan H. Ryan and J. F. Angus, "Arbuscular Mycorrhizae in Wheat and Field Pea Crops on a Low P Soil: Increased Zn-Uptake but No Increase in P-Uptake or Yield," *Plant Soil* 250 (2003): 225–39.

48. E. Graf, "Chemistry and Applications of Phytic Acid: An Overview," in *Phytic Acid: Chemistry and Applications*, ed. E. Graf (Minneapolis, MN: Pilatus Press, 1986), 1–21.

49. H. I. Ali and B. F. Harland, "Effects of Fiber and Phytate in Sorghum Flour on Iron and Zinc in Weanling Rats: A Pilot Study," *Cereal Chemistry* 68, no. 3 (1991): 234–38.

50. A. Buerkert et al., "Phosphorus Application Affects the Nutritional Quality of Millet Grain in the Sahel," *Field Crop Research* 57 (1998): 223–35.

51. Lampe, "Health Effects of Fruits and Vegetables"; Liu, "Additive and Synergistic Combinations."

52. R. Dixon and N. Paiva, "Stress-Induced Phenylpropanoid Metabolism," *Plant Cell* 7 (1995): 1085–97; R. N. Bennett and R. M. Wallsgrove, "Tansley Review No. 72: Secondary Metabolites in Plant Defense Mechanisms," *New Phytologist* 127 (1994): 617–33.

53. Otto Daniel et al., "Selected Phenolic Compound in Cultivated Plants: Ecologic Functions, Health Implications and Modulation by Pesticides," *Environmental Health Perspectives* 107, no. S1 (1999): 109–14.

54. Benbrook et al., "Nutritional Superiority."

55. Shiow Y. Wang et al., "Fruit Quality, Antioxidant Capacity and Flavonoid Content of Organically and Conventionally Grown Blueberries," *Journal of Agricultural and Food Chemistry* 56 (2008): 5788–94.

56. Denison et al., "First Nine years of LTRAS."

57. Mitchell et al., "Ten-Year Comparison."

58. Ramandeep K. Toor, Geoffrey P. Savage, and Anuschka Heeb, "Influence of Different Types of Fertilizers on the Major Antioxidant Components of Tomatoes," *Journal of Food Composition and Analysis* 19 (2006): 20–27.

59. Bourn and Prescott, "Comparison of Organic and Conventional."

60. Alberta Velimirov et al., "The Influence of Biologically and Conventionally Cultivated Food on the Fertility of Rats," *Biology, Agriculture and Horticulture* 8 (1992): 325–37.

61. Marie E. Olsson et al., "Antioxidant Levels and Inhibition of Cancer Cell Proliferation in Vitro by Extracts from Organically and Conventionally Cultivated Strawberries," *Journal of Agricultural and Food Chemistry* 54 (2006): 1248–55.

62. Shiow Y. Wang and Hsin-Shan Lin, "Compost as a Soil Supplement Increases the Level of Anitoxidant Compounds and Oxygen Radical Absorbance Capacity in Strawberries," *Journal of Agricultural and Food Chemistry* 51 (2003): 6844–50.

63. Siriwoharn et al., "Blackberry Maturity and Anthocyanins."

64. Shiow. Y. Wang and Hsin-Shan Lin, "Antioxidant Activity in Fruits and Leaves of Blackberry, Raspberry, and Strawberry Varies with Cultivar and Developmental Stage," *Journal of Agricultural and Food Chemistry* 48 (2000): 140–146; Ronald L Prior et al., "Antioxidant Capacity as Influenced by Total Phenolic and Anthocyanin Content, Maturity, and Variety of Vaccinium Species," *Journal of Agricultural and Food Chemistry* 46 (1998): 2686–93.

RESOURCE GUIDE

Suggested Reading

Benbrook, Charles. "Elevating Antioxidant Levels in Food through Organic Farming and Food Processing." The Organic Center, January 2005. Available at http://www.organic-center.org/science.antiox.php?action=view&report_id=3.

Benbrook, Charles, et al. "New Evidence Confirms the Nutritional Superiority of Plant-Based Organic Foods." The Organic Center, March 2008. Available at http://www.organicenter.org/reportfiles/5367_Nutrient_Content_SSR_FINAL_V2.pdf.

Bourn, Diane, and John Prescott. "A Comparison of the Nutritional Value, Sensory Qualities and Food Safety of Organically and Conventionally Produced Foods." *Critical Reviews in Food Science and Nutrition* 42, no. 1 (2002): 1–34.

Halweil, Brian. "Still No Free Lunch: Nutrient Levels in U.S. Food Supply Eroded by Pursuit of High Yields." The Organic Center, September 2007. Available at http://www.organic-center.org/science.nutri.php?action=view&report_id=115.

Jeavons, John. *How to Grow More Vegetables.* Berkeley, CA: Ten Speed Press, 2006.

Madison, Deborah. *Local Flavors: Cooking and Eating from America's Farmer's Markets.* New York: Broadway Books, 2002.

Pollan, Michael. *In Defense of Food.* New York: The Penguin Press, 2008.

Pollan, Michael. *The Omnivore's Dilemma.* New York: The Penguin Press, 2006.

Rembialkowska, Ewa. "Review: Quality of Plant Products from Organic Agriculture." *Journal of the Science of Food and Agriculture* 87 (2007): 2757–2762.

Worthington, Virginia. "Nutritional Quality of Organic Versus Conventional Fruits, Vegetables, and Grains." *Journal of Alternative and Complementary Medicine* 7 (2001): 161–173.

Web Sites

Center for Science in the Public Interest, http://www.cspinet.org/.

Eat Well, http://www.eatwellguide.org/i.php?pd=Home.

Harvest Plus, http://www.harvestplus.org/index.html.

Local Harvest, http://www.localharvest.org/.

Long-Term Research on Agricultural Systems (LTRAS) Project, http://ltras.ucdavis.edu/.

The Organic Center, http://www.organic-center.org/.

Quality Low Input Food, http://www.qlif.org/about/index.html.

The Rodale Institute, http://www.rodaleinstitute.org/.

13

School Lunch and Breakfast Programs

Sandra M. Stokes

In the summer of 1981, early in President Ronald Reagan's administration, the U.S. Department of Agriculture (USDA) issued a policy directive that would have reclassified ketchup and pickle relish from condiments to vegetables. While this reclassification was proposed as a cost-saving measure (the White House Office of Management and Budget estimated $1 billion annual savings), the ensuing widespread controversy continued to haunt the Reagan administration. One can search online for the phrase "ketchup as a vegetable controversy" even today and find that this proposed policy was never implemented because it became a political lightning rod for charges of indifference to poor children's well-being. Very few Republicans or Democrats wanted to support what turned out to be a huge embarrassment for this Republican administration.[1]

Two important lessons emerge from this controversy: First, school lunches proved to be very popular with the American public, which was outraged by this attempt to "water down" meals for poor children. Because school lunches have been around for almost seventy years, this program has served millions of American citizens. Second, the National School Lunch Program (NSLP) has been the center of controversy many times since its birth in 1946, when the program emerged from the National School Lunch Act.

Another important controversy regarding school lunches had to do with its transformation from a program designed to prop up food commodity prices and employ those who were without jobs to a social welfare program for poor children, a transformation that began in the 1960s. Today, the social welfare aspect of NSLP is firmly entrenched; however, subsequent controversies over funding have ensured that the program has never been well funded and eligibility requirements have proved to be a barrier for families whose children need it the most.[2]

Today, the present controversy over school lunches has to do with their nutritional content: while the original purpose of the NSLP was that children were undernourished because they did not get enough food, today there is a concern that children are getting too much of the wrong foods—which still leads to malnutrition. Now, however, malnutrition is increasingly joined with obesity, and the diseases associated with obesity (e.g., diabetes, heart conditions). This controversy has raised questions that have to do with the original intent of the law, its wording, and how it is implemented. Those debating this issue would do well to keep in mind that school lunches have proven to be sacrosanct to the American public, as evidenced by the steady number of articles published on the topic of school lunches.

ORIGIN OF THE SCHOOL LUNCH PROGRAM

The NSLP had its origins in several factors emerging in American society during and directly following the Great Depression years of the 1930s. At this time of high unemployment, it was discovered that many young people were too undernourished to serve in the military or be gainfully employed despite the existence of farm surpluses.[3] During the time of President Franklin D. Roosevelt's administration, many initiatives to reverse the economic desperation of the Depression were implemented. The Works Progress Administration (WPA) became involved with children's nutrition by hiring workers to prepare and serve food in schools across the United States.[4] The WPA's child nutrition program had several practical goals: it put unemployed people to work; it helped farmers with food surpluses receive more money for their crops by keeping the prices higher than the market otherwise would have done; and, it helped prevent malnutrition in young people, thereby making them fit for military service and employment.[5] When World War II broke out, fitness for military service became a glaring problem, which was noted in Congress. Thus, many legislators worked to make nutrition in schools a national priority.[6]

In 1946, the U.S. Congress voted to create the NSLP through the passage of the National School Lunch Act, which was centered on the surplus food commodities produced in the United States.[7] This act has been reauthorized many times, and is now subsumed within the Child Nutrition Act of 1966; this latter act also includes the Special Milk Program, the Summer Food Service Program, the Child and Adult Care Program, the Special Supplemental Nutrition Program for Women, Infants, and Children (WIC), the Migrant Legal Action Program, and breakfast programs.[8] All of these programs are administered by the USDA's Food and Nutrition Services (FNS).

THE SUCCESSES OF THE NATIONAL SCHOOL LUNCH PROGRAM

The NSLP is the second largest food and nutrition assistance program (the Food Stamp Program is the largest) in the United States.[9] In 2006, the NSLP was available in more than one hundred thousand public and nonprofit private schools; more than twenty-eight million low-cost or free lunches were served in 2006 to children on a typical day.[10] Almost 60 percent of American children ages five to eighteen participate in the program at least once per week; almost half of all lunches served are provided free to students, with an additional 10 percent of the meals available at reduced prices.

Perhaps the NSLP's most important impact has been its impact on learning. A growing body of research has shown the positive impact of proper nutrition on a child's ability to learn.[11] Poor nutrition can interfere with cognitive functioning and is associated with low academic achievement.[12] NSLP mandates vitamin, mineral, fat, and protein requirements in meals served in schools through the program.[13] Breakfast programs have also proven to furnish children the requisite nutrition for learning to take place.[14,15]

One study for the USDA found that "NSLP participants consume more milk and vegetables at lunch and fewer sweets, sweetened beverages, and snack foods than nonparticipants."[16] Among middle-school students, NSLP participants were more likely to derive the recommended daily intake of vitamin A and magnesium, along with higher intakes of calcium and fiber. High school NSLP participants were more likely to receive the recommended daily intakes of vitamins A, B6, C, folate, iron, phosphorus, and thiamin as well as a higher intake of calcium and fiber than found among NSLP nonparticipants.[17]

There also has been financial success for American agriculture, perhaps too much success, as individual farms have been put out of business in favor of large corporations producing agricultural products for home and abroad.[18] In fact, one of NSLP's original purposes was to increase demand for agricultural commodities.[19] According to a USDA study of the NSLP, the bulk of commodities given to schools are what are called entitlement commodities; this includes processed meats, cheeses, grains, and produce as well as chicken fajita strips and nuggets, taco meat, hamburger patties, turkey sausage, canned and frozen fruits and vegetables, salsa, macaroni and cheese, and other pasta. Schools can receive "bonus" commodities—that is, those that become available from surplus agricultural stock and are made available because of an oversupply of these products in the retail market.[20]

THE PRESENT CONTROVERSY OVER SCHOOL LUNCHES

The present controversy over school lunches—in fact over all meals and food served in schools—focuses on three areas: costs and financing, content and supply, and procurement. Since 1946, every controversy has centered either on any one of these areas, or sometimes on all three of them.

Costs and Financing

Local education agencies participating in the NSLP receive reimbursements and donated commodities from the USDA for each meal that they serve. Furthermore, school food services must operate on a nonprofit basis, with their revenue used to support or improve the food service.[21] Schools in the United States are reimbursed just under $2.50 per meal per student daily, even though more money than that is required for labor, transportation of food, utilities, and equipment.[22] While school lunches have never been easy to fund, budgetary pressures on schools increased in the early 1980s, during Reagan's presidency.[23] At that time, cuts in the subsidies were made and have never been fully restored; making it even harder to fund these programs is the fact that costs of transportation and procurement associated with implementing the NSLP have risen, but the USDA reimbursement rate has not kept pace with the growth in these costs.[24] One of the factors that can help with the reimbursement rates is the number of eligible children served: the higher the number of children served, the higher the amount of total reimbursement a school receives.[25]

The problem with funding today has been exacerbated by the present state of the economy. While school districts have always been short of federal funding, the shortage has grown today because more families have found themselves qualifying for government assistance programs—among them the NSLP. Even though the USDA has promised to raise the federal reimbursement rate, the problem remains: even the increased amount of funding buys less food.[26] This problem has further complicated the next area of controversy: content and supply. Generally speaking, when funding is tight, the tendency is to buy the least expensive products. This tendency, coupled with the previous inadequate supply of funding, has made it more difficult for school districts to acquire the most nutritious food, but instead easier to acquire more of the oversupply of commodities that may contribute to obesity while not furnishing much nutritional value.

Content and Supply

The content of school lunches has undergone a number of changes, but has been largely built around agricultural commodity oversupplies. Indeed, as Levine says, the NSLP "was in its goals, structure, and administration, more a subsidy for agriculture than a nutrition program for children."[27] Originally, the NSLP was a welfare program for farmers and a benefit for those middle- and working-class children whose families could pay a subsidized price for their children's meals.[28] According to Levine, "[b]etween 1968 and 1972 the National School Lunch Program was transformed from being primarily an agricultural subsidy into one of the nation's premier poverty programs."[29]

When the NSLP became an antipoverty program, the number of children whose families were paying for lunch declined precipitously because of the stigma attached to participation in a social welfare program.[30] Once the NSLP became a program that guaranteed poor children a free lunch, the quality of school meals also declined, mostly because the amount of money was declining as well, without the money from paying customers. Therefore, "school administrators ... began to look to the private food service industry to keep school cafeterias afloat."[31] Unfortunately, this is a trend that has continued through the present time.

Therefore, school lunches, composed largely of government surplus commodities as well as healthful items such as fruit and vegetables, were forced to compete with such fast food items as Pizza Hut pizza, McDonald's hamburgers, and the like. The problem with this situation can be summed up as follows:

> Nationwide data show that about 10% of school food sold is from the cafeteria reimbursable lunch ... [while] over 70% of school food sold are a la carte items from the cafeteria "Trend" menu, which offers ... burgers, fries, pizza, ice cream, and other snack type foods, and from school stores; over 20% came from vending machines in the schools.[32]

Students have grown increasingly accustomed to fast food meals because their families are purchasing this fare for home consumption. Schools trying to serve more nutritious food have found that students buy fewer lunches or do not eat the fruits and vegetables.[33] Thus, schools have been stuck in an untenable situation. The more difficult it has become to have their school lunches be financially self-sustaining, the more deeply they have gotten into arrangements with such entities as fast food restaurants.[34]

Perhaps the most critical point of this situation can be seen in the contracts—exclusive contracts—schools have signed with soda companies. Nicola Pinson found that 75 percent of U.S. high schools, 65 percent of U.S. middle schools, and 30 percent of elementary schools have these contracts.[35] What these contracts involve is obligating the school districts to purchase an extremely high amount of their products—which have no competition besides the school lunch milk—as well as giving the soda companies the right to advertise and market their products to a captive audience, one the soda companies hope will become "brand loyal."[36]

Meanwhile, the food supplied to schools has increasingly become prepackaged, suitable for reheating only because kitchen equipment in many districts is largely nonexistent. Grants for replacing kitchen equipment were ended during the Reagan administration and never restored so that far too many school districts receive ready-to-serve food, which is reheated in a central kitchen and then sent to the individual schools.[37] Thus, we can see that food supplied to schools has matched the prevailing philosophy of making food cheaper and producing it faster—a philosophy that has driven the fast food industry.[38]

Celebrated school lunch chef Alice Waters, who has been trying to obtain local, nutritious food for schools, has summed up the situation:

> [W]e have a set of agricultural policies that subsidize fast food and makes fresh, wholesome foods, which receive no government support, seem expensive ... [I]ndustrial food is artificially cheap, with its real costs being charged to the public purse, the public health, and the environment.[39]

In theory, the agricultural commodities that the schools receive through the NSLP should be decided on by the farmers producing those commodities. In reality, though, very few farmers actually have a say because the family farm is becoming an anachronism, with large agricultural corporations controlling the marketplace. It is these companies that decide which crops the government will support when the U.S. Congress passes the farm bill every five years. Today, says author Michael Pollan, "that means ... corn and soybeans ... the corn providing the added sugars, the soy providing the added fat, and both providing the feed for the animals ... [so that] the cheapest calories ... are precisely the unhealthiest."[40] The corn and soybeans are fed to animals; these animals are then slaughtered to furnish the country—including children in schools—with food from an unquestionably unsustainable practice, which does not provide a goodly amount of nutrition. For example, pig farms use six pounds of grain for every pound of boneless meat, so that when we feed the grain to the pigs, we lose most of the nutritional value of the grain. Thus, we can see that feedlot beef is high in fat and not as nutritious as the grains themselves. This practice adds to the problem of our nation's children becoming both obese and malnourished at the same time.

In addition to the problem of unsustainable, high-fat food supplied to schools is the problem of synthetic hormones, primarily in use to produce beef, pork, and chicken for consumption—all with the goal of faster production, and therefore cheaper production. This is a particularly American problem: every country in the European Union bans this practice because of research that shows that the "hormone residues in U.S. beef may be linked to high rates of breast and prostate cancer, as well as early onset of puberty in girls."[41]

Producing dairy products cheaply is also a goal supplying food for school lunches, one that has proven to be lucrative for the large dairy corporations, which not only buy milk from farmers but also dictates to those farmers how their dairy cows should be treated.[42] For example, Monsanto Corporation pioneered the use of recombinant bovine growth hormone (rBGH) to increase milk production in dairy cows; this can give cows udder infections, whose pus is often captured in the milk collected. Research also shows that this hormone has been associated with breast, prostate, and colon cancer; such dangers explain why all of the European countries as well as Australia, New Zealand, and Japan have banned the production and sale of milk with rBGH.[43]

The problems of supply for school lunches are not insurmountable, as we will read later in this chapter. However, we first need to examine the problem that school districts have with procuring a nutritious supply of food for school lunches.

Procurement

Schools have had to face the problems associated with finding and keeping a reliable source of food supplies for school lunches. Associated with this problem are increasingly constrained school budgets. It is much cheaper to deal with one central supplier, or as few suppliers as possible, rather than many different ones whose economic survival is not guaranteed. In fact, Jack Kloppenburg found that institutional buyers prefer to deal with as few vendors as possible to maximize the efficiency and costs of ordering and delivery.[44] Schools are required by federal law to receive as much as 80 percent of their food from one central supplier.[45]

Overcoming the problems of procurement is necessary if the United States will be able to change the focus of its school lunch program. This can be seen even when looking at an award-winning school—Richmond Elementary School in Appleton, Wisconsin. This school was recently found to be the fourth healthiest school in the United States by *Health* magazine.[46]

Richmond Elementary School—one of nineteen elementary schools in the school district—is situated on a corner in Appleton, Wisconsin, near Lawrence University. It has occupied much of this same space since its original building in 1887, when it was a two-story wooden schoolhouse, with a kindergarten on the first floor and first and second grades on the second floor.[47]

Today, Richmond Elementary is a neighborhood school with all of its 277 kindergarten through sixth-grade students walking to school. This neighborhood school draws its students from a variety of ethnic and socioeconomic backgrounds, with approximately 33 percent of its students qualifying for free or reduced lunch. The student population has a 17 percent minority representation, primarily Hispanic.[48]

Richmond Elementary, like the other elementary schools in the district, has a health education curriculum that includes nutrition for kindergarten through sixth grade. This education component is especially important in teaching the students about good and healthy foods to eat—at school as well as at home. Research also

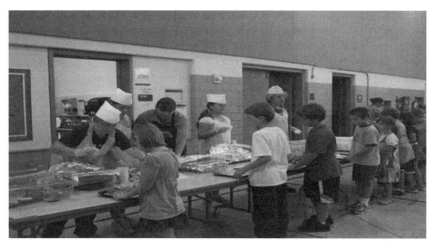

Figure 13.1.
Lunchtime at Richmond Elementary. Photo credit: Sandra Stokes, author.

establishes the importance of students learning about food in school; schools, say Pyles and Lobick, "can shape children's food preferences, and therefore play an important role in helping improve children's diets."[49]

Richmond Elementary works hard to ensure that food served in the school as snacks and for celebrations is also healthy. This is especially important, because as Pyles and Lobick report, preferences for foods increase when those foods are presented as rewards.[50]

Support from parent participation at Richmond Elementary comes from all socioeconomic backgrounds. Parents serve on four committees aimed at school improvement:

- Education for healthy living
- Whole child (which includes bully prevention and character education)
- Responsive Education for All Children (REACH, a collaborative effort between local school districts and Wisconsin's Department of Public Instruction, designed to improve instruction for at-risk students in Title I schools)
- Teaching and learning improvement[51]

Another home-school connection is the newsletter, the *Rocket Reporter*, which Principal Roberta Schmidt composes and sends home to the parents. In every issue of this newsletter, she includes suggestions for sack lunches. For example, for the first week of school, the *Rocket Reporter* included paragraph-size entries for each day of the week:

- Homemade sandwiches and snacks for Monday
- Grilled cheese pockets for Tuesday
- Turkey-cran tortilla bites for Wednesday
- Bite-size offerings with dip for dunking for Thursday
- Layered sandwiches for Friday[52]

These lunch suggestions are written under the heading of "Healthy Kids at Richmond"; in addition, a low-calorie recipe is included for families as well as information about healthy foods.[53]

The activities of Richmond Elementary School's education for healthy living committee and a district-wide initiative designed to improve nutritional offerings in Appleton schools are illustrated in solid qualitative data that show student attitudes toward food choices are evident in the school as well as in the students' homes. Such data were published in a report completed for the Appleton school district measuring student responses to a series of questions. To compose this report, the school district employed the services of Lawrence University, the University of Wisconsin–Fox Valley, and Appleton East High School personnel to conduct a study that grouped results under the following divisions: social influences on nutrition, the culture of food and nutrition, student diets and eating behavior, garbology, and overarching results.[54] Findings from this study not only affect school lunches in Appleton, but also are likely to apply to school districts across the country. Without exposure to certain foods, children most likely will not eat them.[55]

Students in Appleton reported that their family was the biggest social influence on their nutritional behavior. This finding not only explains dinner choices but also explains the choices found in sack lunches. Another finding was that school lunch purchases in Appleton high schools were found to be adversely affected by students being allowed to leave their campus at lunch time; these students most often reported choosing fast food purchases for lunch.[56]

Other salient findings involved sugar, fat, and sodium. The study found that the majority of sugar in students' diets was added sugar rather than the naturally occurring sugar found in milk, fruit, and fruit juices. This result led to the finding that students exceeded the USDA Food Guide recommendations for added sugars, fat, and sodium—the latter by substantial margins. In addition, fiber consumption was found to be well below established guidelines.[57]

The work accomplished by Richmond Elementary has now achieved widespread national recognition.[58] Richmond Elementary's Principal Roberta Schmidt and the pupil services administrator in the Appleton district serve as contact people for the Appleton Area School District's Elementary Food Service Committee. This committee has thirteen members, eight of whom are parents. The dietitian and the district food service director are Aramark employees.

Richmond Elementary has achieved this status without using a farm-to-school philosophy largely because the Appleton school district has partnered with Aramark.[59] Aramark provides food services to more than 420 public and private school districts in the United States.[60] According to Principal Schmidt, Aramark has proved to be cooperative in the district's quest to offer healthy food instead of the commonly found unhealthy school lunches found in many districts.

One method of changing the school lunch menu, according to Schmidt, is for Johnston Elementary School—the designated pilot school for dietary changes in the Appleton district—to test various menu items to discover which ones produce the least plate waste (the term for food that students throw away). Decisions on test items are made by the district and Aramark. Right now, a salad bar is being tested to determine its feasibility in elementary schools; a salad bar is already successfully being offered in Appleton's middle and high schools.

Appleton procures its food for lunches from Sysco Corporation, located in Baraboo, Wisconsin. According to its Web site, Sysco is—

> seeking to respond to this consumer demand for more local and sustainable produced foods by linking the farmer with the customer through the modification of existing procurement and distribution supply chains.[61]

There are four grades of food available from Sysco: supreme, imperial, classic, and reliance. Appleton schools receive reliance-grade food, which Sysco defines as "economy-based products that are specified at a level equal to competitive labels for similar grades or quality."[62]

Of the nine recommendations listed later in this chapter, Richmond Elementary meets seven of them. The only two recommendations not met thus far are ones that apply to the provision of food for school lunches: (1) encouraging local providers to form cooperatives that make it easier for districts to obtain locally grown food, and (2) working to lower the federal requirement that 80 percent of all meal components come from one vendor.

Richmond Elementary has achieved excellent results despite the fact that the whole district has a private firm operating its food services. This arrangement across the country has garnered a great deal of criticism; however, this arrangement can clearly work. In contrast to the situation at Richmond Elementary, another effort to improve school food is known as the farm-to-school approach.

A NEW APPROACH: FARM-TO-SCHOOL PROGRAMS

Nationwide, approximately four hundred farm-to-school (FTS) programs are found in twenty-two states.[63] FTS programs are one initiative in the growing alternative agrifood movement that "brings fresh, local produce into schools."[64] These programs have been defined as follows:

> [T]he ability to connect schools with local and regional farmers to benefit both sets of participants. FTS initiatives connect school food services with local farmers in partnerships that are intended to bring healthier, fresher food to school meals programs while at the same time supporting local farmers by providing an additional source of income and a relatively secure market.[65]

Allen and Guthman argue that FTS programs are unique within the alternative agrifood movement because they, by definition, must work within the NSLP.[66] Nationwide, schools serve some 6.5 billion meals each year to almost 30 million children.[67] The first FTS program, begun in 1994, was called Farm Fresh Start and was located in Hartford, Connecticut.[68] For schools, say Allen and Guthman, having multiple small vendors is a serious problem because this increases the costs of a food program due to higher costs of market intermediaries, insurance requirements, and accounting costs. This has caused some FTS programs to create intermediaries such as farmer collaborations.[69]

The costs of FTS programs cannot be ignored, according to Kloppenburg and Hassanein:

> In an era of straitened or declining budgets many parents, school boards, and state departments of education tend to see FTS programs as potential drains on resources that would best be directed to supporting performance in core academics (or sports).[70]

These authors make the same point about traditional NSLP food: "Food quality continuously degenerates as food services ... are forced to mimic commercial fast food competitors even as they try to cut costs while embracing USDA commodity foods and pre-packaged meal items that are (literally) assembled rather than cooked."[71] To counter the cost constraints, U.S. Senator Tom Harkin of Iowa has included support for FTS in the last two farm bills.[72] The support from Senator Harkin, as well as many others, is based on two concerns—the massive loss of individual family farms (which account for less than 10 percent of all farms in the United States) and the growing recognition that children's nutritional status is problematic today.[73]

Most of the FTS programs are found in California, the Northeast, and Upper Midwest; fresh food for school meals and snacks—usually fruits and vegetables—from local and regional farms provide the food for these programs. FTS programs also involve either individual schools, several schools in a district, or, less commonly, multiple school districts.[74] In most FTS programs:

> Schools may purchase a single crop such as apples or watermelons, or a much broader range of items. Occasionally, dairy products and meats are included. The food may be incorporated into existing lunch menus, presented on a salad bar, or provided to students as part of a snack program ... [and depends] on the types of crops produced in the region and seasonal availability.[75]

According to Kloppenburg and colleagues, there is a vicious circle regarding the costs and supply of local food:[76] "Farmers want a market before they augment production, while food services want to know there is an adequate supply before they commit to buy."[77]

In fact, a study of their Madison-based Wisconsin Homegrown Lunch program found this FTS program was

> seriously constrained by a variety of structural features ... [such as] the overarching food culture, the quasi-privatized character of most school food services, the degree of industrialization of many school food services, issues of price, procurement and supply and the need for processing facilities.[78]

In addition, other problems are associated with FTS programs. Wealthier schools are offering fresh, organic fruits and vegetables in lieu of the fast food model of school lunches typically found in inner-city schools and poor rural areas, because the wealthier schools can afford to absorb the increased costs of eating healthy food, an initiative embraced by the parents of those children.[79] Meanwhile, poor children are relegated to eating the food that is provided to them, largely from surplus commodities instead of healthier foods. The American value of equality in schools is, in reality, turning out to be in contradiction to the basic need all children have for food.

One further characteristic of FTS programs is an education component—from lunchroom to classroom. Education activities include in-class food tasting, field trips to farms, farmer visits to classrooms, school gardening, and the incorporation of food and farm issues into existing curricula. Without such a component, students can all too easily remain fast food customers. As an article in *Rethinking Schools* notes, "When so much of the food that students encounter is transported over long distances, chemical-laden, shrink-wrapped, and processed, students make little connection with the foods' origins."[80]

A SAMPLE OF FTS PROGRAMS

Opelika, Alabama, increased funding for school meals so that those meals can include fresh fruits and vegetables from local farms; the food typically eaten in this community includes such nutritious foods as sweet potatoes, butter cream peas, and black-eyed peas.[81] This fare is all locally produced and often eaten at home.

Olympia, Washington, schools have added salad bars to their cafeterias, stocked with local produce. To reduce costs, the district made a healthy decision: it stopped serving desserts and started serving fresh fruit instead.[82] In fact, Olympia Elementary School has adopted the idea that food should be part of the school's curriculum: On school grounds, one can find a "large organic garden and greenhouse; during the school year, [the] students dig, plant, weed, water, compost, harvest, and cook fresh produce. All classrooms use the garden to help teach measuring, graphing, and weighing."[83]

Berkeley, California, has been a pioneer in school meal changes. The district promotes the consumption of fresh fruits and vegetables; one of its schools has a garden-to-table feature.[84] Every school in Berkeley has a salad bar with ingredients including strawberries, organic chicken or turkey, sunflower seeds, fresh avocado, and other in-season items; 100 percent of the district's food today is fresh and cooked from "scratch." Entrees include organic sushi and organic chicken, and small local businesses supply such food as fresh tamales, muffins, and vegetable calzones.[85]

Six schools in the North Quabbin region in central Massachusetts have partnered with Seeds for Solidarity, a nonprofit organization that has worked with the schools to create and teach a course called Reading, Writing, and Wellness.[86]

Private funding has recently been playing a role, too. Belkin reports on a program called Healthier Options for Public Schoolchildren (HOPS). This program was started by Dr. Arthur Agatston, the creator of the South Beach Diet, and can be found in four of the twenty-nine elementary schools in Osceola County, Florida. The program includes small gardens at each school as well as the inclusion of lesson plans and guides for nutrition lessons to fit into math, science, and social studies curricula.[87]

The W. K. Kellogg Foundation is funding nine communities: Boston and Holyoke, Massachusetts; Detroit, Michigan; New York, New York; Northeast Iowa; Oakland, California; Philadelphia, Pennsylvania; Seattle and King County, Washington; and the Tohono O'odham Nation, Arizona. The funding is intended for planning, implementing, and sustaining changes to improve the quality of life for children and families by providing money to these communities to purchase local, healthy food. Each community is building a collaborative. Foundation Food and Fitness Initiative Co-Director Gail Imig states, "The key issue is that millions of children don't have access to fresh foods that are good for them. Their neighborhoods and communities aren't conducive to exercise and play."[88]

The Wisconsin Homegrown Lunch is an FTS program located in the Madison (Wisconsin) Metropolitan School District (MMSD). The goals of this program are "to increase the amount of locally grown foods served in MMSD cafeterias while also providing meaningful educational opportunities for students."[89] The curricular programming is available on the Web site of the Center for Integrated Agricultural Systems (http://www.cias.wisc.edu/education-and-training/sustainable-agriculture-curriculum-for-high-school-educators-announced/).

One problem encountered by this program was little to no food preparation being performed by the MMSD food service workers; instead, meals served come from ready-to-eat, prepackaged components at a central kitchen facility. This means that the food service department requires fresh food to come in ready-to-use form. Despite this barrier, locally sourced menu items include rhubarb muffins, sweet potato muffins, salad mix, yogurt/cream cheese/dill sauce, vegetarian chili, vegetarian tortilla wrap, cranberry cookies, squash bisque, and baked potatoes.[90]

Another difficulty encountered by this program, consistent with the research on what could improve school lunches, is that the MMSD school district is required to purchase approximately 80 percent of its food products through a national food distributor, meaning that only 20 percent of the food served in school lunches can come from local sources.[91]

The state of California established an initiative called the California Fresh Start Program (CFSP) to encourage and support schools to provide portions of fruit and vegetables, with an emphasis on obtaining the fruit and vegetables from local and regionally grown California produce.[92]

The CFSP provides a $0.10 reimbursement to districts for purchasing fresh fruit and vegetables. More large urban school districts participated in this program than did districts in rural areas. The evaluation of the CFSP found that participating districts had a 46 percent increase in the amount of fresh fruit and vegetables offered; furthermore, students more than doubled their consumption of the fresh fruit and vegetables.[93] Of noteworthy attention was the fact that an evaluation of the program found that its success was far more noticeable in districts that had lower baseline levels of fruit and vegetable consumption by students.[94] Nutrition education, especially regarding the consumption of fresh fruit and vegetables, was part of this program, and it is believed to have contributed to the program's apparent success. Activities included taste testing in classrooms, cooking classes or demonstrations, and nutrition fairs.[95]

Barriers to success were inadequate kitchen facilities and a lack of storage space as well as inadequate time devoted to eating; these findings appear to match the findings in other FTS programs. Yet another barrier was the source of the fresh fruit and vegetables; having to locate and negotiate with multiple growers was perceived as difficult because of concerns about insurance and safety certification issues.[96]

RECOMMENDATIONS FOR HEALTHIER SCHOOL LUNCHES

In compiling a list of recommendations, it should be kept in mind that the areas of cost and funding, content and supply, and procurement are all part of these recommendations.

1. Policies in school districts need to be developed to improve the school lunches served in America's schools.
2. Farmers need to join together to provide a sufficient volume of products as well as to provide the food products in ready-to-use form.

3. Junk food available in programs, school stores, and vending machines needs to be curtailed; schools need to end the use of sweets as incentives for classroom performance.
4. Provide food that is low in fat, calories, and added sugars. Recommended are fruits, vegetables, whole grains, and low-fat or nonfat dairy foods.
5. Provide an adequate amount of time for students to eat school meals; all too many schools offer twenty-five minutes or less to eat lunch.
6. Encourage school meals that contain nutritious food and ensure that all meals meet federal nutrition standards.
7. Effective leadership from principals and food service directors needs to be obtained.
8. An education component that is age-appropriate and culturally sensitive should be included to accompany healthy school lunches. This education should help students develop the knowledge, attitudes, skills, and behaviors needed to adopt and continue healthy eating habits.
9. Drop the federal requirement that school districts must obtain 80 percent of their food from one vendor.

CONCLUSION

If the United States can implement most, if not all, of these recommendations the nation will gain not only a healthier student body, but also a much healthier economy. As Susan Levine concludes,

> School lunch politics for American children has turned out to be more complicated than parents or policy makers ever imagined. For one thing, as nutritionists and parents know all too well, it is difficult, if not impossible, to convince people— whether children or adults—to eat what is good for them, rather than what tastes good. . . .
>
> In crafting a National School Lunch Program, legislators convinced themselves that they could subsidize agricultural markets and at the same time ensure the nutritional well-being of the nation's children.... While policy makers and legislators alike boasted that the National School Lunch Program was intended to protect the nutritional health of all children, no one was willing to appropriate the funds it would take to actually carry out that goal.... But the idea of feeding children in school has brought together unexpected alliances and coalitions that have not always fit with the usual political categories of liberal or conservative. When it comes to children, food, and welfare, school lunch politics challenges all players—agriculture, the food-service industry, nutritionists, children's welfare advocates, and elected officials alike—to serve up balanced meals that include substantive resources along with healthy diets.[97]

An examination of school lunches can be seen either as a glass half-full or as a glass half-empty. There has been much discussion recently about the problems of the food that we eat in the United States. This food comes largely from large corporations instead of from family farms and it is laden with chemicals that harm our health. The issues surrounding school lunches are but one facet of the issues of food, in general. Therefore, as we discuss and plan on creating a healthier supply of food for the general population, procuring safer and healthier food for school lunches should also be improved. Recognition today of the unhealthy food habits that permeate U.S. society can lead to a change from mass-produced food grown with unhealthy methods to a supply of food that is locally grown using sustainable practices.

The large corporations supplying much of the food that we eat are receiving federal government subsidies to produce and supply the food. These subsidies presently are going to a few large corporations and instead could be shifted to individual family farmers who are using sustainable practices. This shift will result in a healthier food supply for society in general, and for children eating food in schools as well.

NOTES

1. Susan Levine, *School Lunch Politics: The Surprising History of America's Favorite Welfare Program* (Princeton, NJ: Princeton University Press, 2008).

2. Ibid.

3. Josephine Martin, "The National School Lunch Program—A Continuing Commitment," *Journal of the American Dietetic Association* 96, no. 9 (1996): 857–858.

4. Ibid.

5. Ibid.

6. Eileen Kennedy and Edward Cooney, "Development of the Child Nutrition Programs in the United States," *The Journal of Nutrition* 131 (2001): 431S–436S.

7. Ibid.

8. Eileen Kennedy, "Public Policy in Nutrition: The U.S. Nutrition Safety Net—Past, Present, and Future," *Food Policy* 24 (1999): 325–333, 343–347.

9. Katherine Ralston et al., "The National School Lunch Program: Background, Trends, and Issues," Economic Research Report No. 61 (Washington, DC: Economic Research Service, U.S. Department of Agriculture, 2008).

10. Ibid.

11. Katherine Alaimo, Christine M. Olson, and Edward A. Frongillo Jr., "Food Insufficiency and American School-Aged Children's Cognitive, Academic, and Psychosocial Development," *Pediatrics* 108, no. 1 (2001): 44–53.

12. Lynn Parker, *The Relationship between Nutrition and Learning: A School Employee's Guide to Information and Action* (Washington, DC: National Education Association, 1989).

13. Alaimo, Olson, and Frongillo Jr., "Food Insufficiency."

14. Laura Rowell, "An Analysis of Green Bay Area Public Schools Breakfast Barriers and Its Impact on Student Nutrition and Program Revenue" (master's thesis, Cardinal Stritch University, 2006).

15. Food Research and Action Center. "School Breakfast Scorecard 2007," http://www.frac.org/pdf/SBP_2007.pdf (accessed July 11, 2008).

16. Ralston et al., "National School Lunch," 22.

17. Ibid.

18. Thomas Reardon and Christopher B. Barrett, "Agroindustrialization, Globalization, and International Development: An Overview of Issues, Patterns, and Determinants," *Agricultural Economics* 23, no. 3 (2000): 195–205.

19. Ralston et al., "National School Lunch."

20. Ibid.

21. Food and Nutrition Service, Office of Research, Nutrition and Analysis, "School Lunch and Breakfast Study—II: Summary of Findings," http://www/fns.usda.gov/OANE/menu/Published/CNP/FILES/MealCostStudySummary.pdf (accessed July 1, 2008).

22. Lisa Belkin, "The School Lunch Test," *New York Times Magazine*, August 20, 2006, Midwest edition.

23. Ralston et al., "National School Lunch."

24. Ibid.

25. Ibid.

26. Emily Gersema, "School Districts Absorb Costs As Free Lunches Soar," *Green Bay Press-Gazette*, August 24, 2006, B5.

27. Levine, *School Lunch Politics*, 39.

28. Ibid.

29. Ibid., 151.

30. Patricia L. Fitzgerald, "Decades of Dedication: The Early Years," *School Foodservice and Nutrition* 2, no. 96 (October 1995): 55–60.

31. Levine, *School Lunch Politics*, 151.

32. Sharron Dalton, "Schools and the Rising Rate of Overweight Children: Prevention and Intervention Strategies," *Topics in Clinical Nutrition* 19, no. 1 (2007): 34–40, 36.

33. Ibid.

34. Ibid.

35. Nicola Pinson, "Who Really Benefits from School Soda Contracts?" *Rethinking Schools* 20, no. 4 (2006): 48–49.

36. Leah Penniman, "Sowing the Seeds of Solidarity," *Rethinking Schools* 20, no. 4 (2006): 34–38.

37. Tom Philpott, "Sucker Lunch: It's Time to Get Serious about Reforming School Lunches," http://www.grist.org/comments.food/2006/09/06schoolmeals/ (accessed July 11, 2008).

38. Jim Hightower, "One Thing to Do about Food," *The Nation* (September 11, 2006): 21.

39. Alice Waters, "One Thing to Do about Food," *The Nation* (September 11, 2006): 13.

40. Michael Pollan, "One Thing to Do about Food," *The Nation* (September 11, 2006): 16.

41. Tim Swinehart, "Got a Little More Than Milk? Students Get a Glimpse into the Corporate-Controlled Food System by Looking at the Politics of Food," *Rethinking Schools* 20, no. 4 (2006): 52–56.

42. Ibid.

43. Ibid.

44. Jack Kloppenburg, Doug Wubben, and Miriam Grunes, *If You Serve It, Will They Come? Farm-to-School Lessons from the Wisconsin Homegrown Lunch Project* (Madison, WI: Center for Integrated Agricultural Systems, 2007).

45. Jack Kloppenburg Jr. and Neva Hassanein, "From Old School to Reform School?" *Agriculture and Human Values* 23 (2006): 417–421.

46. Tracy Minkin, "America's Healthiest Schools," *Health* 22, no. 7 (2008): 142–48.

47. Personal interview with Roberta Schmidt, September 26, 2008.

48. Ibid.

49. Jennifer Pyles and Jennifer Lobick, "Examination of the National School Lunch Program," *Nutritional Anthropology* 24, no. 2 (2001): 15–20.

50. Pyles and Lobick, "Examination."

51. Roberta Schmidt interview.

52. *Rocket Reporter*, Richmond Elementary, Appleton, WI, September 4, 2008.

53. Ibid.

54. Appleton Collaborative Nutrition Project, *Appleton Collaborative Nutrition Project Report* (Appleton, WI: Lawrence University, University of Wisconsin-Fox Valley for Appleton School District, 2008).

55. Pyles and Lobick, "Examination," 18.

56. Appleton Collaborative Nutrition Project. http://www.aasd.k12.wi.us/east/ APPLETON_EAST/Nutrition_Study/nutrition_title.htm.

57. Ibid.

58. Minkin, "America's Healthiest Schools."

59. Aramark, http://www.aramark.com/ContentTemplate.aspx?PostingID=398&Channel ID=228 (accessed November 2, 2008).

60. Ibid.

61. Sysco, http://www.sysco.com/aboutus/aboutus_buylocal.html (accessed November 2, 2008).

62. Ibid.

63. Patricia Allen and Julie Guthman, "From 'Old School' to 'Farm-to-School': Neoliberalization from the Ground Up," *Agriculture and Human Values* 23 (2006): 401–415.

64. Allen and Guthman, "Old School," 412.

65. Ibid.

66. Ibid.

67. Ibid.

68. Ibid.

69. Ibid.

70. Kloppenburg and Hassanein, "From Old School," 419.

71. Ibid.

72. Kloppenburg, Wubben, and Grunes, *If You Serve It.*

73. Ibid.

74. Ibid.

75. Ibid.

76. Ibid.

77. Ibid., 19.

78. Ibid.

79. Allen and Guthman, "Old School," 409.

80. Editors, "Feeding the Children," *Rethinking Schools* 20, no. 4 (2006): 5.

81. Dalton, "Schools."

82. Kathleen Vail, "School Food Revolution," *American School Board Journal* 192, no. 1 (2005): 10–15.

83. Michi Thacker, "There's No Business Like Food Business: Students Explore the Secretive Journey from Farm to Table," *Rethinking Schools* 20, no. 4 (2006): 28–32.

84. Vail, "School Food Revolution."

85. Belkin, "The School Lunch Test."

86. Penniman, "Sowing."

87. Belkin, "The School Lunch Test."

88. W. K. Kellogg Foundation, "Food and Fitness," http://www.wkkf.org/Default. aspz?tabid=90&CID=383&ItemID=5000343&NID=5010343&LanguageID=0 (accessed June 15, 2008).

89. Kloppenburg, Wubben, and Grunes, *If You Serve It,* 6.

90. Ibid.

91. Ibid.

92. Gail Woodward-Lopez and Karen Webb, *Evaluation of the California Fresh Start Program: Report of Findings* (Sacramento: California Department of Education, 2008).

93. Ibid.
94. Ibid.
95. Ibid.
96. Ibid.
97. Levine, *School Lunch Politics*, 190–191.

RESOURCE GUIDE

Suggested Reading

Levine, Susan. *School Lunch Politics: The Surprising History of America's Favorite Welfare Program*. Princeton, NJ: Princeton University Press, 2008.
Philpott, Tom. "Sucker Lunch: It's Time to Get Serious about Reforming School Lunches." Available at http://www.grist.org/comments.food/2006/09/06schoolmeals/ (accessed on July 11, 2008.)

Web Site

Food Research and Action Center, "School Breakfast Scorecard 2007," http://www.frac.org/pdf/SBP_2007.pdf.

14

Disordered Eating and Body Image

Cheryl Toronto Kalny

HISTORICAL OVERVIEW

In the Western Hemisphere, some of the earliest documented cases of voluntary food denial appear in Christian, Medieval Europe, and were interpreted as religious phenomenon. Young, usually unmarried women denied themselves all forms of food except for the consecrated communion wafer they consumed at daily Mass. At a time when the female was considered to be the fountainhead of evil, not only in Church doctrine but also by public opinion, these fasting girls attracted to themselves not only considerable attention, but also positive, public affirmation of their goodness.[1]

Although the motives and goals behind this form of "holy anorexia" were certainly different from the modern mania for excessive thinness, a number of studies have suggested surprising sociocultural similarities through the ages.[2] In the Middle Ages, as today, the onset of food asceticism coincided with the onset of puberty, suggesting a fear of sexual development and an attempt to stunt or curb sexual maturation. Concurrently, these fasting habits can be seen, then and now, as a desire to exert some limited control of one's life, if only through food intake. Young women in both time periods bemoan the inability to achieve satisfying results through strict food asceticism, hence the obsessive compulsion to fast to death.

By the 1600s, the concern with fasting saints had given way to an interest in cultural ideals as well as physical symptomology. Gutierrez examines the convergence in early modern England of fasting women in fact and fiction. The pining away of Shakespeare's Ophelia mirrors the tragic self-induced starvation of one of Queen Elizabeth's ladies-in-waiting, Margaret Ratcliffe, memorialized by the poet Ben Jonson as one "whose grief was out of fashion."[3] Both women are celebrated and mourned not as saints, but as examples of praise-worthy, other-centered females. At this same time, documented cases in London and Paris began to describe illnesses in young women between the ages of fifteen and twenty consisting of diminished food intake, constipation, loss of weight, and, curiously, the patient's unconcern with her condition. Over the next two hundred years, the severe emaciation of these patients was variously attributed to hypopituitarism, nervous consumption, or apepsia hysterica.[4] Generally, it was believed that a lack of appetite was the root cause of these problems, hence the term anorexia (from the Greek, "loss of appetite") was eventually settled on by the turn of the twentieth century.

Not until the post–World War II period, however, did the scientific community begin to explore the psychological causations and implications of eating disorders. Studies from the 1950s discussed the view that the anorexic patient refused food not because of a lack of appetite, but rather from a psychological condition that caused her to lose her appetite for food. During the following decade, further research began to describe features of this disordered eating in terms that continue to resonate today, such as "weight phobia" and "morbid fear of becoming fat."[5] Bruch, in particular, synthesized a forty-year study and treatment of anorexics in 1973, cautioning that although anorexics themselves focused on weight gained and lost, those treating the victims of disordered eating must resist this way of measuring their success and failure, and focus, instead, on the happiness of "the person within."[6]

Disordered eating patterns were subdivided into two separate but interrelated categories by research conducted in the later decades of the twentieth century. Anorexia nervosa referred to the food restrictors, and bulimia to the vomiters.[7] In 1987, the Diagnostic and Statistic Manual of Mental Disorders (DSM) delineated bulimia nervosa as a separate disorder, characterized by binge eating followed by purging.[8] Nevertheless, a common denominator connects these separate phenomena and suggests that these distinct disorders actually may be different reactions to the same psychological stimuli—namely, the fear of fatness. One group of disordered eaters severely restricts calories to keep from getting fat, while the other group may attempt the same strategy, but with less willpower and success—hence the occurrence of bingeing and purging.

PHYSICAL AND PSYCHOLOGICAL ETIOLOGY

Along with fear of fatness, body image, weight, and shape are central factors of concern for disordered eaters, whether bulimic or anorexic. Whether they have a distorted perception of their bodies, or a distorted experience of body weight and shape as the DSM reports, people with eating disorders often deny that they are severely emaciated.[9] In fact, most would insist that they have more weight to lose, which is why they so strongly resist internal or external pressures to eat.

The effects of disordered eating are specific to the disorder. For anorexics, sustained food deprivation and calorie restriction will ultimately result in lowered estrogen levels, leading to the absence of menstrual cycles, causing bone thinning and eventual osteoporosis. All of the muscles of the body diminish in size and strength, including the heart. Fatal arrhythmias are a risk, as well as life-threatening dehydration, and abnormal digestive mechanisms. For bulimics, years of vomiting produce electrolyte imbalance, low potassium levels, esophageal disorders, constipation, and irritable bowel syndrome, all of which may lead to respiratory paralysis or even cardiac arrest.[10]

THEORIES OF CAUSATION

Despite obviously uncomfortable, even painful physical symptoms leading to dire, life-threatening consequences, disordered eaters cling fiercely to their illness and stubbornly resist the attempts at "curing" them made by concerned and well-meaning families and physicians. The psychological components of these disordered behaviors have been variously tied to developmental crises in adolescent females, problems in personal identity and competence, the cultural preference for thinness, and an inordinate desire to please, be recognized, and be rewarded on the part of young women who may have previously felt discounted, powerless, and weak. Their illness gives them not only an individual identity, but also a sense of control over not only themselves, but also over their families, friends, and even the professionals charged with their care.[11]

Alternate theories examine these eating disorders within a broader context, and see the refusal to eat with others as part of a wider refusal of relatedness that permeates every aspect of life.[12] The manner in which anorexics negotiate relatedness in their everyday lives, from relationships with family and food to social rites of passage, their sexuality, and even their own bodies is pivotal to understanding the psychological dimensions of the disease. In effect, disordered eaters avoid and deny traditional forms of relatedness and commensality in favor of forming a relationship with anorexia. Being anorexic gives them not only a personal identity to cling to, but makes them a part of a community, "as if belonging to a secret and powerful group, a religion, or a competitive team sport."[13]

Perhaps one of the most intriguing conceptualizations of the complex problem of disordered eating is to understand the illness as a "dangerous, 'kinky' pleasure" of young women who desire "the pleasure of no pleasure."[14] In a culture that fails to provide women with legitimate and autonomous means of fulfilling individual desire, and that portrays women as the passive object of man's desire, the refusal of those pleasures that are allowed becomes, in itself, a pleasure. Anorexia becomes a means, a tool, for imagining and achieving pleasure, as well as for resisting socialization.[15]

DEMOGRAPHICS

In the United States, eating disorders have been categorized by the general public as a phenomenon affecting primarily white, middle- to upper-class adolescent women. To a large extent, statistics bear out these impressions. The vast majority of anorexics are female, with only about 8 percent of those diagnosed being male, while 15 percent of bulimics are male.[16] More than 89 percent of young women suffering from an eating disorder come from two-parent, double-income families, although there are some studies suggesting that bulimia, specifically, may be more common in lower socioeconomic classes.[17] Similarly, the relatively few studies that have been conducted on eating disorders among minority populations, specifically of African American women, indicate a much lower incidence of anorexia and bulimia within a community that places less value on weight loss, outward appearances, and media images.[18] On the other hand, the incidence of eating disorders among the Hispanic populations in the United States more closely mimics that in the white population.[19]

The demographics of disordered eating are quite alarming, especially considering anorexia nervosa and bulimia nervosa are relative newcomers to the cultural and social scene. Before 1970, few cases of anorexia and bulimia were reported. Between 1970 and the end of the twentieth century, the dimensions of the problem, and the number of reported cases, increased dramatically. Initial responses to this rapidly escalating "social epidemic" questioned whether this increase reflected better diagnostic techniques and greater public awareness, rather than actual increases in new cases.[20] Statistics published by the American Psychiatric Association in 2005, however, show that between 1 to 2 percent of American women begin developing anorexic symptoms in early adolescence, between the ages of fourteen and eighteen, while 2 to 3 percent begin exhibiting bulimic behavior between the ages of sixteen and twenty. Complicating these statistics, however, is the belief that perhaps as high a number as 45 to 50 percent of bulimics start out as anorexics.[21] Whether one considers 2 percent or 3 percent of the adolescent female population in the United States, the fact is that, conservatively speaking, eating disorders affect about seven million young American women today.

Mortality rates for eating disorders are considerably higher than for any other psychiatric disorder. Desiring death, as Warin writes, is the ultimate negation of connectedness, and between 5 and 20 percent of anorexics die each year achieving their goal of being the "perfect anorexic."[22] The National Association of Anorexia Nervosa estimates that 5 to 10 percent of anorexics die within ten years of diagnosis, while 18 to 20 percent will be dead after twenty years. Only about 30 to 40 percent of anorexics can be expected to fully recover, and recovery occurs only after treatment lasting from four to seven years. Relapse remains a problem for more than 25 percent of anorexics.[23]

Statistics on bulimics, especially bulimic anorexics, are even more troubling. Recent studies suggest that while anorexia affects 0.7 percent of the population in Western Hemisphere nations, bulimia rates are closer to 1.6 percent and growing.[24] Superimposed on the already defensive and resistant anorexic pattern is the pronounced difficulty with impulse control and self-destructive behavior of the anorexic bulimic. The intense shame over the chronic pattern of bingeing and purging often leads not only to secretive patterns, but also to suicide attempts. Bulimia remains hard to detect, with only one-tenth of bulimics being treated, and most of them have had the disorder for at least seven years before seeking help. Bulimia continues to pose significant obstacles to treatment and recovery.[25]

Not surprisingly, disordered eating patterns have been reported throughout the Euro-American world in countries that share Western cultural attitudes, values, and influences. In the early 1970s, a Swedish study of high school students in Stockholm found that about 50 percent of the female students felt fat and had tried a rigorous diet, while 10 percent had experienced anorexic symptoms.[26] A survey of college students in England in the 1980s reported similar findings. By the early 1990s, disordered eating studies were being carried out in Australia, Denmark, France, Great Britain, Israel, the Netherlands, Sweden, and Switzerland.[27] Despite cross-national differences, the findings were consistent. Thin is beautiful, and young women were willing to go to extreme lengths, suffering physical and psychological pain, to achieve the desired body image. European statistics on numbers affected, causes, effects, and mortality rates mirror those of the United States.

Eating disorders in Canada received widespread and public attention in the 1980s, when it was reported that anorexia and bulimia affected one in twenty young women.[28] By 2000, studies indicated approximately 10.7 per 100,000 women had sought hospital treatment for an eating disorder. The number of women treated on an out-patient basis, however, or seen in a clinic by a private physician, is not recorded. A data gap also exists in Canada for minority and immigrant women. In

Canada, as in every nation that currently keeps statistics on eating disorders, the largest data gap may represent those anorexics and bulimics who neither seek, nor receive, any treatment at all.

In those non-Western nations that have been most strongly influenced by Western culture, particularly in the post–World War II era, it is perhaps not unexpected to find eating disorders. One of the first studies to suggest a link between westernization and disordered eating was conducted by Mervet Nasser in 1986. Nasser compared the eating patterns of female Egyptian students attending university in London and in Cairo. While 22 percent of the London group exhibited signs of an eating disorder, only 12 percent of those studying in Cairo did so. In addition, none of the Cairo group met the criteria for bulimia, while over 10 percent of the London students qualified for this diagnosis. As further corroborating evidence of a cultural link, Nasser noted that all of the young women in the London group had begun to dress in the European fashion.[29]

Studies in Japan, dating to the 1980s, report an incidence rate of anorexia nervosa as one in five hundred young women.[30] A particularly prevalent form of binge eating in Japan is called *kibarashi* syndrome. Today in Japan, most urban hospitals have opened eating-disorder units and clinics.[31] Similarly, studies conducted in both the Republic of Korea and Singapore in the 1990s reveal the rapid rise of eating disorders in these relatively wealthy, and westernized, Asian countries—despite the smaller body mass of these women. More than 90 percent of schoolgirls in both countries expressed dissatisfaction with their body size and felt they were overweight.[32] In the Republic of Korea, especially, the rise in eating disorders has seemed to parallel the rapid increase of industrialization and urbanization after the 1970s. By the end of the twentieth century, studies indicated that while a majority of Korean school girls felt they were overweight, the average dress size for Korean women was the equivalent of an American size four.[33]

NON-WESTERN WORLD

It had long been assumed that Western-patterned eating disorders would not be found in Asia, Africa, India, Latin America, or even socialist Europe. Economic conditions and limited food supply would seem to make it highly unlikely that many would be affected by an eating pattern dependent on voluntary food rejection and self-starvation. In addition, in many parts of the non-Western, hungry world, fatness, not slimness, is still a sign of affluence and beauty. Recent studies, however, reveal some unexpected findings. Eating disorders are on the rise in the non-Western world.

If, as has been suggested by numerous studies in many parts of the globe, eating disorders are a barometer of cultural change, the political and economic changes occurring in central and eastern European countries following the collapse of Communism and the emergence of capitalism should provide fertile research fields. Unfortunately, however, disordered eating studies were rare in socialist European countries before 1989. Reports of studies conducted in Czechoslovakia and Poland revealed the existence of anorexia nervosa, but little mention was made of bulimia.[34] In 1988, a comparative study of eating disorders conducted between Austria, East Germany, and Hungary showed an almost identical prevalence of disordered eating in the three countries.[35] While these studies suggest the existence of eating disorders in Eastern Europe before the political changes in 1989, these disorders did not receive much attention before the collapse of Communism. There has been some suggestion that given the Soviet insistence on, and rewarding of, thinness in its athletes and ballerinas, the preference for excessive thinness among Eastern Bloc women existed before the onset of Western cultural influences after 1989.[36]

A unique pair of studies examined and compared disordered eating patterns in central and eastern Europe before 1989, with those after the political and economic changes ushered in by the collapse of the Communist system. The eating habits of East and West Berlin school girls were surveyed in the 1980s, before unification.[37] While both groups of girls had similar eating habits, those living in East Berlin had a surprisingly stronger identification with Western body ideals. When this study was replicated after Germany's unification, both groups of school girls evidenced increased focus on, and dissatisfaction with, body image.[38]

Poland, also, presents an interesting case study of the rapidity of the spread of Western body ideals. Two groups of Polish women were studied in 1990: factory workers and school girls. The students scored five times higher than the factory workers on levels of eating disorders, including anorexia and bulimia. Among the general population, bulimia was largely unknown, and Polish words for bingeing and purging did not even exist.[39] The school girls in this study had already been exposed to Western influences and body ideals, and by the end of that decade, the Western fashion industry had nationalized the preference for thinness in Poland. Eastern European models were beginning to appear on the covers of Western fashion magazines, and disordered eating rates in Poland were virtually indistinguishable from those in the West.[40]

An important study conducted in Hong Kong, China, raised questions about the assumed impact of Western culture on eating disorders and their causes and expressions.[41] Sing Lee confirmed the growing number of disordered eating cases coming through his psychiatric practice in the 1980s, but observed interesting contrasts with the Western model of disordered eating. The majority of his patients were from the lower classes, and did not exhibit body image problems or a fear of fatness. In Hong Kong, as in many Asian countries, plumpness represents health and beauty. While rejection of food remains the common denominator, and seems to be a characteristic female reaction to psychological stress, Lee suggests alternate motivations to those commonly accepted in the West. Rather than an obsession with thinness, Lee's young patients starved themselves as a way to express rebellion against their families, and to free themselves from rigid patriarchal control.[42]

Unfortunately, not much information exists on the prevalence of eating disorders throughout China. One survey of medical school students taken in Shanghai in the early 1990s found that approximately 1 percent self-reported bulimic symptoms. American college populations at that time were reporting ranges from 2 to 4 percent.[43] Almost 80 percent of the females who participated in the Chinese study expressed fears of becoming fat or gaining weight. Because these concerns and attitudes about body image and thinness have never been part of traditional Chinese culture, it is surmised that the impact of westernization in the form of media, fast food, and consumerism—particularly in the urban areas—have had a growing impact on China.[44]

In Africa, a 1992 survey of Nigerian women revealed disordered eating prob-lems surprisingly similar to Western society, despite traditional practices that encourage young women to fatten up before marriage.[45] Even though fatness has traditionally been associated with fertility throughout Africa, bulimia, particularly, was quite common among these young Nigerian women. A study of Kenyan women in 1983 revealed this same tension between traditional practices and values and social change. Kenyan immigrant women residing in Great Britain for longer than four years were compared to women still living in Kenya. While traditional Kenyan women preferred a larger body size, those living in England valued a smaller physique—similar to British women.[46] Cultural changes and tensions may, in fact, be the trigger for the development of eating disorders outside of the West.

In South Africa, dominated by white culture and politics until 1994, study results differ from the black population to the white. Before the end of apartheid, eating disorders among black South Africans either did not exist, or were not rec-ognized, treated, or recorded. Among white South Africans, disordered eating pat-terns had been observed and treated since the early 1980s. Rates of anorexia and bulimia among this population were virtually indistinguishable from Western soci-eties. Since the 1990s, however, studies have shown a rise in eating disorders among black South Africans, as rigid segregation has relaxed and cross-cultural contact has increased.[47]

Although it is tempting to theorize that closer association with Western culture and values has been the stimulus for this rise in eating disorders across Africa, the reasons may be far more complex. Shifts of populations from rural to urban areas, along with the attendant changes in lifestyles and values, and political transforma-tions resulting in gender role changes for African women, along with the pressures and stresses of recent empowerment of women, all contribute to a broader cultural understanding of the relatively recent emergence of disordered eating in Africa.[48]

Studies of eating disorders in India began to surface in the 1990s.[49] While access to food is still a major problem in many parts of India, and hunger remains a public health problem the Indian government still struggles to eradicate, eating disorders are on the rise among the growing affluent and professional classes. As Richard Gordon points out, upper-class Indian women have now added weight-control issues to their traditional concerns of skin lightening and hair straighten-ing.[50] The influence of Western body image, as portrayed in films, magazines, and fashions, can be readily seen in these concerns. At the same time, other studies caution that an overreliance on Western-modeled, fat-phobic causation negates different and individually driven cultural diagnosis.[51] Indian culture has a long tra-dition of admiring and encouraging self-sacrifice in women, including practices such as ritual group fasting.

Indeed, a study done among young adults in Jaipur reveals that bulimia rates among this population rival those in Britain, even though these slightly built North Indians express the desire to weigh more than they presently do, not less.[52] Thus, bulimia here does not seem to correlate with a fear of fatness as in the West-ern model. Self-starvation in India, according to Littlewood, might simply be the easiest way for young women to express general distress and attract the attention of family and loved ones in a culture where food preparation and distribution is the expected realm of women.[53]

The reported incidences of disordered eating throughout Latin America vary from place to place. Chile was the first country to report eating disturbances as early as 1982, although the cases referred to in the study dated back to the early 1970s, the same period when similar studies began to emerge in the United States.[54] This was also a time of political turmoil and great social and economic change in Chile, as the Pinochet military regime overthrew the Allende government, and established a commercialized culture and capitalist economy. The transition to a global consumer economy, along with challenges to traditional cultural roles and values, often present women with contradictory and conflicting choices. It is within this milieu, some have theorized, that eating disorders arise in non-Western nations.[55]

In Mexico, the predominant group affected by anorexia and bulimia has been university students living in Mexico City. As has been the case elsewhere, rapid industrialization and urbanization have affected Mexico in many ways, including the rise in eating disorders. Western media images of obsessively thin women have proliferated in Mexico, a nation that traditionally has relied on a high carbohydrate diet. The urban and professional classes have been the first to feel the effects, according to reports published in 1998.[56]

Argentina presents a somewhat unique and interesting study of disordered eating phenomena and causation. In a survey of seven hundred people, 79 percent of women expressed the opinion that slenderness was an important issue, 60 percent considered themselves overweight, and 71 percent were doing something to lose more weight. Numbers such as these have led some researchers to declare an epidemic of eating disorders in Argentina.[57] Argentinians associate being overweight with laziness, while associating slenderness with beauty, sensuality, youth, and attractiveness. Women spend more than $90 million each year on cosmetic surgery, and another $12 million for diet drugs.[58] Restrictive clothing sizes, the largest size in Argentina is the equivalent of size eight in the United States, further reinforce the national preference for slimness and the need to restrict food intake.

Because Argentina has been called the most European of South American nations, it is logical to assume that Western cultural images and preferences have been responsible for Argentina's attitudes and behaviors regarding body image. Today's intense insistence on a culture of beauty might stem more from a reaction to the government repressions of the 1970s, than to external influences. An ongoing neurodevelopmental study by Connan, Katzman, and Treasure suggests that food regulation and emotional restriction can become interrelated adaptive coping mechanisms.[59]

TREATMENT IN THE WESTERN WORLD

One of the first publications in the United States to examine courses of treatment for disordered eating was Hilde Bruch's *Eating Disorders*. While this book was published in 1973, the case studies examined in her work reflected forty years of clinical experience as a psychiatrist specializing in the treatment of eating disorders, specifically obesity and anorexia. Her book continues to be significant, not only for its introduction of her groundbreaking beliefs about best treatment options at that time, but also because it illuminates and critiques the practices commonly in use during the decades before her publication.

Bruch expresses skepticism at the traditional methods of treating anorexic patients, as well as of determining the successful outcomes of that treatment. Her analysis critiques a three-pronged approach: hospitalization, medication, and psychotherapy.

Of the traditional medical approach, hospitalization, Bruch wrote,

> Even if there is no threat to life, anorexia nervosa is such a serious, anxiety-producing condition that sooner or later the question of hospitalization will come up. There has been considerable controversy about the merits of hospitalization. A tradition has developed that it is best to treat these patients away from their families, but in my experience short-term hospitalization to enforce weight gain without attention to the underlying problems is useless, if not harmful.[60]

Similarly, Bruch questions the therapeutic value of medications commonly used at the time, such as insulin (to stimulate the appetite) and thyroid shots (to raise the metabolic rate). It is not unusual even today to find an anorexic who has been receiving thyroid shots for many years, and would not think of giving it up, because the patient is convinced that it helps her keep her weight down. As long as anorexia nervosa was considered of pituitary origin, it was a matter of course to prescribe some glandular extract or even to implant pituitary glands from animals.[61]

Bruch is convinced that even traditional psychotherapy has done more harm than good to patients with disordered eating problems. In spite of gaining insight, some basic disturbance in their approach to life remained beclouded and untouched, or was even reinforced in the traditional psychoanalytic setting in which the patient expresses secret thoughts and feelings, and the analyst interprets their unconscious meanings. This represents in a painful way a repetition of the significant interaction between patient and parents, where "mother always knew how I felt," with the implication that they themselves do not know how they feel. Interpretation to such a patient may mean the devastating re-experience of being told what he thinks and feels, confirming his sense of inadequacy and thus interfering with his developing true self-awareness and trust in his own psychological faculties.[62]

Bruch is particularly critical of the more coercive measures in use at that time, such as enforced isolation, locked rooms, and gastric feeding tubes. Her recommendations for more effective treatment of anorexics included brief hospitalization primarily for those severely emaciated patients in need of life-saving intravenous infusions, the use of psychotropic drugs "under drastic conditions," and more individualized, collaborative therapy where the patient is listened to, rather than told what she "really" feels and means.[63] Bruch cautions that whereas a gain in weight is commonly taken as a sign of recovery, in reality it more likely represents only a temporary remission, especially if the underlying problems persist "below the façade."[64]

Almost twenty years later, a study by another psychiatrist, L. K. George Hsu, reaffirmed some of the same observations Bruch had made in the 1970s. Inpatient treatment, according to Hsu, should be reserved for those anorexics whose body weight has fallen below 70 percent of the average, and should be discontinued shortly after the patient has reached "target weight."[65] Hsu further noted that the use of psychotropic drugs, including antidepressants, appeared to have a "marginal effect" on weight gain, but warned that using weight gain as an "index of improvement" was highly problematic. "Rapid weight gain," Hsu insisted, "is uncomfortable and possibly dangerous to the patient and bears no relationship to long-term outcome."[66]

Treatment goals in the 1990s focused on the physical, emotional, and psychological recovery of the patient, and included the establishment of healthy eating patterns, the resolution of the patient's abnormal fixation on thinness, and the prevention of relapses. Family therapy was believed to hold the key to recovery, because most patients still lived at home and the illness not only originated there, but rather impinged on every member of the family.[67]

Although some of the same treatment goals were identified for both anorexics and bulimics, the latter were not encouraged to gain weight, but rather to maintain a stable weight. A three-stage approach in the 1990s aimed at returning self-control to the patient. First, the binge and purge cycle must be broken through a combination of stimulus control techniques (when, where, and how much to eat) and the self-monitoring of food intake.

Generally speaking, once the bingeing is under control, the purges will cease. The second stage focuses on establishing a regular pattern of eating, and the final stage aims to prevent relapses.[68] Fairburn and Wilson describe a similar three-phase approach known as Interpersonal Psychotherapy (IPT). Once the underlying problems that precipitate the binge-and-purge cycle are identified, a contract is made to work on these issues during treatment sessions.[69]

A slightly different psychotherapy in use by the 1990s was supportive-expressive therapy. Here, disordered eating patterns are seen as disguises for deep-seated interpersonal problems. The patient's past is explored to identify the sources of their relationship conflicts, and the expression of pent-up emotions is encouraged during the treatment sessions.[70]

By the end of the twentieth century, Intensive Outpatient Programs (IOPs) were introduced as an alternative to hospitalization for patients whose health insurance would not cover extensive hospitalization, or for those who needed transition care.[71] In IOPs, treatment focuses on the physical (symptom management) and the psychological (understanding the disorder). Group therapy sessions typically meet weekly for several months and involve attending meals regularly. This has become a popular option for those who want to continue their daily lives and work routines, while attending evening sessions.[72]

The field of psychopharmacology grew rapidly by the end of the century. A range of new drugs was introduced to combat depression, curb binge impulses, and control tension-related behaviors. It was discovered that the neurotransmitter serotonin produced feelings of happiness and satisfaction, while lowered levels of serotonin triggered depression and urges to binge and purge. Medications such as Prozac, Zoloft, and Paxil were commonly prescribed as mood enhancers and antidepressants to control obsessive-compulsive behaviors.[73]

By the advent of the twenty-first century, therapies for disordered eating in the Western world routinely included treatment to change not only the eating behaviors but also body image distortions. Distorted body image is one of the key indicators for both anorexia nervosa and bulimia nervosa, according to the American Psychiatric Association. Patients significantly overestimate their size and shape, imagine or exaggerate feature flaws or defects, and believe their appearance is under intense scrutiny by others. A perceived defect in their appearance makes them believe they are defective people. Common complaints of disordered eating patients focus on specific areas of the body, such as fat thighs, buttocks, upper arms, breasts, neck, or cheeks.[74] Even after body weight is restored, or the cycle of binge eating followed by vomiting is broken, body image dissatisfaction persists.

These cognitive disturbances, whether they are classified as delusional or obsessional, are treated with a variety of cognitive-behavioral procedures. Therapists identify the "negative body talk" of patients, "my thighs are huge and fat and ugly," and encourage cognitive restructuring, "my thighs are strong and muscular." A body image diary continues to monitor the self-conscious statements, beliefs, and perspectives of disordered eaters during therapy. Behavioral procedures are introduced to counter the avoidance habits of patients, the excessive body checking and grooming, the repeated need for reassurance, and the constant comparing that are all hallmarks of disordered eating.[75]

Family therapy, particularly in the treatment of anorexics, has long been an integral component of treatment in the West. As early as Bruch in 1973, therapists have recognized that disordered eating arises within a family context, and family dynamics are as important for the resolution of these disorders as for their conception. Traditional family therapy viewed the family as influencing the personality of the individual, hence treatment focused on correcting the problems in the individual.[76] Structural family therapy works not only with the individual, but also with the family, identifying, altering, or resolving dysfunctional patterns while encouraging open, healthy styles of communication within the family.[77]

Feminist family therapy emphasizes forming a partnership between client and therapist rather than presenting the therapist as the "powerful expert," to address the sociocultural factors that are at the root of disordered eating, namely, the patient's indirect method of gaining power and control while remaining subordinate.[78] Families are encouraged to explore together issues of hierarchy and control, and parents, in particular, are urged to participate in therapy in nonconfrontational ways.

TREATMENT IN THE NON-WESTERN WORLD

As the non-Western world differs in symptomology from the Western world, so, too, do treatment options for disordered eating differ. In cultures where fat phobia does not significantly define disordered eating habits, treatment focuses on other fundamental and underlying issues. Rather than the Western model in which disordered eating is largely regarded as an "appearance disorder" caused by an over-attention to fashion and calorie counting, food refusal in many parts of the world expresses the need for control in situations in which one feels powerless.

In Argentina, mostly because of the lack of insurance coverage for eating disorders, there is a shortage of facilities to treat anorexic and bulimic patients. Anorexia and bulimia are often treated in conjunction with other weight-related illnesses, such as obesity. Patients usually are treated by endocrinologists and nutritionists, with little input by psychologists and psychiatrists.[79] Teamwork is sometimes construed as a breach of patient confidentiality, so professionals are unused to consulting and sharing patients and cases.

Treatment teams are used, however, at the university-based treatment center in Buenos Aires, the largest facility in the country, which opened an Eating Disorders

Clinic in 1993. The treatment program at Hospital Nacional de Clínicas employs teams combining a psychoanalytical approach with family therapy and nutrition education on both an in-patient and out-patient basis. The majority of patients seen at this facility are bulimic, and the dropout rates are more than 50 percent.[80]

In 1996, MET (Motivational Enhancement Therapy) was introduced in Buenos Aires and has experienced some success in the treatment of adolescents with eating disorders, as has CBT (Cognitive Behavioral Therapy), which was introduced in 2000. The cultural preference in Argentina for one-on-one psychoanalytical therapy is gradually yielding to a model that incorporates a number of different therapy options, including patient self-reporting diaries and self-help programs.[81]

The relatively recent and continuing social and political changes occurring in South Africa since the end of apartheid have created a unique treatment profile for disordered eating, especially among the black, rural populations. In general, blacks in South Africa were underserved by the Western-based health care system during apartheid. Eating disorders, specifically, may have been present, but unreported, among black adolescents during these years. Equally possible is the likelihood that in the rural areas, then and now, patients suffering from self-starvation, severe and rapid weight loss, and self-induced vomiting may seek treatment from traditional healers.[82]

Since the end of apartheid, however, an ever-growing percentage of South Africa's rural population has become urbanized. By 1996, the populations of most provinces in South Africa ranged from 50 percent urbanized to 95 percent.[83] The process of urbanization, itself, along with the recent empowerment of black women in South Africa, has created pressures and psychological disturbances that may be factors in the emergence of eating disorders.[84] A cultural understanding of these forces is critical in any treatment and therapy program.

Cultural factors also shape the treatment options and recovery process in parts of the world, such as China, where fat phobia is not an important rationale for not eating. A study of Hong Kong families in 2000 identified five motives for self-starvation, which are relevant to treatment, but are not related to fear of fatness.[85] These motives are reflective of Chinese culture and values, and include self-sacrifice for family well-being, filial piety, bridging of parental conflict, expression of love or control, and camouflage of family conflicts.[86] Psychotherapy and control therapy focuses on helping patients let go of the illusion of control their eating disorder gives them.

Treatment options and preferences differ across Latin America. CBT, which employs such methods as journaling your thoughts and emotions, engaging in activities formerly avoided, and practicing new ways of thinking, reacting, and behaving, is a relatively new treatment in this part of the world and, as such, is accepted and employed in some countries while rejected in others. A shortage of trained and experienced therapists in CBT has been a handicap in some parts of South America.

The latest research and treatment options for disordered eating bring us back to the Western world, to researchers in Canada and the United States. Scientists in both countries are convinced there is a genetic component to anorexia and bulimia and are searching for the genetic links between eating disorders and Obsessive Compulsive Disorder (OCD). Physicians and therapists had previously noted the high rates of OCD in families with eating disorders, and vice versa, and many now believe that eating disorders become one of the ways in which OCD is expressed. As with other psychiatric disorders, such as schizophrenia and autism, it is expected that a genetic component to anorexia and bulimia soon will be identified.

NOTES

1. Rudolph M. Bell, *Holy Anorexia* (Chicago: University of Chicago Press, 1985), 114–16.

2. Caroline Walker Bynum, *Holy Feast and Holy Fast: The Religious Significance of Food to Medieval Women* (Berkeley: University of California Press, 1987).

3. Nancy A. Gutierrez, *"Shall She Famish Then?": Female Food Refusal in Early Modern England* (Burlington, VT: Ashgate, 2003), 30–32.

4. L. K. George Hsu, *Eating Disorders* (New York: Guilford Press, 1990), 1–5.

5. A. H. Crisp, "Anorexia Nervosa," *Hospital Medicine* I (1967): 713–719; G. F. M. Russell, "The Present State of Anorexia Nervosa," *Psychological Medicine* 7 (1977): 353–67.

6. Hilde Bruch, *Eating Disorders: Obesity, Anorexia Nervosa, and the Person Within* (New York: Basic Books, 1973), 211–25.

7. D. M. Garner, P. E. Garfinkel, and M. O'Shaughnessy, "The Validity of the Distinction between Bulimics with and without Anorexia Nervosa," *American Journal of Psychiatry* 142 (1985) 581–87.

8. American Psychiatric Association, *Diagnostic and Statistical Manual of Mental Disorders* (Washington, DC: American Psychiatric Press, 1987).

9. Simona Giordano, *Understanding Eating Disorders: Conceptual and Ethical Issues in the Treatment of Anorexia and Bulimia Nervosa* (Oxford: Clarendon Press, 2005), 23.

10. Ibid., 29.

11. Richard A. Gordon, *Eating Disorders: Anatomy of a Social Epidemic* (Malden, MA: Blackwell Publishers, 2000), 22–23.

12. Megan J. Warin, "Reconfiguring Relatedness in Anorexia," *Anthropology and Medicine* 13 (2006): 42.

13. Ibid., 43.

14. Margaret R. Miles, "Textual Harassment: Desire and the Female Body," in *The Good Body: Asceticism in Contemporary Culture*, ed. Mary G. Winkler and Letha B. Cole (New Haven: Yale University Press, 1994), 50–51.

15. Ibid.

16. Giordano, *Understanding Eating Disorders*, 19.

17. Richard A. Gordon, *Eating Disorders: Anatomy of a Social Epidemic* (Malden, MA: Blackwell Publishers, 2000), 93.

18. Kathryn J. Zerbe, *The Body Betrayed: Women, Eating Disorders, and Treatment* (Washington, DC: American Psychiatric Press, 1993), 108.

19. M. Crago, C. M. Shisslak, and L. S. Estes, "Eating Disturbances among American Minority Groups: A Review," *International Journal of Eating Disorders* 19 (1996): 239–48.

20. Giordano, *Understanding Eating Disorders*, 20.

21. Gordon, *Eating Disorders*, 35.

22. Megan J. Warin, "Reconfiguring Relatedness in Anorexia," *Anthropology and Medicine* 13 (2006): 47.

23. National Association of Anorexia Nervosa and Associated Disorders, http://www.anred.com/stats.html.

24. Ibid.

25. Gordon, *Eating Disorders*, 36–37.

26. I. Nylander, "The Feeling of Being Fat and Dieting in a School Population," *Acta Sociomedica Scandinavica* 3 (1971): 17–26.

27. Gordon, *Eating Disorders*, 86.

28. Veronica Strong-Boag and Gillian Creese, "Canada," in *The Greenwood Encyclopedia of Women's Issues Worldwide: North America and the Caribbean*, ed. Cheryl Kalny (Westport, CT: Greenwood Press, 2003), 49–64.

29. Mervat Nasser, "Comparative Study of the Prevalence of Abnormal Eating Habits among Arab Female Students of Both London and Cairo Universities," *Psychological Medicine* 13 (1986): 829–37.

30. Kathryn J. Zerbe, *The Body Betrayed* (Washington, DC: American Psychiatric Press, 1993), 113.

31. Ibid., 114.

32. Gordon, *Eating Disorders*, 82.

33. Ibid., 8.

34. Gunther Rathner, "Post-Communism and the Marketing of the Thin Ideal," in *Eating Disorders and Cultures in Transition*, ed. Mervat Nasser, Melanie A. Katzman, and Richard Gordon (New York: Brunner-Routledge, 2001), 93–101.

35. Ibid.

36. Noah E. Gotbaum, "Commentary I," in *Eating Disorders and Cultures in Transition*, ed. Nasser et al. (New York: Brunner-Routledge, 2001), 105–7.

37. Rathner, "Post-Communism," 96–98.

38. Ibid.

39. K. Bisaga-Wlodarczyk, B. Dolan, S. McCluskey, and H. Lacey, "Disordered Eating Behavior and Attitudes towards Weight and Shape in Polish Women," *European Eating Disorder Review* 3 (1995): 205–12.

40. Rathner, "Post-Communism," 98.

41. S. Lee, T. P. Ho, and L. K. G. Hsu, "Fat Phobic and Non-Fat Phobic Anorexia Nervosa: A Comparative Study of 70 Chinese Patients in Hong Kong," *Psychological Medicine* 23 (1993): 999–1015.

42. Richard Gordon, "Eating Disorders East and West," in *Eating Disorders and Cultures in Transition*, ed. M. Nasser, M. A. Katzman, R. Gordon (New York: Brunner-Routledge, 2001), 6–7.

43. Z. F. Chun, J. E. Mitchell, K. Li et al., "The Prevalence of Anorexia Nervosa and Bulimia Nervosa among Freshmen Medical College Students in China," *International Journal of Eating Disorders* 12 (1992): 209–14.

44. Gordon, "East and West," 7–8.

45. L. K. Oyewumi and S. S. Kazarian, "Abnormal Eating Attitudes among a Group of Nigerian Youths," *East African Medical Journal* (1992): 663–66.

46. A. Furnham and N. Alibhai, "Cross-Cultural Differences in the Perception of Female Body Shapes," *Psychological Medicine* 13 (1983): 829–37.

47. C. Szabo, M. Berk, et al., "Eating Disorders in Black South African Females," *South African Medical Journal* 85 (1995): 588–90.

48. Ibid.

49. T. N. Srinivasan, T. R. Suresh, and J. Vasantha, "The Emergence of Eating Disorders in India," *International Journal of Social Psychiatry* 44 (1998): 189–98.

50. Gordon, *Eating Disorders*, 83.

51. Roland Littlewood, "Modernity, Culture, Change and Eating Disorders in South Asian Societies," *British Journal of Medical Psychology* 68 (1995): 45–63.

52. Roland Littlewood, "Commentary 1," in *Eating Disorders and Cultures in Transition*, ed. M. Nasser et al. (New York: Brunner-Routledge, 2001), 57–58.

53. Ibid.

54. Gordon,"East and West," 10–11.

55. Ibid.

56. Gordon, *Eating Disorders*, 85.

57. Oscar Meehan and M. A. Katzman, "Argentina: The Social Body at Risk," in *Eating Disorders and Cultures in Transition*, ed. M. Nasser et al. (New York: Brunner-Routledge, 2001), 148–61.

58. Ibid.

59. Ibid.

60. Bruch, *Eating Disorders*, 330.

61. Ibid., 331.

62. Ibid., 336.

63. Ibid., 337.

64. Ibid.

65. Hsu, *Eating Disorders*, 131.

66. Ibid., 156.

67. Ibid., 129.

68. Ibid., 168–69.

69. Christopher G. Fairburn and G. Terence Wilson, *Binge Eating: Nature, Assessment and Treatment* (New York: Guilford Press, 1993), 272.

70. Ibid., 273.

71. M. Siegel, J. Brisman, and M. Weinshel, *Surviving an Eating Disorder* (New York: Harper, 1997), 149.

72. Ibid., 144.

73. Ibid., 146.

74. James C. Rosen, "Cognitive-Behavioral Body Image Therapy," in *Handbook of Treatment for Eating Disorders*, ed. David M. Garner and Paul E. Garfinkel (New York: Guilford, 1997), 189.

75. Ibid., 193–98.

76. Christopher Dare and Ivan Eisler, "Family Therapy for Anorexia Nervosa," in *Handbook of Treatment for Eating Disorders*, ed. Garner and Garfinkel (New York: Guilford, 1997), 309.

77. Ibid., 310.

78. Ibid., 315.

79. Meehan and Katzman, "Argentina,"160.

80. Ibid., 159.

81. Ibid., 160.

82. C. Szabo and D. LeGrange, "Eating Disorders and the Politics of Identity: The South African Experience," in *Eating Disorders and Cultures in Transition*, ed. M. Nasser et al. (New York: Brunner-Routledge, 2001), 26.

83. Ibid., 30.

84. B. Silverstein and D. Perlick, *The Cost of Competence: Why Inequality Causes Depression: Eating Disorders and Illness in Women* (New York: Oxford Press, 1995).

85. S. Lee, "Fat Phobia in Anorexia Nervosa: Whose Obsession Is It?" in *Eating Disorders and Cultures in Transition*, ed. M. Nasser et al. (New York: Brunner-Routledge, 2001), 49.

86. Ibid.

RESOURCE GUIDE

Suggested Reading

Bruch, Hilde. *Eating Disorders: Obesity, Anorexia Nervosa and the Person Within.* New York: Basic Books, 1973.

Giordano, Simona. *Understanding Eating Disorders: Conceptual and Ethical Issues in the Treatment of Anorexia and Bulimia Nervosa.* Oxford: Clarendon Press, 2005.

Gordon, Richard. *Eating Disorders: Anatomy of a Social Epidemic.* Malden, MA: Blackwell Press, 2000.

Nasser, Mervat, M. A. Katzman, and Richard Gordon. *Eating Disorders and Cultures in Transition.* New York: Brunner-Routledge, 2001.

Zerbe, Kathryn J. *The Body Betrayed: Women, Eating Disorders, and Treatment.* Washington, DC: American Psychiatric Press, 1993.

Web Sites

Anorexia Nervosa and Related Eating Disorders, http://www.anred.com.

National Association of Anorexia Nervosa and Associated Disorders, http://www.anad.org.

Eating Disorder Resource Center, http://www.edrcsv.org.

National Eating Disorders Organization, http://www.nationaleatingdisorders.org.

International Association of Eating Disorders, http://www.iaedp.com.

International Eating Disorders Centre, UK, http://www.eatingdisorderscentre.co./uk.

15

Obesity

Joanne Gardner

The obesity epidemic is all around us. For some readers, you can actually feel the adiposity surrounding your waistline. For others, it touches your life indirectly through family, friends, coworkers, clients, or patients. The obesity epidemic is indifferent to geopolitical boundaries, infiltrates all demographic segments, and is changing the course of history. The impact of increasing rates of obesity permeates all aspects of society, creating reactions within the financial, health care, and food industries, as well as social sectors. This chapter explores the current status of the obesity epidemic, describes the interdependent factors that contribute to the disturbing statistics, discusses efforts to curtail the epidemic, and challenges the reader to consider varied perspectives about what might reverse the trend.

OUR CORPULENT PLANET

The World Health Organization (WHO) acknowledged that in 2005 approximately 1.6 billion adults were overweight, and at least four hundred million of them were obese.[1] In response to the alarming fact of increasing obesity, WHO has developed a Global Strategy on Diet, Physical Activity, and Health.[2]

Obesity used to be a problem only in high-income countries, but now the rates are also rising dramatically in low- and middle-income countries as these populations adopt the foods and dietary habits of the high-income countries. Analyses of global economic and food availability data for 1962–1994 revealed an increased availability of cheap vegetable oils and fats, which has facilitated an increased fat consumption among low-income nations.[3] Given that fat enhances flavor and it is human nature to seek flavorful foods, fat consumption may be strongly influenced by the amount of fat available in the food supply moreso than by feelings of hunger and satisfaction. Consequently, the nutrition transition away from traditional foods to a diversified diet, including more refined and processed foods with higher energy density, now occurs more often in countries with lower levels of gross national product. As income increases secondary to economic development, many people experience improved food security and better health. Yet, with rapid nutrition transition catalyzed by easy access to the foods of an industrial diet, the health benefits of economic development are often offset by rising rates of childhood obesity.[4]

THE SUPERSIZING OF THE STATES

A good glimpse into the dietary habits and body weight patterns of U.S. citizens is obtained through the National Health and Nutrition Examination Survey (NHANES), a program designed to assess the nutritional and health status of adults and children in the United States. The periodic survey includes responses from a representative sample of about five thousand persons across the country.[5] Another national survey collects self-reported weight and height data through the Behavioral Risk Factor Surveillance System (BRFSS).[6] According to the NHANES 2003–2004 data, 34.3 and 32 percent of noninstitutionalized adults, age twenty years and older, are either overweight or obese, respectively. In consideration of current U.S. Census Bureau[7] statistics with the current U.S. population approaching 305 million people, the NHANES data imply that with 66.3 percent of the population tipping the scales as overweight or obese, more than 146 million adults are above the range for a healthy weight.

Overweight and obesity in adults are defined in these surveys using body mass index (BMI), a measure of weight relative to height that is closely correlated with total body fat content.[8] According to the National Heart, Lung, and Blood Institute (NHLBI) overweight in adults is defined as a BMI of 25 to 29.9 kilograms per square meters (kg/m^2), obesity is a BMI ≥ 30 kg/m^2, and extreme obesity is a BMI ≥ 40 kg/m^2.[9] The NHLBI also recommends the use of waist circumference in addition to BMI as a screening tool to identify individuals with high intra-abdominal fat, which, when combined with BMI, may be more indicative of increased health risks rather than using only BMI.[10]

NHANES also reported that 17 percent of teenagers age twelve to nineteen and 19 percent of children ages six to eleven are overweight,[11] which implies that there are more than 11.3 million children and teens between six and nineteen years old in the United States who face the possibility of serious psychosocial burdens in addition to the increased health risks associated with being overweight.[12] For children and teens up to age twenty years, the term "overweight" rather than "obese" is currently used by health care organizations, including the Centers for Disease Control and Prevention (CDC). The CDC Growth Charts are used to identify obese youth with a BMI at or above the 95th percentile of gender-specific BMI-for-age values.[13] The CDC defines a BMI between the 85th and 95th percentiles as putting a child or teenager "at risk of [being] overweight," which is the counterpart of the term "overweight" used in adults; however, it has been recommend that this terminology change to be consistent with the terms used for adults.[14]

Data from the 2007 BRFSS represent adult obesity rates, which are stratified by age, gender, race/ethnicity, educational level, and geographic region.[15] The highest rates of obesity occur in black, non-Hispanic women (39 percent), and lower rates of obesity are associated with higher levels of education, especially in women. The lower rates reported by BRFSS, relative to NHANES, partially may be due to the fact that the BRFSS includes eighteen- and nineteen-year-old adults and NHANES reports on adults twenty years and older.[16] As noted by NHANES, obesity rates in teenagers between twelve and nineteen years old average 17 percent,[17] which would shift the rates of adults downward when eighteen- and nineteen-year-olds are included in the adult group.

BRFSS results also reflect ethnic differences in overweight prevalence. Rates of increase in overweight children have been steepest in black, non-Hispanic children compared with Mexican American and white, non-Hispanic children.[18] Socioeconomic differences in obesity in the United States are becoming less apparent in both adults and children.[19] Conversely, a higher occurrence of obesity has been reported in rural populations compared with urban and suburban populations.[20] Rural residency was a risk factor for obesity and overweight in children based on data collected in the 2003 National Survey of Children's Health.[21] Their analysis revealed that rural overweight children five years of age and older were more likely than their urban peers to be white, live below the federal poverty level, and watch television for more than three hours per day.[22] Rural areas seem to be characterized by higher levels of poverty and lack of access to grocery, health, and physical activity resources, which may affect both adult and childhood weight patterns.

One of the most significant trends is that obesity in adults and overweight occurrence for children and teens has accelerated rapidly since 1976–1980 when the data indicated that 15.1 percent of the adult population was obese, and 6.5 percent of children ages six to eleven and 5 percent of teens ages twelve to nineteen were overweight. Meanwhile, adult overweight rates have remained fairly steady at approximately 32 to 33 percent.[23]

The accelerated rate for children and teens may be leveling off, as one report optimistically found that the prevalence of high BMI for age among children and adolescents showed no significant changes when comparing data from 2003–2004 to 2005–2006, and no significant trends emerged between 1999 and 2006.[24] In response to the release of this study, Randy Seeley of the Obesity Research Center said, "Whether this is meaningful data, we don't know yet, but anyone who wants to stick a flag in this and declare victory is just crazy."[25] At this point, it is difficult to ascertain what has contributed to the plateau. It may be that efforts to improve school lunches and educate the public about measures to control childhood obesity are paying off, but on the other hand, it may be that the number of children who are environmentally and genetically susceptible to obesity has reached a saturation point.[26]

DON'T FOLLOW THE LEADER

The United States is a leading exporter of both raw and processed foods, and the influence of these foods around the globe is substantial. The United States also exports technology, marketing, and media-based communications to far reaches of the world, where people can view American images of life and food choices on computer and television screens. For many people, these images exemplify the ideal life they aspire to attain in the land of abundance and plenty. What they don't see are the associated health risks that accompany the adoption of the

average American's diet. If they could see the full impact of these food and lifestyle choices, perhaps they would be viewed less glamorously.

Obesity and overweight pose a major risk for chronic disease, including cardiovascular disease, type 2 diabetes, osteoarthritis, hypertension, stroke, sleep apnea,
and certain forms of cancer—notably, endometrial, esophageal, kidney, prostate,
and postmenopausal breast and colon cancer.[27] Even children are experiencing the
adverse outcomes of being overweight, as demonstrated by an increased incidence
of type 2 diabetes, cardiovascular, orthopedic and pulmonary conditions, and
depressive disorders.[28] A report for the U.S. Department of Agriculture (USDA)
Economic Research Service expressed concern regarding the impact that excess
body weight has on a child's academic success. Overweight children showed less
progress than their non-overweight peers in reading and math skills and were rated
lower on both academic and socioemotional factors by their school teachers. These
academic and social costs must be taken into account when assessing the economic and social impact of childhood overweight.[29]

Health care costs are escalating in the United States. Obesity alone accounts
for as much as 7 percent of health care costs in several industrial countries, yet
the true costs are undoubtedly greater since these calculations do not include all
obesity-related conditions.[30] A large proportion of health care expenditures are
related to chronic conditions, such as diabetes and heart disease, which are linked
to and exacerbated by overweight or obesity. Chronic diseases such as heart disease, cancer, and diabetes are leading causes of disability and death in the United
States. According to the CDC, in 2004, these diseases accounted for more than
70 percent of the $1 trillion spent on health care each year in the United States.[31]

As developing countries strive to improve their economic status and their dietary habits transition to those modeled by the industrial countries, the populations
face the risk of encountering escalating rates of diet-related chronic diseases and
the accompanying costs of treating these conditions. The WHO reports that, if
current trends continue, India and the Middle Eastern region will have the largest
number of diabetics by 2025. Large increases would also be observed in Latin
America, the Caribbean, China, and the rest of Asia.[32] Can these countries afford
the care and treatment of the conditions associated with obesity? Are the food
choices and lifestyle patterns of the United States really enviable if they lead to
such high levels of debilitating chronic diseases with their enormous health care
cost? The WHO is encouraging economically emerging countries to develop policies allowing them to bypass the obesity epidemic and create a healthier food
environment.[33]

WHY ARE OUR COMMUNITIES SO FAT?

Given that the rates of overweight and obesity have soared over the past thirty
years, it is possible to examine what factors have changed and address these
changes in hopes of slowing and reversing the weight gain experienced by our
country's youth. Countless variables contribute to the current obesity epidemic.
For each overweight individual, their body weight is the outward manifestation
of a combination of genetic, metabolic, behavioral, environmental, cultural, economic, and social influences.

The first law of thermodynamics, stating that a system can either store or burn energy, is the underlying principle of food or energy balance; we eat and either burn or store the calories from food. This is the basis for most weight loss recommendations; eat less and move more. In theory it works, but in most people's lives either internal or external interference complicates the body's ability to regulate intake in relation to activity. To maintain a constant weight, the individual must correct energy intake or energy expenditure every few days to counter the imbalances that occurred on previous days. Some people are fortunate to have a strong internal regulatory response, which allows them to maintain their weight for many years. Other people's regulatory response is softer and allows the body weight to gradually creep up each year. And yet for others, it looks as if there is not much of a natural regulatory response, as their weight rapidly balloons in a manner seemingly out of their control. To prevent weight gain, most people need to utilize some method of discipline by either restraining their eating or making adjustments to their intake or activity when they notice a slight weight gain. However, how well an individual can adhere to their intended strategy is what ultimately makes a difference.

One challenge to this perspective is to consider the issue of young children gaining body weight disproportionate to their skeletal growth. What is taking place to diminish their innate regulatory response? Are they are a carrier of the "thrifty genotype"[34] or genetically deficient in a regulatory hormone such as leptin?[35] Perhaps the parents did not follow the infant's signs of hunger and satiety and the child learned to disregard its internal messages.[36] Maybe the mother had diabetes during pregnancy, which contributes to a higher risk of excess weight gain in infants.[37] Exposure to other prenatal toxins may also affect the regulatory system as demonstrated in infants of mothers who smoke during pregnancy and have an increased risk of becoming overweight by age thirty when compared with infants of nonsmoking mothers.[38]

A child's early food experiences are presented by parents and caregivers. The first experience is the liquid nourishment received from the breast or the bottle. When breast milk is the sole source of nutrition for more than three months, obesity risk is significantly reduced in preschool children and in adolescents when compared with infants who are breastfed for three months or less.[39] The transition to table foods is a critical time for children and families to establish patterns of acceptance and familiarity.[40] Are fruits and vegetables a regular part of meals? What kinds of beverages are served? What is the atmosphere around meals? What is the macronutrient quality and content of the meals (referring to the type and amount of fat, carbohydrate, and protein)? Does the family prepare its own foods from "scratch," buy commercially prepared foods, or dine at restaurants? A multitude of issues surround the food environment in which children develop preferences and habits that they carry into the adult years.

THE INFLUENTIAL FOOD ENVIRONMENT IN THE DEVELOPMENT OF OVERWEIGHT AND OBESITY

Since children consume their first calories from liquids, it is a good place to begin to explore the impact of food choices. It is common practice in many places to see a child with some type liquid in a bottle that is not breast milk, water, or commercial baby formula. In many cases, this liquid is a beverage sweetened with high fructose corn syrup (HFCS), such as a fruit "drink" with only a small percentage of juice. One of the most noteworthy changes in food consumption from 1970 to the present is that the intake of HFCS has increased by more than 1,000 percent.[41] HFCS, which represents more than 40 percent of the caloric sweeteners added to foods and beverages, contributes a daily average of 132 calories to the diet of Americans two years and older. The top 20 percent of consumers ingest 316 calories per day (kcal/day) from HFCS,[42] which can be obtained from twenty-seven ounces of soft drink. HFCS-sweetened beverages may contribute to calorie overconsumption and weight gain. If one does not compensate for these extra daily calories, it could result in an annual weight gain of 13.75 to 33 pounds, based on the premise that a positive energy balance of 3,500 calories will result in one pound of weight gain.

Another factor that links HFCS to the accumulation of body fat is that the digestion, absorption, and metabolism of fructose differ from other sugars. The metabolic pathway of fructose favors the production of fat cells in the liver (hepatic lipogenesis) and does not stimulate insulin secretion nor enhance leptin production, two key substances in the regulation of food intake, satiety, and body weight.[43] Parks further contributed to this point of view with a study that revealed that, when fructose was consumed, lipogenesis was twofold greater than in meals without fructose, and this effect carried over until later in the day.[44]

The theory that HFCS is contributing to the obesity epidemic is not universally accepted. Forshee and colleagues reported on the findings of food scientists at the Center for Food, Nutrition, and Agriculture Policy meeting in 2007. This group conducted a review of scientific literature to examine the relationship between consumption of HFCS and weight gain and determined that it is unclear why HFCS would contribute to obesity more so than the sucrose that was more common in the food supply before the 1970s.[45] Another study compared the satiating effects of HFCS and sucrose in various beverages and concluded that the net energy balance from consuming HFCS-sweetened beverages was no different from those of sucrose-sweetened drinks or milk.[46] The role of HFCS in our food supply warrants further study by researchers who are not linked with the production of the corn-based agricultural products from which the HFCS is produced.

One relevant message for all consumers is that beverages containing HFCS, sugar, or alcohol contribute often-overlooked and, sometimes, excessive calories. An appropriate choice is to drink noncaloric beverages more often and obtain dietary fructose from whole fruits, with their naturally occurring fiber and nutrients, rather than from foods and beverages with HFCS. This is especially true when foods and beverages are introduced to young children developing their taste preferences. A review of the relationship between 100 percent fruit juice consumption and weight in youth found that 100 percent fruit juice did not contribute to overweight and that consuming one or two four-ounce daily portions of 100 percent juice can help children meet the recommended fruit servings.[47]

Unfortunately, parents and their children are affected by the media and marketing messages, which are intended to sway buying habits and food choices. Many of the foods marketed to families, children, and teens take a basically nutritious food and alter its taste or image by adding sugar, fat, salt, and flavor or color enhancers. The U.S. food industry is sophisticated and successful, and the scope of its influence can be seen in every grocery cart and garbage dumpster.

Advertising to Children and Teens

Food expenditure data[48] indicate that consumers spent less of their disposable personal income in 2007 on food compared with 1970, (11.4 percent versus 15.3 percent), but this reduction was accompanied by a trend to spend more on foods eaten away from home, especially at quick-serve restaurants (QSRs). Disposable personal income spent to eat at home declined by 43 percent from 11.4 percent in 1970 to 6.5 percent in 2007, combined with a 25 percent increase in disposable money spent on foods away from home. This trend is reflected in the 2007 statistic that nearly 49 percent of food dollars were spent for foods consumed away from home, as compared with 1970 when 33.4 percent of food dollars were spent on foods eaten away from home.[49] In 2007, 37 percent of the dollars spent to eat outside the home was spent at QSRs; a 158 percent increase from the 14.3 percent spent at QSRs in 1967.[50]

Active marketing campaigns certainly have influenced these numbers. Perhaps the media and messages that have been enthusiastically employed to market the food industries' products can be used to spread the message that food choices and activity patterns can play a role in reversing the obesity trend. Messages to influence food buying habits could be modeled after the successful antitobacco campaign in a public crusade to curb the obesity epidemic.[51] A Federal Trade Commission (FTC) report offers recommendations for food and beverage companies, along with the media and entertainment companies they employ, to utilize in their self-regulation.[52] The first recommendation is to join the Children's Food and Beverage Advertising Initiative, established by the Council of Better Business Bureaus in 2006.[53] In response to the FTC report, Susan Linn, director of the Campaign for a Commercial-Free Childhood, said, "It's the marketing industry policing itself, and as is shown over and over and over again, that's problematic."[54]

Do We Really Know What We Are Eating?

With close to 50 percent of the 2007 U.S. food dollars spent on foods prepared and served outside of the home, the type and amount of foods selected at these establishments no doubt influences the nutritional intake and energy balance of U.S. citizens. The Center for Science in the Public Interest (CSPI) released a report in August 2008 addressing the issue of "kids' meals" in restaurants. Their investigation confirmed that good options for feeding kids are hard to find. Ninety-three percent of 1,474 possible choices at the thirteen chains provide more than one-third of the daily calories health professionals recommended for children between the ages of four and eight.[55] A meal of cheese pizza, home-style fries, and lemonade topped out at one thousand calories. Better choices such as a mini-sub, juice box, and a side serving of apple slices, raisins, or yogurt provide less than the 430-calorie benchmark for one-third of a child's daily needs. Criteria for selection specified that nutrition information is available on the restaurant's Web site or upon request.[56]

CSPI Nutrition Policy Director Margo Wootan expressed concern that chain restaurants make it more difficult for parents to feed their children healthy foods when dining out: "Chains are conditioning kids to expect burgers, fried chicken, pizza, french fries, macaroni and cheese, and soda in various combinations at almost every lunch and dinner."[57] Wootan comments that "most of these kid's meals appear to be designed to put America's children on the fast-track to obesity, disability, heart attack, or diabetes."[58] It would be easier to select healthy choices if menus and menu boards listed calories per serving. CSPI has advocated for regulations to require calorie information in visible locations, such as on restaurant menus or menu boards. As of March 2008, the New York City Board of Health mandated restaurants with fifteen locations or more to list calories on their menus or menu boards.[59] Several other cities have passed menu-labeling policies and more than twenty states and cities have introduced menu-labeling legislation in the past two years.

Adults are also challenged to select foods that do not contribute to weight gain. When children and adults are presented a large portion, they are likely to consume more calories.[60] Portion sizes served in restaurants and available in the marketplace began to grow in the 1970s, rose sharply in the 1980s, and have continued to gradually increase in response to consumer expectations for a good value.[61] Fast-food portions are larger in the United States than in Europe, and some chains have increased portion sizes even while health authorities are recommending reduced portion sizes.[62] A 2006 survey of three hundred chefs found that they believe customers expect big platefuls of food when eating out.[63] Overall, 60 percent of chefs serve steaks that are twelve ounces or larger (four times what the government's dietary guidelines cite as a portion), pasta servings that are two to four times the standard half-cup serving, and rather meager vegetable portions that came close to the standard half-cup serving.[64]

Many strategies could be employed to improve the nutritional profile of full-service and fast-food meals, but both the food service industry and consumers must accept these changes. Meals could be prepared according to the Dietary Guidelines for Americans[65] and the American Heart Association (AHA) Dietary Guidelines.[66] These meals would contain more fruits, vegetables, and whole grains and would limit the inclusion of high-fat and sweetened foods that are high energy density and low in nutritional value. This will only happen if consumers demand them and the food industry responds with tasteful, attractive, and reasonably priced options.

RISING FOOD PRICES AFFECT BUYING HABITS

Dining away from home is associated with reduced intake of fruits and vegetables, with the exception of potatoes—either fried or chips.[67] Encouraging Americans to eat more fruit and vegetables has been a primary focus in most dietary guidance messages. Supermarkets stock a broad range of produce year-round and many time-saving, convenient products are widely available. Most fruits and vegetables are naturally low in calories, yet their energy density can be dramatically affected by the addition of fat during preparation and service. Fruit consumption has been found to be associated with lower BMI,[68] probably because most fruit is consumed in its natural low-fat form.

The cost of fresh produce is a commonly cited reason why consumers do not eat more of these healthy foods, and when money is limited, purchasing fruit and vegetable is not a high priority. Drewnowski and colleagues criticized the current structure of food pricing that allows sweet and high-fat food to provide dietary energy at the lowest cost.[69] Consumers trying to save money may buy energy-dense foods high in refined grains, added sugars, and fats.[70] Other researchers found that the most significant impact on fruit and vegetable consumption was education, with college-educated households exhibiting the highest level of consumption.[71]

Among the efforts to increase intake of fruits and vegetables is to improve access, both financial and physical, as quality produce is less likely to be available in low-income neighborhoods. Food assistance programs are being modified and programs, such as the USDA fruit and vegetable pilot program for schools, are expanding.[72] However, it remains to be determined whether these changes spur low-income overweight and obese individuals to eat healthier diets. Many behavioral and economic factors influence the decision to eat fruits and vegetables and, in the end, consumer preference drives the demand and supply for products in the market.[73] The current economic downturn and rise in fuel prices are forcing higher prices for almost everything in the grocery cart. Some people are reacting by changing their food-buying and consumption patterns. Could it be that as Americans trim some superfluous expenses it may also slim their waistlines?

INCHING TOWARD HEALTHIER EATING AND A MORE ACTIVE LIFESTYLE

A July 2008 CDC press release quotes Dr. William Dietz, director of the Division on Nutrition, Physical Activity, and Obesity, as saying,

> The epidemic of adult obesity continues to rise in the United States indicating that we need to step up our efforts at the national, state and local levels. We need to encourage people to eat more fruits and vegetables, engage in more physical activity and reduce the consumption of high calorie foods and sugar sweetened beverages in order to maintain a healthy weight.[74]

An online publication by the Hartman Group, "the leading market research resource for consumer insights, knowledge acquisition and actionable analysis,"[75] discussed the *Problem with Obesity (Hint: It Ain't the Food)*.[76] The comment excerpted from the article addresses the complexity in developing efforts to reverse the obesity epidemic:

> Our research on individual practice and sentiment tells us the ideal solutions to the obesity dilemma may have little at all to do with individual people and a heck of a lot more to do with the larger culture framework within which we live our lives. Quite simply, and we don't mean to sound glib here, but "it is not the food, it's the culture, stupid." ... **And herein lies the most significant and important challenge of all, namely, how to change not individual behavior but the parameters within which such behavior resides—how to change the culture.**[77]

RESOLVING TO CHANGE THE CULTURE SURROUNDING OVEREATING AND INACTIVITY

In 2001, the U.S. Surgeon General issued the *Call to Action to Prevent and Decrease Overweight and Obesity*[78] to spur the development of programs and action plans directed toward this expansive problem. The U.S. Congress delegated the task of developing prevention-focused action plans to decrease the number of overweight children and youth to the Institute of Medicine (IOM). The report, *Preventing Childhood Obesity: Health in the Balance*, describes the committee's action plan[79] and directs attention to communities that experience high rates of obesity and the associated chronic illness and those with environments unsupportive of healthful nutrition and physical activity.[80] Success will not be achieved without the cooperation from all segments of the society, including federal, state, and local governments; the food industry along with their media and marketing agencies; health care providers; community and nonprofit organizations; schools and education institutions; and parents, caregivers, and families.[81]

The AHA released a comprehensive plan for addressing the obesity epidemic.[82] This plan provides a rationale for population-based obesity prevention efforts and research from a public health perspective. It addresses the need to bring together the various arguments for what needs to be done and how, with respect to population-based initiatives, to promote lifestyle, eating, and activity behaviors associated with preventing overweight and obesity.[83]

An example of change that must be explored on the community and cultural level relates to community design, such as public recreation, green spaces, sidewalks, and safe routes to school. This "built environment," as contrasted to naturally occurring features, may either encourage or deter community residents and visitors from increasing their activity. Yancey and colleagues describe the societal changes that contribute to inactivity and identify specific recommendations for policy and environmental changes to facilitate higher levels of energy expenditure.[84] Low-income, inner-city neighborhoods and rural areas both will benefit from exploring the opportunities for exercise, as well as the obstacles that impede their community members from engaging in regular exercise.

Many people find their time available to exercise or their desire to engage in individual or family activity is diminished by long commutes to work, extended work hours or a second job, and a lack of safe places to walk or play. Access to safe places to be active, walkable neighborhoods, and local markets offering healthful food create environments for higher energy expenditure and healthful food selection—two types of behavior that can lead to reduced incidence of chronic disease and help avoid obesity.[85] Framing population-based obesity prevention in the context of finding a balance between healthful eating and increased physical activity will require modification of individual choices, habits, and preferences, yet individuals are responsive to the surrounding environments and are influenced by the actions of their peers at home, school, and the workplace.[86]

DO PEOPLE FEEL EMPOWERED TO CHANGE OR ARE THEY TRAPPED BY THEIR CIRCUMSTANCES?

Frances Moore Lappé, cofounder of Food First: The Institute for Food and Development Policy, and the Small Planet Institute, has argued that global hunger and malnutrition are caused not by the lack of food but rather by the inability of hungry people to gain access to the abundant amount of food that exists in the world because of the maldistribution of power. In essence, it is not that food is lacking, but that people lack power.[87] The concept of lack of power may be applied to the current malnutrition associated with overnutrition and obesity, especially within the many clusters of people living within the demographic, geographic, ethnic, and socioeconomic populations demonstrating high obesity rates. Do people have power over their food choices? Do people have power to take action to change the food culture and the built environment? Do people have power to influence food growers, manufacturers, and food policymakers? Do people have power to create urban green spaces and urban vegetable gardens? Do people have power to obtain healthy food within the radius of their transportation modes? This power goes beyond the willpower needed to refuse the mid-afternoon candy bar or the quick stop at a favorite fast-food restaurant (although the power of self-discipline is necessary at times, too). According to Lappé, "power means simply our capacity to act."[88] She goes on to say that change in the world is a given. In fact, all of our actions create a ripple effect, such that even if we are not consciously choosing to create change, the choices we make can have broad reaching effects. She explains, "So the choice we have is not whether, but only how, we change the world."[89]

As with any epidemic, it takes collective community action as described by the IOM,[90] CDC,[91] and AHA,[92] as well as others to bring it under control. Each person is a valuable member of the greater community, and each person's actions will affect the success of the campaign to rein in obesity. Every person can harness their own personal power to buy the most healthful foods available to them in a given situation, vote for leaders who support creating food and development policies conducive to healthy lifestyles, and engage in regular physical activity. The obesity epidemic may be an undesirable outward manifestation of our modern society, yet the course of this epidemic can be influenced by our individual and collective voice as expressed through conscious political, economic, lifestyle, grocery store, restaurant, and social choices.

NOTES

1. WHO (World Health Organization), "Obesity and Overweight" (Fact Sheet No. 311, 2006), http://www.who.int/mediacentre/factsheets/fs311/en/index.html (accessed July 24, 2008).

2. WHO, "Global Strategy on Diet, Physical Activity and Health, 2004," http://www.who.int/dietphysicalactivity/goals/en/index.html (accessed July 24, 2008).

3. A. Drewnowski and B. Popkin, "The Nutrition Transition: New Trends in the Global Diet," *Nutrition Review* 55 (1997): 31–43.

4. Ibid.

5. NCHS (National Center for Health Statistics), "The National Health and Nutrition Examination Survey, 2003–2004," http://www.cdc.gov/nchs/about/major/nhanes/intro_mec.htm (accessed July 24, 2008).

6. CDC (Centers for Disease Control and Prevention), "State-Specific Prevalence of Obesity among Adults in the United States, 2007," *Morbidity and Mortality Weekly Report*, 57 no. 28 (2008): 765–68, http://www.cdc.gov/mmwr/preview/mmwrhtml/mm5728a1.htm (accessed July 22, 2008).

7. U.S. Census Bureau, "American Factfinder. Age and Sex: 2006 American Community Survey," http://factfinder.census.gov/servlet/STTable?_bm=y&-geo_id=01000US

&-qr_name=ACS_2006_EST_G00_S0101&-ds_name=ACS_2006_EST_G00_9 (accessed July 29, 2008).

8. NIH (National Institutes of Health), "Clinical Guidelines on the Identification, Evaluation, and Treatment of Overweight and Obesity in Adults-the Evidence Report," *Obesity Research* 6 (1998): 51S–209S.

9. Ibid.

10. Ibid.

11. NCHS, "NHANES," 2003–2004.

12. Institute of Medicine, "Focus on Childhood Obesity" (National Academy of Sciences, 2004), http://www.iom.edu (accessed July 23, 2008).

13. R. Kucamarski et al., "CDC Growth Charts: United States," *Advanced Data* 314 (2000): 1–27.

14. S. Barlow, "Expert Committee Recommendations Regarding the Prevention, Assessment and Treatment of Child and Adolescent Overweight and Obesity," Summary Report, *Pediatrics* 120 (2007): S164–S192.

15. CDC, "State-Specific Prevalence of Obesity among Adults in the United States," 2007.

16. CDC, "State-Specific Prevalence"; NCHS, "NHANES," 2003–2004.

17. Ibid.

18. D. Freedman et al., "Racial and Ethnic Differences in Secular Trends for Childhood BMI, Weight and Height," *Obesity* 14 (2006): 301–8.

19. Y. Wang and Q. Zhang, "Are American Children and Adolescents of Low Socioeconomic Status at Increased Risk of Obesity? Changes in the Association between Overweight and Family Income between 1971 and 2002," *American Journal Clinical Nutrition* 84 (2006): 707–16.

20. J. Jackson et al., "A National Study of Obesity Prevalence and Trends by Type of Rural County," *Journal of Rural Health* 21 (2005): 140–48.

21. May Nawal Lutfiyya et al., "Is Rural Residency a Risk Factor for Overweight and Obesity for U.S. Children?" *Obesity* 15 (2007): 2348–56.

22. Ibid.

23. NCHS, "NHANES," 2003–2004.

24. Cynthia Ogden, Margaret Carroll, and Katherine Flegal, "High Body Mass Index for Age among U.S. Children and Adolescents, 2003–2006," *Journal of the American Medical Association* 299 (2008): 2401–5.

25. Jeffery Kluger, "How American's Children Packed on the Pounds," *Time*, June 23, 2008, 69.

26. Ibid.

27. Shiriki K. Kumanyika et al., *American Heart Association Scientific Statement*, "Population-Based Prevention of Obesity: the Need for Comprehensive Promotion of Healthful Eating, Physical Activity and Energy Balance," *Circulation* 118 (2008): 6, http://circ.ahajournals.org (accessed July 10, 2008); WHO, "Obesity and Overweight."

28. S. R. Daniels et al., "Overweight in Children and Adolescents; Pathophysiology, Consequences, Prevention, and Treatment," *Circulation* 111 (2005): 1999–2012.

29. Sara Gable et al., "Ecological Predictors and Developmental Outcomes of Persistent Childhood Overweight" (Economic Research Service, USDA, 2008), http://www.ers.usda.gov (accessed June 14, 2008).

30. WHO, "Overweight and Obesity."

31. CDC, "The Burden of Chronic Diseases and Their Risk Factors: National and State Perspectives 2004" (Atlanta: U.S. Department of Health and Human Services, 2004), http://www.cdc.gov/nccdphp/burdenbook2004 (accessed July 30, 2008).

32. WHO, "Overweight and Obesity."

33. WHO, "Global Strategy on Diet, Physical Activity and Health, 2004."

34. R. Stöger, "The Thrifty Epigeotype: An Acquired and Heritable Predisposition for Obesity and Diabetes?" *Bioessays* 30 (2008): 156–66.

35. Y. Zhang et al., "Positional Cloning of the Mouse Obese Gene and Its Human Homologue," *Nature* 372 (1994): 425–32.

36. Ellyn Satter, *Child of Mine; Feeding with Love and Good Sense* (Boulder, CO: Bull Publishing, 2000).

37. D. Dabelea et al., "Birthweight, Type 2 Diabetes, and Insulin Resistance in Pima Indian Children and Young Adults," *Diabetes Care* 22 (1999): 944–50.

38. A. M. Toschke et al., "Maternal Smoking during Pregnancy and Appetite Control in Offspring," *Journal of Perinatal Medicine* 31 (2003): 251–56; A. Tremblay et al., "Thermogenesis and Weight Loss in Obese Individuals: A Primary Association with Organochlorine Pollution," *International Journal of Obesity Related Metabolic Disorders* 28 (2004): 936–39.

39. R. Von Kries et al., "Breastfeeding and Obesity: Cross Sectional Study," *British Medical Journal* 319 (1999): 147–50.

40. Satter, *Child of Mine.*

41. G. Bray et al., "Consumption of High-Fructose Corn Syrup in Beverages May Play a Role in the Epidemic of Obesity," *American Journal of Clinical Nutrition* 79 (2004): 537–43.

42. Ibid.

43. Ibid.

44. Elizabeth Parks et al., "Dietary Sugars Stimulate Fatty Acid Synthesis in Adults," *Journal of Nutrition* 138 (2008): 1039–46.

45. R. Forshee et al., "A Critical Examination of the Evidence Relating High Fructose Corn Syrup and Weight Gain," *Critical Reviews in Food Science and Nutrition* 47, no. 6 (2007): 561–82.

46. Stijn Soenen and Margriet Weterterp-Plantenga, "No Differences in Satiety or Energy Intake after High-Fructose Corn Syrup, Sucrose or Milk Preloads," *American Journal of Clinical Nutrition* 86 (2007): 1586–94.

47. Carol O'Neil and Theresa A. Nicklas, "A Review of the Relationship Between 100% Fruit Juice Consumption and Weight in Children and Adolescents," *American Journal of Lifestyle Medicine* 2 (2008): 315–54.

48. USDA/ERS (U.S. Department of Agriculture/Economic Research Service), "Consumer Price Index, Food and Expenditure Data 2007," http://www.ers.usda.gov/briefing/CPIFoodAndExpenditures/Data/table8.htm (accessed August 1, 2008).

49. USDA/ERS, "CPI, Food and Expenditure Data 2007," http://www.ers.usda.gov/briefing/CPIFoodAndExpenditures/Data/table1.htm (accessed August 1, 2008).

50. USDA/ERS, "CPI, Food and Expenditure Data 2007."

51. Institute of Medicine of the National Academies, "Advertising, Marketing and the Media: Improving Messages" (2004), http://www.iom.edu (accessed July 22, 2008).

52. William Kovacic et al., *Marketing Food to Children and Adolescents: A Review of Industry Expenditures, Activities, and Self Regulation* (Federal Trade Commission, July 2008), www.ftc.gov/os/2008/07/P064504foodmktingreport.pdf (accessed August 1. 2008).

53. U.S. National Better Business Bureau, "About the Initiative," http://us.bbb.org/WWWRoot/SitePage.aspx?site=113&id=b712b7a7-fcd5-479c-af49-8649107a4b02 (accessed August 6, 2008).

54. Stephanie Clifford, "Tug of War in Food Marketing to Children," *New York Times,* July 30, 2008, http://www.nytimes.com/2008/07/30/business/media/30adco.html (accessed August 1, 2008).

55. CSPI (Center for Science in the Public Interest), "Obesity on the Kids' Menus at Top Chains" (2008), http://www.cspinet.org/new/200808041_print.html (accessed August 4, 2008); USDA, "My Pyramid," http://www.mypyramid.gov/ (accessed Aug. 5, 2008).

56. CSPI, "Obesity on the Kids' Menus at Top Chains."

57. Ibid.

58. Ibid.

59. CNN, "New York Orders Calories on Chain Menus," January 22, 2008, http://edition.cnn.com/2008/HEALTH/diet.fitness/01/22/calories.menus/index.html (accessed August 4, 2008).

60. Barbara Rolls et al., "Larger Portion Sizes Lead to a Sustained Increase in Energy Intake over 2 Days," Journal of the American Dietetic Association 106 (2006): 543–49; J. Fisher et al., "Effects of Portion Size and Energy Density on Young Children's Intake at a Meal," American Journal of Clinical Nutrition 86 (2007): 174–79.

61. Lisa Young and Marion Nestle, "The Contribution of Expanding Portion Sizes to the U.S. Obesity Epidemic," American Journal of Public Health 92 (2002): 246–249; J. Ledikwe et al., "Portion Sizes and the Obesity Epidemic," Journal of Nutrition 135 (2005): 905–9.

62. Lisa Young and Marion Nestle, "Portion Sizes and Obesity: Responses of Fast-Food Companies," Journal of Public Health Policy 28 (2007): 238–48.

63. Marge Condrasky et al., "Chefs' Opinions of Restaurant Portion Sizes," Obesity 15 (2007): 2086–94.

64. Condrasky et al., "Chefs' Opinions"; USDA, "My Pyramid."

65. U.S. Department of Health and Human Services/USDA, "Dietary Guidelines for Americans, 2005," http://www.health.gov/DietaryGuidelines/dga2005/document/default.htm (accessed August 5, 2008).

66. American Heart Association Nutrition Committee, "Diet and Lifestyle Recommendations Revision 2006: A Scientific Statement from the American Heart Association Nutrition Committee," Circulation 114 (2006): 82–96.

67. Joanne Guthrie et al., "Understanding Economic and Behavioral Influences on Fruit and Vegetable Choices," Amber Waves April (2005), http://www.ers.usda.gov/Amberwaves/April05/Features/FruitAndVegChoices.htm (accessed August 6, 2008).

68. Biing-Hwan Lin and Rosanna Morrison, "Higher Fruit Consumption Linked with Lower Body Mass Index" (Food Review 25, UDSA/ERS, 2002), http://www.ers.usda.gov/publications/FoodReview/DEC2002/frvol25i3d.pdf (accessed August 6, 2008).

69. Adam Drewnowski and S. Specter, "Poverty and Obesity: The Role of Energy Density and Energy Costs," American Journal of Clinical Nutrition 79 (2004): 6–16; Adam Drewnowski and Nicole Darmon, "Food Choices and Diet Costs: An Economic Analysis," Journal of Nutrition 135 (2005): 900–904.

70. Nicole Darmon et al., "Energy Dense Diets are Associated with Lower Diet Costs: A Community Study of French Adults," Public Health Nutrition 7 (2004): 21–27.

71. Guthrie et al., "Understanding Economic."

72. USDA, "2008 Farm Bill," http://www.usda.gov/wps/portal/farmbill2008?navid=FARMBILL2008 (accessed August 6, 2008).

73. Guthrie et al., "Understanding Economic."

74. CDC, "Latest CDC Data Show More Americans Report Being Obese," (July 17, 2008), http://www.cdc.gov/media/pressrel/2008/r080717.htm (accessed July 30, 2008).

75. The Hartman-Group, http://www.hartman-group.com (accessed July 30, 2008).

76. Ibid.

77. Ibid.

78. U.S. Surgeon General, "Call to Action to Prevent and Decrease Overweight and Obesity" (2001), http://www.surgeongeneral.gov/topics/obesity/calltoaction/Callto Action.pdf (accessed Aug. 5, 2008).

79. Jeffrey P. Koplan et al., eds., *Preventing Childhood Obesity: Health in the Balance* (Washington, D.C.: National Academy of Sciences, Committee on Prevention of Obesity in Children and Youth, 2005), http://books.nap.edu/catalog.php?record_id=11015#toc.

80. Institute of Medicine, "Focus on Childhood Obesity" (2004), http://www.iom. edu/CMS/22593.aspx (accessed July 23,2008).

81. Ibid.

82. Kumanyika et al., "Population-Based Prevention."

83. Ibid., 3.

84. A. Yancy et al., "Creating a Robust Public Health Infrastructure for Physical Activity Promotion," *American Journal of Preventative Medicine* 32 (2007): 68–78.

85. J. Sallis and K. Glanz, "The Role of Built Environments in Physical Activity, Eating and Obesity in Childhood," *Future Child* 16 (2006): 89–108, http://www.futureofchildren.org/information2826/information_show.htm?doc_id=355433 (accessed August 6, 2008).

86. S. Booth et al., "Environmental and Societal Factors Affect Food Choice and Physical Activity: Rationale, Influences and Leverage Points," *Nutrition Reviews* 59 (2001): S21–S39, S57–S65.

87. Frances Moore Lappé et al., *World Hunger: 12 Myths* (New York: Grove Press, 1998).

88. Frances Moore Lappé, *Getting a Grip: Clarity, Creativity and Courage in a World Gone Mad* (Cambridge: Small Planet Media, 2007), 74.

89. Ibid.

90. Koplan et al., "Preventing Childhood Obesity."

91. CDC, "Obesity and Overweight."

92. Kumanyika et al. "Population-Based Prevention."

RESOURCE GUIDE

Suggested Reading

American Heart Association Nutrition Committee. "Diet and Lifestyle Recommendations Revision 2006; A Scientific Statement from the American Heart Association Nutrition Committee." *Circulation* 114 (2006): 82–96.

Koplan, Jeffrey P., et al., eds. Committee on Prevention of Obesity in Children and Youth. *Preventing Childhood Obesity: Health in the Balance*. (Washington, DC: National Academy of Sciences, 2005. Available at http://books.nap.edu/catalog. php?record_id=11015#toc.

Kumanyika, Shiriki K., et al. American Heart Association Scientific Statement. "Population-Based Prevention of Obesity: the Need for Comprehensive Promotion of Healthful Eating, Physical Activity and Energy Balance." *Circulation*, 118 (2008): 1–37. Available at http://circ.ahajournals.org.

Patel, Raj. *Stuffed and Starved: The Hidden Battle for the World Food System*. Brooklyn, Melville House Publishing, 2007.

Rolls, Barbara. *The Volumetrics Eating Plan: Techniques and Recipes for Feeling Full on Fewer Calories*. New York: Harper Collins Publishing, 2005.

Satter, Ellyn. *Child of Mine; Feeding with Love and Good Sense*. Boulder, CO: Bull Publishing, 2000.

Web Sites

America on the Move, http://www.americaonthemove.org/.
Centers for Disease Control and Prevention, http://www.cdc.gov/.
Center for Science in the Public Interest, http://www.cspinet.org/.
Institute of Medicine, http://www.iom.edu.
U.S. Department of Agriculture, http://www.usda.gov/.
U.S. Department of Agriculture, Economic Research Service, http://www.ers.usda.gov/.
World Health Organization, http://www.WHO.int/.

About the Editor and Contributors

Laurel E. Phoenix is associate professor of Public and Environmental Affairs at the University of Wisconsin-Green Bay and chair of the geography department. She is an executive committee member of the Center for Food in Community and Culture. Laurel teaches courses on sustainable water and land resource management and planning; environment and society; environmental law; and graduate environmental science and policy courses. She is an associate editor of the American Water Resource Association's *Water Resources IMPACT*. Her interest in critical food issues grew from decades of organic gardening as well as researching the synergies of water, air, and soil pollution and the political-corporate structures that perpetuate them.

Richard H. Bernsten is a professor in the Department of Agricultural, Food, and Resource Economics, Michigan State University (MSU), and teaches international development-related undergraduate and graduate courses. His research focuses on the adoption and impact of agricultural technologies, subsector analysis, food security, and agricultural policy analysis. Over the past thirty years, he has conducted research in various countries in Sub-Saharan Africa, Asia, and Latin America. Before joining MSU in 1985, he worked for Winrock International (four years) and the International Rice Research Institute, including four years based in Indonesia. Before earning his doctorate at the University of Illinois (1979), he served as a Peace Corps volunteer in Sierra Leone.

Jim Bingen is a professor of community, food, and agricultural systems. With a degree in political science (University of California–Los Angeles), Jim works on a range of food, farming, and rural development issues from Michigan to Western Europe and French-speaking Africa. He is currently working on several applied research programs that involve studies with farmers market vendors, the transition to organic farming and farmer access to organic markets, and the contribution of place-based and quality food to development in Michigan.

Duncan H. Boughton is associate professor of international development in the Department of Agricultural Economics at Michigan State University (MSU). He has lived and worked for most of his professional life in Sub-Saharan Africa. He worked six years as country coordinator for the department's Agricultural Policy Analysis project in Mozambique. Before moving to Mozambique, Duncan worked as a senior scientist with the International Crops Research Institute for the Semi-Arid Tropics (ICRISAT) based in Malawi. Duncan conducted doctoral and postdoctoral research with the national agricultural research program of Mali (IER) from 1991 to 1996, and prior to beginning his doctorate at MSU worked for the U.K. international aid program in the Gambia for five years.

Dr. Michael Brewer is Field Crops Entomologist at the Texas AgriLife Research and Extension Center at Corpus Christi. He focuses on research of IPM tactics in cropping systems. He was previously coordinator of the Michigan State University IPM Program and Extension Entomologist at the University of Wyoming.

Daniel A. Cibulka is a graduate student in the Environmental Science and Policy Program at the University of Wisconsin–Green Bay. His research interests include sustainable agriculture and its relationship to surface-water quality and community health, fisheries dynamics of inland lakes, and zooplankton interactions within Lake Michigan. His thesis research examines the effects of agricultural changes, implementation of best management practices, and stream restoration projects on the water quality and biotic integrity of streams in the Duck Creek Watershed, Wisconsin.

Kathryn Colasanti is a master's candidate in the Agriculture and Community Food Systems Program within Michigan State University's Department of Community, Agriculture, Recreation, and Resource Studies. Her thesis research relates to the production potential of and community perspectives regarding city-scale urban agriculture in Detroit, Michigan. Before coming to MSU she worked on community garden–based neighborhood health initiatives through Denver Urban Gardens in Denver, Colorado.

John T. Cook is an associate professor of pediatrics in Boston University's School of Medicine researching the causes and consequences of food insecurity and hunger, particularly their impacts on the health, growth, and development of young children under the Children's Sentinel Nutrition Assessment Program (C-SNAP). C-SNAP is a national network of pediatricians and public health researchers conducting original research to inform policy decisions that protect and promote children's health and well-being.

Tracy Dobson, J. D., is professor in the Department of Fisheries and Wildlife at Michigan State University (MSU). Dobson conducts research in fisheries policy and management, primarily regarding the Laurentian Great Lakes basin and the African Great Lakes, especially in Malawi. She teaches in the area of environmental policy and law and gender and environment. She is co-coordinator of MSU's Gender, Justice, and Environmental Change graduate specialization and is a professor in the Department of Fisheries and Wildlife.

Cynthia Donovan is an assistant professor in the Department of Agricultural, Food, and Resource Economics at Michigan State University (MSU). Her research and development interests include market information systems, food security and markets, market development for food staples, impacts of HIV/AIDS on agriculture and rural incomes, and impact monitoring for agricultural sector projects, with a focus in Sub-Saharan Africa. She currently conducts collaborative research and training in Mozambique and Angola, with extensive experience in East and West Africa.

Margaret (Maggie) Fitzpatrick is a native of Cleveland, Ohio, and graduated from John Carroll University, a small Jesuit university on the east side of Cleveland, with a bachelor of science in biology and a concentration in environmental studies. Through environmental studies, she found an interest in sustainable food and agriculture and went on to complete two farm internships, one in Vermont and one in Dayton, Ohio. There she gained cultivation skills and experience as an educator. During this experience, Maggie began to reflect on her previous distance from food production as an urban dweller and how her life has been enriched through participation in food cultivation. She is seeking a master's degree in science with the department of Community, Agriculture, Resource, and Recreation Studies (CARRS) at Michigan State University. Her research interest is the return of small livestock, mainly chicken, to backyards and urban areas through the urban agriculture movement.

Joanne Gardner is a registered dietitian, with a bachelor of science in food science and nutrition, University of Rhode Island, and master's degree in nutritional science from the University of Wisconsin–Stevens Point 1999. Currently, she is an adjunct instructor at the University of Wisconsin–Green Bay in the Nutrition and Dietetics Department. Her previous experience includes Peace Corps volunteer in Colombia, Clinical and Outpatient Dietitian at St. Mary's Hospital, Green Bay, Wisconsin, and individual and group nutrition consulting and writing services for local and international clients.

Marcia Ishii-Eiteman is a senior scientist and coordinator of the Sustainable Agriculture Program at Pesticide Action Network North America (PANNA), and a lead author of the United Nations–sponsored International Assessment of Agricultural Knowledge, Science, and Technology for Development (IAASTD). Before joining PANNA in 1996, Ishii-Eiteman worked in Asia and Africa for more than twelve years, developing farmer field schools in ecological pest management in Thailand, government-farmer-and nongovernmental organization collaborations in sustainable agriculture in Southeast Asia, and women's health, literacy and resource conservation projects in Khmer and Somali refugee camps. Ishii-Eiteman holds a doctorate in ecology and evolutionary biology from Cornell University and a bachelor's degree in women's studies from Yale University.

Cheryl Toronto Kalny received her doctorate in U.S. history from Marquette University. She is an activist-scholar, teaching women's studies courses at the University of Wisconsin–Green Bay, speaking at academic conferences and in public lecture halls, and working through women's organizations for positive change. Her research interests and publications are concerned with the history of women's rights and movements in the United States, and she is the contributing editor of the *North America and Caribbean* volume of *The Greenwood Encyclopedia of Women's Issues Worldwide* (2003).

John M. Kerr is associate professor in the Department of Community, Agriculture, Recreation, and Resource Studies (CARRS) at Michigan State University. His research primarily covers analysis of policies and institutional arrangements related to managing rural natural resources in developing countries. His recent work has addressed the implications of payment for environmental services schemes for conservation and the distribution of benefits to rural people in various parts of the world.

Vicki L. Medland is the associate director of the Cofrin Center for Biodiversity at the University of Wisconsin–Green Bay. She teaches courses related to biodiversity, conservation, and agriculture and has published articles on biodiversity, agro-ecology, and environmental ethics. She is especially interested in issues surrounding the preservation of heritage crops and has led a university program that offers unique heritage vegetables and flowers for sale to the public for ten years.

Katherine Nault is seeking a master's degree in Community, Food, and Agriculture at Michigan State University. Her studies have focused on the engagement of urban youth in research and civic activities around food system issues. She is a former farmers market manager and a founding member of the Michigan Farmers Market Association.

Patricia E. Norris holds the Gordon and Norma Guyer and Gary L. Seevers Chair in Natural Resource Conservation at Michigan State University and is a professor in the Department of Community, Agriculture, Recreation, and Resources Studies and the Department of Agricultural, Food, and Resource Economics. Norris has conducted research and extension education programs addressing issues in soil conservation, water quality, groundwater management, wetland policy, land markets, land-use conflicts, and farmland preservation. She has taught courses in natural resource economics, environmental economics, ecological economics, environmental science, agricultural policy, and public policy analysis. Norris holds her bachelor's degrees in agricultural economics from the University of Georgia and her master's degree and doctorate from Virginia Tech.

Debra Pearson is associate professor of human biology and nutritional sciences and co-director of the Center for Food and Culture at the University of Wisconsin–Green Bay. She received her doctorate in nutritional science from the University of California–Davis. She has conducted research on phytochemicals and heart disease and is the author of several scientific publications, including a recent major review of osteoporosis and vitamin K.

David Pimentel is professor emeritus of insect ecology and agricultural sciences, Department of Entomology and Section of Ecology and Systematics, Cornell University. His multidisciplinary research spans the field of basic population ecology, genetics, ecological and economic aspects of pest control, biological control, energy use and conservation, genetic engineering, sustainable agriculture, soil and water conservation, and natural resource management and environmental policy. He has most recently focused on the relationship between food and fuel.

Sieglinde Snapp is associate professor in soils and cropping system ecology. She is based at the Kellogg Biological Research Station, Department of Crop and Soil Science, Michigan State University (MSU). Sustainable soil management and agro-ecology for smallholder livelihoods are central to her research and teaching, and are the subject of numerous articles and two books. Her deep commitment to science in the service of development in Africa was recently recognized by the Emerging Leader Hudzik International Studies Program Award. She developed the new graduate specialization at MSU in ecological food and farming systems, and teaches the course on international agricultural systems. Before joining MSU in 2000, she was an international scientist based in Malawi and Zimbabwe for close to a decade, and earned her doctorate at the University of California–Davis in 1991.

John M. Staatz is professor of agricultural, food, and resource economics and of African studies at Michigan State University. He has worked on issues of economic development and food security for thirty-three years, with a special focus on West Africa. He teaches graduate courses and conducts research in the areas of food policy, food security, economic development, institutional change, information economics, regional trade, and marketing.

Sandra M. Stokes, professor of education and women's studies at the University of Wisconsin–Green Bay, is an executive committee member of the Center for Food in Community and Culture at the University of Wisconsin–Green Bay and a member of the Mayor of Green Bay's Sustainable Green Bay Task Force and its foods subcommittee. Stokes is the editor of the *WSRA* (Wisconsin State Reading Association) *Journal* and has authored texts on reading assessment and education issues as well as numerous scholarly articles in such publications as *The Reading Teacher*, *The Reading Professor*, *Multicultural Education*, and *Women in Higher Education*.

Index